KOLKATA : TO BE YOUNG WAS PARADISE

KOLKATA
To be Young Was Paradise

H. A. Barari

GYAN PUBLISHING HOUSE
NEW DELHI-110002

Kolkata : To be Young Was Paradise

Rs. 590

ISBN: 81-212-0881-5

Published in 2006 in India by
Gyan Publishing House
5, Ansari Road, Darya Ganj, New Delhi-110002
Phones : 23282060, 23261060
Fax : (011) 23285914
E-mail : gyanbook@vsnl.com
Website : www.gyanbooks.com

Laser Typesetting at : Master Computers, Delhi
Printed at : Salasar Imaging System, Delhi

Dedicated to the people of Kolkata whose cultural outlook and life-style nurtured my adolscent years to make of me the man I became.

Contents

Preface

This is a book of my reminiscences about my college days in Kolkata in the late forties and early fifties of the twentieth century. At the very beginning, I have to bore the reader with my curriculum vitae as some kind of a backdrop against which the events of this phase of my early life are to be viewed. I was said to have been born on April 1, 1929 in a village of the Vikrampur Pargana that formed part of the Dhaka district of undivided Bengal. I have some doubts as to whether this was the true date of my birth – doubts that I have explained in a chapter of my book 'In Sun and Shower'.

In 1945, at the age of 16, I shifted from my village to metropolitan Kolkata to pursue higher education but my home was still in my village. In 1947, we wound up our establishment in the village in the wake of the vivisection of our country and settled down in Kolkata which became our new home town.

I left Kolkata in October, 1953, to join the Indian Police Service. At the fag end of my career in this service, I was chosen to head the Intelligence Bureau of the Government of India as its Director (1984-1987) in the immediate aftermath of the assassination of Prime Minister Indira Gandhi. This was the highest ranking job a police officer could aspire to in India. In this capacity, I had the privilege of presiding over the conferences of the chiefs of the police, intelligence and para-military organisations of the State and Central Governments.

I also served as the Governor of Haryana (1988-1990), when the late Chaudhuri Devi Lal and his son, Om Prakash Chautala, were successively its Chief Ministers. In between, I had doubled as the Governor of Himchal Pradesh for a brief while in December 1989 and January, 1990.

In my earlier book, "In Sun And Shower", I gave an account of the formative years of my life in my native village in east Bengal that has now become Bangladesh. In this companion volume, I have carried forward the narrative till 1953 and focused mainly on Kolkata, my second home and my growing up place, where I spent eight (years 1945–1953) at a stretch and completed my higher education before joining the Indian Police Service. In this book, I have discussed many issues that occupied the center-stage of Kolkata's social, economic and political life, when I lived there in the years preceding and following the partition of our country. I have also dwelt on the cultural ambience of contemporary Kolkata in order to bring out what the Germans call zetgeist or the spirit of those times.

The book brings under the scanner many important events that took place in our country during the years I was a college student and then a college Lecturer in Kolkata. This was a tumultuous period of history that saw the end of the Second World War which was followed by a communal holocaust that rent our country asunder and eventually led to its partition and the migration of vast masses of uprooted humanity across new borders that came to divide the sub-continent. This period was witness to how bravely millions of men, women and children--suddenly rendered homeless by man's cruelty to man and deprived at one stroke of everything they could call their own--moved over to completely new and unknown surroundings and struggled to find their feet and begin their life anew, never giving up hope, but constantly keeping the courage of the quest.

A word about the title of this book would be in place. The expression — to be young was paradise — that forms part of the book's title was inspired by what the English romantic poet William Wordsworth had famously said in his Prelude:

"Bliss was it in that dawn to be alive.
But to be young was very heaven.
The beauty wore of promise, that which sets
(As at some moment might not be unfelt
Among the bowers of paradise itself.)

Wordsworth was thus expressing his sense of idealism and optimism that had gripped the young generation of Europe when the French Revolution broke out in the 18th century. In the latter half of the 1940's, when I was a college student in Kolkata, I shared with the lotus eaters of the country as a whole a similar feeling of hope and optimism in the wake of the end of World War II, the release from prison of India's freedom-fighters, the magic spell cast by the disclosure of the heroic exploits of the Indian National Army and of the supreme sacrifice made by its Prometheus-like leader Netaji Subhas Chandra Bose, the formation of the Interim Government in Delhi under the leadership of Pt. Jawaharlal Nehru and the widespread belief that India's freedom was round the corner, despite the fact that the communal violence and turmoil that engulfed the country put a spanner in the works.

It was extremely difficult to compile this book from Delhi, where I am settled, because many reference books on pre-independence Kolkata are not easily available here. Nor was I in a position to consult many persons with first-hand knowledge of Kolkata of that period for the simple reason that such persons, who, of necessity, have to belong to my generation, are now a first vanishing tribe with very few of them living in Delhi.

This book would not have seen the light of the day but for the help and moral support constantly extended to me by my wife, Anita Barari. I have to thank her for having taken the trouble of going through the manuscript and offering valuable suggestions from time to time. Some others whose assistance I wish to specially acknowledge are the late Pankaj Roy, the famous cricketer of yesteryears, Anirban Chakravarty, Smt. Rani Chatterjee, Smt. Anjalika Chatterjee, Prof. Aparajito Chatterji of the Jawaharlal Nehru University, Delhi, Smt. Sumita Bhattacharya, Dr. Kalyan Sen, my college mate, his sister, Smt. Sova Sengupta and last but not the least P.K.Mitra. I find it difficult to individually mention the names of many others, who have put me in their debt by assisting me in various ways in bringing out this book.

New Delhi **H.A. Barari**
October 2005

1

Forward Face, Unreluctant Soul

In my earlier book, "In Sun and Shower", I have narrated the circumstances leading to my departure for Kolkata in May, 1945, along with the members of our family, from our village Shyamsiddhi in the Vikrampur Pargana of Dhaka district in what was then east Bengal. I had just appeared at the Matriculation examination of the Calcutta University from a village school and the results were expected to come out in a month or two. It was at this stage that our family decided to make a paradigm shift and move over to Kolkata. The idea was to provide for the proper education of my brothers and sisters and to facilitate my higher studies for which I was to join a college there.

How very thoughtful of my father to have conceived of such a venture! He knew that the salary he drew as a teacher of the village school would hardly suffice for the household and educational expenses of his family of eleven members in Kolkata. It was his foresightedness that had led him to take up a job in the Barisal district of east Bengal a few months in advance under the Crop Survey Project of the Indian Statistical Institute headquartered in Kolkata.

My father was, therefore not in our party when we travelled from the village to metropolitan Kolkata. I still vividly recall our journey from the village to Kolkata and my feelings as we entered what was going to be my abode in that city for the next several years. It was well past evening, when we reached the Sealdah Railway Station, dead tired after a journey that involved a lot of walking along rural roads, then a ride in a steamer that crossed the rough waters of the Padma and finally a train journey by third class from

Goalundo to Sealdah on the north eastern periphery of Kolkata. My eldest brother, who knew Kolkata well from his college days, had travelled with us from the village to see through the shift. At Sealdah, he engaged a 'Tonga' (a horse-driven carriage), in which we all squeezed ourselves as well as our luggage with quite some difficulty.

After a couple of hours, we reached Bhowanipore in south Kolkata and then went through a meandering by-lane to reach a comparatively open area that was quite dark. Along with our modest belongings that had been carried by the 'Tonga', we entered a dimly lit small cottage with a tin roof and mud walls which looked hopelessly un-prepossessing, specially because it stood cheek by jowl with many impressive structures in the neighbourhood that were all aglow with blazing lights.

We were welcomed into the house by the family of our uncle, Madhusudan Barari, who was an elder cousin of my father. He was a junior functionary in a court at Baruipur, a small town 25 miles south of Kolkata. His family consisted of his wife and six daughters, of whom two had already got married, the other four living with them and studying in various classes at school. He had taken this house from a landlord, who lived close by, at a monthly rent of Rs. 18/-only. The arrangement now was that we would have two rooms and a kitchen, while he would have the remaining half of the house for his family. As sub-tenants, we were to pay him a hefty sum of Rs. 11/-as monthly rent.

The next morning, I had a look around our new home. There were four rooms in a row with a cement floor, mud walls and a tin roof. An open verandah fronted the rooms. There were two kitchens with mud walls and tiled roofs, one for our uncle's family and the other for us. There was a toilet in one corner of the premises and a tap in the open courtyard, the only source of water supply. All this was to be shared by us with our uncle's family. I felt as if I had come back to another village right in the heart of Kolkata, but one that was rather artificial as compared to our village in Vikrampur, which was a village in the true sense of the term.

For all practical purposes, we lived in a slum, our next-door neighbours being a sweeper and his wife from Bihar and some washermen's families. We had an uncemented courtyard, which became slushy whenever it rained. The courtyard was skirted by an open drain, which separated it from a big open cemented yard that accommodated the cows and buffaloes of the landlord. This yard used to overflow all the time with a semi-solid admixture of bovine dung and urine, which often choked the drain. The whole place stank to high heaven and abounded with flies and mosquitoes, despite efforts made by the landlord's men to maintain a certain standard of cleanliness.

There was some advantage that flowed from such close co-existence with the cattle. A tap in the landlord's yard provided plenty of unfiltered water which, we were told, came straight from the nearby Ganges and was used for washing the cattle and cleaning the yard. We could fall back upon this unfailing source of unfiltered water for our bath, if our supply of filtered water that came through the solitary tap in our courtyard fell short of our requirement for some reason or was interrupted as a result of the Calcutta Municipal Corporation's workers going on a strike. If too hard pressed for water for a bath, we sometimes walked over to a near-by place that boasted a road-side hydrant provided by the Calcutta Municipal Corporation to make available free filtered water for the use of the common man. This had one disadvantage though, which was that you had to go through the motions of your bath under the gaze of the respectable people of the locality – both male and female – whom we often saw peeping through the chinks of their curtained windows for whatever voyeuristic pleasure they as well as we might derive.

Sometimes, for our bath we walked straight to the Ganges, which was about a mile from our place, or to a tank called 'Padmapukur', also about a mile away, though in the opposite direction, which represented a double plus in that you could not only bathe there but also have a good swim for free.

The open drain flowing past our court-yard used to be chockfull of filth and served as the happy breeding ground for insects of all kinds. The choked sewers also harboured big field rats, which one could see frequently running about all over the place. At night, it used to be dark all around our place and once, when I came out into the open in search of some water from the tap, I stepped on a big rat, which sank its teeth into my foot and ran away as fast as it could, because it also must have got hurt and felt scared after being trampled under my foot. I just washed my foot with some water and in a few days, the injury healed up through what must have been nature's own self-healing process. Some members of our family told me to show the injury to a doctor, apprehending that this had the potential of turning into a case of plague. I decided not to make too much fuss about it and just ignored it. The people of Kolkata feared the plague that sometimes broke out in epidemic form at many places in our country. In fact, Kolkata had witnessed an increase in the incidence of plague in the late nineteen forties.

However, this litany of our woes and the shortcomings of our new physical environment give no clue to the real state of my mind at that initial stage of my getting acquainted with and acclimatised to life in Kolkata. I saw many things for the first time, which, therefore, aroused a great deal of curiosity in my mind. The joy of discovering something new every day thrilled me. Every night as I went to bed, I counted my blessings. Each morning, as I woke up to the distant rumble of Kolkata's tram cars, I thought up some fruitful way of spending the day. There were people in our locality who knew Kolkata well and from whom I sought guidance as to where to go, what all to look for and learn and how to make the most of each day.

As I muddled through my new life in Kolkata, seeking to find my feet, I drew considerable moral strength from the following lines of Henry Van Dyke that I had read :

"Let me but live my life from year to year,
With forward face and unreluctant soul;
Not hurrying to, nor returning from, the goal;
Not mourning for the things that disappear
In the dim past, nor holding back in fear
From what the future veils; but with a whole
And happy heart, that pays its toll
To Youth and Age, and travels on with cheer.
So let the way wind up the hill or down
O'er rough or smooth, the journey will be joy:
Still seeking what I sought when but a boy.
New friendship, high adventure, and a crown.
My heart will keep the courage of the quest.
And hope the road's last turn will be the best."

2

Exploring Kolkata

"When one door closes, another opens; but we often look so long and so regretfully upon the closed door that we do not see the one which has opened for us."

— **Alexander Graham Bell**

When I landed in Kolkata in the mid-nineteen forties, it was the proud second city of the British Empire after London. It did not take me very long to realise what new opportunities lay ahead once I settled down in Kolkata and made a determined bid to develop my full potential through hard work and perseverence. Soon I began to go out on my own to explore my new horizons and discover the important landmarks of Kolkata. This helped me to familiarise myself with the streets, find my bearing and know my co-ordinates.

I often wondered how old Kolkata was. When I asked some people who were supposed to be knowledgeable, I got no satisfactory answer. Some one said that long ago (how long ago, nobody knew), a canal that originated in the Ganges to the west of Kolkata flowed eastward through what later came to be known as the Hastings Street and joined another canal that flowed through an area to the east of the city which was later known as creek Row. From the word 'Khal' (Bengali for canal) and another word 'Kata' (Bengali for 'excavated'), the place acquired the name 'Khalkata', which later evolved into Kolkata. I do not think that there is any truth in this surmise.

Another account of how the name Kalikata (or Kolkata) came into vogue has its origin in a revenue map that was got prepared by the Moghul Emperor Akbar in the 16th century A.D. In this map, a village by name 'Kalikata' was found, which was believed to be a corrupt form of Kalighat. This is said to have given rise to the name Calcutta in English. A rather queer account that was also heard sometimes was that numerous Englishmen died in Kolkata during the first 70 years of their occupation of the place. This led the English sailors to call this place Golgotha, a Hebrew word standing for a hill near Jerusalem where Christ was crucified, which in due course came to mean a place of burial or a cemetery or a charnel-house where the bones of the dead are kept. From Golgotha to Kolkata or Calcutta was but a small step.

I used to walk long distances, as going by tram or bus cost money. I managed to get useful tips from some boys of our locality about places that were worth visiting. Some of them even obliged with books about Kolkata's old history and the important landmarks of the city. Around 1535 A.D., some Basaks, Mullicks and Setts had settled down in Govindapur and Sutanati villages close to what was Kalikata. In 1570 A.D. was born Lakshmikanta Ganguly, the first zamindar of Kalikata, whose family subsequently acquired the title of 'Roy Choudhury'. Some important developments took place in the wake of the annexation of Bengal by the Moghuls in 1575 A.D. In 1612 A.D., Emperor Jehangir deputed Man Singh to Bengal to quell the rebellion of Pratapaditya, one of the twelve 'Bhuiyans' (local feudal chiefs). After the defeat of Pratapaditya, Man Singh entrusted the collection of rent in the area to Lakshmikanta, who thus emerged as the zamindar of five Parganas including Kalikata.

Now crops up the name of Job Charnok, who has long been known as the founder of Kolkata city. In 1656 A.D., he came to Bengal from London as the head of the East India Company's 'kothi' at Cossimbazar. In 1686 A.D., the Moghul forces took over the Cossimbazar 'kothi' of the East India Company, which forced Charnok to shift to Hugli and then to Sutanati. Some time later, he had also to quit Sutanati and move over to Balasore. It was on August 24, 1690 A.D. that Job Charnok was said to have returned to Sutanati and founded the city of Kolkata on a site comprising the three villages of Govindapur, Sutanati and Kalikata.

Charnok's personal life was quite colourful. At Sutanati, he had married a very young 15-year old (!) Hindu widow and set up a family there. When her husband died, this girl was about to jump on to the funeral pyre of the former in obsevance of the prevailing social custom. Charnok was so charmed by her beauty that he chivalrously stopped her in her track, rescued her and tied the knot with her. Some children were born to the couple before the hapless girl died in 1693. Charnok was reported to have spent his last days in not very happy circumstances.

In 1698 A.D., Azim, son of the Moghul Emperor Aurangzeb, became the Viceroy of Bengal when the three villages of Sutanati, Kalikata and Govindapur were sold by Sabarna Roy Choudhury, a descendant of Lakshmikanta Roy Choudhury, to the East India Company. Kolkata now became a Presidency of the East India Company and Job Charnok's son-in-law, Charles Eyre became its first Governor, who, however, was placed under the control of the Madras Presidency.

This arrangement continued till 1707 A.D. when Bengal was placed on par with the Presidencies of Madras and Bombay. In 1756 A.D., Nawab Siraj-ud-doula of Bengal stormed Kolkata and captured it from the East India Company. But the next year, Kolkata was recaptured by the English. In 1772 A.D., Warren Hastings became the Governor of Bengal and in 1774 A.D., he became the Governor-General with control over Madras, Bombay and all British possessions in India. He transferred the Treasury from Murshidabad to Kolkata, which thus became the capital of the Englishmen in India.

English poet Rudyard Kipling, in his poem "A Tale of Two Cities", described how Kolkata came into being:

"Where the merchant deals in indigo and tea,
Hides and ghi;
Where the Babu drops inflammatory hints
In his prints;
Stands a City – Charnock chose it – packed away
Near a Bay –
By the sewage rendered fetid, by the sewer
Made impure,
By the Sunderbuns unwholesome, by the swamp
Moist and damp;
Thus the mid-day halt of
Charnock – more is the pity
Grew a city:
As the fungus sprouts chaotic
from its bed.
So it spread

Chance-directed, chance-erected,
Laid and built on the silt,
Palace, byre, hovel, poverty and
Pride,
Side by side
And above the pack and pestilential
Town
Death looked down.

Kipling's utter contempt for Kolkata, as for everything in the east, comes out clearly in these lines.

Recently, however, this account of the origin of Kolkata city was questioned and challenged in a public interest litigation filed before the High Court of Calcutta by a body known as the Roy Chowdhury Paribar Parishad, which contended that the land in question was never sold to Job Charnok but had been leased out at a rent of Rs. 1281/-per year! The lease deed was signed by a member of the Roy Chowdhury family and on behalf of Job Charnok by his son-in-law, Charles Eyre, on November 10, 1698, which was eight years after what has long been observed as the city's foundation day. Many people now believe that Job Charnok was not the founder of the city, because references to its existence are found in 'Manasamangal', a Bengali poetical tract of the 15th century A.D., and in the Ain-I-Akbari, which was written by Abul Fazal in the 16th century A.D.

The Calcutta High Court, which heard the plea of the Sabarna Roy Chowdhury family, appointed a panel headed by the late Nemaisadhan Bose, a former Vice-Chancellor of the Vishwabharati, to go into the question of the origin of Kolkata. In May 2003, the Calcutta High Court passed an order accepting the report of the panel according to which Kolkata did not have a birthday, its origin being a part of the general process of rural settlement, clusters of which agglomerated in the last decade of the 17th century and grew into a town in the 18th century.

Recent excavations undertaken by the Archaeological Survey of India near Dum Dum on the northern outskirts of Kolkata have revealed data pointing to the likelihood of Kolkata being 2000 years old. Artefacts, pot shards and human skeletons that have been unearthed indicate that an urban population lived here for centuries, perhaps since the Sunga Kushana period dating back to the second century B.C. The human skeletons are believed by the scientists to be at least two millennia old and were reportedly under scrutiny at a laboratory. In the light of these discoveries, the view that Kolkata had been founded in the seventeenth century A.D. by Job Charnok may go for a six.

The Bhabisya Purana, an old religious text, gives an account of the origin of Kolkata, which would indicate that this city is fairly old and certainly existed long before Job Charnok set foot upon its soil. It is, however, not possible to relate Kolkata's age to the date of the composition of the Bhabisya Purana simply because there is no commonly accepted date of this Purana.

The Pratisarga Parva of Bhabisya Purana [1] says that once upon a time Gaud was ruled by a king Bhoga Varma, whose sister, Bhogavati, was married to Vikrama (who is sometimes identified with King Vikramaditya, though nobody knows which of the several historical figures known by this name he was). In due course, Bhoga Varma's son, Kali Varma, became the King of Gaud. Once King Kali Varma organized a 'Mahotsava' (a big festival) to pay obeisance to goddess Kali. Pleased with this, the goddess appeared before the king. Simultaneously, numerous Kalika flowers bloomed over a wide area around the place. A beautiful city, which sprang up there, came to be known as Kolikata (i.e. Kolkata of today).

This account is primarily a mythological one, but Kolkata also figures a little later in the same Pratisarga Parva of the Bhabisya Purana[2] where the account is a curious admixture of mythology and history. This latter account mentions the arrival of Nadar (Nadir Shah?), who is described as a 'Daitya' (demon) at a place called Khuraj (Khurja in Uttar Pradesh?) after having killed some Aryans and some gods. (The words 'Aryans' and 'gods' are often used interchangeably in this account). A king by name Madhava is said to have ruled in Delhi for ten years. A 'Mlechchha' (of low caste) by name Aloma (Salim or Jehangir?) later ascended the throne. During his rule, many independent kingdoms arose where local kings ruled.

Then all the gods (Aryans?) came to Krishna Chaitanya. Considering the sad state of affairs prevailing in the world, Krishna Chaitanya went into deep meditation for a while and then said that in earlier times Rama had killed the demon king Ravana and brought the monkeys slain in the battle back to life by sprinkling elixir on them. The monkeys requested Lord Rama to grant them boons. The names of these monkeys were Vikata, Vrijila, Jala, Varaleeno, Simhala, Java, Sumatra etc. Rama assured the gods of his help and told them that some islands which had been set up by Jalandhara, a demon born out of the union of Ravana and his Apsara mistress by name Devangana. These islands, Lord Rama told them, would thenceforth be known by the names of the monkeys and would be governed by a pious king (a well-wisher and a benefactor of the monkeys would rule over those islands.)

In these islands, 'Mlechchhas' or low-caste people known as Gurundas were said to be living for a long time. The Gurundas were believed to have been born out of the head of the mythological cow, Nandini. The gods were told to secure victory over the Gurundas and to establish their rule there. Hearing these words (uttered by Rama and conveyed by Hari, who was perhaps identical with Krisna Chaitanya), the gods felt pleased, prostrated themselves before Hari and then left for those islands. The monkey-faced Gurundas were born in the lineage of Vikata (a monkey mentioned in the preceding paragraph) and had come to those islands for trade. They were followers of Buddhism initially, but later they embraced Christianity. Some of them were sun-worshippers.

The Gurundas were good at heart and truthful and had complete control over their baser instincts. In course of time, they travelled northwards for trade. Hari told the gods to go eastwards and work for the welfare of mankind. Hearing Hari's words, the gods worshipped him out of veneration and proceeded towards Kalikata. In the western islands, there was a ruler by name Vikatavati, who followed the eightfold path (probably Lord Buddha's eightfold path). Her husband, Pulomarchi lived in the city of Kalikata.

In this account, as elsewhere in the Bhabisya Purana, many historical events with deviations from known facts or with distortions in the names of persons and places have been mentioned. For example, names such as those of Humayun, Salim (Jehangir), Nadir Shah, Taimurlang, Sher Shah and Aurangzeb have been distorted as Homayu, Salom, Nadar, Timirlang, Shes Shak and Navrang respectively. References made in the Bhabisya Purana to events of not very old historical times has led some scholars to think that these were latter-day interpolations in the ancient text.

Moreover, there are several manuscripts of the Bhabisya Purana that are still extant, giving rise to legitimate doubts as to which one of them is the authentic text. The fact that these texts differ from one another suggests the possibility that some parts of these manuscripts were interpolated subsequently at different times. It is generally believed that of the four Parvas of the Bhabisya Purana, the first (i.e. the Brahma Parva) mostly conforms to the original text while the other three, specially the Pratsarga Parva (which refers to many historical events including some pertaining to Calcutta), are vitiated by later interpolations.

Some scholars, however, hold the view that since the Bhabisya Purana purported to be a record of what was expected to happen in future, it is but natural that it should touch upon many events of more recent times along with the names of kings and rulers down to the period of British rule in India and the establishment of several Indian cities including Kolkata. These scholars vouch for the absolute sanctity and the authenticity as well as the antiquity of the written text and ascribe the power of clairvoyance and of foreseeing the future to the sages of ancient India whose vision is enshrined in the Bhabisya Purana.

When I lived in Kolkata, it had many relics of the British Raj about which I had read and which I naturally wanted to look up. Some of these were old buildings, which were in a dilapidated condition because these had not been properly maintained. In this category were run-down structures like the house in which Lord Clive used to live, the Old Mint and St. John's Church—none of which I had the opportunity of visiting. But there were many other relics of the Raj which were still in good shape and at which I decided to have a look.

This is how I once reached Dalhousie Square and had a view of the magnificent Government House, the residence of the British Governor. Initially built in 1803 by the Marquis of Wellesley in the neo-Palladian style as the residence of India's Governor-General, it was later converted into the Bengal Governor's residence.

At the far end of the 'Maidan' was the Victoria Memorial Hall, an edifice in white marble built as the Valhalla of Britain's illustrious dead, who had contributed to the building of the empire in India. This monument had lost some of its old splendour after it was painted black during World War II as protective measure against the possibility of bombing by the Japanese. As I went beyond the gateway of this emblem of Italian renaissance architecture walking over the pebbled path, I saw the statues of many English kings and queens including an impressive one of Queen Victoria in whose memory it was built. I had not yet seen the Taj Mahal at Agra, but I was told that the Victoria Memorial Hall bore a striking resemblance to the former and though, unlike the Taj Mahal, it was not meant to be a monument of imperial love, still it served as the meeting place of love-lorn couples belonging to the ordinary strata of society.

The Writers' Buildings on the northern side of the Dalhousie Square, the seat of the Provincial Government, looked quite distinctive with its architecture of "simple lines" that avoided elaborate ornamentation. Close by was Lal Bazar, the headquarters of the Calcutta Police, which was patterned in a general way on the model of London's Scotland Yard.

The GPO (General Post Office), which was housed in a circular building with a big clock at its top, the Indian Museum and the Town Hall in the Chowringhee area were some of the other edifices which greatly impressed me. The GPO was the oldest one of its kind in the country, its clock and bell having been made by the manufacturers of London's Big Ben in the same mould in the year 1897. I was happy to learn that the bell which had stopped chiming was set right and made to clang again from the Christmas eve of its centenary in 1997.

And then I saw the Calcutta High Court, a Gothic structure that proudly thrust its spires high into the sky, as if to proclaim that the judiciary would ever hold its head high, towering above all other man-made institutions. It was necessary for me to see the High Court for the simple reason that I was what in colloquial Bengali was known as a 'Bangal' i.e. a man from east Bengal. People of West Bengal used to pull the legs of their counterparts from east Bengal, disdainfully branding them as 'Bangals', who were said to be so backward that they scarcely knew where the High Court was located! Hence the general saying in Kolkata that the High Court had to be shown to a 'Bangal'. Being a true blue 'Bangal', I, therefore, made a point of seeing the High Court to be able to retort confidently that I had seen the High Court about which there was nothing very mysterious.

Once I walked from Dalhousie Square to the Howrah Bridge, whose silhouette against Kolkata's western sky I had often seen from different points of the city. I walked across the bridge and occasionally stopped to look down at the waters of the Ganges that flowed in their majestic rythm. I walked back to Kolkata from the other end of the bridge that adjoined the ever-noisy Howrah Railway Station complex. It was some years later that I read the following description of the London Bridge by T.S. Eliot, which, I felt, was equally true of the Howrah Bridge:

"A crowd flowed over London
bridge, so many
I had not thought death had
undone so many."

An endless stream of people thronged Burrabazar, Dalhousie Square, Clive Street etc. looking at which poet Bishnu De penned a beautiful poem which was translated into English as follows:

"The turbid stream of men break into foam on Burrabazar. In the air a mingled smoke of biris, cigarettes, ovens, mills. Patches of red spit on the street. Long-drawn sighs. A ceaseless monotonous sound: the confused turmoil of trams and buses and hawkers, of daily passengers to Clive Street, Dalhousie and Lyons Range; a tired silence, and at times, a bitter murmur.[3]

I also explored the Fort William, albeit from outside. It was the fort which, as I learnt from my studies, Nawab Siraj-ud-Doula had once captured by defeating the Englishmen, but had surrendered back to the latter in June 1756, a year before his historic defeat by the British at Plassey. If the disinformation fed by Englishmen were to be believed, the Nawab had enacted the black hole tragedy in June 1756 by causing the death by suffocation of over 100 Bengalee peasants kept imprisoned in a tiny cubicle in inhuman circumstances.

It was in the course of my effort to locate the famous Imperial Library that I saw Belvedere, once the residence of the British Governor-General. This impressive building was later converted into the famous Imperial Library that was renamed as the National Library after independence. When I grew up and joined the Calcutta University for post-graduate studies, I used to visit this library from time to time to consult books that were not available elsewhere.

As I read later, it was in Belvedere that early in the morning of a humid day in June, 1780, Warren Hastings, the British Governor-General, had fought a gun duel with Sir Philip Francis, a member of his Executive Council, to settle a dispute over a personal matter. When Francis arrived in Kolkata in October 1774, he expected to be welcomed with 21 guns, while, in fact, Warren Hastings allowed only 17—a trivial matter which led to a long and bitter acrimony between the two.

Francis usually opposed Governor-General Hastings at the meetings of the Executive Council, which often led the latter to criticize him trenchantly in a tone that, he thought, was highly objectionable.

He challenged Hastings to a duel in which he received a serious injury that confined him to the bed for quite some time. He left India earning the distinction of having his back injured by India's Governor-General. His own account of this duel was preserved in the Hasting's Room of the Victoria Memorial Hall in Kolkata. [4]

It was the same Francis, who, having had to leave behind in England his wife, five daughters and a son, was always on the prowl for romance and on a fateful day in December 1778, took the help of a ladder to scale the wall of a house in order to clandestinely meet his dream girl, a sixteen year-old French beauty – Mrs. Grand – when Mr. Grand was away from home and ended up ignominiously in the hands of Mr. Grand's alert sentry. Francis was hauled up before the Supreme Court under whose orders he had to pay a hefty fine of Rs. 50,000/-to Mr. Grand. So much for the transgressions, minor misdemeanours and licentious ways of some members of the English gentry of Kolkata, who pined for the company of their sweethearts they had to leave behind in England under the strict orders of the East India Company.

One of the Judges of the Supreme Court, who tried Sir Francis Philip, was Robert Chambers, who was frequently mentioned in Boswell's Life of Johnson. He was a member of the Literary Club of Burke, Reynolds and Goldsmith and an intimate friend of Dr. Johnson, who had written a letter introducing Justice Chambers to Warren Hastings, the Governor-General. To quote:

'I am now going to take leave, perhaps a very long leave, of my dear Mr. Chambers; that he is going to live where you govern may justly alleviate the regret of parting; and the hope of seeing you and him again which I am not willing to mingle with doubt must at present console as it can.

Sir, your most humble servant

Sam Johnson."

Dr. Johnson died before either of the two reached Europe. [5]

The literary antecedents of Sir Philip Francis were no less impressive either as he was the author of the 'Letters of Junius', the famous philippics and witty invectives, which made the King of England uneasy. Nobody knew the identity of Junius (who, in fact, was Sir Francis Philip) and the brilliance of the author's style led Dr. Johnson to ascribe them to Burke, who, of course, set the record straight by honestly declaring that he was not 'Junius', the author of the letters. [6]

When I saw Belvedere in the latter half of the nineteen forties, it housed in its substantial premises the 'Burra Sahibs' of English firms as well as many indigenous Marwari business leaders, who had begun to progressively step into the shoes of the departing Englishmen.

Kolkata, though no longer the capital of our country, was still the meeting place of the East and the West, despite whatever Rudyard Kipling had to say. When the Englishmen came to Kolkata in the eighteenth century, there were dense jungles south of Chowringhee. People going to the temple at Kalighat had to pass through this wooded area at some risk to their safety and faced considerable difficulty in the absence of facilities for food, shelter etc. A 'Sadhu' by name Chowringheenath, who lived near the present-day Kolkata 'Maidan', used to extend his helping hand to pilgrims on their way to and back from Kalighat. It is from him that Chowringhee got its name.

When I saw Kolkata in 1945, it was a busy place pulsating with life. There was a fair sprinkling of Englishmen among the people who thronged the city's shopping centres famous for jewellers like Hamiltons and Cooke and Kelvey, tailors like Rankins and Phelps, stores like Hall and Anderson, Whiteaway and Laidlaw and the Army and Navy Stores, hotels like the Grand and Great Eastern and a number of restaurants that offered good tea, apart from snacks and delicious eats. An important landmark was the Firpo's to go where for lunch or dinner was the hallmark of aristocratic living. It was a unique institution that closed down after independence. Hog's Market, alternatively called the New Market, was a hip and happening place where the rich and the sophisticated did their shopping. Cinema halls like Metro and New Empire not only dazzled one's eyes with their blinking red and blue lights, but also showed the latest English films that one could see in any of the world's biggest metropolises.

Sometimes I walked over to the Kolkata 'Maidan' (or 'Gader Math', as the Bengalees call it), which virtually served as the city's lungs and where people used to go there for a breath of fresh air. It was like London's Hyde Park, which I saw many years later. It was here that Kolkata's biggest mass rallies were held at the foot of the Ochterlony Monument that was built by the British in the nineteenth century as a memorial to Sir David Ochterlony, who had helped expand the British Empire. It was here that Kolkata's renowned football clubs and their playgrounds were located, as they still are. Not very far from the 'Maidan', the Eden Gardens then ranked, as it does today, among the world's best cricket grounds.

What made these places additionally attractive and at the same time somewhat forbidding was the presence and frequent movement of a large number of white-skinned Westerners—British and American—who included, apart from the British civilians and their wives, the much bigger presence of military personnel, who dominated the whole scenario during the Second World War years and for some time thereafter. You bumped into them, whether at the Metro or some other cinema hall, showing English movies or on the 'Maidan', where they played various games to keep fit.

There were some pools near the periphery of the 'Maidan', where the white military personnel and their female companions, mostly white, in their scanty swim suits, often beguiled themselves of the tropical tedium with water sports and swimming. It was a pleasant pastime for some local people to throng these spots in the evenings and ogle at the bathing beauties.

A couple of years later, I allowed myself the pleasure of crossing the Ganges in a steam boat when, as I looked at Kolkata from a distance, I was reminded of the tribute that James Atkinson had paid to Kolkata, the city of palaces, in the following lines:

"And gazing around, beheld
the pomp of spires
And palaces ....
All glittering in the sun-beam".

Many years later, I found it much easier to have a coup d'oeil of Kolkata from atop one of the many sky-scrapers that had cropped up in different parts of the city.

In the middle of the nineteen forties, some of the indigenous Maharajas of eastern India still added a touch of glamour to Kolkata's social life, as I gathered from newspapers, which reported on important social and cultural events. One often read of the activities of the Cooch Behar family as also of Uday Chand Mahatab, the doyen of the Burdwan family, who patronised polo and equestrian sport. The Maharajas of Darbhanga and Cossimbazar were known for their patronage of learning and higher education. I benefited personally from a Calcutta University scholarship which the Maharaja of Cossimbazar had instituted.

Once, during a visit to Tollygunge, I had a look at the golf courses from outside-courses which were among the oldest in he world. British company executives played golf there as well as on the courses which, I learnt, were maintained by some jute firms in Kolkata's suburbs. It was not open to Indians to play in some of these courses until the restrictions were withdrawn just on the eve of our independence or soon thereafter.

The Englishmen were fond of club life and among their favorite haunts were the Calcutta Club, Bengal Club, Saturday Club and a couple of clubs in Tollygunge. The Iush green tennis courts of the South Club were immaculately maintained, as I saw during a visit to the area in the course of an expedition to see the houses of Subhas Chandra Bose and his elder brother Sarat Chandra Bose, who lived in the vicinity of the club.

The Calcutta Club did not allow women to be its members, the reason for which might have been the fact that in 1907 when the club was formed, hardly any women would have thought of participating in the kind of activities that the club organized. The rules then framed continue to be in force still now with the result that a woman can now, as then, go to the Calcutta Club not in her own right but as the wife of a man who is a member. A club that sticks to such old conventions thus discriminates against women on the ground of their gender an anachronism in this day and age.

Apart from this British facade, Kolkata had another face, which was entirely indigenous and reflected its Bengali ethos. While Park Street and Chowringhee had their fashionable shops, restaurants, hotels and picture houses, which attracted a cosmopolitan crowd, shops on the Rashbehari Avenue in south Kolkata and along the Cornwallis Road in north Kolkata as well as the markets in different parts of the city catered to the Indian and particularly the Bengalee clientele. There were numerous cinema halls that showed Bengali and Hindi films.

In the field of sports, athletics and gymnastics, Kolkata's 'Para' (neighbourhood) clubs provided facilities of various kinds to the youth that helped some outstanding athletes and gymnasts to come up. Two of India's 'Mr. Universe' title holders in the realm of body building were from Kolkata—Manohar Aich and Manotosh Roy. Manohar Aich, endearingly called 'Pocket Hercules' because of his short stature, had rippling muscles that were a delight to see. They were followed some years later by Arati Saha, who took the world of swimming by storm, being the first Asian girl to cross the English Channel.

I once visited the congested locality of Chor Bagan to see the much-talked-about Marble Palace, which was also known as the Babu Palace. It was built in the third decade of the 19th century by Raja ajendra Lal Mullick, a wealthy bullion merchant of Kolkata. The palace had a Grecian neo-classical façade with mighty columns, but inside, the architecture was largely Indian to suit the life-style of the 'Babus' (Bengalee gentry). Its variegated floors of rare specimens of marble, huge doors and windows, big Belgian mirrors, massive chandeliers, candelbras and lamp-stands, mammoth urns and planters, the original paintings of some European masters and the array of marble statues in the extensive gardens combined to create the ambience of Kolkata of old times when it was aptly called the city of palaces. It was Lord Minto, the Viceroy of India, who gave the name 'Marble Palace' to this edifice after visiting the place when he was highly impressed by the rich collection of a wide variety of precious objects d'art.

An important feature of the city's southern landscape and lakeland was the Dhakuria Lakes, which attracted not only those interested in swimming and rowing, but also many, who wanted to have an evening walk at a leisurely pace in pleasant surroundings. But what made this place specially famous was the fact that it served as an ideal rendezvous for the love-tryst of young romantic couples, already married or at different stages of the run-up to the state of marital bliss. You could see them promenading along secluded pathways or seated on the benches in convenient corners or on the grass below. A delicious snack, the spicy puffed rice called 'Masla Muri' that was hawked around the place served as the spice of life as well as of love.

In 1945, Kolkata was still the commercial capital of the country. The Managing Agency system which the Englishmen had founded as a means of controlling the management of industries in which they had financial stakes was still in full vigour, though some Marwari industrialists had already started taking it over from their English counterparts. Its roads were still uncongested and its air not as polluted as it became some years later. I started liking the place and in the course of the next few years, Kolkata grew on me. I began to feel, like all other Calcuttans, that there was no other place like Kolkata.

Kolkata's downward slide had begun in the early nineteen twenties after it ceased to be the country's political capital. But the real blow was dealt by the partition of the country and of Bengal in 1947, when it ceased to be the capital of undivided Bengal and instead became the capital of a shrunken West Bengal State. I realised how apt poet Wordsworth's famous lines on Venice were:

"Men are we and must grieve
When even the shade
Of that which once was great is
pass'd away".

But for me, as for all others, who have once lived in Kolkata and identified themselves with its spirit and ethos, Kolkata is still great! Kolkata has its problems and its poverty. But it has not lost its amour-propre and its sense of pride in its cultural heritage. That is why I love Kolkata, warts and all. It is like an old love that comes again and again to one's mind even in old age. Like an old melody, it never fails to haunt.

In 1945, I once undertook a particularly tiresome and long journey on foot, which eventually turned out to be a voyage of discovery. This was a visit to the Dakshineshwar temple, sanctified by its association with the name of saint Paramhansa Ramakrishna, and then to the Belur Math founded by his celebrated disciple, Swami Vivekananda, as the headquarters of the Ramakrishna Mission. After reaching Dakshineshwar by bus, I went round and saw the various places associated with the different stages of Ramakrishna's progress towards realising divinity. At the Kali temple, I stopped for a while, head bowed and hands clasped in prayer, before the idol of the goddess that stood over a silver lotus of a thousand petals. It was this goddess whom Ramakrishna had once threatened to beat up, if she did not reveal her true form to him. The threat had worked! I then saw the mighty old banyan tree under whose sprawling branches he had achieved his supreme enlightenment, as if in a flash.

I looked at the sweep of the Ganges, flowing sprightly past the Dakshineshwar temple. As I got down and touched the sacred water, I felt blessed. There, a functionary of the temple administration narrated to me and some other pilgrims the story of Rani Rasmoni, who had helped in building the temple complex in accordance with a divine command she received in a dream. She had become famous also for displaying great courage in taking up the cause of the fishermen of Kolkata whose fishing rights were being encroached upon as a consequence of some arbitrary orders of the British authorities.

From Dakshineshwar, I had a clear view of Belur Math on the other side of the Ganges. I was told—and later I also found it out—that you could see Dakshineshwar as clearly from Belur. I set my sight on Belur and decided to hike the entire distance of about four miles. I started walking towards Belur and crossed the Willingdon Bridge over the Ganges. As ill luck would have it, I took a wrong road and discovered my blunder only after I had already traversed some distance in the opposite direction. I retraced my steps and, trudging along slowly, reached Belur. I was sweating profusely, because it was a hot and humid summer afternoon.

I refreshed myself by having a wash at the Ganges and then proceeded to have a view of the temple's sanctum sanctorum. I was struck by the peacefulness and serenity of the place. It was an elevating experience to be there. It was late in the evening when I returned home by bus.

Over the last half a century, I have read numerous books about Ramakrishna Paramahansa, Swami Vivekananda and the wide range of socio-religious activities undertaken by the Ramakrishna Mission for the benefit of people living on the margins of society. Some years ago, I had the opportunity of going through a report[7] on the Ramakrishna Mission by Sir Charles Tegart, the controversial Commissioner of Kolkata Police, prepared in 1914 when he was the Special Superintedent of Police, Intelligence Branch, C.I.D., Bengal. I was taken aback by some of the statements made by him in his report on the Ramakrishna Mission and several persons associated with it.

The report referred to indications that the Ramakrishna Mission and its followers were connected with " the revolutionary side of the recent political upheaval in India, which has convulsed the student community in Bengal, and has more recently still extended its pernicious influence to even more dangerous ground in the Punjab and Native States of India."

Tegart made some interesting observations on the spiritual life of Shri Ramakrishna. An example: " Towards the end of his career, Ramakrishna appears to have regarded himself as an incarnation of the Deity, and he is now worshipped as such by his disciples. His visions grew more and more and his trances or Samadhi became longer and longer in duration. His disciples at his bidding are reported in several instances to have fallen into similar trances, evidently cases of hypnosis, which resulted in Ramakrishna being credited with supernatural powers.He is said to have possessed the wonderful power of being able to change a man's thoughts by merely touching his body. In some, it is recorded, this touch produced immediate Samadhi, in which they saw visions of gods and goddesses and lost for some time all sensation of the outward world."

The following observation by Prof. Max Muller on Shri Ramakrishna that is quoted by Tegart in his report in this context deserves to be reproduced: "Rama Krishna was in no sense of the word an original thinker, the discoverer of a new idea or the propounder of any new view of the world. But he saw many things which others had not seen. He recognised the Divine presence where it was least suspected. He was a poet, an enthusiast, or, if you like, a dreamer of dreams. But such dreams have also a right to exist and have a claim on our attention and sympathy. Rama Krishna never composed a philosophical treatise. He simply poured out short sayings, and the people came to listen to them, whether the speaker was at the time in full possession of his faculties, or in a dream or a trance. From all we can learn, it is quite clear that he had, by a powerful control of his breath, and by long-continued ascetic exercises, arrived at such a pitch of nervous excitability that he could at any moment faint away or fall into a state of unconsciousness, the so-called Samadhi. With Rama Krishna, it often happened that when he had fallen into the deep sleep, he remained in it so long that his friends were afraid that he would never return to consciousness, and so it was at the time of his death. He had fallen into a trance and he never awoke, but even death could lay hold of his body and his breath only; his Self, no longer his, had recovered its Brahmanhood; had become what it had always been and always will be, the Atman, the Highest Self in all its glory, freed from all the clouds of appearances, and independent of individuality, personality, and of the whole phenomenal world."

Adverting to Swami Vivekananda's spiritual activities and travels abroad, Tegart cited the following paragraph from a report of the Director of Criminal Intelligence,[8] Government of India: "However, spiritual the teachings or the life of Swami Vivekananda may have been, there is no doubt that some false prophets of Vedantism and even some of those who are accepted as genuine Swamis, are attracted to the work in Europe and America by the opportunities it provides for meeting on terms of intimacy with the ladies of the West."

With regard to the political fall-out of Swami Vivekananda's teachings, Tegart again mentioned the view of the Director of Criminal Intelligence, Government of India, that there was not much that could be called directly political in the lectures of the Swami. However, it was observed, since Vivekananda had aspired to put all other religions of the world in their proper place as mere aspects of his reading of Hinduism, he could not have, therefore, reconciled his religious teachings with the political domination of the Christians over the Hindus.

Tegart pointed out that moreover "the family of Swami Vivekanada is tainted with sedition in the person ofhis younger brother, Bhupendra Nath Datta." About Bhupendra Nath, Tegart observed that he was "one of the promoters of the notorious Jugantar newspaper which sowed the seeds of revolution and anarchy in the minds of the youths of Bengal until its suppression by Government in 1908. Bhupendra Nath was the first of its staff to be convicted of sedition, for which he was sentenced to one year's rigorous imprisonment in 1907. On his release in July 1908, he concealed himself or a time at the Belur Math, the headquarters of the Rama Krishna Mission."

After carrying out an extensive and in-depth analysis of the speeches and writings of Swami Vivekananda, Tegart tried to show" how the main principles of the Swami's teachings appealed to the revolutionary party of the present day, and how they have been able to use his sayings and writings to sow the seed of revolution and anarchy in the minds of the Indian youths—how the teachings of Arabinda Ghosh, the leader of the Maniktola conspiracy, were modelled on the same lines as Swami Vivekananda's, but with a more definite appeal to force or Sakti, which, he maintained, was necessary for the regeneration of India."

Tegart made some uncharitable remarks about Sister Nivedita (a name given to Miss Margaret Noble, an American disciple of Swami Vivekananda). It was pointed out that her connection with the Swami had a distinct bearing on the political side of the Swami's work as she was 'undoubtedly strongly imbued with nationalistic ideas.' The following comment made by Tegart on Sister Nivedita's character was in bad taste and highly objectionable: " She dressed in semi-native fashion and went bare-headed and without shoes. She was not looked upon with much favour by the respectable Indians of Kolkata, as from all accounts she did not bear a good moral character and was living in a house with a number of young Bengalis. Her expenses were apparently met by the Rama Krishna Mission."

Tegart also made some critical observations about Swami Abhedananda, a prominent monk of the Ramakrishna Mission. Swami Abhedananda's lectures delivered in America were said to be seditious and a book containing these lectures was, therefore, proscribed.

Tegart also cast aspersions on Swami Abhedananda's character by making the following observation, which was highly objectionable: "His relations with women in America are alleged to be not free from grave suspicion, and it was reported that the United tates Government were enquiring into this matter."

Tegart's report catalogued a number of instances that revealed what he called the close links between the Ramakrishna Mission and the members of revolutionary groups such as the Anushilan Samiti and the Yugantar, which were engaged in the underground freedom movement of our country. He also drew attention to the growth of numerous Ramakrishna Ashrams in the villages all over Bengal and Assam, most of which were not affiliated to the Ramakrishna Mission at Belur and over whose activities, therefore, the latter had no control. Enquiries conducted by the Intelligence Branch, C.I.D., Bengal and interception of the mails of these unaffiliated Ramakrishna Ashrams showed that what they did was to attract the youth under the cover of religious and Ramakrishna Mission-related activities and secretly induct them on the path of revolutionary activity.

Tegart, therefore, observed: " It will be seen from the foregoing that there is evidence to show that the Rama Krishna Mission itself has been used in the past as a revolutionary agency, under the guise of religion and philanthropy, and that the greatest danger at the present time lies in the unaffiliated asrams which have grown up like mushrooms in the affected areas in Eastern Bengal without the knowledge or sanction of the headquarters mission at Belur. In fact, Swami Vivekananda's command to go out and preach the gospel of Sri Rama Krishna and found branch asrams through India has been taken up by the revolutionaries in Bengal to such good effect that it is evident that even admitting the best intentions in the world, the authorities of the mission at Belur are unable to control them."

On the suggestion of the Bengal administration, Swami Saradananda, Secretary, Ramakrishna Math and Mission, Belur, issued a warning to the members of the public, dissociating his organisation from the political and revolutionary activities of the unaffiliated Ramakrishna Ashrams. To quote some excerpts from his statement: " —The Mission, therefore, has all along kept its own work separated from the National Congress, the extremist and such other regular and irregular political movements with the firm conviction that these would never lead to the glorious spiritual regeneration which should be the ideal of India's people. Spirituality and not poltical aggrandisement had been the backbone of the Indian people in the past, and on that inheritance we should stand firm with goodwill and love and peace to all on earth—Let the young men of Bengal and India take heed of the fact, and if in future they find a class of people coming to them in the name of the Rama Krishna Mission and that of the Belur Math, to preach politics to them in any shape whatsoever, let them conclude at once that they are imposters, who are but making cowardly attempts to hide their true colours behind the prestige of the Mission and the Math to serve their own dark purposes.—The second thing against which we want to warn the general public is, never to conclude that a society or a Sevasram belongs to, and is a branch of the Belur Math and Rama Krishna Mission simply for the reason that the name Rama Krishna or Vivekananda is attached to it.— "

Tegart concluded his report with the following observation: "In this note, as stated at the outset, it is the political aspect of the mission to which attention has mainly been directed, and the points against the mission have been set out seriatim. The result may be that an impression has inadvertently been conveyed that there is not another and brighter side of the mission's work. To remove any such impression, it may be said at once that it is not contended that in its essence the Rama Krishna Mission is anything but what it purports to be, a purely religious body, which has undoubtedly done a great deal of good, in a humble way, in affording relief in times of distress, and at all times in giving medical relief gratis to the poor at various Sevasrams referred to above."

"The Swamis, with possibly a few exceptions, do not mix themselves up in political matters. They have stated that they are anxious to exclude political suspects from their mission and have recently given evidence of the good faith in this respect by refusing admission to three members of the revolutionary party who were anxious to join, probably in order to evade the police and carry on their work under the aegis of the math. That the Math authorities were on their guard against revolutionaries is apparent from a declaration form for intending members issued in 1911, in which the applicant is required to sign a declaration to the following effect: " I declare that I have no connection whatever with any political or any secret body."

"On the other hand, it has been shewn that the ranks of the math officials are not free from taint, and it is somewhat disconcerting to find, just at the time of compiling this note, that Saradanada's brother is himself an active and dangerous revolutionary. It has also been shown that several passages of the teachings of Swami Vivekananda are pregnant with sedition, that their potentialities for evil have been fully realized and taken advantage of by the revolutionary party, that the various recognised Maths are resorted to by political refugees and that bogus asrams, which are nothing but centres for the dissemination of revolutionary doctrines, have sprung up with alarming rapidity in Eastern Bengal."

"The authorities at Belur are apparently now fully alive to the dangerous possibilities ahead and are apparently anxious to check this perversion of their teachings as far as possible."

I am sure, many of the offensive statements made in these reports would have caused widespread protest in India, if they had come to light. Let us put all this behind us and express our gratitude to the Ramakrishna Mission for the multifarious activities it has undertaken all over our country and elsewhere for the social and spiritual regeneration of the people. The Ramakrishna Mission's image has remained unsullied despite whatever secret reports the British authorities obtained from their intelligence agencies. In fact, even Tegart recognised in his report the basic fact that the Ramakrishna Mission was primarily a religious organisation that had done immense good to the people at large.

Notes

1. शका नाम तनो राजा महालक्ष्मी सनातनीम्।। त्रिवर्पाते च सा देवी कामाक्षीरूपधारिणी।।८।।
स्वभक्तपालना चैव तत्र वासमकारयत्।। शताद्धाब्दं कृतं राज्यं तेन वै कामवर्यणा।।६।।
मिथुनं जनयामास भोगो भोगवती हि सा।। विक्रमायैव नृपतिः सुतां भोगवंती ददौ।।१०।।
स्वराज्यं च स्वपुत्राय प्रद भोगवर्मणे। पिस्तुल्यं कृतं राज्यं कालिवर्मा सुतोऽभवत्।।११।।
महोत्सवं महाकाल्याः कृतवान्स च भूपतिः।। तस्मै प्रसन्ना वरदा काली भूत्वा स्वयं स्थिता।।१२।।
कलिका बहुपुष्पाणां सा चकार स्वहर्षतः।। ताभिर्भवं च नगरं संजातं च मनोहरम्।।१३।।
कलिकाता पुरी नाम्ना प्रसिद्धाभून्महीतले।। कौशिकस्तस्य तनयः पितुस्तुल्यं कृतं पदम्।।१४।।
Bhabisya Purana, Pratisarga Parva, 4th Khanda, 4, 8-14.

2. तद्राष्ट्रे नादरो नाम दैत्यो देश उपागमत्।। हत्वार्यांश्रव सुराज्जित्वा देशं खुरजमाययौ।।५८।। महामत्स्यो हि मदस्य तनयस्तत्पितुः पदम्।। गृहीत्वा पंचवर्षान्तं स च राज्यं वकार ह।।५६।। मडाराष्ट्रेर्हतो दुष्टस्तालनाम्वयसंभवः।। दहलानगरे राज्य दशाब्दं माधवेन वै।।६०।। कृतं तत्र तदा म्लेच्छ आलोमा राज्यमाप्तवान्।। नद्राष्ट्रे बहवो जाता राजानो निजदेशजाः।।६१।। ग्रामपा बहवो भूपा देशेदेशे वभूविरे।। मण्डलीकपदं तत्राक्षयं जातं महीतले।।६२।। त्रिंशदब्दमतो जातं ग्रामेग्रामे नृपेनृपे।। तदा तु सकला देवाः कृष्णचैतन्यमाययुः।।६३।। यज्ञां शश्रव हरिः साक्षाज्ज्ञात्वा दुःखं महीतले।। मुहूर्तं ध्यानमागम्य देवान्वचनमब्रवीत्।।६४।। पुरा तु राघवो धीमाज्जित्वा रावणराक्षसम्।। कपी नुज्जीवयामास सुधावैस्समंततः।।६५।। विकटो वृजिलो जालो वरलीनो हि सिंहलः।। जवस्तुमात्रश्रव तथा नाम्ना ते क्षुद्रवानराः।।६६।। रामचंद्रं वचः प्राहुर्देहि नो वांछितं प्रभो। रामो दाशरथिः श्रीमाज्ज्ञात्वा तेषां मनोरथम्।।६७।। देवाङ्गनोद्रवाः कन्या रावणाल्लोकरावणात्।। दत्त्वा तेभ्यो हरिस्साक्षाद्ववचनं प्राह हर्षितः।।६८।। भवन्नान्ना च ये द्वीपा जालंधरविनिर्मिताः।। तेषु राज्ञो भविष्यंति भवन्तो हितकारिणः।।६६।। नन्दिंन्या गोश्रव रुंडाद्वै जाता लेच्छा भयानकाः।।गुरुण्डा जातयस्तेपां तास्तु तेषु सदा स्थिताः।।७०।। जित्वा तांश्रव गुरुण्डान्वै कुरुध्वं राज्यमुत्तमम्।। इति श्रुत्वा हरिं नत्व द्वीपेषु प्रययुर्मुदा।।७१।। विकटान्वयसंभूता गुरुण्डा वानराननाः।। वाणिज्यार्थमिहायाता गौरुण्डा बौद्धमार्गिणः।।७२।। ईशपुत्रमते सस्थास्तेषां ह्रदयमुक्तमम्।। सत्यव्रतं कामजितमकोधं सूर्यतत्परम्।।७३।। यूयं तत्रोप्य कार्यं च नृणां कुरुत मा चिरम्।। इति श्रुत्वा तु ते देवाः कुर्युरार्चिकमादसत्।।७४।। नगर्य्यां कलिकातायां स्थापयामासुरुद्यताः।। विकटे पश्रिवमे द्वीपे तत्पनी विकटावती।।७५।। अष्टकौशलमार्गेण राजमंत्रं चकार ह।। तत्पतिस्तु पुलोमार्चिः कलिकातां पुरीं स्थितः।।७६।। विक्रमस्य गते।

Bhabisya Purana, Pratisarga Parva, 4th Khanda, 22, 58-76.

3. Article entitled 'Calcutta in Poetry" by Samar Sen in the Calcutta Municipal Gazette, Anthology Number (1924-1947), pages 94-95.
4. *Ibid.*, article captioned "Calcutta and English Literature" by Rabindra Kumar Dasgupta, p. 73.
5. *Ibid.*, pp. 73-74.
6. *Ibid.*, pp. 71-72.
7. Note dated April 22, 1914 under the caption "The Ramakrishna Mission" prepared by C.A. Tegart, Special Superintendent of Police, Intelligence Branch, C.I.D., Bengal, vide Terrorism in Bengal (1995), Government of West Bengal, Volume IV, pp. 1330-1370.
8. The designation of this officer was changed after some years to "Director, Intelligence Bureau", a designation which still continues and which in the 1980's. I acquired when I held this post.

3

Our Life Style in Kolkata

After we moved over to Kolkata from Vikrampur in 1945, several persons of our village, who came to the city in search of employment or to try their luck in some petty business, visited us from time to time. A few of them lived with us for short periods till they could find some place for themselves. Some of our close relations put up with us for varying periods. All this put a severe strain on our resources because the two small rooms we had were utterly inadequate even for the needs of our own family of eleven members. In such circumstances, there was no privacy for anyone nor was there a small secluded corner which one could call one's own and where one could quietly retire with a book.

My father's cousin, who lived in a part of the house, had six daughters one of whom had married the son of an absentee landlord of Vikrampur, who had a big house in Dhakuria, then a rural suburb of Kolkata. Her name is Rani and the pet name by which we called her was Ranu. She was roughly of the same age as I and, therefore, we had a good rapport. The person Ranu had married was a budding revolutionary poet by name Birendra Chatterjee. When we went to live in Kolkata in 1945, Ranu was a coy Bengalee bride hardly eighteen years of age. Sometimes, her husband, dressed in Khadi 'Dhoti' and 'Kurta' (called 'Punjabi' in Bengal), dropped in along with Ranu and left her behind to spend a day or two with her parents and sisters.

When Ranu went back to her husband's place in Dhakuria, someone had to accompany her, because married girls of middle class families were not expected to go about alone and unchaperoned.

Occasionally, I was asked to drop her back at the place of her husband. The bus in which we travelled stopped short of a Railway level-crossing beyond which we had to walk about a mile through what looked like the countryside with mud roads and ponds all around. An attraction for me to accompany Ranu to this place was the ample and delicious refreshments to which I was treated, because I was a 'Kutum' (Bengali word for a person from a family connected by marriage on whom hospitality of a high order had to be lavished).

Birendra Chatterjee was from Vikrampur in the Dhaka district of undivided Bengal—the place from which I also hailed. He was born in the Bejgaon village of Vikrampur on September 2,1920. Tutturi was his pet name by which his in-laws called him when he visited their place. He was not at all serious in his studies and after passing the Intermediate of Art examination, he made no serious effort to become a graduate. The money given to him by his parents towards his fees for the B.A. examination he magnanimously donated to a poor friend, who had no money to pay his fees!

He dabbled in politics, having been a member even in his school days of the "Anushilan Samiti", a well-known revolutionary group of pre-independence Bengal. He later switched over to the Revolutionary Socialist Party. But his main occupation was the writing of Bengali poetry. For some years after 1945, I met him whenever he visited his parents-in-law along with Ranu. I had, therefore, numerous opportunities of interacting and exchanging pleasantries with him.

When I first met Birendra Chatterjee, two of his books of verses "Grahachyuta"(1943) and "Natun Mas" (1943) had already been published. I read these verses as well as some more that came out in 1946. Another book of verses that came out in 1952 was "Ranur Janya", its title bearing the name of his wife. I was quite impressed by his poetry, though I did not understand much of it at that time. Some of his family members thought that poetry-writing was not going to help him much in life, if the earning of a handsome monthly income was to be regarded as the hall-mark of a person's worldly success.

Birendra Chatterjee toiled hard to eke out an honest living, but fortune did not favour him. He was not a man of the world and did no know how to make money. He was a warm-hearted person, who did not believe in formalities. He was a man in a hurry with a certain degree of impetuosity. He always kept his head high and refused to accept money from any governmental organisation, as he felt that this would curb his freedom of thought and action.

Decades later, when from this poet's pen flowed a steady stream of verses which delighted Bengal's literary world, earning him the much-coveted "Rabindra Puraskar", I realised, with the advantage of hindsight, that even in those far-off days of the nineteen forties, when I had first made my acquaintance with him and his poetical works, he had in him the making of a great poet. As we all know, a poet is not held in much esteem in the early stages of his career, because he does not contribute as much to the family's kitty as other less gifted, but more worldly-wise members do for the upkeep of the family.

Birendra Chatterjee, who blossomed into a well-known literary figure of Bengal in course of time, is, alas, no more, having died prematurely on July 11,1985. That he had earned the love and regard of a wide cross section of people became evident when, after his death, a mammoth funeral procession, carrying his body, wended its way to the Keoratala cremation ground in south Kolkata, braving a heavy downpour that had dislocated normal life in Kolkata. I have highlighted some facets of the life and works of this poet to bring out the kind of atmosphere that prevailed in our house, though it was located in the midst of what was no better than a slum area. I felt very happy when I learnt some years ago that the Government of West Bengal had decided to erect a statue in his memory in Kolkata.

It was inevitable that a country bumpkin like me was to get a rude culture shock in the great metropolis of Kolkata. The customs, etiquettes and traditions of Kolkata diferred radically from those of our village in Vikrampur. For quite some years, we did not imbibe the habit of taking tea, as the people of Kolkata normally did. Gradually, however, we picked up many of the customs of Kolkata's middle class 'Bhadralok' families and adjusted our life-style to the demands of contemporary Kolkata culture. I feel that there is a good side to these age-old niceties of Kolkata in that they reflect the average Bengalee's social grace and his habit of going all out to make his guest feel at home, when he takes the trouble of paying the former a visit, be it a courtesy call or a business errand.

While walking along Kolkata's streets, I was struck by their glistening clean look – something we did not have in our village. But there were many nooks and corners where the filth stank to high heavens. In our village, we did not have any filth of this kind and the environment was remarkably clean. In Kolkata, there were very few public facilities where a person walking along the streets could stop for easing his bladder or bowel if the call of nature was sudden and urgent. At some street corners where the side wall of a house or building provided a convenient foil for a person to direct the flow of his accumulated urine, the authorities, displaying a remarkable capacity for anticipation, had put up notices with the warning: "Commit No Nuisance". But when one's bladder faced the danger of bursting, nobody would bother to heed this warning. At some of these street corners, I saw that the word 'No' had been erased, presumably by street urchins, with the result that the warning now read: "Commit—Nuisance", thus extending an open invitation to one and all to pee in public, no matter whether anybody else was looking at you or not.

Not that Kolkata was the only place where such uncivil or unsightly conduct came to nice or where the people at large were incontinent and had weak bladders. In our village too, we did not hesitate to pee in public in the open spaces that served as our al fresco toilets. The only difference was that the vast expanses of the countryside, ever exposed to the sun, strong winds and rains hardly left any scope for the accumulation of filth and garbage anywhere.

I was fascinated by Kolkata's tram-cars, which proceeded smoothly along fixed tracks with a tan-tan sound. When tram cars first started plying in Kolkata in the latter half of the nineteenth century, with horses brought from Australia drawing them along the meter-gauge track, they must have looked really novel to the city's inhabitants. As the horses found it difficult to stand the hot and humid climate of Kolkata, they were gradually replaced by steam locomotives, which in due course yielded place to electric tram-cars.

In course of time, the tram-cars became an inseparable part of Kolkata's landscape and their movement early in the morning, when it was still dark, produced a gentle drone and a melody to which I became inured over a period of time. It was this sound and the swoosh of water from the hose-pipes used to wash the roads clean which woke you up in the morning and left you in no doubt that it was time to get up.

When Kolkata's political activists had to give vent to their anger, they often chose the tram-car as the target of their fury. In their fit of rage, they not only burnt the tram-car, but also uprooted its track, making the task of restoration of traffic doubly difficult. I was witness to this mood of Kolkata's inhabitants in 1953, when they waged the 'one-pice war' against the authorities to protest against an increase of a pice in tram fares – a movement which was the occasion for the protestors to indulge in large-scale violence and for the police to resort to stringent measures to meet the situation.

I saw the rickshaw for the first time in Kolkata, but it was something to which I never took kindly, because it was pulled by man. I was repelled by the very thought that in pulling a rickshaw a man virtually played the role of a draught animal like the horse and the bullock, which drew the carriages tied behind them. For the common man, though, the rickshaw had several advantages over other modes of transport. It came in handy for short distance journeys; and because it was cheaper than other modes of travel, it was very much in demand.

When Kolkata's streets got flooded by heavy rain, it was the rickshaw alone that could ply, as all mechanised systems of transport became paralysed. On such occasions, it was a sight to see not only dainty damsels or old men and women, but even able-bodied young men imperiously looking all around from their high perch on the fragile vehicle, as the rickety rickshaw-puller strained hard to forge ahead through knee-deep or even waist-deep water, the bell tied to the rickshaw ringing frantically to make sure that no passer-by strayed too close to obstruct its smooth passage.

Since I regarded the very concept of the man-drawn rickshaw as an anathema, I deliberately denied myself the pleasure of ever sitting on one. The pity is that no government has been able to abolish it, as any step in that direction would deprive the numerous rickshaw-pullers of their means of livelihood.

The same consideration, namely that some people will lose their jobs, has stood in the way of doing away with the hand-carts and tram cars, whose fixed tracks obstruct the free and flexible flow of traffic on Kolkata's congested roads.

To my mind, there is a case for the cycle rickshaw, which is pollution-free and environment friendly. No wonder, today the cycle rickshaw has its votaries in many Western countries. Names such as 'Pedicab', 'Velotaxi', 'Metrobike' etc. have been given to the latest incarnations of the cycle rickshaw in several countries of Europe and America.

The West Bengal Government's recent decision to abolish the hand-pulled rickshaw should be welcomed, though it casts on the government the responsibility of providing alternative avenues of employment for the rickshawpullers and simultaneously devising an equally convenient and cheap mode of transport for the people of Kolkata. It is all very well to romanticize the rickshaw-puller in films and literature, but the hard fact is that the hand-pulled rickshaw is the symbol of the grinding poverty and destitution of the city of joy.

What marked a radical departure in Kolkata from our old food habits of Vikrampur in east Bengal was the absence in each meal of fish in ample quantities to which we were accustomed in the village. Moreover, what was sold in Kolkata's markets was fish that was neither alive nor kicking, but was dead, stale and frozen. What amused me was that one did not normally buy a whole fish in Kolkata unless it was of the smaller variety. Big fish like Rohu or Katla was sold in cut pieces and that too by weight. It took me quite a while to get used to this change which I did not like at all. I missed the fish of Shyamsiddhi's ponds and marshes that had a unique taste and flavour.

In the village, we used to take the milk of our own cows. In Kolkata, what we got was the thick and creamy milk of the buffalo, which the milkman passed off as cow's milk, after, of course, diluting it with a certain measure of water about which its taste and gravity left no one in doubt. There was a flexible pricing system which depended on the proportion of water to milk that the customer was prepared to accept and condone.

There was rationing of food in Kolkata and, along with rice, some wheat was also provided by the ration shop. I did not like eating wheat, which I had hardly ever taken in my village, where rice was our staple food. I did not relish the taste of 'Chapati' (our indigenous version of bread) that was made out of wheat flour. However, over the years, I got over my excessive fondness of rice and learnt to like wheat as much as rice. The rice supplied by the ration shops was of poor quality and had a fair admixture of stone chips, which our teeth, strong though they were, found it rather hard to tackle.

There was rationing of cloth as well in Kolkata in view of the unprecedented scarcity of cotton textiles—a problem that highlighted a dismal failure on the part of the Nazimuddin Ministry which was in power in Bengal till March 1945. So serious was the situation that some among the poor could not even cover their shame.

Women sometimes found it embarrassing to come out of their houses, as they were not sufficiently clothed. Even for funeral rites and for weddings, people often had difficulty in arranging the requisite supply of cloth. This situation brought to my mind the following picture of a similar situation that had been painted by Bar, a Sanskrit poet of Bengal :

Gehinyah Sphutitang Shukang Ghatayatuh Kritwa Sakakusmitang

Kupyanti Pratibeshini Praimuhuh Suching Yatha Yachita [1]

It was alleged by many that the scarcity of cloth had been created by the black-marketeers, who were holding the people to ransom after bribing the Ministers and officials. H.S. Suhrawardy, Minister for Civil Supplies, and the officials of his Department came in for trenchant criticism in this context. Not only the opposition parties, but even Lord Wavell,the Governor-General of India, reportedly lambasted the Bengal Government for its failure to put an end to what was basically an artificial and man-made scarcity. In view of the mounting criticism of its policies, the Government of Bengal issued an ordinance authorising the search of godowns to bring out hoarded cloth. During searches that were conducted, hoarded stocks were discovered in about three thousand godowns of north and central Kolkata, which were, therefore, sealed.

These developments, which tarnished the image of the Nazimuddin Government and also affected its strength in the Legislative Assembly, eventually brought about its downfall. During the budget session of the Legislative Assembly, grants for the Department of Agriculture were voted on March 28, 1945.The MLA's supporting Nazimuddin together with the European members of the Assembly were in a majority. However, some businessmen were reportedly found loitering about in the vicinity of the Assembly with bags of money to bribe some of the MLA's into voting out the Nazimuddin Ministry.

Nazimuddin and H.S. Suhrawardy discovered to their dismay that their supporters were not present in full strength. The European MLA's had gone for lunch. There was great concern in the Treasury benches. After lunch, the European MLA's returned to the Assembly. Then, there was a great commotion as 15 supporters of the Nazimuddin Ministry left the Treasury benches to walk across and sit along with the opposition members. Some members of the Treasury benches openly alleged in the Assembly that some businessmen adversely affected by the raids on their godowns had heavily bribed some MLA's to switch their loyalty from the government to the opposition. The Nazimuddin Ministry fell as it could muster only 97 votes as against 106 secured by the opposition. The Governor, R.G. Casey, took over the administration under Section 93 of the Government of India Act, 1935. It became evident that the votes of some members of the Legislative Assembly had been purchased (allegedly by some businessmen) to bring down the Ministry of Nazimuddin for the sin of having raided the godowns of businessmen to unearth hoarded cloth.

This was perhaps one of the earliest examples of the practice of bringing down Ministries by bribing MLA's or by organising defections – a practice that has become an inseparable part of our political culture. Another consequence that followed was that before organising raids on the godowns of the hoarders and black-marketeers in later years, the incumbent Ministry always took the precaution of carefully weighing all the pros and cons.

The main reason for the fall of the Nazimuddin Ministry was that Habibullah, the Nawab of Dhaka, left his party at the last moment, because he was not made the Minister for Supplies. I remember to have seen a statement by Habibullah along with some others, who had left Nazimuddin's Government, that the preceding two years of Nazimuddin's rule had spelt disaster for Bengal because of corruption and inefficiency. They also alleged that the 20 persons, who were authorised to bring supplies of cloth to Bengal from outside the Province, included one Muslim and 19 Hindus most of whom were non-Bengalees, thus seeking to show that the Nazimuddin Government favoured the non-Bengalees.

Strangely enough, H.S. Suhrawardy, a Minister in the Nazimuddin Government, had also put the blame for the Ministry's downfall on the non-Bengalee businessmen. He had alleged in a statement in the Legislative Assembly on the day of the voting (i.e. on March 28, 1945) that in case they lost the vote in the Assembly, it would be on account of some of the Ministry's supporters being bribed by the hoarders and black-marketeers. Since I came to Kolkata very shortly after all this happened, I read lurid accounts of these developments in the press, apart from hearing what people at large used to say.

Kolkata's ambrosial 'Misti Doi' (sweeet curd) was an item of delicatessen that I greatly relished. The confectioners of my native

Vikrampur in east Bengal also made their sweet curd, which, however, was no patch on its Kolkata variant. In fact, the trade secret of Kolkata's 'Misti Doi' had still not leaked out to any other place in India. 'Misti Doi' that formed an essential ingredient of Bengal's dolce vita had a light brown colour and came in earthen pots of various sizes, the smallest one looking like an ice cream cup and its contents matching ice cream in its allure.

Curd of all kinds, sweet or sour, was (and still is) highly prized for its life-extending benefits. Curd probably originated in the middle east many centuries ago. 'Yoghart' meaning curd is a Turkish word, its synonym in the Assyrian language being 'lebeny', which meant 'life'. The longevity-enhancing quality of curd is said to derive from the bacteria which abound in it. According to studies in the field of phagocytosis, these bacteria are transmitted to curd in a perpetual stream through the small doses of seed curd that are inserted into milk as enzyme to make it curdle and coagulate.

Our family did not succumb to the practice of taking tea for quite some years after we shifted to Kolkata. But I occasionally visited one or the other of the many restaurants that dotted our locality to take a cup of tea along with novel snacks and savouries for which Kolkata was famous and which I immensely relished because I had never tasted them before. I can claim, with the advantage of my later experience of life, that such delicacies were not available to the common man anywhere else at prices which they could afford. The famous Sanghu Valley group ran a chain of restaurants all over Kolkata, which were generally manned by people from east Bengal, particularly Chittagong, who spoke a dialect among themselves that we failed to decipher.

A snack which I tasted for the first time in one such restaurant was 'Mamlet', a distorted name given to omlette by the boys of the restaurant, who were innocent of English. Savouries with English and Mughlai names, whose meanings I did not initially understand and which were served in these restaurants included mutton chop, egg devil, fowl cutlet (often wrongly spelt as 'foul' cutlet), mutton cutlet, Biriyani, Murg Masalam, mutton Kaviraji, prawn cutlet, Ragan Josh, Mughlai Parantha (of 'Anadi Cabin' fame), pudding and what have you. The 'Kaviraji', a kind of mutton cutlet, had nothing to do with the 'Kaviraj' or the practitioner of Ayurveda, as he is called in Bengal. The name of this dish derived from the light batter of egg that encrusted the cutlet, the word 'Kaviraji' being a corruption for the word 'covered'. The 'Prawn Kaviraji' was rated as a superior delicacy.

These dishes catered to all tastes and you could order something that suited your purse. If you could not afford a full cup of tea, even though its price was only an anna (one-sixteenth of rupee) in those good old days, you could order what was commonly known a 'double half', which meant that a cup of tea was to be served in two cups to two friends so that the cost per head worked out to half an anna only! I heard many years later that a somewhat similar practice was in vogue in Karnataka, where two not so affluent friends could order "by-two coffee", which meant that a cup of coffee would be split into two cups.

The restaurant is a great social institution of Kolkata, where, in the democratic atmosphere that prevails, the hoi polloi can have, along with tea and snacks of their choice, also a session of 'Adda' (pure gossip, a favourite pastime of the Bengalee), which in those days often reached great intellectual heights, its scope encompassing anything under the sun, ranging from philosophy, politics, national and international developments, Hegelian and Marxist dialectic, economics, sociology and literature, both foreign and indigenous, to art, music, films and sports including football and cricket. I still remember the names of most of these restaurants where I spent many hours of my youth in the delightful company of my numerous friends.

Those belonging to the upper middle class used to patronise restaurants in the Chowringhee area (such as the Quality, Trincas, Firpo's etc.), where the prices were a little higher and the snacks more varied, because they had to cater to a more cosmopolitan clientele that also included non-Bengalees and foreigners. Many of them also drifted to the city's coffee houses, of which more later.

A place where the youngsters of a locality preferred to sit for 'Adda' was the 'Rok' i.e. a narrow strip of open space, usually a small verandah in front of a house, usually facing a road. 'Adda', sometimes described as a 'talkathon', reflected the herd instinct or the gregariousness of the average Bengalee, who joined others for sheer company, after returning from college or office in the evening, though the time might vary on holidays. The cardinal principle of 'Adda' was the acceptance of the democratic principle of equality among its participants and of the freedom of expression, which entitled anyone to express his view on any subject under the sun with an air of authority, whether the others agreed with him or not.

The animated discussions during sessions of 'Adda' on subjects ranging from high philosophy to the politics of the day were quite frank and forthright.

For entertainment, the people flocked to the cinema halls, which showed Bengali, Hindi and English films. I often walked into the foyer of some cinema hall, looking intently at the graffiti that displayed the pictures in various poses of the actors and actresses of the film then on view as well as of those that were expected to be released in the near future. Occasionally, I strolled about near the cinema halls in Chowringhee, which showed English films and whose walls were plastered with the tantalising pictures of the heroines in different degrees of undress. In summer, if you stood in the foyer of a cinema hall, you were vouchsafed a trickle of cool air that escaped through several chinks in the heavy door of the air-conditioned hall or through the gap between the door and the floor below. The blinking coloured lights of the cinema halls that were alternately on and off and were designed to give publicity to the films left a newly arrived rustic like me simply wonder-struck.

In Kolkata, I began to take a good deal of interest in football and in the matches of Kolkata's Football League and the Indian Football Association Shield tournament played by the well-known Kolkata clubs, whose professional standard was rated as the highest in the country. Those were the heady days of Indian soccer whose image was quite good even in the world outside. I often went to the 'Maidan' in the afternoon and waited anxiously outside the enclosed football grounds to get the latest news about the trend of the matches that were being played inside. There were some who went to the 'Maidan' with improvised periscopes with which they could see from outside the match that was being played inside the enclosed ground.

However, I sought entry into the football ground by paying for a ticket to see the final of the I.F.A. Shield tournament or an important match between, say, any two of such famous clubs as the East Bengal, Mohan Bagan and the Mohammedan Sporting.

I was a supporter of the East Bengal Club, as people from east Bengal (called 'Bangals') generally were, while those from West Bengal (called 'Ghatis') mostly identified themselves with the Mohan Bagan Club. I for myself did not, however, harbour any ill feeling towards the supporters of the Mohan Bagan Club or the people of West Bengal. I looked upon the whole thing as a matter of intense rivalry in the realm of sports which should not normally vitiate personal and social equations. It was in a spirit of innocent fun that I approached this issue. I used to admire the whole lot of eminent football players of those days cutting across club lines. The names that readily come to mind are those of Manna, Pugsley, Taj Mohammed, Mewalal, Ahmed Khan, Venkatesh, Saleh and Dhanraj, most of whom were bare-foot players.

The Mohan Bagan Club had established itself in the early years of the twentieth century as the premier indigenous football club. The East Bengal Club was founded at a later date by some people from east Bengal, as they had reportedly felt slighted by some leaders of the Mohan Bagan Club. It was in the year 1911 that the Mohan Bagan Club defeated a crack football team of Englishmen—the East Yorkshire Regiment—in the finals of the Indian Football Association Shield tournament. It was the first time that an Indian football team had defeated an English team—a great achievement that boosted colonial India's national pride and turned the name of the Mohan Bagan club into a symbol of Indian nationalism and national aspirations in the field of sports. In later years, I heard that it was the Shovabazar eam that had earned this honour twentyone years ago in 1890 by defeating the Yorkshire team. I do not still know which account is more reliable.

The East Bengal Club was formed in 1920—long after the Mohan Bagan Club had reached the zenith of its fame and popularity. It drew upon the natural sympathy of those who hailed from the other side of the Padma to emerge as a strong rival to the Mohan Bagan Club. It was on May,28, 1925 that the two teams had their first encounter. In due course, any match between the famed Mohan Bagan and East Bengal clubs became a great sporting as well as a social event of Kolkata and the near-by districts, from which people used to come in their thousands to see it.

A clash between these two giants meant that almost everybody in the employ of the government and of the private companies enjoyed an unofficial holiday at least in the afternoon, when the game was actually played. There was great tension and excitement on the field and sometimes a verdict given by the referee, the guardian of fair play, gave rise to controversies and aroused passions that resulted in his man-handling by the supporters of the club adversely affected by his ruling. This naturally called for prompt action by the police, which made elaborate arrangements in advance and took no chances on such occasions. Not unoften, many horses of the Kolkata Police were seriously injured as a result of pelting of stones and other missiles by unruly crowds. We did not mind braving such situations in order to see a good football match.

Football and fish were the reigning passions of the Bengalees and sometimes the two got interlinked. A football match between the East Bengal and Mohun Bagan teams had an inevitable impact on the price of fish. It is said – rightly or wrongly I do not know – that the people of east Bengal are specially fond of Hilsa fish, while the West Bengal people's hot favourite is the prawn. What actually happened was that, if the East Bengal Club got the better of the Mohan Bagan Club in a match, the price of Hilsa immediately went up; in the reverse case, there was an automatic escalation in the price of prawns. I do not know if the prices of Hilsa and prawns still react in the same old way in Kolkata!

A great merit of the Mohan Bagan Club was that it encouraged local players to come up and in, due course, absorbed the best among them into the team. The East Bengal Club also followed a similar policy in the initial years, but later it started hiring some good players from the other Provinces in order to improve the team's performance. This was an issue on which the Mohan Bagan Club's supporters often criticised the East Bengal Club. But over the years, many of these Kolkata clubs have lost the 'Bengaleeness' or even the 'Indianness' of their football teams as a result of their craze for 'phoren', which has led them to 'import' foreign players from some countries of Asia and Africa and even Russia. Some time ago, Mohan Bagan's Bareto, a foreign footballer, was reported to be a super-hero of Kolkata's football scene.

Though even in the forties of the last century, football in Kolkata had a professional orientation, yet amateur players dominated the show by and large. Things have radically changed now as a result of the advent of the cult of professionalism in all games and sports all over the world. The deadly serious business that sport has now become as a sequel to professional coaching, which is almost Spartan in its emphasis on discipline and performance, has robbed it of much of its earlier charm that derived from its artistic flavour, amateurish orientation and inspirational character.

A fact that has robbed Kolkata's football matches of much of their old appeal is the increasing interest that the new generation has been evincing in cricket in which I personally see nothing wrong, because sporting activity of any kind deserves to be welcomed. In each locality of Kolkata, the boys are now seen playing cricket with a zeal that far surpasses the Calcuttans' traditional enthusiasm for football.

When India became independent in 1947, football in our country, West Bengal included, was not in such a plight as today. In the 1948 Olympic Games held in London, the performance of our bare-foot players had won all-round appreciation. In the 1956 Melbourne Olympic Games, India had ranked fourth in football and in the next Olympics also, our performance was not so unpraiseworthy. India footballers won gold medals at the Asian Games held in 1957 and 1962.True, Kolkata's East Bengal Club lifted the LG Cup ASEAN Club championship at Jakarta in July 2003 and won the Asia Cup in Vietnam in 2004, but these may have been mere flashes in the pan. India now comes very low in the ranking list of the football-playing countries of the world. What ails Indian football today? Unless efforts are made to promote professionalism and make Indian players attain the standards of their peers in the other countries of the world, there is no hope for Indian football

Note

1. This appears in the 'Saduktikarnamrita' composed by Sridharadasa in 1206 A.D. Literally translated, it means: All this did not cause me as much pain as when I saw my wife go to an ill-tempered woman living next door to ask with a plaintive smile on her lips for a needle to repair her torn clothes.

4

Kolkata's B.B.D. Bag : Its Vikrampur Connection

I have referred earlier to my gadding about in Kolkata's famous Dalhouse Square, which has been the nerve-centre of the city's commercial and official life ever since the British colonised in India. It was renamed after independence as Benoy Badal Dinesh Bag or B.B.D.Bag for short. The significance of this new name of Dalhousie Square lies in the fact that it commemorates the martyrdom of three of our country's top-notch revolutionaries of the pre-independence era, namely Benoy Krishna Bose, Badal Gupta and Dinesh Gupta.

It may not be known to many that all three of them hailed from my native Vikrampur that formed part of the Dhaka district of pre-partition east Bengal (now Bangladesh). The fact that they were all from Vikrampur may not have been entirely fortuitous or coincidental. It testified to the fact that Vikrampur had provided a fertile soil for the growth of revolutionary ideas which often found utterance in concrete action. When I lived in Vikrampur in my adolescent years, I used to hear many stories about the patriotic fervour of Benoy, Badal and Dinesh, which reached its apotheosis in their martyrdom in the cause of the country's freedom. When I grew up, I read many detailed accounts of their glorious role in the freedom struggle, which filled my heart with pride.

In the wake of the revolutionary activities of Surya Sen and his disciples, particularly after their role in the Chittagong Armoury Raid of April 18, 1930 became widely known, Bengal turned into a veritable powder keg with the youth itching to do something concrete and ever ready to court death, if that was the price to be paid for achieving their goal of securing the country's freedom. The revolutionary leaders who had been lodged in Alipore Jail for taking part in the non-cooperation movement were greatly exercised in April 1930 because they were made to live in barracks meant for Class III prisoners, most of whom were ordinary criminals. Many of these leaders that included stalwarts such as Subhas Chandra Bose and J.M.Sengupta came out of their wards to ventilate their grievances. The alarm bells started ringing inside the jail and a brutal lathi-charge was made on the prisoners under the orders of one Som Dutt, Superintendent of the Jail. Subhas Chandra Bose suffered grievous injuries, which caused grave apprehension about the chances of his survival. News of this barbaric repression immediately filtered out of the jail and enraged the people all over the country. Bengal's young revolutionaries vowed not to take all this lying down.

The rise in the political temperature of Bengal was clearly reflected in a series of incidents. On August 25,1930, an unsuccessful attempt was made on the life of Charles Tegart, Commissioner, Calcutta Police, by two young revolutionaries. One of them was a young girl, Anuja Sen, who died on the spot as the bomb she was going to hurl at Tegart exploded in her hand before she had time to throw it at the target. The other was Dinesh Mazumdar, a Law student of the Calcutta University, who hurled a bomb at the car of Tegart. The latter escaped, but Dinesh Mazumdar suffered some injuries in his hand and was apprehended along with a revolver and some cartridges and bombs. He was hanged in the Alipore Jail on June 9,1934.

Four days after this incident, Benoy Krishna Bose, a young man of Vikrampur, belonging to the Bengal Volunteers, a group of the revolutionary organisation known as the Dhaka Shri Sangha, made a successful attempt on the life of F.J.Lowman, Inspector-General of Police, in Dhaka on August 29, 1930. Benoy managed to escape and moved from place to place in disguise to evade the police. Units of the British Army were stationed in some schools of Vikrampur to conduct searches and put down the turbulent youth.

Meanwhile, the young revolutionaries of the Bengal Volunteers started chalking out plans of taking revenge on Lt.Col.Simpson, Inspector General of Prisons, whose office was located in the Writers' Buildings, the citadel of the British Raj. Three trusted and reliable workers were chosen for this all-important task of bumping off Lt. Col. Simpson.[1] One of them was Benoy Bose, who was a student of the Mitford Medical School, Dhaka, and had clandestinely reached Kolkata from Dhaka after making the fatal attempt on the life of F.J.Lowman, Inspector General of Police. Born on September 11,1908 in the Routbhog village of Vikrampur in Dhaka district, he had joined the Bengal Volunteers at the tender age of 14, when he was a student of the Collegiate School in Dhaka. As already mentioned, he was also a member of the Shri Sangha, an underground revolutionary organisation of Dhaka. Once when his mother asked him whether he had joined the ranks of the revolutionaries, he kept quiet. When his mother told him that some of their neighbours had spent their whole life in jail after joining the Swadeshi movement, Benoy replied that her son was not born to spend his life in jail. Little did the mother know at that time what Benoy really meant! (After a few years, he was to sacrifice his life in the cause of the country's freedom).

The second person chosen was Badal Gupta, who was born in 1912 in the Purba Shimulia village of Vikrampur. At the age of eight years, he had gone to Patna to live with his uncle, Dharani Nath Gupta, and pursue his studies. Dharani Nath and his brother, Nagendra Gupta, had spent seven years in jail for their complicity in the Manicktola Bomb Case. Badal had his first lessons in revolutionary work from his uncle, who was a member of the Anushilan Samiti in Patna. After some time, Badal came back to Vikrampur and joined the ninth class of the village school at Banari. There, he recieved further indoctrination and training from Nikunja Sen, a famous teacher of the school. He joined the Bengal Volunteers, whose units had sprung up in many schools of Vikrampur at that time.

The third member of the task force was Dinesh Gupta, who was born on December 6, 1911 at Netrakona, where his father was then employed. But the family belonged to Jasholong village of Vikrampur. Dinesh had his early education at Gauripur in Mymensingh district and then at the Dacca Collegiate School. Like Benoy Bose, Dinesh was also a member of the revolutionary organisation, Shri Sangha. Dinesh passed the I.Sc. examination from the Midnapore College and joined the B.Sc. class at the Dacca University. He enlisted himself in the University Training Corps and then formed a revolutionary group along with his intimate friends. Even while he was at Midnapore, he had come in close touch with the Abhay Ashram and the Tilak Library and had formed a revolutionary group, which in later years contributed hundreds of dedicated workers to the freedom movement. Though still rather young, he was a budding poet with a flair for literature and philosophy. A many-splendoured personality, he excelled in the fine arts as well as in the pyrotechnics of a fire-brand revolutionary.

It was in December, 1930, that some revolutionary leaders chalked out a plan to mount an attack on the Writers' Buildings in Kolkata in order to avenge the repression that had been unleashed on Subhas Chandra Bose and the other leaders in jail. Benoy Bose was chosen as the leader and was to be assisted by Badal Gupta and Dinesh Gupta. It was generally believed at that time that Subhas Chandra Bose was aware of this plan and had approved of it.

On December 7,1930, Nikunja Sen, the teacher of Vikrampur's Banari School, went to the Writers' Buildings along with Badal Gupta and Dinesh Gupta and made a reconnaissance of the rooms. The next day, Benoy Bose took a taxi to reach the rendezvous on Pipe Road in Kidderpore, where Badal and Dinesh also arrived in another taxi. They were dressed as European military officers and carried with them loaded revolvers, potassium cyanide and the tri-colour national flag. They entered the Writers' Buildings dressed as Major Benoy Bose, Captain Dinesh Gupta and Lieutenant Badal Gupta and went up the stairs, shouting 'Vande Mataram'. They entered the room of Lt.Col.Simpson, Inspector General of Prisons, who was seated at his office table and fired at him, killing him on the spot.

They proceeded to take a shot at Albion Mar, Revenue Secretary, but were interrupted by another official at whom they immediately fired. On hearing the sound of gun-shot, T.J. Craig, the new Inspector General of Police, who had replaced the just assassinated F.J. Lowman, came rushing out of his room and fired at the revolutionaries, but missed all his targets. It was the same Craig whom two revolutionaries, namely Ramakrishna Biswas and Kalipada Chakraborti, had tried to assassinate some time ago at the Chandpur Railway Station, but had ended up killing a Police Inspector, Tarini Mukherjee, mistaking him for Craig.

At this point, Jones, Assistant Inspector General of Police, snatched the revolver from Craig and came forward to give chase to the revolutionaries. But finding the situation rather confusing, Jones beat a hasty retreat. The revolutionaries then fired at Nelson, Judicial Secretary and Townend, Deputy Secretary to the Government of Bengal. Nelson was hit on the leg.

Benoy, Badal and Dinesh now attacked the Passport Officer, when they saw Johnson, an American clergyman, frantically trying to escape by climbing down a water-pipe of the building. The staccato sound of gun-shot created great consternation among the government employees at the Writers' Buildings, who began to run helter skelter in order to escape and save their precious lives. Dinesh Gupta's left arm had suffered a gun shot injury, but nevertheless he went on shooting his way forward.

Lal Bazar, the headquarters of the Calcutta Police at a stone's throw from the Writers' Buildings, at once got the news of the shoot-out. Charles Tegart, Commissioner of Police, and two Deputy Commissioners, namely Gordon and Burt, appeared on the scene with a posse a policemen. There was virtually a pitched battle. It was an unequal fight because the police had their long-range rifles, while the revolutionaries had just three revolvers. Very soon, the latter realised that they had almost run through their stock of cartridges!

The young revolutionaries entered an empty room, and after closing its doors, they all consumed potassium cyanide. Badal Gupta [2] succeeded in taking his own life. Benoy Bose and Dinesh Gupta, who did not die immediately, fired their revolvers at themselves to accelerate their death. Their bodies collapsed on the hard floor of the Writers' Buildings. They were removed to the hospital of the Calcutta Medical College. There, Dinesh Gupta recovered, but Benoy, who had no intention of surviving, deliberately ran his fingers through the wounds on his body to make them turn septic. With no co-operation from the recalcitrant patient, the doctors failed to save his life. Benoy's dead body was handed over to a relative.

Pending trial by a Special Tribunal, Dinesh Gupta, the lone survivor, was kept in the Alipore Jail. Ramakrishna Biswas and Kalipada Chakraborti, who had made an unsuccessful bid to kill T.J.Craig, Inspector General of Police at Chandpur, were also lodged in the same ward of the jail. From the jail, Dinesh wrote a series of letters under his pet name Nosu to his mother and other close relations. These letters in which he poured out his heart, expressing highly philosophical and spiritual ideas, showed the depth of his emotion and political conviction. When I grew up, I read these letters which were extremely touching and apt to bring tears in the eyes of any discerning reader. A few specimens of these letters in Bengali would translate into English as below:

Alipore Central Jail
June 17, 1931, Calcutta

My Dear Mother,

Give up your love for me. Don't think of me day and night............ Nobody belongs to anybody else. Everything in this world is a part of 'Maya'. Pray to God heart and soul so that he can dispel the illusion of Maya and give you peace of mind...........

Think that in place of your one son, you have got all the children of India as your sons. You are the mother of them all. Love them as you love your Nosu (pet name of Dinesh). If you can expand your heart, you will get peace. Love the sick and the suffering, the poor, the orphans. Love them as your own children. You will get boundless joy if you distribute your love beyond the narrow confines of your small family.

Yours Nosu

Alipore Central Jail
Calcutta
June 30,1931

Mother ....

Perhaps you are thinking that despite all your prayers, God has turned a deaf ear to you .... I understand one thing. In God's dispensation, there can be no injustice in this world. Do not lose your faith in His justice, but try to accept it with a contented heart. How shall we comprehend what He wants to do through what means? He can strike fear in our minds because we magnify the importance of death........... Some day, everybody will have to welcome death. Are we so deeply grieved and worked up because death has come a couple of days in advance? Do we regard death as a great enemy because, instead of coming without notice, it has come with notice? It is wrong, utterly wrong; death has come to me as a friend ....

Yours Nosu

—

Alipore central jail
5.30 P.M.
6.7.1931

Mother,

I shall see you no more. But in the hereafter, I shall wait for you. I have never been able to do anything for you. No one would be able to understand how much grief this inability on my part is causing me. Do not try to explain it to any one. Kindly pardon me for all my lapses and all the wrongs I have done. My love and salutation to you.

Yours Nosu

—

This last letter was written in the evening preceding the day of his execution i.e. on July 7, 1931. Before he was hanged, he was asked to have his bath, as required under the rules. Armed guards stood around him. As he poured the water over his body, he uttered the Mantra in obeisance to the sun-god: "Om Jabakusuma....Sankasham Kashyapeyam Mahadyutim Dhwantarim Sarvapapaghnam Pranatohasmi Divakaram" (i.e. I salute the sun, the son of Kashyapa, who is crimson like the hibiscus, full of energy, the dispeller of darkness and the destrcyer of all sins).

As Dinesh had conquered the fear of death, he was full of cheer when he was being readied for the gallows. When a member of the armed guard asked him if he was not afraid of death, he cited the verse from the Geeta, which, translated into English means: "As a man leaves an old garment and puts on one that is new, the soul leaves its mortal body and then puts on one that is new". Then he sprightly walked forward to mount the gallows with not a trace of bitterness or regret. He shouted 'Vande Mataram' as the hangman dutifully performed his assigned task.

The body of Dinesh Gupta was cremated in the jail compound to avoid the risk of unforeseen consequences in view of the fact that there was a strong public demand for his acquittal. The Calcutta Corporation under the leadership of the then Mayor, Dr.B.C.Roy, adjourned its meeting for the day as a mark of respect to his sacred memory. Ramakrishana Biswas was also hanged on August 4,1931.

Dinesh Gupta had a good following among there volutionary workers of Midnapore, where he had his college education and had set up a branch of the revolutionary organisation 'Bengal Volunteers'. His as well as Ramakrishna's death by hanging greatly agitated the public mind, particularly in Midnapore. The young revolutionaries of Bengal wanted to do away with R.R. Garlick, I.C.S.,Senior Sessions Judge, 24-Parganas, who, as the President of the Special Tribunal, had passed the sentences on Dinesh and Ramakrishna. They wanted to get rid of Garlick before Dinesh was hanged so that he could die with the knowledge that the judge had already been despatched.

But this wish of the revolutionaries was not fulfilled, as Dinesh was hanged on July 7,1931, while it was on July 27, 1931 that Kanai Lal Bhattacharya, a young revolutionary of Majilpur, Police Station Joynagar, District 24-Parganas, could kill Garlick, firing at him from a point blank range after entering the Alipore Sessions Court, where the latter was then trying a case. Kanai was immediately shot down by the Sergeant on duty, but he committed suicide while lying wounded under the table by swallowing potassium cyanide from a phial which was later found on the floor. In the hip pocket of Kanai was found a slip of paper, with a bullet hole made through it, on which was written: "Vande Mataram. Cursed be your Court, whose injustice condemned Dinesh Gupta to execution. Receive the reward for it." [3]

It was in Midnapore that the reaction to the arrest and trial of Dinesh Gupta took its most virulent form. Three District Magistrates of Midnapore were done to death by the revolutionaries—James Pedie on April 8, 1931, Robert Douglas on April 30,1932 and B.E.J.Burge on Sptember 2, 1933![4]

When I moved over to Kolkata from Vikrampur in the latter half of the nineteen forties, I often passed through Dalhousie Square, the hub of the city, and looked in awe at the mighty structures of the Writers' Buildings and Lal Bazar. Memories of what I had heard and read about the bravery and patriotism of Benoy, Badal and Dinesh came rushing to my mind whenever I could take time off for a walk around the Lal Dighi, the tank at the heart of the Dalhousie Square.

Vikrampur continued to throw up revolutionary workers, who thought nothing of sacrificing their lives in the cause of the freedom movement. Kamala Das, who was born in a Vaidya family of Vikrampur on March 11, 1907, had become a household name in our villages by virtue of her revolutionary exploits. She was a member of the Yugantar, a revolutionary outfit, and had helped Bina Das in making an attempt on the life of the Governor of Bengal, Sir Stanely Jackson, at the Convocation of the Calcutta University on the 6th February, 1932.

Bina Das, a fresh graduate, who was to receive the degree, fired several shots at the Governor, till the ammunition was exhausted. The shots whizzed past the Governor, who survived the bid to kill him. Bina Das was arrested, tried and convicted. Kamala Das was also arrested, but released for lack of evidence. She went to jail on many occasions. She joined the Congress Party and was imprisoned for her role in the Quit India movement in 1942. During 1946-47, she worked in Noakhali and other riot-affected districts of Bengal along with Mahatma Gandhi's disciples. She died in 2000 A.D. at the ripe old age of 93 years, leaving behind several books which bring out her patriotic fervour.

Ujjala Mazumdar, a girl from Vikrampur, was in a group of revolutionaries, who fired at Sir John Anderson, the Governor of Bengal, on May 8, 1934 at the race course at Lebong near Darjeeling. They failed in their attempt to kill the Governor. Of those involved in this case, Bhawani Bhattacharya was hanged inside a jail, Manoranjan Banerji and Rabindranath Banerji were sentenced to transportation for life and Ujjala to 14 years' rigorous imprisonment.

When I lived in Vikrampur, I used to hear from the elders many glowing accounts of the patriotism and martyrdom of these heroes and heroines of our country's freedom struggle. Their sacrifices did not go in vain.

Notes

1. Page 163, Surya Sener Sonali Swapna by Rupmoy Pal.
2. *Ibid.*, pages 175-176.
3. A Chronological Account of Violent Incidents from 1907 to 1939 prepared by the Government of pre-independence Bengal vide Terrorism in Bengal (1995), Government of West Bengal, Volume VI, page 757.
4. Surya Sener Sonali Swapna by Rupmoy Pal, pages 175-176.

5

Ghati and Bangal : Glimpses of My College Life : Kolkata's Religious Festivals

The Bengali language that I spoke in Vikrampur was a dialect used in the rural areas of Dhaka district and was different from the language spoken in Kolkata, which was regarded as Bengali proper and which, besides Sanskritised Bengali, formed the language of Bengali literature. My Vikrampur dialect was of no use in Kolkata where you were expected to speak the Kolkata dialect of which I was quite innocent. The difficulty I, therefore, experienced in making a proper conversation with most people in Kolkata bred in me a feeling of shyness and inferiority complex. People, who belonged to Kolkata, often taunted us by branding us as 'Bangals' (people from east Bengal), who could not speak properly. Sometimes, they uttered a few words of an east Bengal dialect in a distorted and even a mocking tone in order to pull our legs and provoke derisory laughter all around.

The 'Bangals' countered this by branding the Kolkata people as 'Ghatis'. The relationship between them corresponded to what I saw many years later in Germany where the 'Ossis' and 'Wessis' i.e. the easterners and the westerners stood respectively for the people of the German Democratic Republic (i.e. east Germany) and the Federal Republic of Germany (i.e. West Germany).The distinction between 'them' and 'us' in Kolkata had, however, a purely social connotation, devoid of any deeper political or ideological overtone and was usually invoked out of a spirit of innocent fun.

The differentiation between the 'Ghatis' and 'Bangals' dates back to ancient times. The word 'Bangal' was derived from 'Vanga' or 'Banga' which meant east Bengal. In his 'Raghuvansham' (canto 4), poet Kalidasa referred to Vanga or Banga (Nichakhaya Vangan). In the 'Kavikankan' of Mukundaram, the word 'Bangal' appears in the line "Aar Bangal Kande Shokey Shirey Diye Haat" (And the Bangal weeps in grief, with his hand placed on the head). The word 'Ghati' originated from 'Bandyaghati' i.e. a resident of 'Bandyghat', a village of West Bengal which was known as 'Rahr'. The 'Bandyghatis' were Brahmins.

So initially, the term 'Ghati' referred to a Brahmin of West Bengal. Later, it came to denote the people of West Bengal in general. In days of yore, the people of West Bengal did not go in for matrimonial alliance with those from east Bengal. Even in ancient Bengali literature, references have been made to the tradition of the people of West Bengal not seeking marital relations with families from east Bengal. All this changed considerably after the partition of Bengal in 1947, when the migration of most of the Hindu families from east Bengal to West Bengal resulted in close social intermingling and gradually broke down many artificial barriers.

In Kolkata, my surname Barari caused a lot of curiosity among those with whom I came in touch. Many of them referred to the surnames 'Brar' and 'Brari' of some Sikh residents of Bhowanipur in southern Kolkata of whom they had heard and when they asked me if I had any linkage with the Sikhs, I naturally told them that I had none.

I had once heard a learned discussion on the word 'Barari' which a Sanskrit scholar of Vikrampur, my native place in east Bengal, had with some teachers of my village school there. According to what I recall about that discussion, the word 'Barari' is the name of a Raga of Indian classical music in which the Mantras were chanted at the time of Durga Puja – to be more specific, at the time of what is known as the 'Mahasnan' of the goddess. 'Mahasnan' is the ritual bathing of Durga with the sprinkling of water to the accompaniment of music and the playing of many musical instruments that include drums, conches etc. The word Barari is said to be the name of the Raga of the music produced when conches are blown on this occasion! Going by this account, I should be a highly musical person! But, alas, according to my memory of the scholarly discussion that I heard, my surname had nothing to do with this Raga or with any other Raga for that matter.

What I know for sure is that my surname Barari is a corrupt form of 'Bandopadhyay'. Over the centuries, Bandopadhyay came to be pronounced as 'Barujye' for the simple reason that it was easier to pronounce it that way. In course of time, 'Barujye' began to be pronounced as 'Baruri' 'Barori' or 'Barari' in some areas of Vikrampur that formed part of the Dhaka district of undivided Bengal. Come to think of it, we 'Bararis' were the orginal 'Ghatis' from Rahr or West Bengal, because that is where all Bandopadhyays initially hailed from. In course of time, we came to be branded as 'Bangals', because we had migrated to and settled down in east Bengal—at what point of time nobody knows!

Experts have divided Bengal's dialects into four groups: i) Rarhi, spoken in West Bengal and regarded as standard colloquial Bengali; ii) Varendri spoken in north Bengal; iii) Kamrupi, spoken in north-eastern Bengal and parts of Assam; and iv) Vanga spoken in east Bengal. In fact, the fourth dialect, Vanga was not identical all over east Bengal, but differed from district to district. The Vikrampur-Manikganj dialect of Dhaka district was said to be the standard colloquial Bengali of east Bengal and this was the dialect that I spoke. It was quite different from the south eastern variety of Vanga spoken in Chittagong and some adjacent districts, which even a 'Bangal' like me found rather difficult to understand.

Dr. Grierson, an authority on linguistics, has pointed out that the Bengali dialect spoken in east Bengal exhibits a cockney-like avoidance of pre-existing aspirates. The eastern Bengali always drops his aspirates (i.e. does not pronounce the aspirate 'h'). I was reminded of our practice of dropping our aspirates in eastBengal years later, when I saw the film 'My Fair Lady' based on George Bernard Shaw's 'Pygmalion'. In this film, Henry Higgins tries to make his ward Eliza Dolittle get rid of her cockney habit of "dropping aitches" by dinning into her ears the words "In Hertford Hereford and Hampshire hurricanes hardly happen".

The people of east Bengal, besides sharing this habit of the cockneys, also substitute an aspirate for a sibilant. As Dr. Grierson has explained, while the people of West Bengal are generally unable to pronounce 'shibboleth', except as 'sibboleth', the eastern Bengali avoids the sound of 'sh' and pronounces the word as 'hibboleth'.

Dr. Grierson has also rightly observed that the eastern Bengali cannot pronounce the letters 'ch', 'chh' and 'j' for which he substitutes 'ts', 's' and 'z' respectively.

Soon after I landed in Kolkata, I applied myself whole-heartedly to the task of picking up the 'Rarhi' dialect, which was the standard colloquial language of West Bengal, apart from being the language of the cultured Bengalee that was often the language of Bengali books. It took a good deal of effort on my part to be able in due course to speak the Kolkata dialect.

An important factor that contributed to bringing about a big change in my outlook in Kolkata was the newspaper with which I had practically no acquaintance during the first sixteen years of my life that I spent in a village. We started subscribing to the daily Statesman and sometimes switched over to the Amrita Bazar Patrika, which then cost an anna per copy – a big amount no doubt in that day and age. Gradually, I got addicted to the newspaper.

The boys of our neighbourhood and some of our relations who had been living in Kolkata since long had an advantage over me since they had the radio, which gave them access, without much effort on their part, to news and views on various matters, apart from music and cultural programmes. We did not have the radio nor the telephone, which an average family in Kolkata counted among its basic amenities.

Towards the middle of 1945, the results of the Matriculation examination were hung up on the walls of the Calcutta University's premises on College Street. I rushed there by tram car early that morning and saw the result with my own eyes. I had passed in the First Division (which meant that I had secured at least 60% marks). I was thrilled with my result, even though no indication was provided as to whether I had achieved distinction in any subject.

I felt so excited that I wanted to go back home as soon as possible to break the news to all the members of our family. Rather than wait for a bus or tram, I walked back home – a distance of seven miles!

Soon I joined the Asutosh College that was nearest to our place. My father took the view that it was not necessary for me to get into any other college, say, the famous Presidency College, to do well in examination, for, as he said – and I agreed with him – what mattered more than anything else was one's own effort. Moreover, my father and elder brothers thought that the Asutosh College that I was joining was a good institution, besides being within a convenient walking distance, which would eliminate travel expenses and also the hassles of journeying by tram or bus.

To tell the truth, I myself felt quite happy with my college. For the first time, I found that it was not necessary to attend a class and that presence at 75% of the classes was all that was required. There was a system of'proxy', which meant that a boy, though not present in the class, could get his presence marked by asking a friend, who was going to attend the class, to respond for him, when his roll number was called out by the Lecturer at the beginning of period. This mode of deception could pass muster in view of the fact that the Lecturer did not know most of the large number of students by name or face.

For the first time in my life, I heard lectures that were delivered in English, generally extempore, by Lecturers, who knew their subjects very well. I came to know in due course that the Lecturers were all brilliant students once upon a time and that many of them had authored learned tomes on their respective subjects.

I joined the Intermediate Arts course and took up, apart from English and Bengali, which were compulsory, Civics (which included both economics and political science), Logic and Sanskrit. I also opted for Mathematics as an additional subject, since a certain percentage of the marks obtained in it was to be added to the total score, thus raising my average marks.

The little Sanskrit that I learnt in college (up to the Intermediate Arts standard) proved very useful later in life. Apart from the vast treasure of its literature, Sanskrit is the bed-rock of Hindu and Buddhist religions because most of their original texts are in this language. Sanskrit lies at the root of most of the modern Indian languages and is in fact the basis of India's culture and civilisation.

Some Lecturers such as Bijon Kumar Bhattacharya (Bengali), Nirode Kumar Bhattacharya (Political Science), Sibnath Chakraboti (Political Science), K.N.Sen (Economics), J.N. Chakraborti (English), Debabrata Mukherjee (English), who later became a Judge of the Calcutta High Court, Jamini Kar (Mathematics) and A.P. Chatterjee (English), had made a deep impression on me. The last-named Lecturer who used to take some of our tutorial classes, evolved in due course into an important communist leader and a Member of Parliament belonging to the CPM, though he later switched over to the CPI. He had attracted nation-wide notice by spear-heading a movement in protest against what he characterised as the frequent foreign trips of Jyoti Basu, West Bengal Chief Minister, at the government's expense. Our Principal, Panchanan Sinha, was a great authority on Economics and Geography. Most of the Lecturers were so conscientious and committed to their academic work that they inspired not only respect but also reverence.

One of the pieces in our English text-book contained references to William Makepeace Thackeray, the famous 19th-century English novelist, who was born in Kolkata in 1811. His father, Richard Thackeray, who had become Secretary to the Board of Revenue, lived at one time along with William Makepeace in a house in Alipur, which earlier used to be the residence of the notorious Sir Philip Francis, a member of the Governor-General of India to whom I have already referred in Chapter II. Our learned professor, Debabrata Mukherjee, who taught us English told us about the tomb of William Makepeace Thackeray that one could still see in Kolkata.

In this context, our professor gave us a low-down on the literary heritage of Kolkata during the days of the Raj. He referred us to some fine specimens of English writing in the old issues of the Calcutta Municipal Gazette that pertained to several leading figures of the 19th-century English society of Kolkata. This is how I chanced upon the December 1939 issue of the Calcutta Municipal Gazette going through which proved highly rewarding. A write-up in this issue by Rabindra Kumar Dasgupta [1] dilated upon some prominent Englishmen of Kolkata who had been associated with well-known English writers. For example, the tomb in Kolkata's South Park cemetery of a young English girl, Rose Aylmer, was reported to have an inscription on it which had been described as "the brightest gem of English elegy". [2] She was said to have "caused the first stirrings of love" in the English poet Walter Savage Landor's breast. On hearing the news of her death in the bloom of her youth, Landor was driven into despondency

Rose Aylmer figured in some of Landor's poems, one of which captioned "Three Roses" read:

"When the buds began to burst
Long ago with Rose the first,
I was walking joyous then,
Far above all other men,

Til before us up there stood
Britonferries oaken wood,
Whispering, 'happy as Thou art,
Happiness and thou must part."

Soon I discovered another poem by Landor captioned "Rose Aylmer", which is also worth reproducing:

"Ah, what avails the sceptred race!
Ah! What the form divine!
What every virtue, every grace!
Rose Aylmer, all were thine.
Rose Aylmer, whom these wakeful eyes
May weep, but never see,
A night of memories and of sighs
I consecrate to thee.
I strove with none, for none was worth my strife.
Nature I loved and, next to nature, Art:
I warmed both hands before the fire of life;
It sinks, and I am ready to depart."

Another poem on Rose Aylmer which bore the title "Abertawy" shows how deeply Landor "felt the sad death of a young maid, who, sick for home, languished in an alien clime" [3] To quote:

"Where is she now? Called far away
By one she dared not disobey,
To those proud halls for youth unfit
Where Princes stand and Judges sit.
Where Ganges rolls hid widest wave
She dropped her blossom in the grave
Her noble name she never changed
Nor was her nobler heart estranged."

Close to Rose Aylmer's tomb was the tomb of a young sailor, Captain William Mackay, who was involved in a ship-wreck in the Indian waters that caused the death of several persons. The account of the memorable ship-wreck of Juno given in a book by Captain Mackay was said to be a very beautiful piece of literature on which Byron drew liberally when describing a ship-wreck in his 'Don Juan'.[4]

Another tomb in Kolkata which figures in Rabindra Kumar Dasgupta's write-up in the Calcutta Municipal Gazette (December 1939) is that of Lt. Col. James Achilies Kirpatrick, the Resident of

Hyderabad, who married a Begum of the Nizam and later shifted to Kolkata. His daughter, the beautiful Kitty Kirpatrick was a friend of Carlyle's and was thought by many to be the original of 'Blumine' in Carlyle's Sartor Resartus.

Thomas Babington Macaulay, one of the greatest figures in the history of English prose, who came to Kolkata as a Member of the Supreme Council, lived in a house in Chowringhee. His lasting contribution lay in his 'Minute on Education' and the Indian Penal Code. It was in Kolkata that Macaulay penned his best literary essay on Francis Bacon.

Macaulay did not think very highly of India and Bengal. His description of the Bengalis was highly derisive: "The physical organization of the Bengalees is feeble, even to effeminacy. He lives in a constant vapour bath. His pursuits are sedentary, his limbs delicate, his movements languid. During many ages, he has been trampled upon by men of bolder and more hardy breeds."

There were several other leading British figures of the Raj whose remarks on Indians smacked of utter racial prejudice. For example, a judgement of the Lahore High Court delivered in 1925 had described the Punjabis as "habitual liars even in the face of death." Two British Indian judges had observed: "It is well-known that inhabitants of Punjab will often in dying declaration not only accuse offenders but will also add the names of other enemies." Recently, some advocates took up the matter with the Supreme Court of India with the plea that these humiliating remarks against the Punjabis be over-ruled.

In his article, Rabindra Kumar Dasgupta suggests that one should not take Macaulay's remarks on the Bengalis too seriously. He says: "And we must remember that he was as much critical of the character of Siraj-u-dulla and Nanda Coomar as of Clive and Warren Hastings; that a man habitually fond of rhetoric is frequently driven to excess and that he was one of the most honest Englishmen that ever came to India. His educational policy led not only to literary renascence, but also to an awakened political consciousness in Bengal. The obloquy to which he exposed himself by advocating the freedom of the Press and equality of law in India shows that Macaulay did not come to our country merely to scoff."[5]

Macaulay did not like our climate nor our fruits. This is what he wrote about our fruits: "The tropical fruits are wretched. The best of them are inferior to our apricot or gooseberry. A plantain is very like a rotten pear. A yam is better. It is like an indifferent potato. I tried palm wine, it was like ginger beer into which ginger has been sparingly used." [6]

About our climate, Macaulay wrote: "We are annually baked four months, boiled four more and allowed the remaining four to become cool if we can." [7]

It was in Kolkata that Macaulay wrote his best literary essay on Francis Bacon.

Rudyard Kipling was born in Bombay, but had come to Kolkata. His description of Kolkata in his "City of the Dreadful Night" clearly brought out his contempt for Kolkata: "It seems not only a wrong but a criminal thing to allow natives to have any voice in the control of such a city adorned, docked, wharfed, fronted and reclaimed by Englishmen, existing only because England lives and dependent for its life on England. All India knows of the Calcutta Municipality. But h as any one thoroughly investigated the Calcutta Stink?" [8]

Commenting on Kipling's arrogant attitude towards Kolkata, Rabindra Kumar Dasgupta points out with unconcealed glee: "And those Indians who do not much like the man might remember with satisfaction that he had a good slap, in Calcutta, from the stinking hand of a 'native'; and that his unmannerliness angered even Queen Victoria, who never gave him the honour of the Poet Laureate.' [9]

Since our Asutosh College was a private one, it had to make itself financially viable by enrolling a good number of students and holding classes in three shifts. The morning shift was exclusively for girls and the day shift for boys. The night shift was for I.Com (Intermediate of Commerce) and B.Com. (Bachelor of Commerce) classes, which were attended mostly by those who worked in offices during the day and were keen on brightening their career prospects by improving their qualification.

The Kolkata girls whom I saw in college and elsewhere in the latter half of the nineteen forties were a graceful lot, their bearing and deportment looking so different from what I had seen in Vikrampur's belles. They were quite well groomed even without going to the present-day finishing schools. Their powdered cheeks and special hair-do, the dark glasses which some of them wore, the 'vanity bag', which almost all of them carried, and the smart demureness with which they wove their way through the crowd on the street or through the dense masses of menfolk inside the bus or the tram invested them with a simple charm, though, by and large, they still shunned the lip stick and refused to bare their mid-riffs.

In Dalhousie Square, the commercial zone of Kolkata, I sometimes saw many working girls, many of whom Anglo-Indians, the like of whom I had not encountered in my village. I read a description of these girls in a write-up in the Calcutta Municipal Gazette, which is worth reproducing: "Trim and smart, these girls give an air of gay femininity that relieves the rigid decorum of Clive Street. With powder-puff and rouge-tube and lip-stick they repair the damages of work and heat and emerge after office hours almost as self-preserved as when they enter. They board trams and buses with joyous abandon and make their man feel the worm he is outside office jurisdiction. And then to cinemas and dinners sans peur but not sans raproche." [10]

On the whole, for the young lotus-eaters, college life, despite its minor hassles, was full of good cheer and fun, with occasional openings for romance also thrown in for those who were inclined that way. I very much liked the liberal atmosphere of the college and the personal freedom that I came to enjoy for the first time in my life.

The atmosphere in the class room was quite serious, as the Lecturers laid a good deal of emphasis on discipline and good behaviour. However, minor deviations from the code of conduct often came to notice. It was not rare to find an odd boy dozing off in the class. I knew a boy who came ready for this purpose with a pair of dark glasses that he wore and then closed his eyes, sitting in the very first row right under the nose of the Lecturer. He generally went undetected except on an odd occasion when he began to snore. Once a Lecturer with a fine sense of humour observed that sleep was the most inexpensive means of relaxation and when a person snored it meant that he had accumulated a large backlog of sleep. I remember having read about the characterisation by George Bernard Shaw of sleep as an opinion, when someone asked him why he had slept through a drama he had gone to see.

I was thus settling down to college life as an average good student, taking keen interest in the subjects of the syllabus that I had taken up. Then, one day, something happened, which was perhaps the greatest surprise of my life and which, I feel, was the turning point of my academic career. That day, someone showed me a magazine, which had published the names of the 'first ten' students, who had been awarded merit scholarships on the basis of the Matriculation examination results. And lo and behold! In that list, both Sambhu Nath, my class-mate at school, and I figured at the seventh place, which meant that we had secured equal marks in the compulsory subjects and were to get a monthly scholarship of Rs. 16/-each. This was an unexpectedly good result indeed, of which I was blissfully unaware all this time. I must add here that in the merit list prepared by the University some months ago, Sambhu Nath and not I figured because he had done better than I in an optional subject. My good performance in the Matriculation examination boosted my self-confidence and gave me the feeling that, if I tried hard, there was nothing that could stop me from doing better.

Hearing of my good academic performance and the valiant effort I was making to forge ahead with my studies despite all odds, our landlord sent word that he was willing to provide some facilities for my study. He was Nandalal Roy, a highly benevolent and kind-hearted person. He and his eldest brother, a learned man, who mostly lived at Puri, were the scions of a famous Zamindar family of Choumohuni in the Noakhali district of east Bengal, who were known for their interest in literature, art and culture. They had provided living accommodation to a few students in the out-house of their premises. My elder brother, who was a B.A. student in the Asutosh College, and I were given a room in their premises for our study. This was a god-send that enabled us to concentrate on our studies.

Since there was no electricity even in this room, we had still to depend on the good old hurricane lantern. This room on the ground floor was so located in a corner of the house that no daylight could have entered it ever since the building was constructed many decades ago. It was damp and swanky and, therefore, had one advantage, namely that it was cool in summer. So we did not miss the electric fan too much. Adjacent to this room were several others, rented out to tenants among whom were a truck driver, a shop-keeper and a newspaper hawker. I often bumped into them because they were my neighbours. They were good and courteous people and were highly appreciative of my sincere effort to excel in studies.

Adjoining our room were the premises of another landlord, where a rotary press used to turn out printed material from morning till evening, filling the whole environment with the clanking noise of the machine, apart from the constant chatter and conversation by the sizeable number of its workers. I sometimes wondered if the high decibel level was going to affect my hearing over the long haul, but my auditory nerves were quite strong and did not give in. I had never gone inside that press nor met or seen any of the workers or the members of the supervisory staff and yet, constantly hearing what they said day in and day out, I knew the character and functions of each of them, a faculty which a blind man acquires in relation to all other persons, who form part of his immediate environment.

In mentioning the short-comings of the room given to us for study I have no intention of running down the kind gesture of the landlord, who did us such a good turn; it would be highly improper and unfair of me to look a gift horse in the month. I am only narrating the facts as they were without meaning to be ungrateful to our landlord. He gave us what he could spare out of sheer generosity, for which I felt obliged to him all through my life. In fact, he saved my career.

Meanwhile, I had been steadily gaining knowledge of political affairs and national and international developments by virtue of my regular study of newspapers and magazines. Two books by Pt. Nehru, which I read with great interest, were the 'Glimpses of World History' and the 'Discovery of India'. Another book which I studied very thoroughly was Mahatma Gandhi's autobiography. By now, I was bold enough to pen an article in English on apartheid in South Africa, the inhuman treatment meted out to the Indians there and Mahatma Gandhi's non-violent struggle against it. I sent it on to the editor of the college magazine in which, to my surprise, it was duly published—a matter of great pride for me and something which boosted my morale and self-confidence. I thought that this was not a mean achievement, considering that this happened within just a year of my coming to Kolkata, when I had started reading newspapers and periodicals for the first time.

Soon I became aware that Durga Puja was drawing near, because there was no mistaking the nip in the air in the mornings. Brisk shopping expeditions by groups of men and women, usually accompanied by children, were a common sight in Kolkata's markets, as the Pujas aproached. One day, very early in the morning, when it was still dark outside, I was suddenly awakened from my deep slumber by the magnificent strains of Mahalaya—a programme of devotional music accompanied by the chanting of Sanskrit verses in a stentorian voice that was coming over the radio from all the neighbours' houses. We had no radio of our own, but since practically every radio in the locality had been switched on, there was no difficulty in deciphering and lapping up the rich fare that was being served. The voice over the radio that kept me spell-bound was, I learnt later, the voice of Birendra Kishore Bhadra—a voice that I never failed to recognise in subsequent years on this occasion—Mahalaya, the last day of the waning moon in the Hindu month of Bhadrapada (September-October).

Mahalaya marks the end of 'Pitri Paksha' and is also called Sarvapitri Amavasya. It is the last day of fortnight-long offerings of oblations of water by devout Hindus to their ancestors. The Pitri Paksha ceremony which consists of many rituals of Shraddha symbolises the obeisance paid by the Hindus to their forefathers as a token of gratitude for all that they have imbibed and inherited from the latter. This is the occasion for the Hindus to seek the blessings of their departed ancestors.

There is a special reason for offering Shraddha on the occasion of Amavasya. Among the numerous rays of the sun, there is one called 'Ama', which is specially powerful and with which the sun illuminates the three worlds i.e. heaven, earth and the lower regions. It is in this 'Ama' that the moon-god is present on the occasion of Amavasya. So, on the night of new moon, the sun and the moon dwell together. It is, therefore, said that the new moon provides a specially significant and auspicious occasion for all kinds of religious activity, particularly the Shraddha ceremony.

Some years later, I came to know a Christian boy in Kolkata, who told me about a similar custom prevalent among the Roman Catholics. This is the All Souls Day observed by them on November 2 each year as the day of supplication for the eternal repose of the souls of all the faithful departed. On this day, the Catholics offer prayers in commemoration of their deceased near and dear relatives and friends. A person gives to the priest of the parish a list of the names of his deceased relatives and friends and the priest says masses for their souls.

Mahalaya also signals the commencement of Devi Paksha or the arrival of mother Durga on earth, which means the beginning of Durga Puja. On this occasion, Durga or Parvati, as she is alternatively called, is said to come to her father's abode on earth along with her two sons and two daughters for a short stay, after which she departs on Vijaya Dashami day or the day of Dussehra for the Himalayan abode of her divine spouse, Lord Shiva.

I lay quietly on my bed, trying for the first time in my life to listen with rapt attention to the rendition of the songs, which alternated with the musical and masterly chanting by Birendra Krishna Bhadra of the Sanskrit verses typified by the most famous of them all: Ya Devi Sarvabhuteshu ...... Samsthita (the goddess who in inheres in all beings). It gave me a blissful feeling. It was something new which I had not experienced in Vikrampur. The composition was by Bani Kumar and the music by Pankaj Kumar Mullick.

O Tempora O Mores! Birendra Krishna Bhadra, Bani Kumar and Pakaj Mullick have all left the cage of the mortal coil. The voices that once used to cast their spell on the people from all walks of life in Bengal have fallen silent for evermore. And so my generation of Bengalees – in whatever part of the globe they may be – now misses on this occasion every year the religious fervour and the majesty of Birendra Krishna Bhadra's live baritone and Pankaj Kumar Mullick's music.

In Kolkata, I had the opportunity of attending several Durga Pujas in localities close to where I lived. Apart from taking part in the celebration and performing some of the religious rites such as offering 'Anjali', I also closely observed how the priests went through the rituals and often tried to understand the meanings of the many 'Mantras' that were chanted on this occasion. My studies in Sanskrit at college and getting to know a couple of learned priests who lived close by, besides the subsequent study of some religious texts helped me to get acquainted with the subtler theosophical aspects of this all-important Puja.

Durga symbolizes the concept of the goddess as Devi or Shakti (energy) or Mother. The discovery of the idols of female deities at the sites of the Indus Valley Civilisation such as Mohenjodaro and Harappa testify to the antiquity of this concept. References to the worship of Devi or Mother are to be found in the Vedas and in the ancient scriptural texts such as the Devi Mahatayam. Shankarachaya, in his Soundaryalahari, had thus described the beauty of Devi or the Mother: "May she who is the pride of Shiva appear before us with large full breasts like the temples of a young elephant, with slender waist girdled with tingling bells, Her face like the full moon, holding bow, arrow, noose and a goad in Her hands."

The Chandi that forms part of Markandeya Purana specifically mentions the vanquishing of Mahishasura or the buffalo demon by Durga. The Devi Suktam of the Rig Veda says:

ध्यानम्

ॐ सिंहस्था शशिशेखरा मरकतप्रख्यैश्चतुर्भिर्भुजैः

शङ्ख चक्रधनुःशरांश्च दधती नेत्रैस्त्रिभिः शोभिता।

आमुक्ताङ्गदहारकङ्कणरणत्काश्रीरणन्नूपुरा

दुर्गा दुर्गतिहारिणी भवतु नो रत्नोल्लसत्कुण्डला।।

देवीसूक्तम्

This gives a description of goddess Durga, the remover of all forms of distress, seated on a lion, with the moon as her crown, weapons in her four arms, three eyes and various ornaments adorning her body. The Taittiriya Aranyaka calls her Durgi: कात्यायनाय विद्म्हे, कन्याकुमारीं धीमहि तन्मो दुर्गिः प्रचोदयात्।

This means that Durga is someone who can be attained with great difficulty through long penance, meditation, good deeds etc. It is also said that Durga got her name after killing a demon by name 'Durgaw' (pronounced differently from Durga). In the Chandi, the goddess herself said that she had got this name after killing the demon Durga:

शाकम्भरीति विख्यातिं तदा यास्याम्यहं भुवि।

तत्रैव च वधिष्यामि दुर्गमाख्यं महासुरम।।४६।।

दुर्गादेवीति विख्यातं तन्मे नाम भविष्यति।

पुनश्चाहं यदा भीमं रूपं कृत्वा हिमाचले।।५०।।

– Devi-Mahatyam, chapter 11, verses 49-50

The Mahabharata says that both Yudhisthira and Arjuna had prayed to goddess Durga. The Virat Parva of this epic mentions Yudhisthira's eulogy of Durga, describing her as the redeemer of sinners, the vanquisher of Mahishasuramardini and the bestower of victory on her devotees. He said that she was called Durga because she saved people from unbearable distress:

दुर्गात् तारयसे दुर्गे तत् त्वं दुर्गा स्मृता जनैः।

कान्तारेष्ववसन्नानां मग्नानांच महार्णवे।।

– Verse 20, Virat Parva, chapter 6, Mahabharata.

He prayed to the goddess seeking her blessings for the Pandavas' victory over the Kauravas. Pleased with Yudhisthira, Durga appeared before him and assured him of victory over the Kauravas:

भविष्यत्यचिरादेव संग्रामे विजयस्तव।
मम प्रसादान्निर्जित्य हत्वा कौरववाहिनीम।।
राज्यं निष्कटंकं कृत्वा भोक्ष्यसे मेदिनीं पुनः।
भ्रातृभिः सहितो राजन् प्रीतिं प्राप्स्यसि पुष्कलाम्।।

—Verses 28-29, chapter 6, Virat Parva, Mahabharata.

She also said that by her grace neither the Kauravas nor the people of Viratnagar would get to know that the Pandavas were living in disguise there:

तस्य सर्वाणि कर्याणि सिद्धिं यास्यन्ति पाण्डवाः।
मत्प्रसादाच्च वः सर्वान्ः विराटनगरे स्थितान्।।

—Verse 34, chapter 6, Virat Parva, Mahabharata.

The Mahabharata also mentions the fact that on the eve of the battle of Kurukshetra, Lord Krishna advised Arjuna to read the eulogy of goddess Durga in order to ensure the defeat of the Kauravas.

श्रीभगवानुवाच
शुचिर्भूत्वा महाबाहो संग्रामाभिमुखे स्थितः।
पराजयाय शत्रूणां दुर्गास्तोत्रमुदीरय।।२।।

—Verse 2, chapter 23, Bhisma Parva, Mahabharata.

Arjuna acted accordingly and concluded his eulogy with a prayer seeking the blessings of the goddess so that he might always be victorious on the field of battle:

स्तुताऽसि त्वं महादेवि विशुद्धेनान्तरात्मना।
जयो भवतु मे नित्यं त्वत्प्रसादाद रणाजिरे।।१३।।

—Verse 13, chapter 23, Bhisma Parva, Mahabharata.

Then the goddess spoke to Arjuna from heaven assuring him of the Pandavas' victory over their enemies because he was a valorous person, who had Lord Indra as his patron:

स्वल्पेनैव तु कालेन शत्रूञ्ज्येष्यसि पाण्डव।
नरस्त्वमसि दुर्धर्ष नारायणसहायवान्।।१८।।
अजेयस्त्वं रणेऽरीणामपि वज्रभृतः स्वयम्।
इत्येवमुक्त्वा वरदा क्षणेनान्तरधीयता।।१९।।

—Verse 18-19, chapter 23, Bhisma Parva, Mahabharata.

The Devi Bhagawat and the Kalika Purana mention the worship of Durga by Lord Rama. The Bengali version of the Ramayana by Krittivasa has mentioned that Lord Rama had vorshipped Durga in autumn to seek her blessings before proceeding to kill Ravana. This was called 'Akalbodhan' or untimely worship because the goddess was traditionally worshipped in spring. It is generally believed that Valmiki's Ramayana does not refer to Lord Rama's worship of Durga in autumn.

However, I think that one can take an alternative view in this regard. Rama's worship of Durga can be said to have found mention, though rather brief, in the following verse that figures in the Yuddha (Lanka) Kand of Valmiki's Ramayana:

ससंप्राप्यधनुष्पा णिर्मायायोगमरिंदमः ।।

तस्थैब्रह्मविधानेनविजेतुंरघुनंदन ।।३४

—Valmiki Ramayana, Yuddha (Lanka) Kand, chapter 85, verse 34.

A literal translation of this verse would read: The suppressor of foes, Lakshmana, the illustrious son of Raghu lineage, carrying a bow in his hand, reached there and kept waiting in the hope of achieving victory. However, this verse leaves enough scope for an alternative interpretation because what is mentioned in it is 'Raghunandana', son of Raghu lineage, but not Lakshmana specifically. Who was waiting to vanquish Ravana—Lakshmana or Rama?

An alternative interpretation that can be put on this verse would imply that it was Rama, not Lakshmana, who was waiting there. This would mean that Lord Brahma had acted as the priest in worshipping Durga in autumn with a view to getting Ravana vanquished. This worship can be said to have been performed by Rama as he was its beneficiary. After achieving the favour (through close proximity) of Maya (i.e. goddess Sarada or Durga) as a result of Lord Brahma's worship of the goddess, Rama kept waiting in the hope of victory. The word "Maya' here refers to Durga as has been explained in verse12, chapter 2 of the tenth canto of Bhagawat Purana:

कुमुदा चण्डिका कृष्णा माधवी कन्यकंति च। माया नारायणीशानी शारदेत्यम्बिकेति च।।१२।।

The Valmiki Ramayana also explains why Ravana got killed by Rama even though the former had been blessed by Lord Brahma with the boon of invincibility, which, however, had a loophole. Ravana had pleaded with Lord Brahma to grant him the boon of immortality:

भगवन्! प्राणिनां नित्यं नान्यत्र मरणाद्रयम्।
नास्ति मृत्युसमः शत्रुय्मरत्वमहं वृणे।।१६

—Verse 16, chapter 10, Uttarkand, Valmiki Ramayana.

Brahma turned this down and told Ravana to ask for some other boon:

एवमुक्तस्तदा ब्रह्मा दशग्रीवमुवाच ह !
नास्ति सर्वामरत्वन्ते वरमन्यं वृणीष्व मे।।१७

—*Ibid.*, **verse 17.**

Ravana then said to Brahma: "May I be unconquerable by the Gandharvas (celestial singers), Yakshas (sprites), gods and demons' He did not mention men for whom he had utter contempt and from whom, therefore, he did not expect any harm to come to him:

एवमुक्ते तदा राम! ब्रह्मणा लोककर्त्तृणा।
दशग्रीव उवाचेदं कृतांजलिस्थाग्रतः।।१८
सुपर्ण–नाग–यक्षाणां दैत्य–दानव–रक्षसाम्।
अवध्योऽहं प्रजाध्यक्ष देवतानांश्च शाश्वत।।१६
नहि चिन्ता ममान्येष प्राणिष्वमरपूजित।
तृणभूता हि ते मन्ये प्राणिनो मानुषादयः।।२०

—*Ibid.*, **verses 18-20.**

This was readily granted by Brahma which meant that Ravana could be killed by a man.

I saw that the period of nine days after Mahalaya was almost universally celebrated by the non-Bengalees resident in Kolkata as Navaratra which was followed on the tenth day by observing Dussehra with the burning Ravana's effigy. Though this celebration differed from the way the Bengalees did it, they all drew upon the same spiritual and scriptural traditions. On the first three days of Navaratra, Durga was worshipped as Mahakali, on the next three days as Mahalaxmi and on the remaining days as Mahasaraswati——the three names of Durga mentioned in Devi Mahatyam. Lord Brahma had given nine names to Durga which are collectively referred to as Navadurga. These names are Shailaputri, Brahmacharini, Chandaghanta, Ksmanda, Skandamata, Katyayani, Kalaratri, Mahagouri and Siddhidatri.

In Kolkata many rich and aristocratic families had their own private pujas to which we the hoi polloi had no access. I used to hear and read a lot about the lavish style of these celebrations, though, as I heard, many of these pujas strictly conformed to the prescribed rituals. After the Englishmen came to Kolkata as the masters of the John Company, many of them began to participate in the festivities, feasts and, above all, the famous nautch that were the hallmark of the celebration of Durga Puja by many Bengalee nouveaux riches.

In course of time, ordinary people belonging to various localities of Kolkata began to organize what came to be called 'Baroari' pujas as distinct from the private pujas at the houses of individuals. I had heard an anecdote that a group of twelve persons who had taken umbrage at their exclusion from the puja at he home of a rich individual had organized the first group or community puja which was the precursor of this kind of puja that derived its nomenclature from the 12 pioneers. When the number of participants in a particular locality increased, this began to be called 'Sarvajanin' Puja (i. e. meant for all people).

To assert this all-inclusive view of Durga Puja, the organizers drew upon a pristine ritual which enjoined that a material which had something to do with the prostitutes, a generally despised section of humanity, would be required for the performance of Durga Puja. This much-needed material was a clod of earth from under the threshold at the door-step of a prostitute's quarters! This was one of the many articles that had to be used for Durga's 'Mahasnan' or the grand bath of the goddess. No wonder that poet Tagore had said:

Make haste and come to Mother's coronation, the vessel auspicious
Is still to be filled
With the sacred water sanctified by the touch of all
By the shore of the sea of Bharata's Great Humanity. [11]

Poet Nazrul Islam wrote in the same vein and in the famous lines[12] of his poem onthis subject, he called upon all, even those who were unclean and sinful, to join the Mother's worship that would give people of all castes an opportunity of touching the Mother's feet.

Over time, Durga Puja took on the character of an occasion for flaunting the Bengalee identity. This is, of course a religious occasion but is also a social festival in which the culture of Bengal finds expression in a variety of ways-in the social camaraderie, in the musical soirees, dance, drama etc. and even in the typically Bengalee a la carte offered by eating houses and food stalls that mushroom in Kolkata during puja.

Durga Puja had an impact on the literary scene of Kolkata as was evident from the publication by many newspapers, English as well as vernacular, of Puja numbers featuring a rich crop of literary creations such as novels, short stories, poems, essays etc. I often went to the pavement book corners to leaf through some of these magazines as long as I could till I was politely asked by the stall owner to either buy one or quit. I did not normally buy any of these publications which I sometimes borrowed from my acquaintances in the neighbourhood, most of whom lost their interest in them after a week or so.

The Puja Committees of various localities also came out with their souvenirs on the eve of Durga Puja, which contained all forms of literary compositions, besides, of course, a plethora of advertisements on which the committees came to increasingly depend for meeting the growing expenses of Durga Puja, as subscriptions from the participants proved inadequate for this purpose. These souvenirs also published all kinds writings by the budding writers of a locality which were often marked by literary excellence.

All over Bengal as well as in Kolkata, most Bengalees worshipped goddess Lakshmi about five days after Dussehra on the full moon evening. Unlike Durga Puja, this puja was held not on a community basis jointly by the residents of a locality but by each family at home. This was called Kojagari Lakshmi Puja because on this night people were expected to keep awake in order to receive the blessings of goddess Lakshmi. In this context, the Lingapurana says: "आश्विने पौर्णमास्यास्तु चरेत् जागरणं निशि।" This means that one should keep awake on the full moon night in the month of Ashwin. It is believed that in the month of Ashwin, Lakshmi moves about at night to see who was keeping awake after drinking coconut water and was playing with dice. She is said to bestow wealth and prosperity on such a person, as the Lingapurana says:

निशीये वरदा लक्षीः को जागर्त्ति महीतले।
जरत् प्रक्रमते तस्यां लोकचेष्टावलोकिनी।।

नरिकेलोदकं पीत्वा अक्षैर्ज्जागरणं निशि,
तस्मै वित्तं प्रयच्छामि को जागर्त्ति महीतले।।

The importance of Lakshmi Puja in Bengal derives from this widely held belief that Lakshmi is the dispenser of wealth and all-round prosperity. Sri Suktam that forms part of the Rig Veda is a sacred hymn to goddess Lakshmi which brings out this aspect of her role as the giver of wealth and happiness. As Lord Indra's hymn in praise of Lakshmi makes it clear, the very sight of this goddess blesses a person with wife, son, home, friends and wealth:

दाराः पुत्रास्तथागारं सुहृद्धान्यधनादिकम्।
भवत्येतन्महाभागे नित्यं त्वद्वीक्षणान्नृणाम्।।७।।

In his eulogy of Lakshmi, Purandara (as Indra is alternatively known) describes her as dwelling in a lotus (Kamalavasini), with eyes like the leaf of the lotus plant (Padmapatreksshna), with a face like a lotus (Padmasya) and seated on a lotus (Padmasana). She is very beautiful, fair-complexioned, holding a lotus of gold in her right hand and adorned with many ornaments, as the traditional prayer to the goddess explains:

गौरवर्णां सुरूपांच सर्वालंकार भूषिताम।
रौक्म्यपंद्माव्यग्रकरां वरदां दक्षिणेन तु
ॐ श्री लक्षीदेव्यै नमः

According to Hindu mythology, Lakshmi or Kamala is the wife of Lord Vishnu. Once Durvasa, the ever angry sage of yore, pronounced a curse on Indra, lord of heaven, as a result of which all the three worlds lost their sheen and Lakshmi left heaven to seek refuge in the ocean. Lakshmi's absence turned heaven into a lack-lustre place. It was only after the gods churned the ocean that Lakshmi came out and heaven regained its pristine glory. It is said that in one of her incarnations Lakshmi was born as Sita to become Lord Rama's spouse.

I observed that some of the customs relating to Lakshmi Puja in Kolkata differed from those in my native Vikrampur in east Bengal (now Bangladesh). For our village Lakshmi Puja in Vikrampur, some householders made a clay idol of the goddess; some others had an image of the goddess painted in white on a terracotta 'Sara' (a hollow earthen lid that served as a convenient canvas for the painter). In Kolkata, no such idol or 'Sara' was normally worshipped. What was worshipped was an 'Adi' made of cane, which once upon a time was used as a device for measuring paddy. Inside this 'Adi' that served as the symbol of goddess Lakshmi various articles were kept such as Shankha (bangles made of shell), Alta (lac-dye), Sindur (vermilion) and paddy. This Adi was mounted on a small wooden stool in front of which was placed a small earthen pot filled with water that sported a twig of the mango tree with five leaves. This puja ended with a good meal whose menu included many special delicacies offered as 'Bhog' to the deity.

A fortnight after Lakshmi Puja that took place on the evening of Purnima in the month of Ashwin (October-November) came the noisy Diwali on the following new moon night, which in fact synchronised with Kali Puja. Diwali, the festival of lights was celebrated with great enthusiasm in Kolkata as in the rest of our country. On this occasion goddess Kali was worshipped not only in the temples but also on a community basis in various localities of Kolkata. In many other parts of our country, however, the goddess generally worshipped during Diwali is Lakshmi, the goddess of wealth and prosperity, as I have mentioned earlier. The Hindu scriptures in fact provide for Lakshmi Puja on Diwali or Deepanwita night, the rituals for which are almost the same as for Kojagari Lakshmi Puja.

I learnt that some non-Bengalees resident in Kolkata, like people in different parts of our country, worshipped Lord Ganesh along with Lakshmi on the occasion of Diwali. One of the reasons for this practice is that Ganesh, the god of wealth, is the icon of businessmen, who invariably seek his blessings before embarking upon any new business venture. Another reason for worshipping Ganesh is that he is the symbol of 'Vivek" or discernment. As is generally known, wealth unaccompanied by the capacity to judge what is right or wrong does not last long. That is why the worship of Ganesh alongside Lakshmi has come into vogue in our country. In fact, Ganesh, the remover of all obstacles, is compulsorily worshipped before any other god or goddess can be worshipped.

In Kolkata, as in the rest of Bengal, some worshippers of Lakshmi observe on the occasion of Diwali a custom called 'Alakshmi Vidaya' or the driving away of Alakshmi, a rather unsavoury character, who is the elder sister of Lakshmi. Dark-complexioned and clad in dark clothes, she was said to instigate quarrels between spouses and went about riding an ass and carrying in her hand a broom. Alakshmi is supposed to be driven away by the devotees who set fire to some dry stalks of the jute plant (which are highly combustible) and hold them in their hands, as they go round the place, while some others create a peculiar din by beating the 'Kula' (a winnowing device made with bamboo reeds). After 'Alakshmi Vidaya', Lakshmi is worshipped in the evening and the lamps are lighted as indicated below:

प्रदोषसमये लक्ष्मीं पूजयित्वा यथाक्रमम्
दीपरक्षा तया कार्य्या भक्तया देवगृहेष्वपि

At the Kali temple of Kalighat in southern Kolkata, Diwali was a big occasion. The members of our family visited this temple on several occasions during the year and more particularly on the day of Diwali. A fact that struck me was that, on the occasion of Diwali, goddess Kali was worshipped at the Kalighat temple as on all other days round the year, but it was goddess Lakshmi whose worship at this temple on the Diwali evening was the more important event. I have drawn extensively on a write-up on this subject by Suman Gupta in the Bengali weekly 'Bartaman' (Kolkata) dated November 6, 2004.

How did the custom of worshipping Lakshmi at the Kali temple of Kalighat come into vogue? To comprehend this we have to go back into the history of this temple and scrutinize the roles of the various families and individuals who played an important part in prescribing the rules and rituals that came to be followed by this institution. Centuries ago, Kalighat was located in the midst of a dense jungle on the bank of Adi Ganga. Peethamala, an ancient religious text, mentions this location of Kalighat and places it on par with Benares from the point of view of religious sanctity, saying that, not to speak of human beings, even insects which lose their lives here secure liberation:

कालीक्षेत्रे काशीक्षेत्र अतोदोऽपि
कीटोऽपि मरणे मुक्त किन्न पुनः महेश्वर मनवाह्य।

The Bhabishya Purana had mentioned this temple about 2000 years ago. Those traveling to the far east for commercial ventures used to course along the Adi Ganga before entering the bay of Bengal and invariably stopped at Kalighat to worship Kali. In course of time, the forest was cleared which paved the way for human habitations to come up around Kalighat. According to local tradition, two ascetics by name Brahmananda Giri and Atmaram Brahmachari succeeded in retrieving from under the water of a pond a slab of stone bearing the imprint of a finger of Sati's foot, which was nothing but what had made Kalighat a Peethasthan – one of the several sacred places of India where some limb or other of Parvati had fallen from above after her body was cut to pieces by the rotating discus of Lord Vishnu. This footprint is still preserved in a silver box kept below goddess Kali's idol at Kalighat.

In course of time, a new temple of goddess Kali came up at Kalighat towards the end of the 18th century, thanks to the generosity of the family of Sabarna Roy Choudhury of Barisha. It is said that this temple had been built after pulling down an old temple that had been built by Basanta Roy Chowdhury, the uncle of Pratapadity the illustrious Bhuinya of Jessore, who had fought against the Mughal Emperor Akbar. After Sabarna Roy Choudhury built this new Kali temple, a member of the famous Haldar family of Kalighat became the 'Sevait' of the temple (i.e.took over the priestly duties at the Kali temple in lieu of food and clothing).

It is now necessary to bring in the name of one Bhabanidas Chakraborti, who belonged to a village of Jessore district. Once his father Srinath disappeared from their house. This led Bhabanidas to go to various places in search of his father. Bhabanidas arrived at Kalighat in the hope of finding his father Srinath who used to worship Kali. Bhabanidas was, however, a devotee of Vasudev or Krishna. He stayed on at Kalighat and, after some time, married the daughter of Bhubaneshwar Giri, who was then the Mohunt (or abbot) of the Kali temple. In course of time, Bhubaneshwar Giri handed over the responsibility of worshipping Kali at the temple to his son-in-law Bhabanidas Chakraborti. This how a householder became the priest at the Kali temple in place of a Sannyasi (ascetic).

Till this time, Kalighat was the epitome of'Shaktism', where even human sacrifice had reportedly taken place. There was no system of worshipping goddess Lakshmi at this temple. It was Bhabanidas Chakraborti who first introduced Lakshmi Puja here on the evening of Diwali because, as already mentioned, he was a Vaishnavite. It is said that once Bhabanidas had a dream in which he saw that Vasudev, of whom he was a devotee, was not being worshipped properly at his village home in Jessore district. He went to his village, brought the idol of Vasudev to Kalighat and placed it in a niche on the western side of the Kali temple. He worshipped Vasudev every day and started the practice of offering 'Bhog' (cooked food) to the deity – a practice that is still in vogue.

One night something miraculous happened. Bhabandas had a dream which showed that there was a 'Tilak' (mark made usually with sandal paste) on the nose of goddess Kali's idol. He got up at once, had a quick bath and then entered the temple where he saw that Mother Kali's idol was sporting a 'Tilak' on the nose! He was at a loss to understand who had painted the 'Tilak' on the Mother's nose. He thought that the Mother looked very happy to flaunt this image of a Vaishnavi. He looked at the idol of Vasudev close by and saw that its body was daubed all over with sandal paste and vermilion. The realization dawned on him that there was no difference between Kali and Krishna, between Shyama and Shyam. Vaishnavism and Shaktism were no different from each other. From that day onward, the 'Tilak' found a permanent place on the nose of goddess Kali in the Kalighat temple – something which is unique because no such thing is to be found at any other temple in our country.

This paved the way for commencing Lakshmi Puja at the Kalighat temple on the evening of Deepanwita or Diwali. On this occasion, Kali is worshipped as on all other days, there being no special puja for the goddess. It is goddess Lakshmi that is worshipped here with great fanfare on the evening of Diwali. But no idol of Lakshmi is put up on this occasion. The idol of goddess Kali is worshipped as Lakshmi! The ritual of Alakshmi Vidaya is also observed here on this occasion as during Kojagari Lakshmi Puja mentioned earlier. Even on the day of Lakshmi Puja at the Kalighat temple on the occasion of Diwali, goats are sacrificed here as part of the prescribed ritual.

As already mentioned, since the days of Sabarna Roy Chowdhury, priestly duties at the Kalghat temple have been entrusted to the Haldar family, the 'Sevait' of the temple. So it is the members of this family who organize Lakshmi Puja at the Kali temple of Kalighat.

Most of the houses of Kolkata were illuminated with earthen lamps, as was the practice in our village in east Bengal as well. But there was a difference in the pattern of Kolkata's illumination, because some houses were lit up with candles, while some others looked resplendent with electric lights and even with now-on-now-off multi-coloured lights. As I learnt later, this was the day when Lord Rama, Sita and Lakshmana had returned to Ayodhya at the end of their fourteen-year long exile. The people of Ayodhya, therefore, celebrated the occasion by illuminating their houses-—a custom that has been observed ever since by the people in different parts of India.

However, in south India, this occasion is said to commemorate the slaying of the demon Narakasura by Lord Krishna. According to the Bhagawat Purana, this demon, who lived in Pragjyotishapura (a place now in Assam), had joined hands with Kansa and some demons to oppress innocent people. Lord Krishna killed Narakasura on the 14th day of the dark fortnight in the month of Kartik (October-November), which began to be observed as Naraka Chaturdashi. Krishna also freed 16000 princesses whom Narakasura had thrown into his prison, brought them along with him to Dwaraka and married them. This event which took place on the new moon night was celebrated with the lighting of numerous lamps and came to be known as Deepavali or Diwali.

When I grew up, I learnt that the Jains celebrate Diwali because it was on this day that Lord Mahavira had attained liberation. In Bengal, Deepavali is observed as the night of the 'Pitris" (departed souls) and the lamps lighted on this occasion are believed to be guides to the 'Pitris'.

In our village in east Bengal, we had fireworks on the occasion of Diwali. This was a much quieter affair than in Kolkata, where fireworks during Diwali lent a highly explosive touch to the situation as the bursting of powerful crackers rent the air with loud noise that was ear-shattering and reminded me of what I later came to learn about Guy Fawkes' Night in London.

Diwali now brings to my mind what I have read in Brihadaranyaka Upanishad. King Janaka asked Yajnavalkya what light a person would have when both the sun and the moon set, bringing about a state of total darkness. Yajnavalkya replied that it was fire that would provide light in such an eventuality. The lamps lit on the occasion of Diwali symbolised that light. To a further question by Janaka as to what light a person would have if fire also went out, Yajnavalkya answered that one could in that case depend on speech or sound which would enable one to make one's presence felt when it was dark all around. It is as true now as it was in the days of King Janaka. On the dark night of Diwali, the deafening sound of crackers helps one register one's presence with a big bang!

In our Kolkata home, we celebrated Saraswati Puja, as we used to do in our village home in Vikrampur. Our devotion to the goddess stemmed largely from our whole-hearted commitment to education, which we looked upon as the only means whereby one could make good in life and which, moreover, represented the only field where, with sincere effort, one could surpass all others, howsoever rich or socially important they might be. As the saying in Bengali went:

"One that for studies cares,
In carriage and pair fares."

A lot of effort went into the arrangements we made for Saraswati Puja. Among the articles required for the rituals of the Puja were flowers and the tender blossoms of the mango tree that began to flower at this time of the year. In Kolkata of those days, there were still some beautiful gardens, public parks, where flowers of all kinds bloomed in the different seasons. Early in the morning on the day of Saraswati Puja, I went out to look for flowers. As I plucked some blossoms from the outstretched branches of a mango tree that stood in the corner of a park, I remembered the famous lines from poet Kalidasa's Ritusamharam: [13]

Sprays of full blown mango blossoms –
His sharp arrows, honey bees in rows –
The humming bow string;
Warrior-Spring set to break the hearts
Of Love's devotees, is now approaching, my love.

I also gathered a basketful of flowers including the seasonal marigold from the garden of a kind-hearted neighbour. Spring was in the air. I again remembered Kalidasa's lines in the Ritusamharam:[14]

Trees put forth flowers,
Waters abound in lotuses
Women's thoughts turn to love;
The air is sweetly scented.
Mornings are pleasant, days are delightful.
All things are more alluring in spring time, my love.

Since most of the people of our locality had come to know of our academic accomplishments, some of them belonging to much better off families came to attend our Puja, which made us feel rather proud and grateful to them.The way they behaved with us and spoke to us strengthened my conviction that the rich were not necessarily bad people.

On the streets of Kolkata, I saw girls dressed in Saris that dyed yellow with the pigment extracted from the stalk of Shefali flowers (Nyctanthers Arbortristis). Kalidasa's imagery in the Ritusamharam again leapt up before my eyes: [15]

Fine woven silks dyed scarlet with mallow juice
Swathe round hips; delicate silks saffron-dyed
Shining pale gold, veil the perfect orbs of breasts.
Women now dress with light-hearted grace.

Notes

1. Article captioned "Calcutta And English Literature" by Rabindra Kumar Dasgupta in the Calcutta municipal Gazette, Anthology Number (1924–1947), pages 70-79.
2. *Ibid.*, page 74.
3. *Ibid.*, page 74.
4. *Ibid.*, page 75.
5. *Ibid.*, page 77.
6. *Ibid.*, page 77.
7. *Ibid.*, page 77.
8. *Ibid.*, page 78.
9. *Ibid.*, pages 78-79.
10. *Ibid.*, Article entitled "A City Cosmopolitan" by R. Dhara, page 116.
11. Ma'r Abhisheke Eso Eso Twara
    Mangalghat Hoyni Je Bhara
    Sabar Parashe Pavitra Kara Tirthe neere
    Ei Bharater Mahamanaber Sagarateere
12. Aay Ashuchi Aayre Patit Ebar
    Mayer Puja Habey
    Jetha Sakal Jatir Sakal Manush
    Nirbhaye Maar Charan Chhonbe
13. Verse 1 of Chapter 6 of Kalidasa's Ritusamhara.
14. *Ibid.*, verse 2.
15. *Ibid.*, verse 5.

6

The Gory End of A Friend's Father

One of my class mates in Asutosh College, Kolkata, whom I have special reason to remember, was Kalyan Prasad Sengupta. After getting acquainted with him, I gradually developed a liking for him because of his friendly nature and more importantly because, like me, he also hailed from Vikrampur (now in Bangladesh), to be precise, from Beltali village, which was not very far from my village.

There was another reason for which he came to occupy a soft corner of my heart. It was the gory death years ago of his father and the cruel fate that befell Kalyan, then still a small child, after his father was gunned down in rather tragic circumstances by some persons, who were first class patriots, but name-called terrorists in the good old days of the Raj. His father, Kamakhya Prasad Sengupta had acquired a rather unsavoury reputation in pre-independence Bengal as a tormentor of the freedom-fighters. However, as I learnt from Kalyan, his father was after all not as bad a man as he came to be painted as. There was also a positive side to his character that was not known to most people.

Kalyan belonged to a well-known family of Vikrampur's Beltali village, whose members had distinguished themselves in the professions as well as in the service of the government. Some of them had worked in the Railways in Assam. Their philanthropic activities had earned them the gratitude of the people of their village in Vikrampur.

Kalyan's grandfather, Annada Prasad, was a good physician, who occupied a high position in the Assam Bengal Railways. He was benevolent by nature and had offered jobs to many in the Railways. He had founded the Kalibari (with a temple of goddess Kali) at Lumding in Assam. His patriotic fervour found expression in his patronage of the 'Charkha' (indigenous spinning wheel) and in the 'Khadi' clothes (rough hand-woven clothes) that he wore. He had identified himself with many social causes such as spreading education amongst girls, abolition of the dowry system, stoppage of child marriage etc. In his Beltali village, he had established an impressive "Pancharatna Mutt" in memory of his mother. A Shivalinga was installed inside the Mutt and a big Mela (fair) used to be held there every year during Shivaratri.

Kalyan's father, Kamakhya Prasad Sengupta was the eldest of the three sons of Annada Prasad. Born in 1895 in Beltali village, he spent his early life with his father in Assam. He left home at a young age and went to Burma to seek his fortune, as many young people of eastern India were wont to do in those good old days when Burma was known to be the land of the pagoda tree. However, with hardly any educational qualification worth the name, he had no alternative but to join the ranks of unskilled labourers, breaking stones on the Railway track in order to earn his livelihood.

An Englishman, who was a high government official, developed a liking for him in view of his sincere and hard work. Looking at his face and seeing his bearing, the Englishman got a feeling that Kamakhya hailed from a good family.His guess proved correct as he soon discovered that Kamakhya was a fugitive from home. He persuaded Kamakhya to go back home and devote himself to studies, assuring him of a good job in due course if he could become a graduate. He told Kamakhya to get back to him, wherever he might be, but after his graduation.

So, Kamakhya left Burma and went in for further studies in colleges at Serampore and Dhaka. He became a graduate and then got in touch with the Englishman, who had not forgotten the promise he had made to Kamakhya. The Englishman redeemed his pledge and helped Kamakhya in all possible ways. During World War I, Kamakhya worked for some time in the Indian Recruitment Department. In 1920, he became a Sub-Deputy Collector, a very high post indeed in the administrative hierarchy of the Raj. After a stint in the Settlement Department for some time, he was posted as the

Sub-Deputy Magistrate at Narayanganj and then at Munshiganj where he tried in various ways to promote the welfare of the people. When communal riots broke out in Dhaka, he rescued many affected persons. One Mukul Banerjee, a famous Zamindar of Murapara, who was well-known all over Bengal, was killed in the riots. Kamakhya managed to get his dead body salvaged and transported to Narayanganj at considerable risk to his own life.

The anti-British revolutionary movement that swept across Bengal in the wake of the partition of the Province in 1905 did not subside even after this plan was jettisoned. The underground movement spearheaded by secret radical groups known as the Anushilan Samiti and the Yugantar reached its peak in the late nineteen twenties. The branches of these two organisations, which sprang up all over Bengal, attracted many middle class Bengalees into their folds.

Shree Sangha, an underground revolutionary group became active in Dhaka district including Vikrampur. Another similar body styled as the Suhrid Samiti, which had its headquarters at Mymensingh, set up its branches in several districts of east Bengal including Dhaka and was particularly active in Vikrampur. As early as on December 14, 1908, in a report[1] on the situation in Bengal, R. Nathan, Commissioner, Dhaka Division, had drawn pointed attention to Vikrampur and referred to the following extract from a letter written by a leader of the Suhrid Samiti to another member: "Came to Munshiganj and talked with the Secretary, the Captain and the leading members. Talked also with the men of Bajrajogini and Sonarang. The result is that I have come to the conclusion that work will not prosper if Mymensingh is made the centre. Accordingly, after taking the opinion of all, I have settled to make Malkhanagar the centre. Malkhanagar is the central place in this quarter, and work is also going on well here, as there are some energetic and zealous workers in this village. It is only owing to their zeal that whatever work was done in Vikrampur, was done. The centre should be made therefore in that village. I am shortly going to Malkhanagar to talk with all about this matter. If you and others agree to my proposal then write to Chandra Kanta Basu of the village. I hope that work will go on nicely if that village be made the centre."

The Commissioner of Dhaka Division had also observed in his report: "Malkhanagar has always been regarded as one of the worst localities in the Dhaka district, and persistent reports have been received of the secretion of arms in this place. The members of the Malkhanagar Bose family are among the most mischievous of our agitators, and the above allusions to this locality and this family are most sinister. The "work" here referred to must be secret and criminal work."

Bengal thus became the epi-centre of revolutionary activities that sometimes led to the killing of government officials, particularly Englishmen. Political dacoities were committed to raise funds for financing revolutionary activities as well as for the purchase weapons from abroad. In the latter half of the nineteen twenties, the focus of the revolutionary movement began to shift, as the Anushilan Samiti and the Yugantar lost some of their cadres to the nascent communist movement.

In 1930, the Chittagong Armoury Raid organised by Surya Sen and his band of patriotic workers struck a big blow to the British authorities and boosted the morale of the revolutionaries. In 1931-32, armed dacoities by the revolutionaries were reported from Munishiganj and some other places of Vikrampur. On October 28, 1931, Durno, the District Magistrate of Dhaka, was shot dead by Saroj Guha and Ramen Bhowmick. By the end of that year, the non-co-operation movement against British rule had spread all over the country.

In this highly surcharged atmosphere, Kamakhya Prasad was chosen by the British Government as the Special Magistrate of Munshiganj to deal with the civil disobedience movement. Special camps were set up in many villages of Vikrampur such as Solaghar, Paikpara, Hashara and Taltala to suppress the movement. (Incidentally, I attended school in Solaghar village from 1936 to 1945.) Kamakhya Prasad's official conduct was perceived to be rather oppressive by the revolutionaries, who, therefore, decided to have him despatched. Some people reportedly gave expression to their feeling of revulsion against Kamakhya Prasad in private. Kamakhya knew that he had earned the wrath of the revolutionaries and become their target.

Kamakhya sent his old mother, wife and children away to Comilla, apprehending danger to their lives. A warning of the impending catastrophe came, when Kamakhya's wife received a postal parcel that contained some sunned rice and an unbleached and borderless white Saree—articles that are meant for the use of widows in Bengal. This was the revolutionaries' way of forewarning Kamakhya's wife of her approaching widowhood, since her husband was soon going to be killed by them.

The climactic event took place in June,1932. Kamakhya Prasad had gone to Dhaka and put up in the house of Sachindra Nath Chatterjee, Sub-divisional Officer (South), Dhaka, on Rankin Street, Police Station Sutrapur. The revolutionaries came to know of his presence in Dhaka and started looking for an opportunity to bump him off. On June 27, 1932, at about 4 A.M., while Kamakhya Prasad was asleep in a room on the ground floor of his guest's house, some revolutionaries went in through a window and fired several shots at him from a close range, killing him on the spot. His host, Sachindra Nath Chatterjee, who heard the sound of gun-fire, came running down the stairs from the first floor to find his guest lying dead in a pool of blood. According to a slightly different version, the revolutionaries had entered the room and remained in hiding for some time before Kamakhya Prasad had retired there for the night. Kamakhya was the first Indian Magistrate to be killed by the revolutionaries. His dead body was taken to Comilla for cremation.

The British authorities sent telegrams to Kamakhya's old mother and wife placing on record their appreciation of his services as a "brave and able officer of the Government". Government offices were ordered closed at Dhaka, Narayanganj, Munshiganj and Comilla.

Police and the sleuths of the Criminal Investigation Department at once swung into action to track down the killers, but had no luck for some time. Then suddenly there was a breakthrough. One of the revolutionaries, who was involved in the plot, was so elated by the success of their mission that he went to the telegraph office to send a wire to a person in the Ichhapura village of Vikrampur. The telegram was worded as follows: "Kamakhya's operation successful. No need to worry". The Post Master became suspicious on seeing the name of Kamakhya in the telegram. He sent word to the police and kept the sender of the telegram engaged in some idle gossip. The police came in no time and arrested him.

Interrogation of this revolutionary revealed the names of several persons, who had a hand in the plot. The police also raided and searched many places in Dhaka and Kolkata and arrested some persons who were interrogated. One of the suspects, Kalipada Mukherjee, admitted having killed Kamakhya Prasad to avenge the oppression that the latter had let loose on the people. During his trial, Kalipada readily admitted his guilt and was, therefore, sentenced to death. He was hanged on February 16,1933 at the Dhaka Jail. Kalipada was the only son of his father. Before he was hanged, his wife had died on January 7,1933 after giving birth to a son. Some people were of the view that Kalipada was not the real killer, but had owned up to having killed Kamakhya Prasad in order to save all the others involved in the plot.

A contemporary report[2] on this case prepared by the Government of Bengal mentioned the following facts: "The Magistrate was on special duty in the Munshiganj subdivision in connection with the civil disobedience movement and secret information showed that the terrorists were annoyed with him. Five fired pistol cartridges bearing the mark "U.M.C. 32 A.E.P." were found in the room where the occurrence took place.

Thirty-eight persons were arrested during investigation including Kalipada Mukherji, son of Matilal, of Ichhapura, police station Serajdikhan, Dhaka, who confessed to having committed the murder. He was sent up for trial under section 302, I.P.C. before a Special Tribunal, and sentenced to death on he 8th November, 1932. An appeal against his conviction before the Hon'ble High Court was dismissed on the 19th December, 1932 as was a petition for mercy to His Majesty the King, and he was hanged on the 16th February, 1933.

The under-mentioned were dealt with under the Bengal Criminal Law Amendment Act, 1930, on their discharge in the case:-

(1) Ranjan Mohan De, son of Bhagaban, of Majipara, police station Srinagar, Dacca.

(2) Jogesh Chandra Datta, son of the late Mahesh Chandra, of 3, Iswar Das Lane,Dacca.

(3) Santosh Ganguly, son of Umesh, of 28/7, North Gendaria, police station Sutrapur, Dacca.
(4) Fatik Chandra Goswami, son of Nikunja Behari, of 20, Rajani Chaudhuri Road, police station Sutrapur, Dacca.
(5) Phanindra Goswami alias Fuli, son of Nikunja Behari, of 20, Rajani Chaudhuri Road, police station Sutrapur, Dacca.
(6) Prafulla Chandra Pyne, son of the late Ambika Charan, of Madhapara, police station Serajdikhan.
(7) Santi Bhusan Chatarji, son of Ramani Mohan, of Ichhapura, police station Serajdikhan.
(8) Amulya Charan Chakran Chakrabartti, son of Haralal, of Madhyapara, police station Serajdikhan.
(9) Madhu Sudan Bhattacharji, son of Haridas, of Rajdia, police station Serajdikhan.
(10) Pran Gopal Ganguly, son of Narendra Chandra, of Betka, police station Tangibari.
(11) Nikhil Chandra Sen, son of Kaviraj Srish Chandra, of Hashara, police station Srinagar.
(12) Shiva Priya Basu, son of Rajendra Kumar, of 14, Miratar Lane, police station Kotwali, Dhaka.
(13) Purna Chandra Basak, son of Govindra Chandra, of 56, Radhika Mohan Basak Lane, police station Kotwali, Dhaka.
(14) Nirode Behari Chakrabatti, son of Khirode Behari, of Mattagram, police station Kashba, Tippera.

Members of the Anushilan were responsible for this outrage, but the Sree Sangha was also concerned."

Incidentally, Nikhil Chandra Sen figuring at serial number(11) above was the son of Srish Chandra Sen, the fabulous Kaviraj (a practitioner of Ayurveda) of Vikrampur to whom I as well as some other members of our family used to go for treatment.

My friend, Kalyan, told me that he was about three years of age at that time and did not comprehend what had happened. It was after some years that he came to know how the revolutionaries had killed his father whom he began to miss.

According to Kalyan, for some time before his death, his father had started feeling uneasy in his job because patriotic urges had begun to stir his soul. Kamakhya Prasad used to wear 'Khadi', while his younger brother openly professed his commitment to Gandhian ideals and life style.

In a Bengali book "Vikrampur" (page 215, Volume III, published in 1944), its author, Himangshu Mohan Chattopadhyay, had some good words for Kamakhya Prasad Sengupta's life . A rough and ready translation of what he wrote would read as below:

"The untimely death of Kamakhya Prasad has been the cause of great harm for Beltali. He strove to improve the condition of the village in various ways. He sought to relieve the scarcity of water by getting some tube wells bored in Beltali. Personally, he was efficient, noble, strong in character and kind-hearted. For a few months before his death, he became a tool in the hands of the higher authorities and finally departed, acquiring the notoriety of having been an oppressive administrator; but those who knew him intimately, were deeply hurt by the premature and tragic end of a life that was full of possibilities."

Kamakhya Prasad left behind a son (Kalyan) and five daughters, besides his wife, mother and a widowed sister. The British Government looked after them by providing monthly pensions for all of them—Rs.150/-for his wife and Rs.30/-each for his mother and sister for life and Rs.20/-for each of the six children—till the age of 25 for Kalyan and the age of 20 for each daughter. In case Kalyan's mother died before he attained the age of 25 years, his monthly pension was to be raised to Rs.50/-till he was 25. Obviously, the idea was that each daughter was to get married by the age of 20, while the son could go in for higher studies or take a few years more to get settled in life. In the case of the daughters, no pension was to be paid after marriage, but a lump sum grant of Rs.1000/-was to be made for the marriage of each daughter.

Kalyan shifted to Kolkata after his father's death and had his schooling in the Jagabandhu Institution. Then he joined the Asutosh College for the Intermediate of Arts course, as I had done. But he could not graduate as he gave up his studies some time after his mother expired in 1948, which meant the stoppage of her monthly pension of Rs.150/-. This made the family's economic condition rather precarious.

Kalyan left home for Bombay in 1949 almost penniless. In 1950, he went to Delhi and joined the New Delhi Municipal Committee as a menial worker in which capacity he had to go from bungalow to bungalow, spraying DDTas part of an anti-mosquito campaign. He also served as a Vaccinator in the Health Department of the Municipal Committee. Later, he worked as a private tutor to a school girl whom he taught English. In 1951, he joined the office of the Chief Inspector of Explosives, Government of India as a Lower Division Clerk, shifting later on transfer to Nagpur, where he spent long years. As a second string to his bow, he picked up homoeopathy and built up a sizable practice, acquiring a great reputation. He moved over to Kolkata in 1985, but continued to visit Nagpur from time to time to look after his numerous patients there.

My point in mentioning these facts is to show how Kalyan's life came to follow the rough and uneven course that it did as a result of the shattering impact of his father's violent death in the early nineteen thirties and then his mother's untimely death immediately after the partition of Bengal in 1947.

One of Kalyan's elder sisters, Abha Sengupta had passed the Matriculation Examination of the pre-independence Calcutta University from Gauhati, standing first among all the girl students from Assam. Since she hailed from Vikrampur, Haripada Banerji, the Head Master of my school in the Solaghar village of Vikrampur, was highly elated when he heard this news. Though he did not know the girl or her family members, yet he felt so happy over her performance that he walked several miles to go to her house in the Beltali village of Vikrampur to personally congratulate her.

Our Head Master carried with him several presents for Abha Sengupta, which included a few scores of live 'Koi' fish, whose value as an item of gastronomic delight only the fish-loving people of Vikrampur and Bengal can properly judge! Needless to say, Abha Di (I am addressing her as such because she is the elder sister of my college friend) and the members of her family were delighted. But the point that I wish to emphasise is how much interest the Head Master of a school took in those days in examinations and their results and what importance he attached to the good performance of a student, irrespective of which school she belonged to and whether or not he knew her personally! Even today, my friend Kalyan and his sisters proudly recall the visit that Haripada Banerjee, our Head Master, had paid to their house and narrate this story to those who care to listen, long after our Head Master has left his mortal coil.

Notes

1. Terrorism in Bengal (1995),Government of West Bengal, Volume II, page 810. The places mentioned in this extract are villages of Vikrampur. I personally knew some members of the Bose family of Malkhanagar mentioned above. It was one of the most respectable families of Vikrampur and I am sure, the people of Vikrampur would not have agreed with the assessment of the Divisional Commissioner.
2. A Chronological Account of Violent Incidents from 1907 to 1939 vide Terrorism in Bengal (1995),Government of West Bengal, Volume VI, pages 906-907.

7

End of World War II : The I.N.A. Saga

Soon after we moved over to Kolkata from Vikrampur, the Second World War came to an end with Germany's surrender in May 1945 and the dropping of atom bombs by the U.S.A. on Hiroshima on August 6, 1945 and on Nagasaki three days later, which compelled Japan also to surrender. A few weeks before that—on July 15, 1945, to be precise—a test of the atom bomb conducted at Almagarado, New Mexico, United States of America, had failed. But the next day, the test succeeded, thanks to the efforts of Gen. Leslie Groves, the administrative head of the project and J. Robert Oppenheimer, the American physicist and Director of the project. Of course, the development of the bomb was not the handiwork of the American scientists alone but was the result of successful co-operation among them and the scientists of several European countries.

What an irony that it was the same Oppenheimer who, years later, opposed the development of the hydrogen bomb on moral grounds, as a result of which he became a suspect from the security angle and his loyalty to his country came under a cloud!

Incidentally, according to information that has recently come to light, Albert Einstein, the great scientist, also blamed himself for the use of the atom bomb at Hiroshima and Nagasaki and was greatly pained by the misuse of his idea.

With regular access to newspapers in Kolkata, I was now in a position to keep myself posted with developments on the national and international planes. What struck me was that the name of the place, Almagarado, where the test was carried out, had a close similarity with the word 'Armageddon' that stands for a devastating conflict between nations. The Trinity site in the desert that stood the brunt of the test witnessed a massive blinding flash of light that was visible at a distance of 420 kilometres, a roar that was audible 80 kilometres away and a mushroom cloud that rose 12,192 metres (about 40,000 feet) above the ground.

A repentant Oppenheimer, who was well versed in Sanskrit, recited two verses from the Gita when he saw the big blaze set off by the atomic explosion. A couple of months later, when I began to read Chapter 11 of the Gita prescribed for study in my college, I understood the significance of these two verses, one of which (stanza 12, Chapter 11, Gita) reads :

दिवि सूर्यसहस्रस्य भवेद्युगपदुत्थिता।
यदि भाः सदृशी सा स्याभ्दासस्तस्य महात्मनः।।१२।।

(What brilliance there would have been if a thousand suns were to blaze forth all of a sudden in the sky — to that was comparable the splendour of that great Being). It was this idea that had led Robert Jungk, who wrote a book on this subject, to give it the title " Brighter Than a Thousand Suns ".

The second verse quoted by Oppenheimer (stanza 32,Chapter 11, Gita) reads :

श्रीभगवानुवाच
कालोऽस्मि लोकक्षयकृत्प्रवृद्धो लोकान् समाहर्तुमिह प्रवृत्तः।
ऋतेऽपि त्वां न भविष्यन्ति सर्वे येऽवस्थिताः प्रत्यनीकेषु योधाः।।३२।।

(I am the mighty world-destroying Time, engaged in annihilating all beings. Even without you, not one of all the warriors arrayed in these rival armies will survive).

Through these verses figuring in Chapter II of the Gita entitled "Viswaroopdarshanayogah", Lord Krishna had vousafed to Arjuna a vision of his cosmic form, his luminous splendour as well as his all-destroying power — attributes that were now sought to be usurped by the man of science, whose creation — the atom bomb — made it possible for the USA to enact an unprecedented spectacle of death and destruction at Hiroshima and Nagasaki. In fact, the three worst tragedies for which humanity will remember World War II were the dropping of the atom bomb on Hiroshima and Nagasaki, the holocaust that resulted in the mass murder of six million Jews in Nazi Germany and the man-made Bengal Famine of 1943 during British rule in which the number of those who lost their lives ranged between 1.5 million (official estimates) and 3.5 to 5 million (unofficial estimates).

The dropping of atom bombs at Hiroshima and Nagasaki triggered world-wide condemnation, but not in the USA. Nor did the man who dropped the first atom bomb on Hiroshima nurse any sense of guilt or remorse. Decades later, I read a piece by Joerg-Michael Dettmer in the New Delhi Hindustan Times of November 13, 2000, which bore me out. Paul Tibbets was the ace American bomber pilot who dropped the bomb on Hiroshima from a plane "Enola Gay" named after his mother. On August 6, 1945, the plane took off at 2.45 a.m. from Tinian and dropped the bomb above the centre of Hiroshima city just after 8.15 a.m. Decades later, in a speech delivered at a convention of social studies teachers in Dallas, Texas, in the latter half of 2000, Tibbets, then 85 years old, said: "After the war, I met President Truman. He told me I had done my duty and that if anyone criticised me for dropping the bomb, I should send that person to see him because he gave me the order to do so".

"Yes I would do it again if the war situation and the circumstances demanded it", Tibbets told the convention. A thunderous applause greeted his observation. There is no doubt that most Americans regard him as a hero!

Some years later, on July 19, 2004, I read a news item in the New Delhi edition of the daily Times of India, which said that Charles Sweeny, a retired Air Force general, who had piloted the plane that dropped the atomic bomb on Nagasaki on August 9, 1945, had died at the age of 84 at a hospital in Boston. The cause of his death was not disclosed. Sweeny was also said to be an outspoken defender of the bombing, which became evident from his speeches at colleges and universities. My mind raced back to those tension-filled days sixty years ago when this news greeted my eyes.

It has often been claimed that the USA had used the atom bomb in Japan with a view to forcing the latter to surrender and thus bringing about a swift end to the war. It has also been said that this measure was the least abhorrent because it ensured the minimum loss of life and property. Recent studies, however, indicate that the USA's main motive in using the bomb at Hiroshima and Nagasaki was to intimidate the USSR and limit Soviet expansionism in Japan and Asia. The USA was aware that Japan was already looking for peace and so there was no military need for the USA to resort to the bomb. Viewedinthi light, the USA's cold war strategy that was to dominate world politics for the next half century.

The end of World War II changed the whole international scenario and had its inevitable impact on the question of India's freedom. Leaders of the Indian National Congress, who had been put behind bars in the wake of the Quit India movement, started coming out of jails. I attended many mammoth public meetings which became the order of the day in Kolkata, because they were addressed by leaders of the stature of Mahatma Gandhi, Pt. Jawaharlal Nehru, Sardar Vallabhbhai Patel, Acharya J.B. Kripalini and Sarat Chandra Bose.

It was at this juncture that, like all others in our country, I started becoming aware of the full facts about the valorous deeds of the Indian National Army under the leadership of Netaji Subhas Chandra Bose. These received wide publicity through the press and platform and won the instantaneous acclaim of all sections of the people throughout the country. Earlier, many Indians had been misled by the propaganda offensive of the Allied Powers into believing that the Japanese attack on India's north eastern region was nothing but a Fascist attempt to conquer Indian territory. Even Pandit Jawahar Lal Nehru was reported to have said that he would fight and repel these forces. It is only now that the common people came to learn that the INA and the Japanese forces had joined hands in this invasion which, therefore, formed part of the INA's struggle to free India.

The news of Netaji having perished in a plane crash at Taihoku in Taiwan on August 18, 1945 was treated by us with utter contempt, because we did not have a scintilla of doubt that this was a false story circulated by the British. We all believed that Netaji was alive and in hiding, perhaps in the U.S.S.R., biding his time to make a dramatic appearance on the Indian soil at a time of his choosing.

Kolkata, which derived its pre-eminent position by virtue not only of once having been the capital of British India but also of its having always been in the fore-front of the freedom struggle, now lived up to its reputation and captured the right political mood to become the focal point of the people's fervour which found daily expression in numerous overt acts that shook the very foundation of the Raj.

Kolkata witnessed mammoth processions with big, larger-than-life cut-outs of Netaji Subhas Chandra Bose in the INA uniform towering head and shoulders over milling crowds and with young boys and girls marching to the tune of bands that blared out I.N.A. songs. "Kadam Kadam Barhaye Ja, Khushise Geet Gaye Ja" (March ahead, step by step, go forward as you sing happily) – this was the most favourite marching song of the I.N.A., which, chorussed to the drum-beat of the band, created a feeling of great euphoria among the people, specially among the youth and the students. Netaji's slogans "Chalo Dilli" (On to Delhi), "Lal Quila Leyenge, Tiranga Lehraenge" (We shall occupy the Red Fort and fly the tri-colour), "Jai Hind" (Victory to India) etc. stirred our souls. The excitement of the people knew no bounds and their anger against the colonial rulers rose steadily throughout the country. Living in those stirring times, I often recalled English poet Wordsworth's memorable words: "Bliss was it in that dawn to be alive. But to be young was paradise".

The country's political leaders voiced the unanimous demand of the people for the immediate and honourable release of the I.N.A. heroes without trial, on which the British authorities insisted, as they accused the I.N.A. personnel of being traitors, who had betrayed their masters in violation of all canons of military discipline. In Kolkata, a big public meeting organised in defence of the I.N.A. heroes' cause was addressed by many important leaders of the Congress Party including Pandit Jawahar Lal Nehru and Sardar Patel, besides Sarat Chandra Bose, elder brother of Netaji.

I attended this meeting held in the Deshabandhu Park in south Kolkata, reaching the venue several hours in advance to be sure of getting a place where I would be able to sit on the bare ground. It was a huge gathering with numerous streams of people converging there from all parts of the city and its suburbs. In the continuous jostling by the crowd, which created frequent stampedes, many fainted, many had their shirts torn and many lost their shoes.

At this meeting, I saw how strained the relationship between the leaders of the Congress and the I.N.A. on the one hand and the communists on the other was. The Congress leaders came out openly to give vent to their displeasure over the latter's collaboration with the British and the Allied Powers during the country's freedom struggle.

It was at this time that our college – Asutosh College – gave a reception to Uttam Chand Malhotra, an Indian national settled in Kabul, where he had his own business. He had given shelter to Subhas Chandra Bose, when the latter reached Kabul via Peshawar in January 1941 after his dramatic escape from his Elgin Road house in Kolkata, where he had been interned by the British authorities. In an address he delivered to the students and teachers of our college, Uttam Chand narrated the details of Netaji's journey through Kabul into Russia on his way to Berlin. It was for the first time that I heard a first-hand account of Netaji's escapade. There was pin-drop silence as he spoke and we lapped up in rapt attention whatever he said. He cast a spell on us with the lurid details of Netaji's exploits, the many hazards that he faced on his fateful trek to Berlin and the diverse stratagems that he employed to keep up the cover he had adopted and throw dust in the eyes of the British authorities, who got on his trail as soon as they realised that Bose had fooled them by making good his escape.

As we learnt from Uttam Chand, one Mian Akbar Shah of the North West Frontier Province, who was a member of the Forward Bloc, came to Kolkata for the ostensible purpose of attending a meeting of the party's Working Committee and utilised this opportunity to buy some clothes for Bose to give him the appearance of a Muslim. Bose assumed the name of Mohd. Ziauddin and took the cover of an itinerant Inspector of an Insurance Company based at Jabalpur. It was Sisir Bose, his nephew, who drove him in his car at dead of night to a place called Bararee near Dhanbad, where they put up with another of Bose's nephews, Asoke Bose. (I can legitimately lay claim to a feeling of some pride in the name of this place which is identical with my surname). From there, Bose travelled by car to Gomoh, where he took the Kalka Mail to reach a place near Delhi. Here, Bose got into the Frontier Mail along with Mian Akbar Shah and reached Peshawar.

At Peshawar, Subhas Chandra Bose was met by one Bhagat Ram Talwar of the Kirti Nishan Party. Then the two proceeded to Kabul, travelling by a car, a truck, a horse-drawn 'Tonga' and sometimes on foot or on mule back, through a bleak and inhospitable terrain, braving the severe cold of that cruel January winter.

In Kabul, Bose and Mian Akbar Shah put up in a 'Serai' (rest house) under the assumed names of Ziauddin and Rahamat Khan respectively. Their conduct soon aroused the suspicion of an Afghan policeman, which compelled Bhagat Ram Talwar to seek the help of a relation of his, who was none other than our honoured guest speaker—Uttam Chand Malhotra, who was a scrap dealer.

Uttam Chand, who had a background of participation in the freedom struggle in India, put up Bose in his own house. He and his wife looked after Bose with great care to ensure that the whole matter was kept under wraps. Soon thereafter, Bose left for Moscow en route to Berlin. Netaji's stature, which was already very high in our estimation, rose a few notches higher, after we heard Uttam Chand's fascinating talk, which strengthened our conviction that Netaji was not dead. We were all admiration for Uttam Chand for the signal contribution he had made to the cause of the contry's freedom by rendering the much-needed help to Netaji during the latter's sojourn in Kabul.

Bose adopted the pseudonym Orlando Matsoda while traveling from Kabul to Moscow and then to Berlin I April 1945. In Berlin, Subhas tried to enlist the co-operation of the German authorities in the task of securing India's freedom. He met Von Ribbentrop, the German Foreign Minister, who agreed to allow him to organise propaganda against the British. But, by and large, the Germans were not greatly interested in the plans that Subhas had chalked out mainly because they thought that India was too remote a place to count in their scheme of things and their plans for the war. During his sojourn in Germany, Subhas became intimately acquainted with Emily Shenkell, an Austrian, whom he married before leaving Germany in February, 1943. He proceeded to the south eastern theatre of the war after a long submarine journey and established contact with the Japanese. He met Tojo, Prime Minister of Japan, in June, 1943, who gave him assurances of support to India's freedom struggle.

Just before this, some Indian soldiers of the British Army had surrendered to the Japanese and formed the Indian National Army under the leadership of Captain Mohan Singh. There also existed an Indian Independence League that had been set up by Rash Behari Bose, a veteran revolutionary leader from Bengal. These bodies were not fully functional when Bose appeared on the scene. Arriving at Singapore in July 1943, he took over the leadership of the I.N.A. and the Indian Independence League and breathed fresh life into them.

His broadcasts over the radio addressed to the people of India from time to time assured them that their liberation from British rule was to materialise very soon.

In December 1943, the INA liberated the Andaman and Nicober Islands from British control and hoisted the flag of free India on the two islands which were then named as 'Shaheed' and 'Swaraj'. The INA soldiers crossed into India and hoisted the national flag at Imphal on March 18,1944. India's tricolour flag was also hoisted at Kohima on April 8, 1944 by Col. Thakur Singh of the Subhas Brigade and at Moirang on April 14, 1944 by Colonel Mullick. Then a bid was made to capture Bishenpur at a distance of only three miles. But the attempt failed, as the rains set in prematurely early, disrupting communication and supply lines. They had no alternative but to retreat. Many years later, I had the opportunity of seeing a statue of Netaji erected in the special complex built at Moirang after independence. I felt rather bad when I learnt that this statue was destroyed by some miscreants in July 1993. It was a matter of some consolation that 'Bandhs' were observed at some places in Manipur in protest against this vandalism.

The British built a war cemetery in Kohima as a memorial to their soldiers who had laid down their lives in the fierce and final battle that they and the Japanese fought on the famous Garrison Hill from the opposite sides of a tennis court in the bungalow of the British Deputy Commissioner. In April 1944, the British ultimately won the battle. More than three decades later, when I had occasion to visit this cemetery in Kohima, I was deeply moved by the following words inscribed there: When you go home, tell them of us and say: "For your tomorrow, we gave our today".

Even in the ranks of the I.N.A., there were a few black sheep, who were not patriotic. The I.N.A. had an intelligence network and an espionage school of which N. Rajbavan was the Director. Some of the spies trained by this school had clandestinely entered India, but were intercepted by the British, tried and executed. One Col. Mohammed Khan Durrani had betrayed the I.N.A. and divulged its secret plans of espionage, for which he was rewarded with the Victoria Cross by the grateful British authorities. In mentioning these facts I have no intention whatsoever of belittling the glorious achievements of the I.N.A.

After World War II ended, the I.N.A. movement was adopted by the Congress Party as its own, though its leader, Subhas Chandra Bose, and his brother, Sarat Chandra Bose, had left the party earlier. Sarat Chandra Bose now rejoined the Congress and helped it in usurping the goodwill created by the I.N.A. saga. Mahatma Gandhi, despite his critical attitude towards Subhas Chandra Bose, now admitted that Netaji's name "is one to conjure with". But he openly disagreed with Subhas Chandra's political line and maintained that violence should be abjured. Gandhiji did not believe that Netaji had captured the imagination of the people as a whole; in his view, Netaji had cast his spell only on sections of the youth and women. This stand of Mahatma Gandhi did not find support among the youth and the student community, particularly in Bengal.

In fact, Bengalee sentiment at that time was deeply hurt by the resolution that the Congress Working Committee had adopted, extending the party's help in defending the I.N.A. heroes put on trial, but making it clear at the same time that this did not mean any deviation from the party's policy of seeking to gain independence by peaceful means alone.

Mahatma Gandhi's as well as the Congress Party's disapproval of the political line of Netaji and the INA was of a piece with their critical attitude towards the martyrdom of Bhagat Singh, Raj Guru and Sukhdev, who were hanged by the British rulers on March 23, 1931 for their role in the shooting down of an English policeman in Lahore in 1928. They did not agree with Subhash Chandra Bose, who wanted the Congress Party to make serious efforts towards securing the commutation of the death sentences passed upon Bhagat Singh and his compatriots. After 1947, however, the Congress Party had no hesitation in identifying itself with Bhagat Singh and taking over the latter's legacy as its own, as it did in the case of Netaji and the INA also. Earlier, Mahatma Gandhi had also characterized the martyrdom of Surya Sen and the other heroes of the 1930 Chittagong Armoury Raid as "regrettable" because, as he thought, violence was bound to impede the progress towards independence.

Realising that the saga of the I.N.A. and Netaji had deeply moved the people at large, the Congress Party decided to take up the cause of the I.N.A. and defend its three top leaders namely, Shah Nawaz Khan, Capt. P.K. Sahgal and Col. G.S. Dhillon, whose trial on the charge of treason started in Delhi's Red Fort on November 21, 1945. The I.N.A. heroes—a Hindu, a Muslim and a Sikh—were defended by a team of eminent lawyers led by Bhulabhai Desai and even Jawahar Lal Nehru, who had given up legal practice for long years, joined the team.

The trial triggered country-wide protests and demonstrations, particularly in Kolkata, where there was serious trouble as the workers of almost all political parties including even the Muslim League took part in the agitation. Firing had to be ordered on Kolkata's Dharmatolla Street on November 21, 1945 to disperse the student agitators. This resulted in the death of a student, Rameshwar Bannerjee, whose name instantaneously became a household word in Bengal. In protest, the people of Kolkata organised a complete 'Hartal' the next day with all political parties and the people of all communities—Hindus, Muslims and Sikhs—joining hands to make a big success of the occasion. We observed Hartal in our college. I vividly remember how enthusiastically I joined some of my friends and went out to see what was happening on the streets..

The trial of another I.N.A. leader, Capt. Abdul Rashid, was held in February 1946. The students of Kolkata, both Hindu and Muslim, organised mammoth protest meetings on the occasion of this trial, making it necessary for the authorities to call in the Army to deal with the explosive situation. There were pitched battles on the streets between the students and the police and the military which resulted in some deaths and injuries to a few hundred. Hindu-Muslim unity was seen at its best in Kolkata during this protest action.

The popular upsurge in the wake of the trials of the I.N.A. heroes had a great impact on the Indian members of the Armed Forces, which soon found expression in the mutiny by the personnel of the Royal Indian Navy at Bombay and Karachi on February 18,1946. They shouted slogans demanding the release of the INA leaders, apart from better food for themselves. Some came down to Bombay streets, where they were joined by the local people and the naval personnel on the shore. The Maratha Guards refused to fire on the naval mutineers. The disturbances in Bombay were so serious that the army had to be called in to help the police. About 200 persons lost their lives in the disturbances. There was also trouble in the Royal Indian Air Force and in the Indian Army. We were thrilled to read accounts of these developments which led us to believe that the British would not be able to keep India in bondage for long.

There is no doubt that the contribution of Netaji and the INA in the last phase of our freedom struggle was very great – much greater than that of most other heroes of that struggle. The disaffection that the INA saga created in the ranks of the Indian personnel of the Army, Navy and Air Force shook the confidence of the British imperialists and produced a psychological impact – on the British authorities as well as on the Indian masses – that spelled the doom of the British Empire in the Indian sub-continent. This is what I, like most students of those days, genuinely believed.

Attempts have been made by some people from time to time to play down Netaji's role in securing the freedom of our country because of his refusal to abjure the path of violence as opposed to the Congress Party's official line that reposed its faith in non-violence. Yet, the fact remains that non-violence was not the means through which our country became free. The British handed over power as a result of the concatenation of a host of historical forces that were unleashed at the end of the Second World War such as the grim economic problems faced by Great Britain at that time that made it difficult for her to hold on to India and solve its many problems; the INA trials that led to great discontent among the Indian people as well as among the armed forces; and last but not the least, the communal conflagration that engulfed India and assumed the dimensions of a civil war, which the British were themselves largely responsible for creating, but which, being something of the nature of a Frankenstein, they were not confident of handling. There was large-scale violence that led the British authorities to decide in favour of quitting the country.

Even now tit-bits of information about Netaji that become available attract public attention in our country. For example, there was a great furore over the Centre's farcical decision to honour Netaji with the award of the Bharat Ratna in 1992 apparently as a gesture to make up for the historical lapses of the Congress Party's Central leaders in dealing with him during his life-time. The people at large looked upon this move as an insult to Netaji's memory for the simple reason that it sought to equate him with the other recipients of this honour, thus bringing him down from the highest pedestal on which they had placed him for ever. The Supreme Court's action in 1997 in cancelling the official communiqué regarding the award was greeted with great relief by the people in general.

Or take, for example, the move that had been made by the Indian Government to bring to our country the so-called 'ashes' of Netaji preserved in the Renkoji Temple near Tokyo in order to honour his memory in the centenary year (1996) of his birth. This naturally aroused resentment in West Bengal because the story of his death in the air crash at Taihoku in Taiwan on August 18, 1945 is not generally believed. It was argued by the detractors of such a move that these were not the ashes of Netaji whose death was still to be conclusively established.

The proposal to bring the ashes of Netaji from Japan to India was generally interpreted as a ploy on the part of the Congress Party to exploit his name for deriving political mileage during the elections that were to be held in 1996. That was the reason behind the virulently hostile reaction to the speech of a prominent Congress leader at a Kolkata gathering on January 23,1996, who had hinted that Netaji was dead. The police had to intervene and whisk the Congress leader away.

During a trip to Japan in December, 2001, Prime minister Atal Behari Vajpayee visited the Renkoji Temple, where the so-called ashes of Netaji have been preserved. When a former Japanese official observed that the ashes should be taken to Netaji's home, Vajpayee had reportedly said that he also felt the same way. The Prime Minister's remark evoked critical reactions in Kolkata's political circles. Several political leaders of West Bengal expressed surprise that the Prime Minister had accepted the ashes as being those of Netaji, when a definite conclusion in this regard was still to be arrived at by the Mukherjee Commission that had been appointed by Vajpayee's own government.

In January 1996, the authorities of the Presidency College, Kolkata, revoked the order of rustication that had been served on Subhas Chandra Bose in 1916 by H.R. James, the then Principal of the college, for his alleged involvement in an assault on a professor. This step which was aimed at retrospectively vindicating Bose's position did not go down well with the intelligentsia, because nobody knew what purpose was served by such action. The rustication of Bose by the Principal of the Presidency College in 1916 is a fact of history which cannot be changed by such a measure.

Did Netaji really perish in the so-called air-crash at Taihoku on August 18, 1945? Or is he still alive? We all fervently hope that he did not die in 1945. But the Shah Nawaz Enquiry Committee as well as the later G.D. Khosla Commission gave the finding that Netaji was dead. Despite this, however, doubts have continued to assail the public mind in our country and there is a general reluctance to accept the story of his death in a plane crash.

Scepticism about Netaji's death often fed upon the doubts over this issue that Lord Wavell, the Viceroy of India in the mid-1940's, was said to have expressed in his diary. According to Ashwini Kumar of the Delhi Hindi daily 'Punjab Kesari' (dated February 7, 2005), Sir R.F.Mudie, Home Member, Government of India when Lord Wavell was the Viceroy, had sent a secret note to Wavell pointing out that the news of Netaji's death was false, but he added that it was in their interest to propagate it as true.

Netaji's elder brother, the late Sarat Bose was reported to have said in 1947 after meeting a number of persons in South East Asia that Subhas was alive and that Pandit Nehru was aware of it. That the INA was anathema to the ruling Congress Party was evident from several facts – denial of re-induction of the INA personnel in free India's army, disapproval of the display of Netaji's portraits in Government offices, refusal to declare a government holiday on Netaji's birthday and delaying the display of a portrait of Netaji in India's Parliament till the fault was rectified in 1978 when Morarji Desai became the Prime Minister. In 1950, Praful Chakravarty, Professor of History, University of Calcutta, had submitted a report to Prime Minister Nehru about the disappearance of Netaji but the Prime Minister's office refused to release it.

Doubts about Netaji's death got a fillip when in 1964 a Buddhist Bhiksu, who bore close resemblance to Netaji, turned up to offer obeisance to Pandit Nehru after the latter's demise.But nobody knew the Bhiksu's identity nor could anyone say where he disappeared. The Hindustan Times of August 16, 2001 referred to several reports suggesting that even as late as in 1964, the American Central Intelligence Agency had been talking about the possibility of Netaji Subhas Chandra Bose's return to India. People sometimes refer to the statement made by Prime Minister Morarji Desai in the Parliament in 1978 raising some doubts in this regard in view of the many contradictions in the testimonies of several persons and in some documents that became available from time to time.

Doubts about the validity of the Shah Nawaz Enquiry Committee's finding continued to persist since its report was not unanimous. Suresh Bose, elder brother of Netaji, who was a member of this Committee, did not agree with the finding, which, he alleged, had been dictated from above by Prime Minister Pt. Jawaharlal Nehru. Public opinion in the country and in Bengal particularly did not accept the verdict of the G.D. Khosla Commission primarily because the Judge had gone out of the way to make a value judgement of Subhas Chandra Bose's political ideology, which rendered his report suspect.

Reports continue to appear in the press drawing attention to a host of relevant facts that call for further enquiry. According to the Hindustan Times of March 4, 2001, Shyam Lal Jain, Confidential Secretary of Asaf Ali, who had functioned as the Secretary to the INA Defence Committee, had told the Khosla Commission under oath that on December 26 or 27, 1945, he was summoned to Asaf Ali's residence where Pandit Nehru asked him to make out typed copies of a hand-written note, which said that Bose had reached Russia via Dairen. Jain also alleged that Pandit Nehru asked him to type out a letter to the British Prime Minister Clement Attlee which said: "Bose, your war criminal, has been allowed to enter Russian territory by Stalin. This is a clear treachery and betrayal of faith by the Russians, as Russia has been an ally of the British-Americans. Please take note of it and do what you consider proper and fit". Justice Khosla is said to have attached no importance to this allegation.

Adverting to this matter, Ashwini Kumar of the Punjab Kesari (dated February 7, 2005) pointed out that in reply to a question in the British Parliament, Prime Minister Clement Attlee had replied that the British Government had entered into a pact with the Government of India stipulating that if Netaji was ever arrested, he would have to be handed over to the British Government. Ashwini Kumar even quoted 'Confidential 10 (INA) 279' as the number of the Government of India file in which this matter was dealt with.

The probable fate of Netaji used to be a favourite subject matter of speculation among the student community, when I was a college student in Kolkata in the latter half of the 1940's. I had heard many people say that Netaji had been captured and killed by the British after the Japanese surrendered. Very recently, on August 14, 2005, Eunan O'Halpin of the Trinity College, Dublin,, while delivering a lecture at the Netaji Research Bureau, Kolkata, disclosed that the British Foreign Office had ordered the assassination of Netaji Subhas Chandra Bose in 1941 just after he had made his 'grand escape' from Kolkata (Times of India, Delhi, dated August 16, 2005). He said that the British Special Operation Executive (formed in 1940 to carry out sabotage and underground activities) had asked its representatives in Cairo and Istanbul to wire about the arrangements made for Netaji's assassination. O'Halpin observed: "Even in the midst of war, this was a remarkable instruction................The fact that any trace of London's orders to assassinate Bose remains in official records is just as striking."

Whether Netaji's name continued to figure on the Allied Powers' list of war criminals was an issue that was also the subject matter of speculation for many years. Kofi Annan, the U.N. Secretary-General, declared in 1998 that from then on, Netaji would not be referred to as a war criminal and that he was not responsible for what had been done in the past. The British Government clarified that his name was not on their list of war criminals.

The possibility of Netaji having escaped into the Soviet Union via Manchuria after Japan's surrender in 1945 has been a recurring theme in many reports and in the press. The SACSEA Commission No. 1 of the South East Asia Commission, Saigon, had reported in November 1945 that right from the end of 1944, Netaji had been trying to proceed from Japan to the USSR as part of his efforts to enlist Russian help in the cause of India's independence.

A Hamburg-based association of expatriate-Indians submitted a memorandum to Prime Minister Atal Bihari Vajpayee on August 15, 1998, demanding a serious probe into the Netaji affair. It cited several post-war documents unearthed from the archives of the USA and erstwhile East Germany and the Soviet Union to show that there was no plane crash at Taihoku within a week before or after August 18, 1945 and that Netaji was alive in the Soviet Union in July 1946.

A few years ago, three research scholars from Kolkata, who were in Russia in connection with their work on the history of the communist movement in India, had stumbled upon declassified documents in the Russian and British archives which indicated that Netaji was very much alive till at least 1946.

I also read a press report[1] in January 2001, according to which Rai Singh, a former diplomat, had met one Ram Rahul, who had visited the Soviet Union several times. The latter reportedly told the former that he (Ram Rahul) had met Gafurov, who headed the Soviet Institute of Oriental and African Studies. Gafurov is said to have told Ram Rahul that Netaji had crossed over to the Soviet Union via Manchuria in 1945 and had been detained in a labour camp in Seberia as Stalin wanted to make him a bargaining chip in future dealings with Britain and India. According to Gafurov, India's Ambassador to the USSR was permitted to have a glimpse of Netaji in the labour camp on the condition that no word was exchanged with him. Rahul Ram, a former Professor of the Jawaharlal Nehru University, Delhi, was a scholar of Central Asian Studies, who had given all this information to Rai Singh in July, 2000 before his death.

Rai Singh was said to be of the view that the Indian Ambassador to Moscow, who had seen Netaji, could have been Dr. S. Radhakrishnan, who became the President of India.

According to a news-report (circulated by Linux, Lucknow, September 18, 2005), a team of Indian experts, who had visited Russia in 1996, had seen de-classified KGB files which mentioned that Stalin had considered the possibility of using Netaji as an alternative to Pt. Nehru in 1946, a year after his alleged death. Some Russian agents were said to have disclosed that Netaji was incarcerated in the Irkhutsk Gulag for many years by Stalin and that Pandit Nehru and Gandhiji were aware of Bose's fate but did not want him back in India.The report even hinted that Stalin might have used Bose as a pawn to blackmail Pandit Nehru into taking the favourable stand he did with Russia and communist China.

According to Dipak Basu, Professor of International Economics, Nagasaki University, Japan (Organiser,June 19, 2005), Netaji was possibly killed by Stalin. Basu also said: "The Soviet Union had acknowledged that Stalin had killed two other Indian freedom-fighters – Abani Mukherjee, founder of the Communist Party of India, and Virendranath Chattopadhyay, brother of Sarojini Naidu and an associate of Veer Savarkar, who had attempted to kill M.N. Roy. All of them, just like Netaji, had escaped to the Soviet Union from the British clutches, but ultimately suffered at the hands of Stalin as a result. The Indian government has never asked the Soviet Union in this matter."

In this context, it is worth mentioning that the Russian Ambassador in India had issued a statement in February 1996 to emphasise the point that there was no document with the KGB about the presence of Netaji in the USSR. It was also reported in the press in 1999 that the Russian authorities had informed Shri Ranen Sen, then India's Ambassador to Russia, that there was nothing in their archives suggesting Netaji's survival after the plane crash at Taihokn on August 18, 1945.

Some Indian experts, who had probed the possibility of Netaji having sought refuge in Russia after Japan's surrender in 1945, approached the court, which compelled the Government of India to appoint in 1999 Justice M.K. Mukherjee, a retired Judge of the Supreme Court of India, as the one-man commission to enquire into the disappearance of Netaji Subhas Chandra Bose and his alleged death in a plane crash. Reports that have appeared in the press indicate that several persons have deposed before the Mukherjee Commission. One of them is Pritam Singh, a former Colonel of the INA and a trusted Lieutenant of Netaji. He is said to have told the Commission the reasons for not believing the story of the plane crash at Taihoku on August 18, 1945 in which Netaji was alleged to have perished. According to Col. Pritam Singh, Netaji had gone to Russia via Manchuria. Another important person to have deposed before the Commission is E. Bhaskaran, Stenographer and Private Secretary to Netaji, when the latter was the chief of the INA. His evidence in believed to have emphasised the same points as were made by Col. Pritam Singh. Anuj Dhar, author of a book 'Back From The Dead', who has deposed before the Commission, has reportedly pointed out that one should look into the records of the KGB and the private papers of Stalin to get at the truth about the whereabouts of Netaji.

According to what I have read in the press, Purabi Roy, Professor of the Jadavpur University, has deposed before the Mukherjee Commission. During her visits to Russia in connection with her research projects, she is said to have met several functionaries of the Institute of Oriental Studies, Moscow, including a former member of the KGB, who is said to have had access to the secret files of the agency pertaining to Netaji. She is believed to have submitted to the Mukherjee Commission several documents to show that Netaji had not perished in the so-called plane crash but had in fact been in the Soviet Union even after that incident. Purabi Roy has observed that one Maj. General Kolesnikov of the Oriental faculty at St. Petersburg University (who is now on a diplomatic mission to Central Asia) had claimed during the Warsaw Pact in 1946 that Stalin had discussed with his lieutenants–Voroshillov, Molotov and Jacob Mallik–the question of where to lodge "Chandra Bose", who was in their custody.

A report in the Hindustan Times (March 4, 2001) stated that Prof. Purabi Roy had come out with some startling facts about the vast funds of the INA, whose whereabouts held the key to the mystery surrounding Netaji. She was said to have come across documents indicating that a young Major of the MI-5 had been shadowing Bose in Afghanistan. This agent, who retired as a Colonel dealing with INA affairs, was stationed in Herat, which played a key role during Bose's flight to Germany. The Hindustan Times claimed to have cross-checked the MI-5 agent's story independently and found nothing to contradict Purabi Roy's claims. Purabi Roy met the agent, who was living in Oxford. He told Purabi Roy that a huge sum of INA money— —about Rs. 70,000 crore (in those days!)— —was handed over to Lord Mountbatten and a senior Congress leader in Singapore and that the mystery of Bose's disappearance could be unravelled by ascertaining the route along which these funds travelled. It is said that the Shah Nawaz Committee had also observed that a part of the assets carried by Netaji had been kept in the National Archives and that this matter should be subjected to a separate enquiry. The Government of India did not act on this recommendation of the Shah Nawaz Committee.

How true these reports in the press are I do not know. I am sure that the Mukherjee Commission is sifting through these reports to ascertain their truth or otherwise. Some time ago, I had seen a press report which suggested that the Mukherjee Commission was likely to face many problems arising from the non-co-operative attitude of the Central and West Bengal Governments as a result of which many vital and relevant documents at the disposal of the two Governments might not be made available to it.

According to Dr. P.N. Chopra[2], a research scholar of the Indian Council of Historical Research, the British Government had some secret papers about Netaji which it was unwilling to part with, giving rise to a feeling that it had something to hide about its role. Kamal Pande, Union Home Secretary, refused to give access to the Mukherjee Commission to the documents at the disposal of the Government of India. In April 2002, a report[3] in the press quoted him as having explained the stance of the Government of India to the Mukherjee Commission as follows: "I have examined the documents; the disclosure will lower Netaji's image; cause injury to the public interest; hurt the sentiments of the people at large. Diplomatic ties with friendly countries may also be adversely affected".

According to reports in the Kolkata press, the Mukherjee Commission had publicly expressed unhappiness over the refusal of the Central Government to make available all relevant files, thus thwarting its task of unraveling the whole truth. Justice Mukherjee even complained during a hearing that the Central Government as well as the Government of West Bengal had not been extending full co-operation to it in the matter of sending replies to its queries.

The Hindustan Times of June 26, 2001 reproduced a Press Trust of India report from Kolkata to say that the Justice M.K.Mukherjee Commission had recorded an affidavit by one Mubarak Mazdoor, a freedom-fighter, who claimed to have met Netaji several times in 1954 in Myanmar, where the latter was said to be living in the guise of a Buddhist monk.

It has sometimes been claimed that Netaji had been hiding somewhere in our country in the guise of a Sadhu. A story that was long in circulation was that one Shoulmari Baba was none else but Netaji in disguise. Some time ago, a reporter of the Hindustan Times by name Anuj Dhar undertook a thorough enquiry into the mystery surrounding Netaji's disappearance in 1945 and launched a public probe on the internet (http://www.hindustantimes.com). It was revealed that Netaji had entered India from Nepal in the mid-1950's and after remaining in hiding for many years, he spent the last few years of his life disguised as Bhagawanji or Gumnami Baba (which means one whose name was lost) in a house called Ramabhawan at Faizabad in Uttar Pradesh till his death on September 16, 1985, at the age of 88 years. Bhagawanji had a striking resemblance with Netaji. He was equally tall and of the same age as Netaji, besides having some peculiar physical features of Netaji such as gaps between the teeth and a scalpel mark on the abdomen.

Many documents, photographs, specimens of Bhagawanji's hand-writing and a few of his teeth were found in his Faizabad house. Since many people said that Bhagawanji was none other than Netaji in disguise, the Allahabad High Court sealed his belongings which were kept at the Treasury of Faizabad district. Many people interested in getting to the bottom of the Netaji mystery suggested an analysis of Bhagawanji's hand-writing and a DNA test of his teeth with a view to establishing his real identity. The Mukherjee Commission was reported to have sent some articles belonging to Bhagawanji to the Central Forensic Laboratory for technical examination. An expert on handwriting to whom the Commission had referred some specimens of Gumnami Baba's handwriting has reportedly pointed out some striking similarities with Netaji;s handwriting.

On January 23, 2005, the birthday of Netaji, Justice Mukherjee proceeded to Taihoku where Netaji was said to have perished in a plane crash on August 18, 1945. In February,2005, it was reported that the Taiwan Government had informed the Mukherjee Commission that there was no record of any air-crash at Taihoku on August 18, 1945. This new fact that has now come to light has added a further twist to the mystery about Netaji's death.

If there was no plane crash at Taihoku and if, therefore, Netaji did not die there, then why do so many persons persist in claiming that Netaji had perished there? The Pakistan Cricket Board Chairman, Brig (Retd.) Shahryar Khan has claimed in his book 'Cricket: A Bridge of Peace' that Col. Habib-ur-Rehman, a close aide of Netaji, who had traveled with Netaji in the plane that was said to have crashed, had told him that Netaji had died in the crash because his shirt was of an inflammable material. Brig (Retd.) Khan also disclosed that Col. Rehman had seen Netaji's charred body. Lakshmi Sehgal, another associate of Netaji, has also said that she has no doubt about Netaji's death in the plane crash.

Even Netaji's daughter, Anita (Bose) Pfaff, a Professor of Economics at the Augsburg University, is convinced that Netaji is not alive[4]. She "wonders how many fact-finding commissions it would take to convince the "believers"—the flock that refuses to allow anyone to celebrate Netaji's death anniversary or award him the Bharat Ratna posthumously". According to her, those who think that he is alive are being "irrational aid nonsensical". She feels that the plane crash was "the only reasonably consistent theory".

The Mukherjee Commission decided to visit Russia with view to finding out the truth or otherwise about the many reports pointing to the probability of Netaji having proceeded to the Soviet Union after Japan's surrender at the end of World War II. The Commission was reported to be unhappy over the Central Government dragging its feet in according the requisite sanction for this visit and also over the delay on its part of the in extending its term beyond May 31, 2005 to enable it to proceed to Russia. It was after considerable delay that the Central Government gave another six-month extension to the Commission till November 14, 2005. Justice Mukherjee proceeded to Russia on September 19, 2005 accompanied by Purabi Roy, Subrata Bose, Netaji's nephew, and several other deponents before the Commission.

The Mukherjee Commission met the scholars of the Institute of Oriental Studies in Moscow, one of whom, Felix Yurlov, was reported to have said that by inviting Netaji, the Soviet Union, then a close ally of the USA and Great Britain, would have incurred the displeasure of those countries. Yurlov also dismissed as baseless the Taiwan authorities' denial of a plane crash at Taihoku in which Netaji was supposed to have lost his life. Though the Taiwan Government's announcement was reported to have been backed by the CIA, Yurlov said that this information could not be relied upon because it was based on the mere fact that there was no mention of such a plane crash in the newspapers. The scholars of the Institute of Oriental Studies were also reported to have posed the question as to why, instead of ransacking the archives in Russia, nobody had so far carried out a DNA test of the ashes kept at the Renkoji Temple in Japan with a view to finding out whether these were Netaji's ashes.

On return to Kolkata in the first week of October 2005, Justice Mukherjee disclosed that he had not come across any material in Russia which was relevant to the enquiry. He did not visit the KGB archives as the KGB had informed him that there was no relevant document in its archives.

Subrata Bose, a member of the group that visited Russia, said on return to Kolkata that he was disappointed over the commission being denied access to classified KGB files and also because the

Russian deponents were not prepared to speak. Purabi Roy, another member of the group, also expressed her disappointment as the Russian deponents were either not available or did not reveal anything. According to her, Raikov, a Russian deponent, denied everything and another deponent, Kolesnikov was away on an assignment in Turkey. But she said that a third deponent, Turadzev disclosed that there was classified information on Netaji Bose in the KGB archives.

Without access to the relevant documents at the disposal of the Government of India as also those in the archives of Russia, the United Kingdom and the USA, the Mukherjee Commission may find itself seriously handicapped in coming out with the last word about the decades-old Netaji mystery. It is not known if the Commission has derived any worthwhile evidence about Netaji's identity from DNA and other scientific tests carried out on the ashes kept in the Renkoji Temple in Japan and on the hand-writing of Gumnami Baba and his teeth recovered from his residence in Faizabad. We have to wait with baited breath till November 14, 2005, the last working day of the Mukherjee Commission, to hear the truth about Netaji that has eluded us for over half a century.

I now turn my attention to the political scene in Bengal towards the end of 1945, when the people's euphoria over the INA issue was at its peak. At that time, I came in touch with some young communists, who lived in our neighbourhood or were students of the Asutosh College which I had joined. Most people in Bengal did not approve of the C.P.I.'s characterisation of the I.N.A. as mercenaries and of Netaji Subhas Chandra Bose as one who had joined hands with the Fascists in the vain hope that Germany and Japan would help India achieve independence. To quote from a resolution adopted by the First Congress of the C.P.I. held in 1943 : " The groups which make up the fifth column are the Forward Bloc, the party of the traitor Bose, the Congress Socialist Party which betrayed socialism at the beginning of the war – and finally, the Trotskyite groups which are criminal groups in the pay of Fascists. The Communist Party declares that all these groups must be treated by every honest Indian as the worst enemy of the nation and driven out of political life and exterminated."

The People's War, the mouthpiece of the C.P.I., often carried disparaging observations about Subhas Chandra Bose that ran counter to the prevailing sentiment in our country. In its issue of July 19, 1942, it called Bose as "a blood-thirsty devil riding on the back of the Japanese militarists." On September 13, 1942, it called Bose "a dog with a Gandhi cap under the control and command of Hitler." On December 6, 1942, it quoted B.T. Ranadive, the communist leader, as having called Bose "a henchman of Japanese imperialism." On December 13, 1943, it slandered Bose as " the running dog of Japanese Fascism."

Towards the end of December, 1945, in view of the fact that a general election was going to be held in the near future, the communists realised the need to adopt a stance that was not too much at variance with popular feelings. Therefore, the CPI gave a call for the observance of "I.N.A. Defence Day" in December 1945, saying that though the I.N.A. had chosen a wrong path, yet its members were "misguided patriots" and that the British Government had no right to try them. As a matter of fact, such quibbling cut no ice with the ordinary people, who saw through the smoke-screen of their opportunistic jugglery with words.

Like other people in different walks of life, Kolkata's student community in general had not approved of the communists' opposition to the Quit India movement and of its criticism of Netaji and the INA. The CPI's support for the Muslim League's demand for Pakistan was another reason for the party's unpopularity among sections of the student community. This was the reason for the decrease in the strength and influence of the CPI-controlled All-India Students' Federation among the students of Kolkata.

The communists were expelled from the Congress Party in December 1945—a step that many of my communist friends criticised vehemently. The Congress workers' revulsion against the role of the communists found expression in violent demonstrations in Bombay and Kolkata in January 1946 and attacks on the workers and offices of the CPI, which resulted in injuries to many.

The communists understood the popular mood and tried desperately to gain public sympathy by gradually changing their policies on various issues. In February 1946, the party's student supporters got an opportunity of showing their patriotic credentials by organising large-scale violence in the course of demonstrations and a general strike in Kolkata in protest against the trial of Capt. Abdul Rashid, the I.N.A. hero, in Delhi's Red Fort. Destruction of public property on a considerable scale and the killing of many persons in the wake of these disturbances, which lasted several days, gave the communist students some ground to claim credit for their role. I remember that on this occasion, the young Bengali poet, Sukanta Bhattacharya, who had a communist outlook, had composed a poem, which went down very well with Kolkata's student community and literary circles.

In recent years, the communists admitted that their evaluation of the INA and Netaji was wrong. Jyoti Basu and Buddhadeb Bhattacharya, who succeeded Jyoti Basu as the Chief Minister of West Bengal, have expressed regret for having cast aspersions on Netaji.

As the popular upsurge over the trial of the INA heroes swept the country, the British rulers understood the gravity of the situation and sent post haste a Cabinet Mission consisting of Lord Pethick Lawrence, Secretary of State for India, Sir Stafford Cripps, President of the Board of Trade, and A.V. Alexander, First Lord of Admiralty, who reached India on March 23, 1946 to go immediately into the question of transferring power to Indian hands.

Another factor which lent a sense of urgency to the question of transferring power to India was the explosive communal situation in the country about which more in the next chapter.

Notes

1. See his letter to the Editor of the Hindustan Times dated February 7, 2001.
2. Letter to the Editor, Hindustan Times dated January 2, 2001.
3. Hindustan Times dated April 24, 2002.

8

Pre-independence Communal Scene : A Historical Retrospective

The Cabinet Mission that came to India in March 1946 found it difficult to evolve a proposal acceptable to the Congress as well as the Muslim League, because the relationship between the two parties, which by then had come to be perceived as the representatives of the Hindus and Muslims respectively, had undergone a radical transformation in the preceding few years. We all knew that the Congress Party did not want to be regarded as a party of the Hindus alone; but that is how it was perceived by many.

The story of how the Muslims and Hindus came to harbour the intense mutual antipathy that vitiated the communal scene in the latter half of the 1940's is a long one to understand which one has to go far back into our country's history. There is no doubt that most of the Muslims of our country were converts from Hinduism. In Bengal particularly, very few of the Muslims were descended from those who had come to India from outside to establish their rule, because the latter did not generally like the damp and humid climate of Bengal and preferred to colonise in and around places like Delhi and Agra with their comparatively drier climate. How were the Hindus converted to Islam? Some Hindu scholars believe that the Mohammedans used the sword to spread Islam. Some also mention the allurements of office and the prospect of material gain from embracing the religion of the rulers as other important factors that tilted the scale in favour of embracing Islam.

Many Muslim scholars do not accept these views and prefer to rely on the theory of 'social liberation' to explain the conversion of millions of Hindus to Islam in India. Their main argument is that the down-trodden lower strata of Hindu society, suffering from oppression over the centuries by the upper castes, sought liberation by merging their identity in the democratic fraternity of Islam. The eclipse of Bengal's Pala rulers marked the decline of Buddhist influence and was followed by the ascendancy of the Sena dynasty in the twelfth century A.D., when the Hindu caste system with its inequitous distinctions aggressively asserted itself, generating an atmosphere of hostility between the Hindus and Buddhists. At the time of the Muslim conquest of Bengal, the prevailing Hindu-Buddhist rivalry is said to have led many Buddhists to welcome the Muslim conquerors and in due course embrace Islam. It is said that while many low-caste Hindus also converted to Islam, there were others whom Islam found it difficult to win over because of their strong commitment to their religion and the institution of the family.

Muslim leaders in general claim that Islam is a liberal religion and cite in support the observation by H.G. Wells that Islam offered the best social order and the broadest, freshest and cleanest political idea to mankind. Wells had also said: "The Islamic teachings have left great traditions for equitable and gentle dealings and behaviour; and inspire people with nobility and tolerance.......Islam is replete with gentleness, courtesy and fraternity."[1]

About the greatness of Islam, George Bernard Shaw had said; "I have always held the religion of Prophet Muhammad in high estimation because of its wonderful vitality. It is the only religion which appears to me to possess that assimilating capacity to the changing phase of existence which can make itself appeal to every age."[2]

Napoleon Bonaparte had paid the following tribute to Islam: "I hope the time is not far off when I shall be able to unite all the wise and educated men of all the countries and establish a uniform regime based on the principles of the Qu'ran which alone are true and which alone can lead men to happiness."[3]

Bertrand Russel's observation also bears quotation in this context: "Our use of the phrase 'The Dark Ages' to cover the period from 699 to 1000 marks our undue concentration on Western Europe..... From India to Spain, the brilliant civilization of Islam flourished. What was lost to Christendom at this time was not lost to civilization, but quite the contrary......To us it seems that West European civilization is civilization, but this is a narrow view."[4]

It is beyond my competence to adjudicate the claims of different religions to greatness or the rival theories about the conversion of the Hindus to Islam. What can, however, be safely asserted is that all these factors—co-ercion, allurement and the urge for social liberation—must have contributed in different degrees to the conversion of the Hindus to Islam.

The Hindus in general did not welcome the advent of Muslim rule in India, because, as Al-beruni, a foreign traveller, pointed out, "the Hindus were a very proud and self-conscious people, somewhat arrogant and high-brow in their attitude towards the Muslims." [5]However, according to Dr.Niharranjan Ray, the noted historian, the Hindus of earlier periods were not only very friendly, but most accommodating as well towards all foreigners. The Hindus' hostile attitude towards the Muslims was, in the view of Dr. Ray, traceable to the "aggressively militant and destructive nature of early Muslim adventurers in India as illustrated in the activities of individual Muslim kings and emperors and the discriminatory character of the general policy of the state and administration in respect of the Hindus through the long centuries of their rule".

It is true that Indian culture has all along had a multi-ethnic character; Indian society has been an assimilative one right from the days of the Vedas and Upanishads. The Jats, Hoons, Gujjars and Rajputs—all came from outside and merged their identities in the composite whole that is India. But Dr. Niharranjan Ray probably thought that there was an exception to this general rule in that Hinduism was not able to assimilate Islam, which retained its distinctive identity in India. As he says, "in Islam the Hindus had found for the first time a religion and a way of life that admitted of no compromise, were militant and aggressive in its behaviour pattern and aimed at controlling the entire area of man's life including the political and the economic."

However, with regard to this view about our past history, we have to remember that the Muslims of our country are full-fledged Indian nationals, who deserve a place of honour in our multi-ethnic society. They are the dominant minority of our polity and the fact that their number is greater than that of the Muslim population of Pakistan clearly brings out the strength of our pluralistic culture. When Islam first came to Bengal, the new rulers as well as the Ulemas took the lead in spreading their religion. Alongside, came the Sufis, whose syncretist line aimed at bridging the gulf between the Muslims and the Hindus and,within the parameters of their over-all loyalty to the tenets of Islam, highlighted certain basic human values which were universal in their appeal.

Sufism came to Bengal in several garbs that differed subtly from one another, as has been ably brought out in special studies made by Md. Enamul Huq and M.R. Tarafdar. They first came as warrior Sufis and later as reforming Sufis. The warrior Sufis came soon after the Turks conquered Bihar and Bengal. The names and heroic exploits of many warrior Sufis are well known, though there is no clear evidence about their historicity. I have referred in a chapter of my earlier book 'In Sun And Shower' to a warrior Sufi by name Baba Adam Shahid, who was instrumental in spreading Islam in my native place Vikrampur, which is now in Bangladesh. From the middle of the thirteenth till about the end of the fourteenth century, the warrior Sufis helped the Muslim rulers in annexing new territory.

When Muslim rule was sufficiently well established in Bengal, the reforming Sufis entered the field, perhaps after Ilyas Shah united the whole of Bengal under his rule in 1352 A.D. and took the titles of Shah-i-Bengal, Shah-i-Bangaliyan and Sultan-i-Bangla. In the serene atmosphere of Ilyas Shah's rule, the reforming Sufis played a peaceful role and helped in achieving a good measure of reconciliation with the local Hindus.

During the rule of Hussein Shah (1494-1538), who was a contemporary of Shri Chaitanya Mahaprabhu, the Sufis started building Dargahs, which not only the Muslims but also the Hindus visited during fairs and festivals. In course of time, the Sufi literature of Bengal started drawing upon non-Muslim concepts and practices such as those based on Yoga and Tantra. Bengalees will never forget the contribution made by Husein Shah to the development of their language.

We have also to take into account the fact that in Bengal, Islam was, by and large, a syncretist religion. This was due to the fact that most of the new converts from Hinduism and Buddhism continued to retain many of their old social and religious customs even after conversion. Their language was the same, namely, Bengali. With hardly any knowledge of Arabic or Persian, they could scarcely comprehend the theological concepts of Islam that came from the Arab world and preferred instead to stick as long as possible to their old gods and goddesses of the Hindu pantheon. That is why, a Muslim of Bengal had more in common with the Bengalee Hindu than with his co-religionist in Delhi or Agra.

The Hindus and Muslims also influenced each other's religious and social practices and outlook. While the Muslims newly converted from Hinduism and Buddhism retained some of their old customs, the Hindus were also influenced by some of the former's practices, thus leading to the fusion of their cultures and customs. From the Hindus, the Muslims even imbibed something similar to the patently un-Islamic caste system with the Ashrafs or higher class Muslims distancing themselves from the lower class Altafs, who again sub-divided themselves into castes like Jolaha, Teli, Yogi etc., like the Hindus.

In the field of education, alongside the rise of a Persian-knowing Hindu intelligentsia, a Muslim educated class committed to expressing itself in Bengali language signalled the beginning of an era of Muslim poets and writers vying with their Hindu brethren and coming forward with a considerable amount of literary output of a high order that bore the imprint of syncretism. Despite all this, however, and notwithstanding the people's appreciation of the eclectism of the Sufis, the Hindus and Muslims at large maintained their divergent social, cultural and religious attitudes. As Dr.Niharranjan Ray says, the Sufis' contribution "was recognised neither by the orthodox Muslims nor by the orthodox Hindus, who together formed by far the largest segment of the Indian population".[6]

During the rule of Nawab Siraj-ud-Daula, Hindu-Muslim amity was largely maintained in Bengal. The Hindus learnt Persian and soaked in a good deal of Muslim culture. Among the Muslims, the Sheikhs, the Saiyids and the Ulamas wielded considerable social influence. During the Nawabs' rule in Bengal, the Hindus occupied an important place in the industrial, commercial and economic fields.

However, during the rule of the Mughals and the Nawabs, notwithstanding the intimate mingling of the Hindus and Muslims on the social plane, which resulted in a considerable transformation of their religious outlook and social practices, they continued, by and large, to hold their own and preserve their respective identities.

After the advent of the East India Company, Hindu Sannyasis and Muslim Faqirs had joined hands in an armed struggle against the policies of the company in different parts of Bengal—a fact which helped in cementing Hindu-Muslim unity for some time. But this was nothing more than a passing phase.

Gradually, the differences in the outlook of the Hindus and Muslims began to reveal themselves and in course of time got accentuated. When the British snatched political authority from the Muslims, the latter naturally resented it and suffered from a sense of deprivation. The Hindus had no particular reason to feel unhappy over the change of guard, which only meant that political authority had passed on from the Muslims to Englishmen. With the lapse of time, the Hindus of Bengal began to take advantage of the changed situation to improve their socio-economic position. The Muslims reacted by beginning to withdraw into a shell to lick their wounds. The Hindu Zamindars were dispossessed, but their places were taken over by other Hindus from among the rich classes. As Sirajul Islam has pointed out, "under the Nawabs, the power was shared between the Mughals and Bengalee Hindu elites and when the colonial state was formed on the basis of the supremacy of the white race, it was the Mughals and Hindu elites, who were deprived of powers and privileges.The Bengalee Muslims had little to lose." [7]

The Hindus went in for western education, which enabled them to grab most of the jobs in the administration. The Muslims, with their penchant for Persian, were generally cool towards English education and thus lost out to the Hindus, as had happened during the earlier regime of the Nawabs, when too the Hindus were preferred. Thus a sense of 'grievance' started building up among the Muslims. During the Mughal period, the need for both Muslims and Hindus to know the Persian language had helped in the growth of a composite culture. A set-back was caused to this process with the advent of the British, the introduction of English as the language of the court in place of Persian.

A consequence of the establishment of British political authority in India was the growth of an English-educated, urban middle class in different parts of the country, particularly in Kolkata, Bombay and Madras. In Bengal, this process that started with the endeavours of Raja Rammohan Roy, got accelerated by the efforts of men like Iswar Chandra Vidyasagar, Devendranath Tagore and Michael Madhusudan Datta. They harked back to the cultural heritage of ancient India that was essentially Hindu in character. Rejection of the old obscurantist socio-religious practices of the Hindus after retaining the rationalist core of traditional Hindu religion and philosophy and the acceptance of Western learning with its emphasis on rationalism were the important characteristics of this new awakening among the Hindus that came to be labelled as the Bengal Renaissance. But this was basically a Hindu movement in which the Muslims had hardly any place.

In the meantime, the Muslims launched the Wahabi movement, a reformist religious movement that was led by Shah Sayyid Ahmad of Rai Bareilly. It started exhorting the Muslims to not only defend Islam, but also to reject the symbols of Hindu customs and practices. A section of the Muslims came to believe that their pitiable condition during British rule was traceable to their failure to stick to the tenets of Islam. One Shariatullah, a Muslim leader from the Faridpur district of east Bengal, entered the field in a bid to remove Hindu influences from Islam as practised in Bengal. This was the beginning of the Faraizi movement which was led initially by Shariatullah and subsequently—and more violently—by his son Dadu Miyan. They fought against the oppression of the Zamindars (who were mostly Hindus), the British indigo planters and the officials of the East India Company.

This, however, created a breach between the Faraizis, who were all Muslims and the Hindu ryots, who, while reeling under the oppression of the Zamindars, generally refused to identify themselves with the Muslim ryots. The Faraizis also attempted to impart an Arab image to Islam in Bengal, though they did not go to the same extent in this venture as the followers of Sayyid Ahmad Barelvi, who instituted 'Jihad' in India.

Some Muslim reformers, like Sir Syed Ahmad Khan (1817-1898 A.D.) tried to tone down the orthodoxy of Islam in India by spreading the ideas of Western liberalism among the Muslims and making them learn the English language. In Bengal, Nawab Abdul Latif and Syed Amir Ali sought to do the same thing. Initially, Sir Syed Ahmed believed in the unity of the Hindus and Muslims, but gradually he came to dislike the Congress Party, which he dubbed as a seditious movement led by the Bengalees, who,in his view, being highly educated, were bound to dominate the less educated Muslims. Some even say that it was Sir Syed and not M.A.Jinnah, who first propagated the view that the Hindus and Muslims were two separate nations.

The class of Zamindars created by Lord Cornwallis in Bengal under the Permanent Settlement of 1793 consisted mostly of Hindus. Out of the emerging bourgeois class in Bengal, he created a new class of feudal landlords and a new culture—the 'Babu' culture of the Bengalee 'Bhadralok' (or gentleman). This new culture basically reflected the outlook of the Hindus rather than that of the Muslims, most of whom wer oppressed by the Zamindars and continued to follow the lead given by Haji Shariatullah and Dadu Miyan as well as Titumir, another Muslim leader, whose activities in the Barasat area of the 24 Parganas district of Bengal had to be quelled with a heavy hand by the British authorities. Titumir had become a legendary figure of Bengal in the first half of the 19th century by organising the rural people against the British as well as Hindu oppressors. He was killed by the British forces in a pitched battle in 1831 in which they used cannons to destroy a fort that he had built with bamboo sticks!

The upper-strata Muslims of Bengal including the Zamindars did not like the activities of Shariatullah, Dadu Miyan or Titumir. For centuries, they had flaunted their racial superiority, priding themselves on their noble blood and claiming to be Ashrafs. They looked down upon the ordinary Muslims of Bengal as racially inferior converts from Hinduism.

The reformist movement led by the Brahmo leaders of Bengal succeeded in a certain measure in imparting a Western liberal orientation to the local Hindus' outlook. In the Punjab, the Arya Samaj movement launched by Swami Dayanand Saraswati was informed by the same spirit and inspired by similar ideas. The Muslim reformist leaders were not able to do much in this regard in respect of Muslim society.

Some Muslim intellectuals of Bengal did not accept the view, held by historians like Sir Jadunath Sarkar, that the new Hindu culture was a renaissance on the European pattern, since, as they explained, the renaissance in Europe had an anti-feudal thrust and stood for the liberal ideals of the French revolution derived from the doctrines of Mill, Bentham, Rousseau and Voltaire, while the new Hindu culture of Bengal failed to break free of the old religious traditions of the Vedas and the Upanishads.

In pre-independence Bengal, a section of the Muslim intelligentsia had sought to foster an attitude of liberalism among the Muslim masses. Writers such as Mir Musharaf Hussain, Kaikobad, Ismail Hussain Siraji, Lutfar Rahman, Sayed Emdad Ali, Kazi Emdadul Huq and Mozammel Huq brought to the fore themes such as the Muslims' history and theology, religious reforms, Hindu-Muslim relations, spread of education among the Muslims, liberation of women etc. Some of them advocated pro-Western reforms, while the others favoured an approach in keeping with Islamic traditions.

In Dhaka, some progressive Muslim intellectuals propagated secular values. Abul Hussain (1897-1938) and Kazi Abdul Odud

1898-1970), Professors of Dacca University, were great admirers of Raja Rammohun Roy and worked for establishing harmonious relations between the Hindus and Muslims. But these efforts remained confined to the periphery of Muslim society and failed to touch the greater bulk of the Muslim masses.

The British rulers' policy of 'divide and rule' exacerbated the differences between the Hindus and Muslims. A series of steps taken by them beginning with the partition of Bengal(1905) had the effect of creating a deep cleavage between the Hindus and Muslims. The partition of Bengal received widespread support among the Muslims, but was fiercely opposed by the Hindus. The movement against the partition of Bengal was inspired largely by the spirit of Hindu sub-nationalism. The slogans, songs and symbols of the movement were almost wholly Hindu in spirit.

The partition of Bengal fostered among the Muslims the idea of the feasibility, in fact the desirability, of the division of Bengal on communal lines and the creation of a Muslim-majority province of east Bengal. The seeds of the future partition of India can be said to have been sown by this move of the British rulers – long before the idea of Pakistan was formally put forward by some Muslim leaders. The intense agitation against it worked up by the Hindus re-inforced the Muslims' consciousness of their communal identity. Annulment of the partition in 1912 aroused the wrath of the Muslims and vitiated the communal atmosphere.

The Morley Minto Reforms of 1909, which provided for separate electorates for the Muslims and Hindus, put a premium on communal feelings. The Lucknow Pact (1916) between the Congress and the Muslim League, which proposed the allocation of specific numbers of seats in the legislative bodies for the Muslims and non-Muslims, helped to keep communal feelings on the boil. In Bengal, the Muslims, who constituted more than 50% of the population, felt unhappy because they were allotted only 40% of the seats. The Hindus in the Congress Party riposted that in Bengal they were superior in education and political consciousness and hence deserved a greater number of seats. The Montagu Chelmsford Reforms of 1919 conceded only 45% of the seats to the Muslims, which did not fully satisfy them.

To mollify Muslim sentiment, the British authorities came out with a proposal for the establishment of a University at Dhaka. But the agitation launched by the Hindu leaders of Bengal against this proposal led to the postponement of its implementation for several years and it was only in 1921 that the University of Dacca could be set up with its jurisdiction limited to Dhaka town and a small area around it. Even after this, the Hindu Ministers of the Bengal Government had allegedly thwarted its functioning through various devices including the withholding of funds.

After World War I, when the Muslims of India launched the Khilafat movement in support of the demand for the continuation of the Caliphate in Turkey, Mahatma Gandhi included this demand as a plank of his non-cooperation movement. This brought the Hindus and Muslims nearer to each other, but this unity did not reflect a union of hearts, since it was based on the opportunistic considerations of the Hindus and Muslims alike. Moreover, when Gandhiji called off the non-cooperation movement in 1921 to express his disapproval of the violence resorted to by the supporters of the movement at Chaura Chauri near Gorakhpur, the Muslim leaders of the Khilafat movement were left high and dry and felt disillusioned.

The Bengal Pact mooted by Deshbandhu C.R.Das and signed in December, 1923 provided for a higher percentage of representation to the Muslims in the various institutions of local self-government and in government jobs in Bengal, a ban on the playing of music by processions passing in front of mosques, freedom of the Muslims to slaughter cows on religious occasions, etc. This helped to garner considerable support among the Muslims, though at the cost of annoying many die-hard Hindus. But the refusal of the All India Congress Committee to approve of the Bengal Pact and the untimely demise of C.R.Das in 1925 marked the end of a period of considerable Hindu-Muslim rapport in Bengal's political milieu. Soon Bengal witnessed a series of communal riots during 1925-26 which resulted in the death of and injuries to many persons, apart from the desecration of many temples, Gurdwaras and mosques.

In 1928, the Congress leaders of Bengal, who were mostly Hindus, supported a Bill for amending the Bengal Tenancy Act with a view to conferring greater powers on the Zamindars, which were tilted against the interests of the ordinary people. Those who opposed the Bill were mostly Muslims, thus bringing into sharp focus the fact the Congress leaders were generally in favour of furthering the interests of the Zamindars, who were mostly Hindus. This development made many nationalist Muslim leaders such as Akram Khan, Syed Nausher Ali, A.K.Fazlul Huq and H.S.Subrawardy leave the Congress Party and form the Krishak Praja Party.

The revolutionary underground movement that convulsed Bengal during the nineteen twenties and thirties was looked upon by the Muslims at large as being pro-Hindu in its orientation, which, they alleged, was clearly reflected in their equating the country with the Divine Mother or 'Shakti'. The revolutionary movement did not, therefore, evoke much response from the Muslims, who dubbed it as an off-shoot of the Congress Party's pro-Hindu outlook.

The Round Table Conference held in London in 1931 failed to solve the problem of communal representation and gave way to Ramsay McDonald's Communal Award (August 1932) which allotted 119 seats to the Muslims and 80 to the Hindus in the Bengal Legislative Assembly. Of the 80 seats earmarked for the Hindus, 30 were reserved for the Scheduled Castes under the Poona Pact hammered out after Gandhiji went on a fast to protest against the scheme of a separate electorate for the Scheduled Castes under the McDonald Award. This Award provoked the Hindus of Bengal into launching an intense agitation, leading to their alienation from the Muslim community as well as from the central leadership of the Congress Party. A Congress Nationalist Party formed in Bengal in the wake of this development created a rift in the political organisation of the Hindus. Sarat Chandra Chatterjee, the Bengalee novelist, spoke strongly against the Communal Award in which he perceived a distinct threat to Bengal's culture and literature.

It is known thatsome Pakistani historians(e.g. Aitzaz Ahsan, The Indus Saga) have of late been trying to trace the roots of a Pakistani identify at Mohenjodaro in the Indus Valley. But the fact remains that a concerete proposal for carving out separate homeland of the Indian Muslims out of India was conceptualised by Muhammad Iqbal, the man who gave us the song 'Sare Jahan Se Achchha'. In 1930, in his presidential address at the All-India Muslim Conference held in Allahabad, he criticised the view that the Hindus and Muslims of India could live together and put forward the plea for the creation of a separate State consisting of the Muslim-majority Provinces of the Punjab, Sind, Baluchistan and the North West Frontier Province. Initially, Bengal was not included in this new State to be created, but a few years later, Iqbal suggested the inclusion of Bengal as well in this Muslim-majority State. He did not use the term Pakistan for this State. Later, Rahamat Ali, the Cambridge-educated intellectual, coined this expression and prevailed upon M A. Jinnah to take up this issue.

The working of the Government of India Act, 1935, which incorporated the provisions of the Communal Award and the elections held in 1937 under the Act gave the Congress Party in Bengal an opportunity to form a government in coalition with the Krishak Praja Party of A.K.Fazlul Huq, but the policy of the Congress Party's national leadership stood in the way of such a move. This thwarted the possibility of working out a political arrangement that would have made for a certain measure of communal rapprochement. In the event, Huq had no alternative but to seek the help of the Muslim League in forming a government dominated by the latter, which marked the beginning of an era of Muslim League ascendancy in Bengal. The League asserted its dominant position in the day-to-day working of the government, thus helping the communalisation of Bengal politics.

A.K. Fazlul Huq, the most charismatic Muslim leader of Bengal, hailed from Barisal district of east Bengal and belonged to a middle class family of lawyers with modest landed interests. He took up the cause of the oppressed peasants of Bengal. His contribution towards ridding the ordinary Hindu and Muslim peasant of the curse of indebtedness enhanced his mass appeal among Hindus as well as Muslims. He projected himself as a pro-peasant Bengalee nationalist leader, who stood for radical reforms that included spreading education among the masses. In the nineteen twenties, he had joined hands with Deshbandhu Chittaranjan Das, the veteran Congress leader known for his progressive and secular outlook. They had jointly formulated certain principles for resolving Hindu-Muslim differences in the working of the Calcutta Municipal Corporation. Even his arch political rival, H.S.Suhrawardy concedes in his memoirs that Fazlul Huq was a "remarkable man", "of acutely active intelligence, colossal memory, great erudition and a deep insight into human character and mass psychology", who "swayed the emotions and captured the imagination of the people of Bengal with his remarkable gift of oratory and fluency of language".

Fazlul Huq was a kind-hearted man, whom many ordinary people approached for government jobs. In the last decade of the 19th century, he was a student of the Presidency College, Kolkata, which I joined decades later in the late 1940's. He gifted away his government scholarship to one Moulvi Masudal Husain Saheb – an act that showed what a kind soul he was. But since this money could not be gifted directly, all that Huq did was to authorise the

Moulvi to receive his scholarship from the college authorities. The facsimile of Huq's letter of authority dated January 10, 1896 is reproduced below: [8]

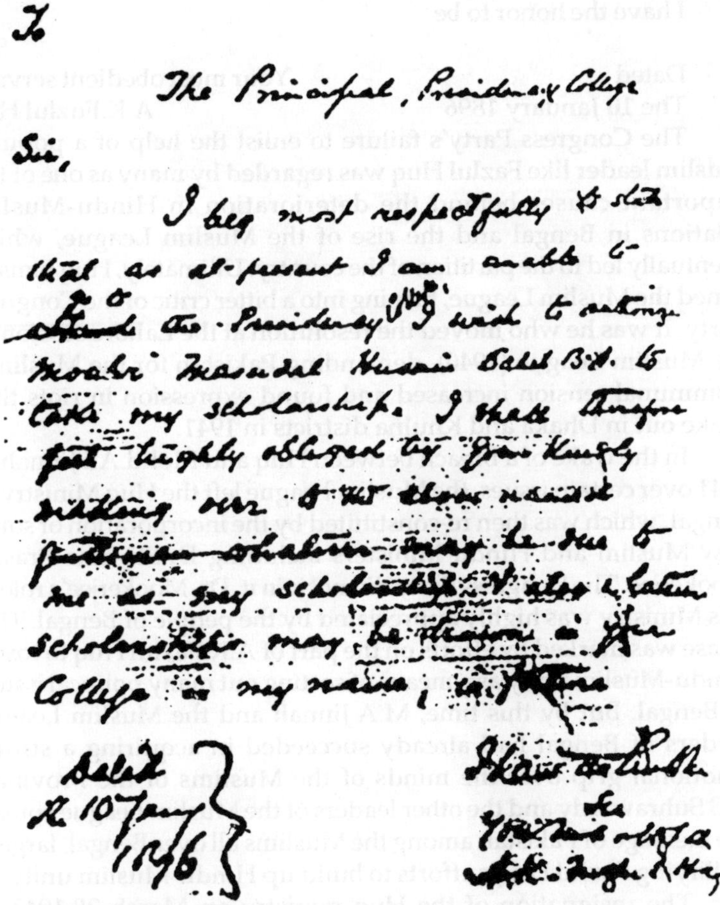

To

The Principal, Presidency College

Sir,

I beg most respectfully to state

that as at present I am unable to

go to the Presidency College I wish to authorize

Moulvi Masudal Husain Saheb B.A. to

take my scholarship. I shall therefore

feel highly obliged by your kindly

making over to the above mentioned

[illegible]

[illegible] my scholarship [illegible]

scholarship may be [illegible]

College [illegible] my name, [illegible]

Dated

the 10 Jany

1896

I have the honor to be

Your most obedient [illegible]

[illegible] Huq

To facilitate perusal, this letter is reproduced below in print:

To

The Principal, Presidency College

Sir,

I beg most respectfully to state that as at present I am unable to go to the Presidency College, I wish to authorize Moulvi Masudal Husain Saheb B.A. to take my scholarship. I shall, therefore, feel highly obliged by your kindly making over to the above mentioned gentleman whatever may be due to me as my scholarship and also whatever scholarships may be drawn in your college in my name, in future.

I have the honor to be

Sir,

Dated Your most obedient servant

The 10 January 1896 A.K.Fuzlul Haq

The Congress Party's failure to enlist the help of a popular Muslim leader like Fazlul Huq was regarded by many as one of the important causes behind the deterioration in Hindu-Muslim relations in Bengal and the rise of the Muslim League, which eventually led to the partition of the country. Ultimately, Huq himself joined the Muslim League, turning into a bitter critic of the Congress Party. It was he who moved the resolution at the Lahore session of the Muslim League (1940), demanding Pakistan for the Muslims. Communal tension increased and found expression in riots that broke out in Dhaka and Khulna districts in 1941.

In the wake of a breach between Huq and Mohd.Ali Jinnah in 1941 over certain issues, the Muslim League left the Huq Ministry in Bengal, which was then re-constituted by the incorporation of some new Muslim and Hindu Ministers including Dr.Shyama Prasad Mookerjee. The Congress Party did not join it. Dr. Mookerjee's role in this Ministry was highly appreciated by the people of Bengal. This phase was marked by efforts on the part of A.K.Fazlul Huq to foster Hindu-Muslim unity as a means of sorting out many political issues of Bengal. But by this time, M.A.Jinnah and the Muslim League leaders of Bengal had already succeeded in acquiring a strong emotional grip over the minds of the Muslims of the Province. H.S.Suhrawardy and the other leaders of the Muslim League spread the message of Pakistan among the Muslims all over Bengal, largely nullifying Fazlul Huq's efforts to build up Hindu-Muslim unity.

The resignation of the Huq ministry on March 28,1943 in dubious circumstances that made it look synonymous with his virtual dismissal by the British Governor of Bengal and its replacement by a Muslim League Ministry headed by Sir Khwaja Nazimuddin (1943-1945) helped the trend towards the progressive communalisation of the political scene in Bengal. Nazimuddin, belonged to the Nawab family of Dhaka, that had come to Bengal from Kashmir centuries ago. Educated at Aligarh and Cambridge, he did not have much in common with the ordinary Bengalee Muslim.

The Muslim League's mass mobilization programme during the years of the Second World War when the Congress leaders remained shut up in jails was crowned with success that was reflected in the results of the elections held in November 1945 to the Central Assembly and in March 1946 to the Provincial Assembly of Bengal. The party captured all the 30 seats earmarked for the Muslims in the Central Assembly and 113 out of the 119 Muslim seats in the Bengal Legislative Assembly. A.K.Fazlul Huq's party was almost obliterated.

The formation of another Muslim League Ministry led by H.S. Suhrawardy in April 1946 was a development that gave rise to misgivings among the Bengalee Hindus that from then on, there was hardly any possibility of their gaining power. Yet, it must be said in fairness to Suhrawardy that he had tried to get the Congress Party to join his ministry. His efforts failed as the high commands of both the Congress and the Muslim League did not approve of such an arrangement.

Suhrawardy, a rich, roly-poly politician, who hailed from an aristocratic family of West Bengal, was an Oxford graduate and a barrister to boot. After the death of his wife, Naiz Fatima in 1940, he married Vera Tiscenko, a former actress of the Moscow Arts Theatre,"who had led a life almost as colourful and unusual as the man she was soon to marry".[9] Many have attributed the creation of Pakistan to the determined bid that Suhrawardy made for it.

Thus, the chasm between the Hindus and Muslims of Bengal continued to widen and in the course of just a decade (1937-1947), the Muslim League emerged from its insignificant position to reach a point where it was perceived as the undisputed mouthpiece of the Muslim community, negating the claims in this regard that used to be made on behalf of the Congress Party and Huq's Krishak Praja Party, which virtually became a non-entity.

The Muslim League's emergence on the eve of the partition of the country as the dominant party that spoke on behalf of the Muslims has been attributed by some scholars to two main factors, namely, the communal twist given to the anti-feudal peasant struggle and the communal outlook of the leaders of Bengal's Muslim bourgeoisie.[10] The British rulers welcomed this development, which led to the division of the Indian electorate on communal lines. This was evident from the contents of a contemporary telegram said to have been despatched to the British authorities by Governor R.G.

Casey of Bengal, predicting that "the Muslim League and the Congress would sweep the Moslem and caste Hindu polls respectively".

Notes

1. This quotation has been taken from "Sacred Space" in the Times of India, New Delhi, dated September 8, 2004.
2. *Ibid.*
3. *Ibid.*
4. *Ibid.*
5. Nationalism In India by Dr. Niharranjan Ray (Aligarh Muslim University, 1973).
6. *Ibid.* page 60.
7. History Of Bangladesh by Sirajul Islam, Vol. I, page 15.
8. Taken from the brochure published in 1998 by the Kolkata Presidency College Alumni Association, Delhi.
9. 'Memoirs Of Huseyn Shaheed Suhrawardy' edited by Mohammad H.R. Talukdar.
10. 'A History Of Pakistan, 1947-1948' by Y.V. Gankovsky and M.A. Wilcox, page 80. Also 'Ideological Dilemmas In Pakistan's Political Culture' in Donald Eugene Smith's 'South Asian Politics And Religion', page 344.

9

Cabinet Mission Proposals : 'Direct Action'

The Cabinet Mission led by Lord Pethick Lawrence spent more than a month and a half meeting the leaders of various political parties and the representatives of all shades of public opinion and formulated its plan of transferring power to a Federal Government of a united India, which was made public on May 16, 1946. From newspaper reports, the salient features of the scheme appeared to be somewhat as follows. The Provincial legislatures were to elect the members of a Constituent Assembly that would draw up free India's constitution. The Federal Government would deal with foreign affairs, defence and communications, important issues being decided by a majority of the Hindu members as well as by a majority of the Muslim members of the Central legislature.

The country was to be divided into three zones, called Sections A, B and C. Section B would be a Muslim-majority area comprising Punjab, Sindh, North West Frontier Province and British Baluchistan. In Section C, which was to include Bengal and Assam Provinces, the Muslims would have a small majority over the Hindus. The rest of the country would be in Section A, where the Hindus would be preponderant. The Mission thought that this arrangement would contain sufficient guarantees to safeguard the interests of the Muslim minority and allay its fears of being swamped by the Hindu majority. It also allotted the majority of the subjects to the Provinces so that the Muslims could exercise almost complete autonomy in the Provinces, where they were in a majority.

Initially, both the Congress and the Muslim League seemed willing to seriously consider the Plan, which, some Indians thought, offered the last chance of guaranteeing the country's unity and simultaneously assuring the Mulsim minority of substantial satisfaction. At this stage, the Congress Party did something which was regarded by many as unfortunate and even dishonest. A declaration by Pandit Jawaharlal Nehru in Bombay on July 10, 1946 that the Congress Party would enter the Constituent Assembly "completely unfettered by agreements and free to meet all situations as they arise" in effect amounted to saying that his party would have the freedom to unilaterally alter the Cabinet Mission Plan, as it thought necessary.

Many considered the Congress Party's stand as a negative one that naturally gave rise to serious doubts in the Muslim mind about the bonafides of the Congress leaders. Independent political observers saw considerable justification in the League's stand that the Congress Party was deviating from the proposals of the Cabinet Mission in regard to the grouping of Provinces. The League, they thought, was justified in holding that the Constituent Assembly had no right to change the basic structure of the Plan, of which the grouping of Provinces was an important provision.

I became aware of a similar feeling on the part of Maulana Abul Kalam Azad when, many years later, I read the 1988 edition of his book "India Wins Freedom". This contained certain paragraphs that had been omitted from the earlier edition in accordance with his wish. These paragraphs included in the 1988 edition revealed the fact that Azad had squarely blamed Pt.Jawaharlal Nehru for having arbitrarily sought to modify the Cabinet Mission Plan. To quote: "I must place on record that Jahawarlal's statement was wrong. It was not correct to say that Congress was free to modify the Plan ..... . Jahaharlal's statement came to him (Jinnah) as a bombshell. .... Mr.Jinnah re-iterated the demand for Pakistan as the only course left open to the Muslim League." Maulana Azad thought that Pt. Nehru's unhelpful statement was " one of those unfortunate events which changed the course of history."

I had heard some people say that Maulana Azad's assessment had attached an exaggerated importance to Jawaharlal's statement which was not the real cause that led Jinnah and the Muslim League to behave in the manner they did. It has been pointed out by some that there were much deeper causes which had exacerbated Congress-Muslim League relations to such a great extent that the hope of any rapprochement between them looked misplaced.

M.A. Jinnah felt extremely unhappy and lambasted the Congress Party's stand that it could modify the Cabinet Mission Plan by virtue of the majority it would have in the Constituent Assembly. He apprehended that such unilateral action on the part of the Congress Party would place the minorities at the mercy of the Hindu majority. He, therefore, concluded that partitioning the country to form Pakistan as a home-land for the Muslims had become inevitable—a stand that was put forward in a resolution adopted by the Muslim League on July 29, 1946. The Muslim League not only rejected the Cabinet Mission Plan, but also gave a call to the Muslims to resort to Direct Action as a step towards achieving Pakistan. On July 30, 1946, the Muslim League declared that Direct Action Day would be observed all over India on August 16,1946, which was a Friday.

Like many of my college friends, I considered this decision of the Muslim League to be rather ominous, because in the meantime, the relations between the Congress and the Muslim League had already become quite strained in Bengal over the question of the formation of a government in the wake of the elections to the Provincial Assembly held in March 1946 in which the Muslim League had got 115 seats and the Congress 87 out of a total number of 250 seats. H.S. Suhrawardy, leader of the Muslim League group, suggested to Congress leader Kiran Shankar Roy the formation of the coalition Ministry. The Congress High Command vacillated for some time and then agreed to consider such a move but at the same time laid down certain conditions which the Muslim League did not find acceptable.

Ultimately, the proposal for a coalition Ministry in Bengal fell through and Suhrawardy formed a Muslim League Ministry in which some Hindu members were included. Many in Bengal pointed out at that time that it was a blunder on the part of the Congress not to give more serious thought to Suhrawardy's offer to form a coalition Ministry that could have helped in building up and maintaining harmonious relations between the Hindus and the Muslims.

The political situation in the country took on a new dimension with the Muslim League's call for the observance of Direct Action Day all over India on August 16, 1946. Significantly, it was declared a public holiday by H.S. Suhrawardy, Chief Minister of Bengal. While speaking in Delhi on August 10, 1946, Suhrawardy held out the threat that in case the Congress Party formed an Interim Government at the Centre excluding the Muslim League from it, the Government of Bengal would not only defy the Centre and have nothing to do with it, but also see to it that the Centre could collect no revenue from Bengal. The slogan 'Ladke Lenge Pakistan' (we will achieve Pakistan by fighting for it), which was often raised by the Muslim League workers of Bengal, was a pointer to the mood of the party and its Government.

On August 16, 1946, a large public meeting was held by the Muslim League at the Kolkata maidan, where the Muslim masses were called upon to organise themselves and join the fight to achieve their goal of Pakistan. This meeting was followed by widespread communal violence in different parts of Kolkata that resulted in unprecedented casualities. The Hindus started retaliating against the Muslims in those parts of the city where they were in a majority.

I distinctly remember the events of that humid and muggy afternoon of August 16, 1946. Since it was declared a holiday, I did not go to college, but stayed at home, pre-occupied with my studies, as usual. All of a sudden, I heard a big noise, which was accompanied by the shouting of slogans by a crowd. I did not understand what was happening. Then, in a few minutes, I saw that some people of the slum area came running very fast, apparently happy with the head-loads of clothes, shoes and other precious articles they had looted from the shops.

I rushed out to the main street to see what the matter was. About a furlong from our place was Jagu Babu's Bazar, where I saw a big crowd milling around several shops, trying to break them open. The crowd moved from shop to shop, selecting the shops of the Muslims as their targets and, after breaking their locks and doors, looted all the articles. The Muslims had all fled in fear. This was the pattern in our area, where the Hindus were in a majority. In areas with the opposite communal composition, the Hindu shops were looted and burnt.

Later, I heard some people say – on what basis I did not know – that, apart from open exhortations to violence, there was also a clear warning given by the then Commissioner of Police to the Bengal Government, on the basis of intelligence reports, of the impending catastrophe. Even the London Times had editorially prognosticated as early as the 30th of July, 1946 the ominous significance of the Muslim League's call for Direct Action.[1] The same day, Sardar J.J.Singh, President of the India League in the USA, had openly appealed to the United Nations Organisation to intervene so that

India was not engulfed in violence and bloodshed.[2] In view of all these forebodings, why the Central Government and the Bengal Government did not take adequate preventive measures had surprised many.

The whole of Kolkata became a cauldron, boiling over with the poison of communal hatred. The city got automatically divided into distinct zones, in which either the Hindus or the Muslims were in pre-ponderance. Those in a minority in a particular zone fled to another zone where their own community was numerically stronger. Initially, it was the Muslims who took the offensive, but later the situation became really serious when the Hindus, being in an over-all majority in the city, launched their counter-offensive against the Muslims, which proved more brutal. It was then that, following consultations between Lord Wavell, the Governor-General and Sir Frederick Burrows, Governor of Bengal, the Army was pressed into service from August 18, 1946, to stop the dance macabre of the demon of communalism and bring the situation under control. From August 20 onward, the situation started improving. A mammoth peace procession led by the important representatives of all communities such as Muhammad Ali of Bogra, Khwaja Nazimuddin, H.S. Suhrawardy, Sarat Bose and Kiran Shankar Roy, which passed through the disturbed areas on August 21, 1946, helped a great deal in the restoration of normalcy. A rough estimate put the number killed in the carnage at 10,000!

Many Sikh taxi drivers and mechanics, armed with their long swords and sometimes with guns, mostly from Bhowanipore, where I lived, did a wonderful job, rescuing people from Muslim pockets, of course, for money, but at great risk to their own lives. There must have been similar cases of Muslims being rescued from Hindu-majority areas. There were also many cases of Hindus going out of the way to save Muslims in Hindu-majority pockets and of Muslims doing the same in respect of their Hindu neighbours, who were in trouble. The newspapers highlighted the case of Dr. Qudrat-I-Khuda, Principal of the prestigious PresidencyCollege, whose residence in my Bhowanipore locality was attacked by the hooligans. His Hindu neighbours intervened effectively to save his life.

In each area, young men organised defence squads to resist likely attacks at night from members of the other community, who lived in near-by areas. I remember having performed night duty as a member of a vigilante group for a month or so.

In Hindu areas, even a genuine Hindu stood the risk of being killed by brother Hindus, if his dress or conduct aroused suspicion that he was a Muslim masquerading as a Hindu. If he claimed to be a Hindu, he was sometimes stripped to check if he was circumcised which was counted as proof positive that he was a Muslim. Sometimes, a Hindu, finding himself in such distress, volunteered to strip in order to prove himself.

Close to where I lived, there was a small cluster of houses where some Muslims lived. They were businessmen and perhaps hailed from respectable families of Uttar Pradesh or Punjab as was apparent from their dress, language, life style and physical appearance. Some hoodlums surrounded these houses, shouted anti-Muslim slogans and hurled all kinds of abuses at these unfortunate Muslims. Soon, they started dragging the Muslims out of their houses on to the road, where a crowd had assembled. Driven to the wall, one of the Muslims, who had a gun, took his position on roof-top and opened fire at the mob, injuring a few persons.

I was standing at a distance along with some other curious onlookers. Suddenly, I saw that the person standing next to me was bleeding profusely, because a bullet had pierced through his body. This was in a sense a near-death experience for me and gave me the fright of my life. I realised that I had just narrowly missed being hit and killed by a bullet. And so I ran for my life. Meanwhile, one of the Muslims rang up the police, which arrived there very promptly, rescued the Muslims after beating up the miscreants, and then drove away with the victims in their vehicles.

A version of the Great Calcutta Killing of August 1946, which is now available in Mohammad H.R.Talukdar's account given in the "Memoirs of Huseyn Shaheed Suhrawardy", makes interesting reading. The justification given for declaring a holiday on August 16,1946 is that on a previous occasion, when no holiday was declared, people were dragged out their cars and insulted, thus leading to clashes between the Hindus and Muslims. Talukdar laments that neither the Intelligence Branch nor the Criminal Investigation Department of the police, which were almost exclusively manned by the Hindus, had given Suhrawardy any information about the preparations made to create trouble with the result that he was caught unawares.

Suhrawardy alleges in his memoirs that "on 16 August, 1946 which the Muslim League High Command had designated Direct Action Day and which thousands of Muslims of Kolkata observed by attending a public and wholly peaceful meeting, the Hindus, who appeared to have been well-prepared, attacked the Muslims who were taken wholly by surprise". According to Talukdar, the Commissioner of Calcutta Police, an Englishman, did not know Calcutta and was unable to deal with the situation with the small force at his command.

Further on, the account in Suhrawardy's memoirs reads: "The Riot Commission, which was set up by the British government as a result of the riot, reports that immediately after the riot began, the Prime Minister[3] rushed to Lalbazar Police Headquarters to obtain first hand information and, being apprised of the grave situation, demanded deployment of the army on the very first day of the riot. But Governor Burrows rejected the demand, primarily to divert the strong anti-British sentiments generated during the Rashid Ali Day, observed in Kolkata in June 1945 and which he hoped would worsen Hindu-Muslim relations........"

"The Governor also turned down Suhrawardy's suggestion to put pickets between Hindu and Muslim localities, creating a bulwark which would help to separate the two communities .... Instead, Burrows heeded the advice of the Commissioner of Police that the civil power was capable of dealing with the situation and that there was no need to deploy the army. It was only when Suhrawardy threatened to resign that the Governor reluctantly pretended to agree and three or four days later merely ordered the army to stand by".

"At that time Calcutta was a city of 6 million people, but it had only a 1200-man police force, of whom only 63 were Muslims....... The 1200-man police force was, therefore, not only small to cope with the situation, but suspect in its loyalty as well. In this situation, Suhrawardy decided to appoint 1200 trained Muslim Punjabi Sepahis to achieve equity in the balance of the city's police force. Hindu leaders protested against this to the Governor, who asked Suhrawardy to desist from recruiting Muslim Punjabi Sepahis. Suhrawardy argued that trained Muslim Bengali Sepahis could not easily be found and that he needed trained forces immediately to contain the riots .... Burrows finally consented to his proposal only when the Prime Minister again threatened to resign on this issue. Suhrawardy immediately recruited 1200 trained Muslim Punjabi Sepahis .... and ordered Muslim Officers-in-Charge to be posted in 21 of the 22 thanas. Hc personally took charge of the Police Control Room from one British Officer and mobilized the police force himself to quell the riots".

"There were hundreds of occasions when Suhrawardy himself, often clandestinely clad in the uniform of a European military officer, drove through the affected localities to save the lives of the defenceless victims, Muslims and Hindus alike ..... he arranged free lodging and food for many Hindu families ....

"Viceroy Lord Wavell visited Calcutta on 25 August and saw the carnage himself..... Suhrawardy explained that the riot was a consequence of the formation of the interim government without Muslim League representation and the deeply held Muslim belief of a deliberate British creation of Hindu-Muslim misunderstanding as a rationale to hand over power only to the Congress Party. He further warned that what had happened in Calcutta would repeat itself all over India unless the British government changed its policy. Suhrawardy also convinced him that a united India was impossible and cooperation of the Muslim League was essential if India was to be saved from civil war. Before he left Bengal, Lord Wavell asked Suhrawardy to work as an emissary between himsel and Jinnah".

"Suhrawardy saw Jinnah in Bombay on 6 September and Lord Wavell in Delhi two days later, and succeeded in bringing about a rapprochement between them. They first met on 16 September in Delhi. Lord Wavell assured Jinnah that he was ready to accept the Muslim League demand, and the Muslim League announced on 15 October its decision to join the interim government headed by Pandit Nehru. On this occasion Jinnah admitted that Suhrawardy had saved the country from a perilous situation".

I have quoted extensively from Talukdar's account as it brings out clearly how different this version is from what the Hindus of Kolkata generally thought at that time about these grim happenings. Talukdar goes on to observe that Suhrawardy's contribution to the creation of Pakistan was greater than anybody else's because, as he says, quoting from an article by Abdul Mansur Ahmad: "Had Suhrawardy not won the general election in 1946, in the light of total failure of the Muslim League in all the other Muslim majority provinces, there would have been no Pakistan." Talukdar also says that "Jinnah's Direct Action strategy, bathed in the blood of the Muslims of Calcutta, won him a great political victory and made Pakistan inevitable". Suhrawardy's contribution in organising the Direct Action Day in Kolkata and in handling the civil war as a sequel to the Great Calcutta Killing was no doubt the most potent blow for the creation of the Pakistan.

Needless to say, the views expressed by the Hindu and Muslim political leaders and intellectuals differ sharply and mostly suffer from bias. For example, Suhrawardy's presence in the Police Control Room at Lal Bazar, when the riots were at their worst, was interpreted differently by his critics and supporters, the former alleging that from his vantage position in the Control Room he was issuing instructions to the police officers that harmed the Hindus, while the latter justified his role in the Control Room by asserting that he was thus trying his best to bring the situation under control.

There is no doubt that Suhrawardy had at one time been very close to secular-minded national leaders like C.R. Das and had tried to enlist the co-operation of the Congress Party in forming a coalition government in Bengal in the wake of the Assembly elections held in 1946. It would be hard to believe that he had changed all of a sudden into such a rabid hater of the Hindus as to go all out to organise their mass killing. He had definitely chalked out an elaborate plan of organising a massive protest action to press the demand for Pakistan as also to show his political prowess in Bengal not only to the Congress Party but also to M.A. Jinnah whom he did not particularly like and who in turn suspected Suhrawardy of harbouring the secret ambition of creating a sovereign Bengal outside Jinnah's Pakistan.

But it appeared to me even at that time that Suhrawardy had not foreseen that the observance of Direct Action would result in such disastrous consequences and lead to communal violence on such a large scale. He admitted as much in a statement he made in the Bengal Legislative Assembly, when he practically said that he had miscalculated the explosive potential of the call for Direct Action, but absolved himself of the charge of deliberate mischief on his part. There were several instances of Suhrawardy himself rushing to trouble spots to bring the situation under control or to save innocent lives.

Suhrawardy seems to have suffered pangs of remorse for the large-scale violence and the killings that took place and that is why he sought refuge in Gandhiji's elevating company, though many Hindus taunted him at that time for what they thought was rank hypocrisy on his part. It must not be forgotten that as a disciple of C.R. Das, Suhrawardy had championed the cause of Hind-Muslim unity in pre-partition Bengal and had, on the eve of the country's partition, joined hands with Sarat Chandra Bose to work for the creation of a sovereign Bengal where the Hindus and the Muslims would live together in amity. Even after partition, he continued to uphold the cause of the Hindu minority in Pakistan, especially in east Bengal.

The Communist Party of India, which had realised the mistake it had committed by distancing itself from the Quit India movement in 1942, again made a blunder in 1946, when it called upon its workers to participate in the observance of "Direct Action Day" by the Muslim League on August 16, 1946. The C.P.I.'s ostensible reason for adopting such a course was to identify itself with the Muslim working class and to demonstrate the anti-imperialist unity of the working class. It tried to justify its stand by blaming the communal riots on the bourgeois leadership of the various political parties and the machinations of the imperialists to split the national liberation struggle. Party workers were told to ensure that Hindus and Muslims did not clash during the observance of the day. Muslim workers of the party struck work in Kolkata, bringing the trams and railways to a grinding halt. On the ground, however, the party's ordinary workers got divided on communal lines with the result that there was utter confusion among its rank and file.

Many of my communist friends, while seeking to justify the party line, failed to convince the student-followers of other parties, who often bad-mouthed the former by branding them as the stooges of a foreign power.

Notes

1. Ashok Mitra, Three Score and Ten, Volume II, page 279.
2. *Ibid.*
3. Suhrawardy was then designated as th Prime Minister of Bengal.

10

Noakhali and After

Lord Wavell, Governor-General of India, had been trying since July,1946 to persuade the Congress and the Muslim League to join an Interim Government at the Centre, pending finalisation of arrangements for the transfer of power in the near future. Initially, both the parties refused to join the Government. But Lord Wavell continued his efforts and was able to persuade the Congress to join the Interim Government on September 2, 1946. In his capacity as Deputy Chairman of the Executive Council, Pt. Nehru virtually became the Prime Minister in this new dispensation. The Muslim League, however, refused to join the Interim Government on the ground that the Congress had been allowed to nominate two Muslims as Ministers, thus negating the Muslim League's claim of being the sole representative of the Muslim community.

Later, Wavell was able to persuade the Muslim League also to join the Interim Government on October 26, 1946. As a counter to the Congress Party nominating two Muslim Ministers, Jinnah managed to get a Scheduled Caste leader from Bengal—Jogendra Nath Mandal—included in the Ministry, thus posing a challenge to the Congress Party's claim of being the sole representative of the Hindus.

In the mean time, the Great Calcutta Killing of August 1946 was already leading to a chain of reaction and counter-reaction at other places engulfing many parts of the country in competitive communal frenzy marked by brutality and savagery of the worst kind. From Kolkata, the trouble spread to Noakhali, a district of east Bengal, where the Muslims far out-numbered the Hindus. The killing of some Imams and Muezzins of mosques in Kolkata, who hailed from Noakhali inflamed Muslim passions at the latter place. Soon, reports of communal killings and acts of bestial violence started pouring in from Bihar, U.P., Punjab and Delhi.

Under the leadership of Ghulam Sarwar, an erstwhile Congressman, who had switched over to the Muslim League, the Noakhali Muslims sought to avenge the killing of their brethren in Kolkata, moving from village to village, armed with deadly weapons and indulging in loot, murder, arson and rape and abduction of Hindu women.

They desecrated Hindu temples and organised mass conversion of Hindus, forcing them to take beef and other forbidden food. Though the trouble in Noakhali started on October 10, 1946, the auspicious day on which the Hindus were to celebrate their 'Lakshmi Puja' (worship of the goddess of wealth), reports of rioting and hooliganism took about a week to reach the outside world, as communication facilities were utterly lacking in this district criss-crossed by rivers, canals and waterways. When the newspapers started reporting on the communal holocaust in Noakhali, there was widespread anguish and resentment among the Hindus in Kolkata and elsewhere in the country.

In Noakhali district, the Hindus were less than 20% and the Muslims more than 80% of the population. The presence of numerous Hajees, who had made it to Mecca, had helped to foster a highly orthodox religious outlook among the Muslims of the district. Their commitment to fundamentalism was clearly reflected in the large number of students from Noakhali, who used to attend the Muslim theological school at Deoband in Uttar Pradesh. The Imams of many mosques in different parts of Bengal hailed from Noakhali. A factor which contributed to the aggravation of communal tension was the presence in the district of a large number of ex-servicemen discharged after the Second World War—people who provided the technical know-how for disrupting communication and thwarting the operations of the police.

I learnt about some of the barbaric acts directly from people, who had fled from Choumohoni in Noakhali district—a place to which our landlord, Nanda Lal Roy, belonged. Unable to face the onslaught of the Muslim marauders, some Hindus from Choumohoni and other places of Noakhali district drifted to Kolkata and were given shelter by our benevolent landlord. It is from these hapless victims of communal hatred that I heard first-hand accounts of the orgies of communal frenzy and of man's inhuman behaviour towards man that reminded me of the barbarism of the middle ages.

The most blood-curdling incident of which an account was given to me by a Hindu refugee from Noakhali took place on the 11th of October, 1946 at Karpara, where the house of Rai Saheb Rajendra Lal Chowdhury, President of the District Bar Association, was attacked by a Muslim mob at the instigation of Ghulam Sarwar. Rajendra Lal and all other members of his family including women and children took shelter on the roof of their house. When the mob advanced menacingly towards them and then surrounded the house, Rajendra Lal's men opened fire, stalling the onward march of the crowd. The firing went on for some time, but when there was no more ammunition to go round, the crowd rushed forward and set fire to the building.

The hooligans seized Rajendra Lal and his family members.The frenzied mob chopped off Rajendra Lal's head and carried it away, displaying it all around as a highly valued trophy and a visible symbol of victory. Some members of the family were killed, while Rajendra Lal's wife and some other women were dragged away to unknown places; two girls of the family were taken away and reportedly raped by some ruffians.

A monk of the Bharat Sevashram Sangh by name Tryambakananda, who had been living in Rajendra Lal's house for some time, managed to escape from this ordeal with great difficulty and reached Kolkata after walking long distances through jungles and swimming across canals and rivulets. Once in Kolkata, he narrated these incidents in all their gory details, which were promptly flashed by the press.

From Noakhali, the trouble spread to places in south eastern Tripura, such as Hajiganj, Chandpur and Laksham police stations. The disturbances in Noakhali and Tripura, which continued from October 10 to 21, 1946, resulted in innumerable casualties among the Hindus that took the form of killings, destruction of their property, forcible conversion to Islam, rape and abduction of women and indignities of various kinds.

It was Mahatma Gandhi, who had the courage to roundly condemn the beastly behaviour of the Hindus as well as the Muslims in different parts of the country. He rushed to Noakhali, where he trekked from village to village from November 1946 till early March 1947, when he left for Bihar, which also needed his attention, as the Hindu majority there had turned against the Muslims in the wake of reports of Muslim atrocities on the Hindus of Noakhali and Tripura.

Gandhiji organised prayer meetings in the villages of Noakhali, exhorting Hindus and Muslims to live in peace and amity. The whole area reverberated with the strains of Tagore's famous song " Ekla Chalo Re" and the 'Ramdhun' i.e. "Raghupati Raghava Rajaram". When he camped in a village, he usually put up in the hut of a Muslim and subsisted on whatever fruits and vegetables grew locally, supplementing them with goat's milk, where available. His bare feet, on which he walked long distances, developed painful blisters.

Gandhiji had to face the daily ordeal of crossing ramshackle foot-bridges over village streams, which were so unsteady and shaky that he often risked falling down into the muddy and swirling waters below. Some of his associates were laid up with malaria. But he refused to leave Noakhali district or give up his pilgrimage of peace, as he called it. He carried on with his programme with missionary zeal.

Gandhiji launched a vigorous programme of restoring Hindu women, who had been abducted by Muslim hooligans, to their families and getting them accepted by the latter as well as by Hindu society. This was a difficult task, as many Hindus were reluctant to take back these unfortunate and innocent women, whose modesty had been outraged.

Acharya J.B. Kripalani, the then President of the All-India Congress Committee, visited some of the affected areas of Noakhali district and personally brought the grimness of the situation to the notice of the Governor of Bengal.

The late Nirmal Kumar Bose, a staunch follower of Gandhiji, pointed out in an account of the latter's 'walking pilgrimage' in Noakhali, that, in accordance with his principle of non-violence, Gandhiji advised the Hindus not to attack the Muslims, even if they were attacked by the latter. The Hindus were told to sacrifice their lives rather than embrace Islam out of fear and not to run away from their homes. Similarly, Hindu women were told to give up their lives rather than allow their chastity to be violated.

Gandhiji also called upon the Muslims to love the Hindus as their brothers. According to Nirmal Kumar Bose, whatever might have been the impact of Gandhiji's advice on the Hindus, his appeal to the Muslims appeared to bear even less fruit. By February 1947, the Muslims started expressing their resentment against Gandhiji's stay in Noakhali by deliberately placing dirt and filth on the paths which he was to take in the course of his peregrination.

H.S. Suhrawardy, Chief Minister of Bengal, had to take measures for the restoration of normalcy in Noakhali, which, however, did not go down well with the Muslims there. Suhrawardy was bitterly criticised by A.K. Fazlul Huq, a former Chief Minister of Bengal, who had once fallen foul of the Muslim League for his defiance of the dictates of M.A. Jinnah but was allowed re-entry into the Muslim League in the wake of the programme of Direct Action in Kolkata.

On February 9, 1946, at a meeting of the Bengal Muslim League leaders, Suhrawardy was taken to task for his failure to stop what was characterised as the oppression of the Muslims of Noakhali by the police. Suhrawardy defended himself by saying that the number of Muslims arrested in Noakhali was only about 800 and not 3000, as alleged, and that there was also no truth in another allegation that any police officer of the district had been dismissed from service for failure to take action against the Muslim rioters.

Simpson, a judge, who had been sent by the Government of Bengal, to Noakhali and Tripura to enquire into the communal situation, submitted a report in November, 1946, which was, however, not made public. But Simpson's main findings, which found their way into the newspapers, by and large, confirmed what was generally known about the loss of life and property, forcible conversion of the Hindus, abduction and rape of Hindu women etc. The Commissioner of the Chittagong Division, who had enquired into the Noakhali situation after the riots, had submitted a report to the Government of Bengal in May, 1947, pointing out that an uneasy calm prevailed in the district, with the Hindus being in a state of panic as a result of the continuing oppression and humiliation by the Muslims in the remote areas away from the towns. The police was said to be behaving in a partisan manner and refusing to take action against the Muslim culprits. The Muslims, aided by the goondas, were said to be targetting the property and the business establishments of the Hindus.

In the memoirs[1] of H.S..Suhrawardy published a few years ago,the extent of violence that took place during the Noakhali riots has been shown to be much less serious than what is generally believed to have been the case. It has been said that the Muslims had burnt a number of Hindu villages, killed 282 persons and abducted four women of whom three were subsequently restored. It has been further added: "The Amrita Bazar Patrika and other Congress papers flashed a statement by the Secretary of the Bengal Provincial Committee that 50,000 Hindus had been killed and numberless women abducted. Excited by such reports, the Hindus massacred and humiliated the Muslims in Garmukteswar in the United Provinces and throughout the Province of Bihar where they are believed to have killed as many as 1,00,000 Muslims – men, women and children – with unbelievable savagery."

In Bihar, where Gandhiji went in March 1947 to pacify the Hindus, who were mercilessly killing the Muslims, he chided the former at prayer meetings he organised to restore in them a semblance of sanity. By this time, the situation in Bengal and the North West Frontier Province had started deteriorating very fast. While Badshah Khan had gone away to Bihar to join Gandhiji there, his brother Dr. Khan Saheb, the then Congress Chief Minister of North West Frontier Province, and the Khudai Khidmatgars (or Red Shirts, as they were ordinarily called) tried their best to provide some measure of security to the non-Muslims of their Province.

In the Punjab, where a coalition government of the Unionist Party, Congress and the Akalis headed by Khizar Hyat Khan of the Unionist Party was in power, the Muslim League, which was in opposition, realised that Pakistan was in the offing and took the lead in organising widespread communal trouble. As the Hindus led by the Rashtriya Swayam Sevak Sangh and militant Sikhs under the leadership of Master Tara Singh resisted the Muslim rioters, a situation akin to almost a civil war developed in the Punjab. Khizar Hyat Khan's government resigned as it could not deal effectively with such a situation and Governor's rule had to be imposed in the Province.

The Ashram that Gandhiji set up in Noakhali still exists and has over the past decades undertaken several programmes of rural development, besides running a school. Branches of the Abhoy Ashram that had been set up at Chittagong, Comilla and Brahmanbaria (now in Bangladesh) still carry on the legacy of the Mahatma.

Sailen Chatterji, a well-known journalist, who worked for the United Press of India, was in Noakhali during those troubled times and used to accompany Gandhiji during his visits to the villages. He had reportedly gone to Noakhali in 1999 and visited the Ashram with which Gandhiji's hallowed memory is associated. Naturally, it was quite an emotional moment for him. In the year 2000, I had met this veteran disciple of Gandhiji at a reception at the Rashtrapati Bhavan in New Delhi, when he told me how nostalgic he had felt during his visit to Noakhali. It now appears that he had undertaken this pilgrimage just in time, because in 2001 A.D. he was to be no more!

Notes

1. Memoirs of Huseyn Suhrawardy edited by Mohammad H.R. Talukdar, page 107.

11

The British Decide to Quit: My Last Eve-of-partition Visit to My Village in East Bengal

The Congress leaders understood the reality that existed on the ground and started preparing for the vivisection of the country. The All-India Congress Committee adopted a resolution on January 6,1947 agreeing to accept those sections of the Cabinet Mission's Plan, which would in effect give the Muslim-majority Provinces the right to secede from India and join hands to form Pakistan. This resolution was against Gandhiji's specific advice to the contrary, since this would result in the vivisection of the country, which he was unwilling to accept at that stage. The Congress High Command was of the view that, if these proposals were not accepted, there was a likelihood of the whole country sliding into chaos and anarchy to which the prevailing communal situation was a pointer.

The British authorities realised, particularly after the communal conflagrations in Kolkata and Noakhali, that the situation in India was getting too hot for them. In fact, Lord Wavell, the British Governor-General, had kept ready a contingency plan for the evacuation of all British civilians from India, if the circumstances warranted such a step. He had also chalked out another plan (designated as Operation Ebb-Tide) for the departure of all British civil and military personnel from the Provinces with a view to assembling them at the port cities of Bombay and Karachi before they finally left en masse from India.

On February 20, 1947, Prime Minister Attlee declared that Great Britain would leave India as early as possible and definitely before June 1948. He also announced that Lord Wavell, the incumbent Viceroy, would be replaced by Admiral Lord Louis Mountbatten as India's next and last British Viceroy. I had heard at that time that Lord Wavell did not welcome the announcement of a date for British withdrawal from India. He was said to be in favour of persisting with the Cabinet Mission Plan which, he thought, was the only possible solution of the Indian problem. Withdrawal of British forces from India in the situation then prevailing was bound, in his view, to result in large-scale riots and disturbances. According to the account of these developments given by Maulana Abul Kalam Azad, Prime Minister Attlee did not agree with Lord Wavell.

Maulana Azad was of the view that if Wavell's advice was followed and a solution of the Indian problem deferred by some time, there was a possibility of the Muslim League getting tired of its opposition to the Cabinet Mission Plan, which could have meant the avoidance of the tragedy of India's partition. Many people thought at that time that Wavell was making a serious effort towards averting the partition of the country. Azad's perception was completely antithetical to the Muslim League's view that partition was the only alternative to a prolonged civil war.

I remember how thrilled I felt when we learnt that the British were ultimately going to leave our country, which would bring us freedom. At the same time, I had uncanny fears about the future, as we did not still know for certain what we were heading for. We were not sure if the country would remain one or was going to be vivisected, in which case either the whole of Bengal or at least its Muslim-majority eastern districts would form part of Pakistan. Both scenarios looked equally dismal to me, because my native village in the Dhaka district of east Bengal would be in Pakistan in either case. An uncertain future thus stared me in the face and robbed me of much of the joy which I otherwise felt over the prospect of freedom in the not-too-distant future. However, gradually I reconciled myself to the idea of partition with all its destabilising consequences.

It was in the midst of this atmosphere of political uncertainty that I appeared at the Intermediate Arts examination held in February-March, 1947. With the examination over, I took the opportunity of the respite I got from my college studies to pay a visit in March 1947 to my native village of Shyamsiddhi in Vikrampur which was in the Dhaka district of east Bengal. I made a point of visiting my school that was located a couple of miles away from my village. I remember how affectionately I was received by my teachers.

In my village, I met a relation of mine who was a Tantrik i.e. a practitioner of Tantra, an important school of Hindu religion. As I have explained in some chapters of my earlier book, Tantra had a long history in Vikrampur (east Bengal) to which I belonged. It was home to the old heritage of both Hindu and Buddhist Tantrism that occupied an important place in the lives of the people during the time of the Buddhist Pala rulers and some Hindu rulers of the Sena dynasty. Kedar Roy, the ruler of Vikrampur in the 16th and 17th centuries A.D. was the disciple of a Guru, who was a votary of the Virachara cult of Tantra.

Unsurprisingly, one, therefore, came across Tantriks in the villages of Vikrampur. If one had the inclination, one could get books on Tantrism for a study of the subject from the historical and religious points of view. Moreover, there were Tantriks at the cutting edge level, who, when approached by the people, used their myriad mystical powers to cure the latter of their multifarious mundane ailments of the body and the mind. I was, therefore, aware in my early life of the influence of Tantrism in Vikrampur at both the intellectual and practical planes. I kept up my interest in this subject through the study of books that came my way later in life. It is for this reason that I now go into this matter at some length.

My Tantrik relation, with whom I had developed a special rapport, used to lend me some books on Tantra. I read and re-read these books for the simple reason that they were hard nuts to crack. My relation had once told me to read Rabindranath Tagore's 'Bashikaran', which I now did. It has been written as a drama that depicts how the wife of a disenchanted husband succeeds in winning back the latter's love through the performance of Tantric rituals. One of the strange Mantras uttered by the wife refers to mother Vajrayogini as a Tantric deity. This had a familiar ring for me, because Vajrajogini was a village in Vikrampur, where, centuries ago, Dipamkara Atisa, the pioneer of Buddhist Tantricism, was born.

I was not sure if Tagore was aware of the existence of this village in Vikrampur or whether this fact had anything at all to do with the invocation of mother Vajrajogini in the Tantric Mantra that is mentioned in his story. Terms such as 'Maran', 'Uchchatan', 'Bashikaran' etc., are used in this book by Tagore to create an appropriate Tantric ambience for his story. Years later, when I saw the Vajrayogini temple at Khajuraho with the beautiful figures of divine damsels carved on its walls, I again remembered the name of Vikrampur's famous Vajrayogini village.

Studies in Tantra that I undertook many years later brought home to me that Tantrism, whether Hindu or Buddhist, had not added any new religious or spiritual philosophy to either of these religions. The basis of Tantric and non-Tantric religion is, for all practical purposes, identical, as is the case with Tantric and non-Tantric forms of Buddhism. The difference between the Tantric and non-Tantric forms of both these religions lies primarily in the fact that the Tantrics lay much greater store than the orthodox followers of these religions by various practices and rituals that form part of their Sadhana.

The difference is methodological as Tantra is the psycho-experimental interpretation of non-Tantric lore. As I read more about Tantra when I grew up, I became aware that Tantra was more value-free than non-Tantric traditions and that "moralizing and other be-good clichés are set aside to a far greater extent in Tantrism than in other doctrine."[1] Tantra pays initial homage to conventional morality but all Tantriks flout traditional orthodoxy as the situation demands. Tantra is, therefore, claimed to be a short-cut to liberation.2 In this respect there is no difference between the Tantric Sadhana of the Hindus and Vajrayana Buddhists, despite the wide divergence between their philosophies.3

Tantric Sadhana attaches considerable importance to Panchamakara that involves the use of Madya (liquor), Matsya (fish), Mamsa (meat), and Mudra (parched grain) leading to the fifth 'M' or Maithuna (copulation). From studies that I undertook later, I learnt that the elaborate and detailed instructions were given in the Tantric texts about preparations for the performance of the five 'M'-related tasks. One of these steps pertains to Vijaya-Grahana or the taking of some drug, usually hemp, that creates a feeling of euphoria in the Tantrik. Hemp (called Bhang in Hindi and Siddhi in Bengali) is, according to Mahamahopadhyaya Gopinath Kaviraj, mentioned in the Shatapatha Brahmana, which shows the old vintage of this practice.4 Among the Mantras chanted during Panchamakara Sadhana are some that invoke Shiva and Shakti.

After drinking liquor and eating the other articles of Panchamakara Sadhana, the devotee then proceeds to perform the last act of Maithuna, strictly adhering to the drill that has been prescribed and viewing himself as Shiva and his partner as Shakti, whose union he constantly aims at achieving. The climax of this event has been described in the following words by Agehananda Bharati; "In the end, he 'abandons his sperm' (Sukratyag Kare) with the following Mantra: "Om with light and ether as my two hands, I, the exulting one, relying on the ladle, I, who take dharma as his sacrificial ingredients, offer (this oblation) lovingly into the fire, svaha."5 In Buddhist Tantric Sadhana, however, the Tantrik does not eject his semen, the Vajrayana injunction being: "Nispidya Kamale Vajram BodhichittamNotsrjet" (i.e. having brought down the thunderbolt in the lotus, he should not let go the Bodhi-mind).6

As I read more about Tantra in later years, I formed the impression that it was Panchamakara Sadhana which was largely responsible for tarnishing its public image. The justification given for this form of Sadhana is that Tantra does not favour the suppression of basic human desires, but allows a Sadhaka to satisfy them by enjoying wine, meat, fish, parched rice and sexual union—the five 'M's' as they are called. The idea is that the Sadhaka thus gets over his desires in due course and can finally renounce them so as to be in a position to concentrate whole-heartedly on the truly spiritual goal. Lord Krishna has said in the Gita: "Prakrting Yanti Bhutani Nigrahang King Karisyati" (All beings follow the dictates of nature; there is no point in suppressing it).

The Panchamakara Sadhaka also puts a mystic interpretation on the meaning of the five 'M's'. It is said that the terminology used in Tantra has a meaning different from the ordinary meaning of the words. It is, therefore, wrong—so the argument runs—to regard these practices as obscene and immoral. For example, the Hindu Tantric tradition makes a distinction between Sadhana that is performed on a purely mental plane and that which involves the physical handling of the various ingredients of Panchamakara Sadhana including women. In Hindu Tantra, the latter is called Vamachara (left-handed tradition) and the former Dakshinachara (right-handed tradition).

There is a third tradition called Pratinidhi (substitute) in which the actual ingredients namely wine, meat fish etc. are replaced by substitutes like vegetables and Maithuna is symbolically performed by meditating on the conjunction of the Kundalini Shakti with Shiva at the Sahasrara Chakra.7

I remember that when I was spending my vacation in my village, my Tantrik relation used to tell me not to get misled by the many double entendres that abounded in Tantrik literature. Later when I undertook further studies in Tantra as an intellectual pastime, I came across a double entendre in the following Shloka of the Kularnava Tantra; "Alinganag Chumbanang Stanyormardanang Tatha Darshanang Sparshanang Yonorvikashe Lingagharsanam Praveshah Sthapanang Shakternabapuspani Pujana". The deeper meaning of this Shloka refers to nine 'flowers' to be offered during Tantra Sadhana, though in a literal sense, the words refer to the various stages and modes of the sex act beginning from kissing and ending in copulation and, therefore, appear to be highly obscene and vulgar, besides being untranslatable into English.

Or take for example the following Shloka; "Peetwa Peetwa Punah Patitang Dharanitale Utthaya Cha Punah Peetwa Punarjanmang Na Vidyate". The apparent reference here is to a drunkard who goes on drinking and falling on the ground because of intoxication and again gets up to have his drink. To appreciate the true meaning of this Shloka one has to understand how, according to Tantric belief, Kundalini energy rises from the Muladhara Chakra at the base of the spinal cord and passes through five other Chakras before reaching the seventh Chakra called Sahasrara, the thousand-petalled lotus, when the Tantra Sadhaka is said to attain his goal of Samadhi or self-realisation.

According to Tantra, the deeper meaning of the Shloka mentioned above is that it is the Kundalini that drinks the nectar oozing out of the Sahasrara Chakra, then comes down to the Muladhara Chakra and again goes up to the Sahasrara Chakra to drink the nectar—a process which ensures that the Sadhaka does not have to be born again. But in such cases, the underlying significance that the Tantriks attach to ordinary language is not obvious to the uninitiated, who go by the literal meaning of the ambiguous words to justify their drinking habit, thereby giving a bad name to Tantra.

A Tantric saying which has often been wrongly interpreted is "Maithunena Mahayogi Mama Tulyo Na Samshayah". The literal meaning here is that through the sexual union or copulation the Mahayogi becomes the equal of Shiva. Obviously, this is an absurd interpretation. How can one attain equality with Shiva by merely practicing coition? The true meaning of Maithuna here is'action and reaction' and'coupling', sexual intercourse being only one form of such coupling. In Yoga, there is a coupling of the active and changeless principles of the universe. The saying means that the mahayogi, who unites the Kundalini Shakti in his body with Paramshiva, himself becomes Shiva.16 (change number).

The following Tantric verse has similarly been sometimes grossly misinterpreted:

"Matr-Yanou Ksipet Lingam Bhaginyah Stanamardanam
Guror-Murdhni Padam Dattva Punarjanma Na Vidyate".

Taken literally, this means that if anybody commits incest with his mother and sister and places his foot on the head of his Guru, he is liberated from re-birth. On the face of it this is absurd. In the correct Tantric parlance, the word 'Lingam' here means the Jivatma. The triangle located at the Muladhara center with the Swayambhulinga in it is called Matriyoni. The verse thus refers to the placing of the Jivatma at the Muladhara center. The Jivatma and the Kundalini, after getting united here, move upward to the Sahasrara Chakra or the thousand-petalled lotus in the head situated above the twelve-petalled lotus, which again is the abode of his Guru. When the Yogi is above the twelve-petalled lotus, his feet may be described as being on the head of the Guru.9

The Tantriks mention the strict rules which govern the use of the five 'M's' in order to stress the point that the main object of these practices is to attain spiritual goals rather than to derive sensual pleasure. It is claimed that desire itself is subjected to rigorous discipline in order to ultimately conquer desire. 'Bisasya Bisousadham' (like cures like or poison neutralizes poison) and 'Samah Samang Shamayati' (Similia Similibus Curantur, which is the underlying principle of Homoeopathy) are the principles cited in support of the practices of Panchamakara Sadhana.

Among the restrictions imposed by Mahanirvan Tantra is one which forbids during Kali-Yuga a house-holder to partake of wine and permits only a concoction of milk, sugar and honey. The woman to be used in Panchamakara Sadhana is to be the wife of the Sadhaka. That the Tantras have counseled sexual restraint is clear from the dictum; "Maranag Bindupatena Jeevanang Bindudharanat" (the secret of good life lies in controlling the sex urge; sexual indulgence means sure death).

Without going into the metaphysical interpretation that the Sadhaka puts on the enjoyment of each of the five 'M's' and keeping aside all verbiage, it can be said that the Tantrik's main aim is to sublimate his passion rather than suppress it. The objective is to awaken the Kundalini, which is the basic energy from which man's desires, mental make-up, bahavioural pattern, sex urge etc. are derived. There is considerable similarity between this approach and the view of Dr. Freud that all behaviour is motivated by "an inner and unconscious principle, sexuality or libido". In the Indian Tantric literature, the Kundalini has a similar connotation in a rough and ready sense. Prof. Jung, a disciple of Dr. Freud, has called the sex urge the 'divine energy' – a characterization that re-inforces the same view.

While I was enjoying my study of Tantra, naturally confining myself to the intellectual plane, a serious development that took place, which reflected the reality on the ground and shook my faith not so much in the theoretical validity of Tantra as in the integrity of those who went about preaching its greatness with a view to making the ordinary people go by its precepts in actual life. A Tantrik from a neighbouring village, who had been visiting our house from time to time, prevailed upon our elders to organise a religious function with some rituals in order to ensure that there was no theft in our house thereafter. To make the house theft-proof, four 'Trishuls' (tridents) were planted in the four corners of our house.

It was also stipulated that small quantities of precious metals like gold, silver, copper etc were to be kept buried under the ground at these four corners. This was to be done by the Tantrik at night so that nobody would come to know the exact spots where the precious metals were kept, because in that case these would certainly be stolen. On the appointed day, the rituals were gone through by the Tantrik, who was sumptuously fed and paid a decent sum of money as his priestly fee. The nocturnal assignment was also completed in great secrecy, though one of the elders of our family was privy to it.

Our family felt very secure after this insurance of the household done according to Tantric rites. But within a month, there was a burglary, which involved the theft of many valuables. This came as a rude shock to all of us and dealt a serious blow to the prestige of Tantra. The Tantrik who had fed our elders on high hopes was nowhere to be found! It was then decided, in violation of the dire warning the Tantrik had previously given, to dig up the four spots where the precious metals had been buried under the ground. When the ground was opened up, there was no trace of the precious metals!

As I have already said, it would not be appropriate to form any opinion about the validity of Tantra on the basis of this incident, which no doubt showed the Tantrik in question in poor light. Many years later, I read a book which referred to some magical and mystical practices of the Tantriks of Bengal. For counteracting the menace of theft, the Tantriks suggested the following measure: "Under Pusya naksatra, in the bright half, one should collect the root of the gunja plant, which should be tied on the head."10

A fact that I noticed at this time was the atmosphere of communal harmony that prevailed in my village and in the rest of Vikrampur. While serious communal trouble had vitiated the atmosphere in many parts of Bengal, no untoward incident took place in my village or elsewhere in Vikrampur. Nothing destroyed the even tenor of life in our village. It was a sharp contrast to what happened in Kolkata, Noakhali, Tripura and at many other places of our country.

One reason for this was that in our village there was no economic rivalry or the clash of economic interests between the Muslim peasant or weaver on the one hand and the Hindu blacksmith, potter, carpenter, goldsmith, barber, milkman and cobbler on the other. The poorer sections of both communities, who were equally exploited by the upper caste Hindus, had an affinity that defied the differences of religion.

The down-trodden Hindus at the lowest rung of the caste hierarchy were in the same position as the famished and illiterate Muslim peasants whose unremitting toil provided the basis for the imposing super-structure of Bengal's economy and culture. Poverty, illiteracy and lack of consciousness accounted for their submissiveness and failure to react.

With the partition of the country, the wheels of history turned, if not full circle, at least to a degree that assured a more equitable dispensation to the millions, who had been at the receiving end for centuries. The creation of Bangladesh in 1971 was a further big step towards the fulfilment of that promise. How prophetic were poet Rabindranath Tagore's famous lines, which would translate as below:

"Oh my luckless country, those whom you have dishonoured, with them you will have to be equated in dishonour.

He, whom you pull down on the ground, will bring you down;

He, whom you have pulled from behind, is ever pulling you back."

After spending about a month in my village, I put aside the books on Tantra and returned to Kolkata. Naturally, I missed my home, my village and particularly my cousins who still lived there and in whose company I had a really good time because we were roughly of the same age group. Soon I made a trip to Dinajpur in north Bengal, where my father had been transferred from Barisal. I immensely liked this change. It was for the first time that I saw a district town of north Bengal.

Notes

1. The Tantric Tradition by Agehananda Bharati, page 20.
2. *Ibid.*, page 21.
3. *Ibid.*, page 27.
4. *Ibid.*, page 250.
5. *Ibid.*, page 265.
6. *Ibid.*, page 296.
7. *Ibid.*, page 228.
8. Arthur Avlon (Woodroffe), as cited by M.P. Pandit in his 'Lights on the Tantra', page 61.
9. *Ibid.*, page 61-62.
10. Tantra in Bengal by Dr. S.C. Banerji, page 206.

12

Plans for the Country's Vivisection

In the meantime, events on the country's political plane were moving very fast. After the British Government's declaration on February 20, 1947 that power would be transferred to Indian hands before June 1948, the Congress Party gradually reconciled itself to the fact that partition of the country was inevitable. In a letter dated March 9, 1947, addressed to Lord Wavell, Governor-General of India, Pandit Jawaharlal Nehru demanded the division of the Punjab into two Provinces—one for the Muslims and the other for the non-Muslims.

The Hindus of Bengal also started demanding a similar division of their Province. In fact, a demand on these lines had begun to be heard in the immediate aftermath of the Great Kolkata Killing of August 1946. Now that the country was going to be divided and the partition of the Punjab was being demanded by the Congress, a plea for the partition of Bengal as well on the basis of religion was put forward by the leaders of the Congress as well as the Hindu Mahasabha. It was the Hindu Mahasabha leaders of Bengal, particularly Dr. Shyama Prasad Mookerjee and N.C. Chatterjee, who played a leading role in the campaign over this issue.

How strange to think that the Hindu leaders, who had fought hard in the first decade of the 20th century to nullify the partition of Bengal, were now seeking desperately to have the Province partitioned! The Congress and the Hindu Mahasabha, which were at one time bitterly opposed to the partition of India, were now demanding the partition of Bengal, once it was known that the whole country was going to be divided on a religious basis!

Lord Mountbatten, who took over as the last British Viceroy of India on March 24, 1947, addressed himself to his task in right earnest and in a business-like manner. He held numerous meetings with political leaders of all hues before working out his plan of transferring power. During a meeting Pandit Nehru had with Lord Mountbatten on April 1, 1947, when the latter raised the question of the partition of the Punjab, Pandit Nehru mentioned the issue of the partition of Bengal as well.

The Hindu Mahasabha organised a three-day conference at Tarakeshwar in the Hooghly district of Bengal from April 4, 1947 to voice its demand for the partition of Bengal. Addressing the conference, N.C. Chatterjee, Working President of the party's Bengal unit, observed that as the Muslim League was persisting in its fantastic idea of establishing Pakistan in Bengal, the Hindus of Bengal had no alternative but to ask for a separate Province under a strong National Government. Dr. Shyama Prasad Mookerjee, who spoke at the conference on April 5, 1947, declared: " I can conceive of no other solution of the communal problem in Bengal than to divide the province and let the two major communities residing herein live in peace and freedom." He also welcomed the resolution adopted on April 4, 1947 by the Bengal Provincial Congress Committee demanding the partition of Bengal. The Bengal Congress had also demanded, pending the final transfer of power by the British to Indian hands, the formation of two separate interim governments in the Hindu-majority and the Muslim-majority regions of Bengal. The Hindu Mahasabha leaders of Bengal upped the ante by demanding that even if India was not partitioned, a separate Province should be formed comprising the Hindu-majority areas of Bengal. On April 23, 1947, Dr. Shyama Prasad Mookerjee called on Lord Mountbatten in Delhi and explained the case for the partition of Bengal.

M.A. Jinnah met Lord Mountbatten a number of times during the first half of April, 1947 and demanded the partition of India. Mountbatten told him that if he accepted Jinnah's arguments on the need for the partition of India, then he would not be in a position to resist the arguments the Congress Party was putting forward for the partition of the Punjab and Bengal.

H.S. Suhrawardy, Chief Minister of the Muslim League-led Government of Bengal, fought hard against the move to partition Bengal and to counter this, he announced, at a press conference in

Delhi on April 27,1947, a plan for a 'sovereign independent united Bengal', a third entity outside both India and Pakistan. The Shurawardy faction of the Muslim League had some reservations about Jinnah's plea for the establishment of a sovereign Pakistan encompassing the two Muslim-majority wings in the west and the east, which would lack geographical contiguity.

A year earlier, on April 7, 1946, at the Delhi convention of Muslim League leaders, the language of the Lahore Resolution, which had demanded the creation of two separate sovereign Muslim states—one in the west and another in the east—had been changed at the instance of M.A. Jinnah by substituting the word 'state' for 'states', thus making it clear that the party now demanded a single, unified state of Pakistan. Many Bengalee Muslim leaders such as Abdul Hashim, General Secretary of the Bengal Muslim League, and Maulana Abdul Hamid Khan Bhashani, President of the Assam Muslim League, had strongly protested against this change in the wording of the Lahore Resolution and pleaded for the creation of a separate independent state of Bengal in view of the lack of geographical contiguity between the two wings and cultural and linguistic differences between them. The Bengalee Muslim leaders were, however, over-ruled.

Meanwhile, H.S. Suhrawardy and the other Muslim League leaders of Bengal mounted a vigorous campaign in favour of a united sovereign Bengal where, they hoped, the Muslims and the Hindus would live in amity. One of the promises held out to make the proposal attractive to the Hindus was a system of joint electorates. Abul Hashim, Secretary of the Bengal Muslim League, promised that the Hindus and the Muslims would be guaranteed scrupulous implementation of "C.R. Das's formula of 50:50 enjoyment of political power and economic privileges." A factor that weighed with Suhrawardy was that he could not contemplate with equanimity the loss of Kolkata to Pakistan if Bengal was divided. Suhrawardy was also reported to have proposed to include in the undivided Bengal as visualised by him some areas from Bihar such as Manbhum, Singhbhum and Purnea as well as the Surma Valley of Assam. This was a sop he was said to be willing to offer to the Hindus, as in an enlarged united Bengal of this kind, the Hindus and the Muslims would have been almost equal in number.

Some Hindu leaders like Sarat Chandra Bose and Kiran Shankar Roy (of the Congress Party) fell in line with Suhrawardy and extended their active support to the demand for a united sovereign Bengal. Sir Frederick Burrows, Governor of Bengal,was in favour of this proposal and plumped for the Congress joining hands with the Muslim League to form a coalition Government in the Province. But the Congress was not persuaded.

The Communist Party of India did not support the demand for the partition of Bengal and was in favour of the creation of Pakistan with an undivided Bengal forming part of it. During the party-led 'Tebhaga' movement which was in progress in some districts of Bengal at this time, many Hindu and Muslim peasants were voicing the demand for preserving the unity of Bengal. But this was a passing phase, because later the party changed its line.

Sarat Chandra Bose and H.S. Suhrawardy had several meetings with Mahatma Gandhi, then camping at the Sodepur Ashram, not very far from Kolkata, and pleaded for his support. Gandhiji initially took a stand which appeared to be supportive of the idea of a united Bengal, he later said that he would have the proposal placed before the Congress Working Committee for taking a decision. When asked by Lord Mountbatten for his views on this matter, Pandit Jawaharlal Nehru was believed to have replied that the Congress Party would accept the proposal only if a united Bengal remained in India.

The Muslim League leaders of Bengal along with some from the Congress Party organised a series of public meetings to mobilise public opinion in favour of their proposal for a sovereign united Bengal. They hammered out a tentative agreement which they signed on May 20,1947. Suhrawardy forwarded the proposal to Jinnah and Sarat Bose to Gandhiji. After discussions with Pandit Nehru and Sardar Patel, Gandhiji advised Sarat Bose in a letter dated June 1,1947 to give up the proposal. Bose and Kiran Shankar Roy later met Sardar Patel, who disagreed with them. Some years later, I learnt that the Congress Party had agreed to the partition of India and the creation of Pakistan on the condition that Bengal would be partitioned with Kolkata remaining in India[1].

Sarat Bose felt disappointed and reacted by recalling the many sacrifices the Hindus of Bengal had made during their struggle to undo the partition of Bengal in 1905. He also criticised the Central leaders of the Congress Party for "the ill-treatment C.R.Das and Netaji

Subhas Chandra Bose, his brother, had received from North Indian leaders", forcing them to leave the Congress and respectively form the Swarajya Party and the Forward Bloc. But Sarat Chandra Bose's feelings were not reciprocated by most of the Hindus of Bengal as contemporary writings in the Hindu press made it obvious. In those days, I used to read the Amrita Bazar Patrika, the Kolkata daily, which published a "Survey of Opinion" that brought out the Bengalee Hindus' overwhelming support for the partition of Bengal and the retention of West Bengal in India.

There was another proposal made by Sir Frederick Burrows, Governor of Bengal, which suggested the conversion of Kolkata into a free city and port outside Bengal, catering to the economic requirements of both India and Pakistan. It was generally believed that the proposal was aimed at safeguarding the interests of Englishmen, who at that time had a dominant say in the trade and industry of Kolkata. Burrows argued that if Kolkata was included in West Bengal on the basis of its Hindu majority, it would amount to ignoring the great contribution that east Bengal had made to the city's prosperity. Moreover, the Governor urged, Kolkata's merger with West Bengal would adversely affect the fortunes of east Bengal whose economy was vitally dependent on that city. However, the industrialists of Bengal, both Hindu and Muslim, did not generally support the proposal for a free city of Kolkata. On April 28, 1947, Lord Mountbatten communicated to Governor Sir Frederick Burrows that he did not like the idea of a free city of Kolkata, because it went against all the principles on which the plan for the whole country was going to be based.

The Hindus of Bengal generally believed that, after an independent State of Bengal was formed, Suhrawardy was likely to take advantage of the Muslim community's majority in such a State to drag the whole of Bengal into Pakistan. This became quite clear from what Jinnah told Lord Mountbatten during a meeting on April 26, 1947. Though Jinnah was initially opposed to the idea of a united sovereign Bengal and had in fact opposed a coalition between the Muslim League and the Congress to form a government in Bengal after the elections held in 1946, Suhrawardy was able to persuade him to change his mind by telling him that a united sovereign Bengal could eventually join Pakistan. When Jinnah met Lord Moutbatten in Delhi on April 26, 1947, the latter sought his views about a sovereign independent Bengal. Jinnah had welcomed the proposal saying that he was sure that such a state would be on friendly terms with Pakistan. Lord Mountbatten thought that Jinnah was prepared to accept Suhrawardy's plan, because an independent Bengal with its Muslim majority would be a sort of subsidiary Pakistan.

On June 3, 1947, when Lord Mountbatten announced the plan for the partition of the country, I was still at Dinajpur. I recall our excitement when we gathered around the radio to hear Lord Mountbatten disclose the features of this plan. The reception on the radio set was not very clear. This, along with our inability to properly comprehend the English that Mountbatten spoke, left most of us in doubt as to what the details of the plan were. We kept on debating about it till late in the night. It was from next morning's newspapers that we got a true version of the plan, which, I then realised, was going to seal our fate for ever.

Mountbatten's plan provided for the partition of India and the creation of a new State of Pakistan consisting of the Muslim-majority Provinces with the proviso that the Hindu-majority areas of Bengal and the Punjab would have the option of joining the Indian Union. Provisions were also made for plebiscites in the North West Frontier Province and in the Sylhet district of Assam to decide whether they would join Pakistan. Boundary Commissions were to go into the question of demarcating the boundaries of the Hindu-majority and Muslim-majority areas of Bengal and the Punjab which would respectively be merged with India and Pakistan. Immediately after Lord Mountbatten, Pandit Nehru, M.A. Jinnah and Sardar Baldev Singh spoke over the All-India Radio to signify their acceptance of the plan for the vivisection of the country. The next morning (i.e. on June 4, 1947), Lord Mountbatten announced at a press conference that the date of the British withdrawal from India had been advanced to August 15, 1947 from June 1948, which had been declared earlier.

Suhrawardy and Sarat Bose continued to pursue the idea of an independent Bengal even after the Cabinet Mission Plan was announced on June 3, 1947. But the Central leaders of the Muslim League did not favour the creation of an independent Bengal and asked for a united Pakistan comprising all territories where the Muslims were in a majority. The Hindus of West Bengal naturally did not favour a united Bengal where they would have been reduced to the status of a minority.

The realisation that I would lose my home in east Bengal where I was born and where I had lived more than16 of the 18 years that was my age then left me cold and robbed me of quite some share of the joy which freedom was otherwise going to bring for me as for all the people of the Indian sub-continent.

I soon returned to Kolkata from Dinajpur and waited for August 15, 1947, the date fixed by Mountbatten for the transfer of power to India, which would mean the creation of two Dominions within the British Commonwealth of Nations—India and Pakistan—with Bengal and Punjab divided on the basis of religion, one part of each joining India and the other Pakistan.

The Congress Working Committee signified its acceptance of the plan. Mahatma Gandhi was opposed to it because it would result in the partition of the country. He had made his views known to the Congress High Command. And yet on the 14th of June, 1947, when the All-India Congress Committee met at Bombay to consider this matter, Gandhiji advised the delegates to support the Congress Working Committee's stand and accept the plan. The general impression in the country at that time was that, though Gandhiji was opposed to the vivisection of the country, it was his sense of party discipline and loyalty to the party, apart from his sense of pragmatism, that had led him to tender this advice.

Maulana Abul Kalam Azad persisted in his opposition to partition and was shocked to find that even Gandhiji had changed his mind. Khan Abdul Ghaffar Khan, the North West Frontier Province leader, was stunned when he found that that the Congress Working Committee had accepted partition—a stance which, Khan felt, the North West Frontier Province would consider as an act of treachery on the part of the Congress.

When the All-India Congress Committee met on June 14, 1947 to consider the Congress Working Committee's proposal for the acceptance of partition, Gandhiji threw his weight behind the Working Committee, because he felt that there was no other alternative. When the resolution was put to vote, according to Azad, 29 voted for it and 15 against, despite Gandhiji's appeal for support to the resolution.

Mutually conflicting reports about Mahatma Gandhi's stand vis-à-vis the partition of India continued to surface in later years. For example, Pyarelal, Private Secretary to the Mahatma, has argued in his book 'Mahatma Gandhi-The Last Phase' that the latter had serious misgivings about partition, while the Congress leaders generally favoured it. At a meeting of the Congress Working Committee held on June 25,1946, Gandhiji, according to Pyarelal, told them: "I admit defeat. You are not bound to act on my unsupported suspicion. You should follow the dictates of your reason." Further, in the words of Pyarelal: "In that hour of decision, they had no use for Bapu. They decided to drop the pilot. Bapu returned to his residence. At noon, the Cabinet Mission invited the members of the Working Committee to meet them. Bapu, not being a member, was not sent for and did not go. On their return, nobody told Bapu a word about what had happened at the meeting."

An American expert on South Asia, Prof. Stanely Wolpert, in a lecture delivered at Rawalpindi on March 27, 1998, was reported as having observed that Gandhiji was not in favour of the partition of India and had in fact offered Jinnah the Prime Ministership of an undivided India, but both Pandit Nehru and Lord Moutbatten, Viceroy of India, had opposed the proposal. But all these arguments cannot explain certain facts which favour the other view that Gandhiji had in fact accepted the proposal for partition in the then prevailing circumstances, though he would have been happier if partition could have been avoided. In this context, it is pertinent to quote what Gandhiji had written in the Harijan dated April 6,1940: "The Muslims must have the same right of self-determination that the rest of India has. We are at present a joint family. Any member may claim a division."

The members of the A.I.C.C. from Sind opposed the proposal for partition, while Kiran Shankar Roy, an important Congress leader from east Bengal, remained unreconciled to the idea till the end.

I was in Kolkata on June 20, 1947, when the majority of the members of Bengal's Legislative Assembly voted to join Pakistan. Then the members from the Hindu-majority districts of Bengal voted to express their preference for joining the Indian Union. This meant that Bengal would be partitioned and the Hindu-majority districts and Kolkata would remain in the Indian Union, while the Muslim-majority districts would form part of Pakistan. The communist members of the Assembly, including Jyoti Basu, who had once been in the vanguard of the agitation against the partition of Bengal, also voted in favour of partition.

The fate of Kolkata was decided by the Partition Council of Bengal, which had an equal number of Hindu and Muslim members with Governor Burrows as its Chairman. The Muslim representatives generally wanted Kolkata to be included in East Pakistan, claiming that the city's economic prosperity was primarily linked with jute grown mainly in east Bengal. The Hindus, of course, wanted Kolkata to remain in West Bengal. Governor Burrows was reported to have supported the Muslim viewpoint and offered to vote for Kolkata's inclusion in East Pakistan in case of a tie. But since a Muslim member of the Partition Council joined the Hindus at the time of voting, Kolkata was given to West Bengal. It was a slender margin indeed by which Kolkata's umbilical link with West Bengal was preserved! Some among the Muslim League representatives from east Bengal did not feel particularly unhappy over this development, because, by excluding Kolkata from east Pakistan, they hoped to cut at the root of Suhrawardy's political strength which largely depended on his hold among the Muslim masses of Kolkata. This was a good example of the old English saw about cutting one's nose to spite one's face.

A shadow cabinet for West Bengal with Dr. P.C. Ghosh, a veteran Congress leader and a Gandhian, as Chief Minister, was formed on July 3, 1947. Though formally H. S. Suhrawardy continued to be the Chief Minister of Bengal as a whole till August 15, 1947, before any action was taken on matters concerning the districts of West Bengal, the concurrence of the shadow cabinet for West Bengal was sought.

Two Boundary Commissions, both headed by sir Cyril Radcliffe, a British judge, demarcated the boundaries between the two Bengals and the two Punjabs and submitted the reports to Lord Mountbatten on August 9, 1947. However, it was only after August 15, 1947 i.e. after the transfer of power that the recommendations of the two Commissions were made public and then implemented. Though some of these recommendations were considered to be arbitrary by both Hindus and Muslims, these were generally accepted by all concerned as they were in the nature of an award.

Soon Khwaja Nazimuddin was elected as the Chief Minister of East Bengal that was to form part of Pakistan. H.S. Suhrawardy to whom Pakistan owed so much became a nonentity for some time, but after a few years, he made his presence felt in East Pakistan.

I realised that the die had been cast and that I would have to bid adieu for ever to our home in Vikrampur. The prospect of living in Kolkata without any piece of land which we would be able to regard as our own homestead filled my mind with the fear of facing an uncertain future. I started feeling 'homeless' already and many of our acquaintances in Kolkata called us 'refugees' – or sometimes a little more euphemistically – 'displaced persons'. However, most of the people of Kolkata displayed no such condescension but rather made friendly gestures to us in view of the catastrophe that had befallen us.

Notes

1. Raghib Ahsan, A note on the Inner History of the United Bengal Scheme, cited at page 30 of the Memoirs of Huseyn Shaheed Suhrawardy edited by Mohammad H.R.Talukdar.

13

Presidency College : Our Dreaming Spire

One fine morning, some time in the middle of 1947, I was pleasantly surprised to see my name in a boxed news item on the front pages of newspapers. The precious news was that I had passed the Intermediate Arts examination quite creditably, my name figuring at the second place in the list of the 'first ten' that was published. I was naturally overjoyed. It was a shot in the arm for me and a matter of great pride for the members of my family. This, I realised, was a reward for the very hard work that I had put in. Some of my college friends tried to seek me out to congratulate me, but failed to do so because they could not simply locate the place where I lived.

Back home in Vikrampur (east Bengal), the news of my good result in the I.A. examination was greeted with great jubilation by the teachers and students of my school and was the occasion for the headmaster of my school to pen a congratulatory letter addressed to me on behalf of the members of the staff and the students—a letter which I read again and again when I received it in Kolkata.

My father agreed with me that I could now join the famous Presidency College for my Bachelor of Arts course. So one day in the month of July 1947—-if memory serves me aright—I paid a visit to the Presidency College to explore the possibility and the modalities of getting admission into the B.A. course. It was a thrilling experience, as I entered its hallowed precincts. I could hardly believe that I was now standing before a college that had become a part of Bengal's history as the symbol of the Bengal Renaissance and the cradle of intellectualism. The Dorian edifice of the college looked distinctive and impressive and the verdure of the extensive playing fields soothed one's eyes. An atmosphere of academic serenity hung around the place with very little of the hustle and bustle that one saw in most of the other Kolkata colleges.

Inside the cloistered college building, the atmosphere was almost monastic. The ancientness of its look was re-inforced by the tattered remnants of graffiti splattered on the outer walls, the rickety latticed notice board on the walls along the long corridors displaying outdated orders on old paper that looked sepia and brittle, and the unpolished but sturdy furniture in the rooms to whose high ceilings old cowebs clung so tenaciously that they refused to flutter even when the creaking electric fans went full blast.

I had heard and read a lot about the glorious history of this premier educational institution of Asia. Initially started by the British in 1817 as the Hindu College, it was renamed as the Presidency College in 1855, two years before the Calcutta University was established in 1857. The junior section of the Hindu College was then converted into a school and named as the Hindu School.

James Sutcliffe was the last Principal of the Hindu College and the first Prinicipal of the Presidency College. At that time, Pandit Ishwar Chandra Vidyasagar was the Principal of the Sanskrit College on the other side of the College Square. The Hindu College was meant for the Hindu students only just as the Calcutta Madrasa established in 1785 A.D. was exclusively for the Muslim students. The renaming of the Hindu College as the Presidency College in 1855 A.D. meant that its doors were now thrown open to students from all communities.

The Hindu College and the Young Bengal Society consisting of a group of some progressive students of the college played a pioneering role in spreading Western ideas and the spirit of free enquiry in Bengal. Henry Louis V. Derozio, a young poet and critic in his early twenties, who was appointed a teacher of the Hindu College in view of his extraordinary brilliance, was the leader of the Young Bengal Society. He inculcated in the students the values of liberalism and freethinking, which often bordered on the glorification of atheism. As he said in a poem he had composed:

" I watch the gentle opening of your minds
And the sweet loosening of the spell that binds
Your intellectual energies and powers."

Derozio became a highly controversial figure in Bengal because of his ultra-modernism that led him to encourage his student followers to take Western food and imbibe alcohol. Naturally, he drew flak from the conservative section of Hindu society for ridiculing what he regarded as the irrational religious practices of the Hindus. But his student disciples worshipped him for his rational thinking, his patriotism (which was unexpected in a Firangi, as he was generally called) and his fierce opposition to the use of authoritarian methods by the British in holding India under the imperialist yoke. He was eventually compelled to give up his college job. He died prematurely at the age of just 22 years on December 23, 1831.

Among the alumni of the Presidency College, there were several eminent Bengalees of that period as will be seen from a facsimile of the college's attendance register of 1858, which is reproduced below[1] :

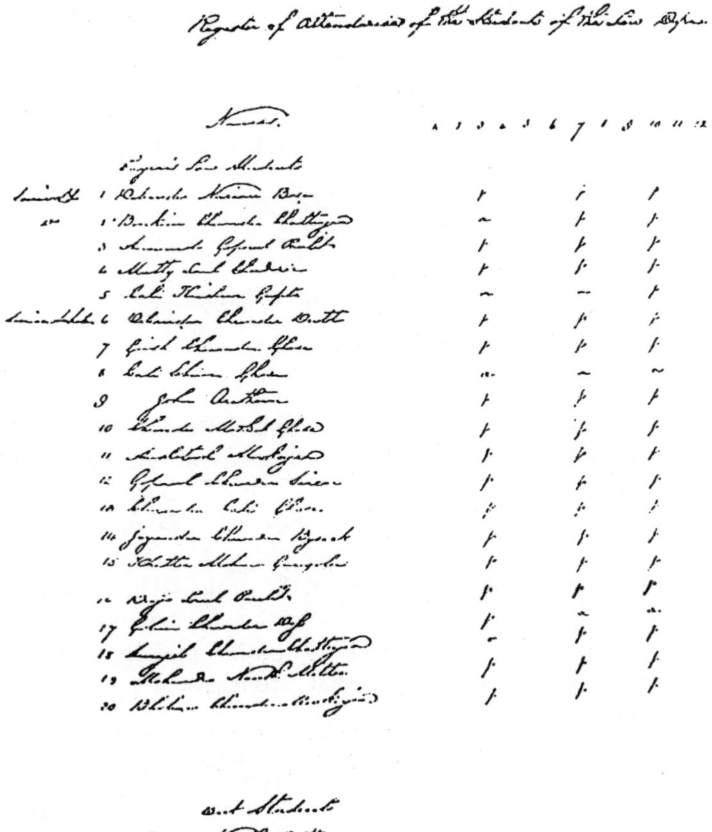

Bankim Chandra Chatterjee, Chandra Madhab Ghose and Sanjeev Chandra Chatterjee figure at roll numbers 2,10 and 18 respectively of the third year law class. Bankim Chandra and Jadunath Basu were the first graduates of the Calcutta University, who passed the first B.A. examination held in 1858 A.D.

The Hindu College (later renamed Presidency College) functioned from several buildings after its inception in 1817 A.D. It was on March 31, 1874 that the Presidency College shifted to its present location, the event being inaugurated by the Lt. Governor of Bengal in the presence of the Viceroy of India. It was a great event indeed!

Today, when I think of the majestic building of the Presidency College, what leaps up before my eyes is the clock at the top of the turret. The cost of this clock was met from a donation of Rs. 4000/- made in August 1874 by Baboo Naffar Chandra Pal Chowdhuri, Zamindar of Latoodak, Krishnagar. The procurement of the clock from London and its installation involved long correspondence among various departments of the government. A copy of a letter written in this regard by one of the concerned officials to another is reproduced below[2]:

No. 4272

From : The Offg. Director of Public Instructions

To

The Secretary to the Government of Bengal,
General Department,
Fort Willam, the 14 September, 1874.

Sir,

I have the honor to forward in original letter No. 1486 from the Offg. Principal of the Presidency College with enclosure and to request that as suggested in para 3 of Mr. Tawney's letter, Government will be pleased to allow the clock to be procured direct from England by the Babu or the Principal without the intervention of the Secretary of State I may add that the Principal has in his hands the necessary details and estimates for the construction of a first-class Turret clock by one of the best London makers and that an order from him will receive immediate attention.

I have the honor to be

Sir
Your most obedient servant
Sd/-J.Sutcliffe
Offg. Director of Public Instn.

I had never seen this clock in working condition, because it had gone out of order in 1927 and had not been repaired ever since. I understand that it was repaired in 1997 – after a gap of 70 years! I hope that it continues to tick.

The rich traditions of the college were built over a long period as much by the galaxy of its dedicated teachers as by its brilliant students for whom the purity of learning and the desire to excel counted for more than anything else. Like the scholars of European renaissance typified by Robert Browning's Grammarian, they had held aloft the torch of classical learning and unceasing endeavour in their quest for knowledge. Many of its students were careerists all right, as witness the number it has contributed to the country's civil services – the Indian Civil Service, the Indian Police, the Central and Provincial services and the judiciary as well as the corresponding services that came into being after our country attained independence. They constituted a formidable number among the boxwallahs as well. This was a shining example of how Macaulay's plan to churn out English-knowing 'Babus' reached fruition.

To counter the charge of careerism that is often hurled at its students, you have to look at the large number of those who passed through its portals and did well in the professions including the bar as well as in the political field. They were in the fore-front of the country's freedom struggle. Most of the important political leaders of Bengal and of India at one time were its students. Among those who figured on the rolls of this college were Netaji Subhas Chandra Bose, Dr. P.C. Ghosh, West Bengal's Chief Minister at the time of partition and Dr Rajendra Prasad, who later became the first President of the Indian Republic.

Did Subhas Chandra Bose not give up a career in the Indian Civil Service and fling himself heart and soul in the struggle for his motherland's freedom? Did he think of his career when he 'oatenised' E.F. Oaten, Professor of History, for having the audacity of boasting before the students of Great Britain's historic mission of civilising the Indians as the Greeks had, centuries ago, Hellenised the barbarians outside Greece? It is another matter that the historians subsequently came to the conclusion that he had not assaulted Oaten and that, decades later, this very professor spoke affectionately of Bose after he heard that the latter had allegedly perished in an air-crash at Taihoku. Students of the Presidency College would readily recall in this context the professor's touching tribute to Bose in a sonnet that he had composed:

" Did I once suffer, Subhas, at your hand ?
Your patriot heart is stilled. I would forget."

It has been rightly said that almost everybody, who was somebody in Bengal, was associated with the Presidency College – men of letters like Bankim Chandra Chatterjee and Michael Madhusudan Dutta, the great spiritual leader Swami Vivekananda and scientists of the stature of Jagadish Chandra Bose, Meghnad Saha and Acharya Prafulla Chandra Ray. Even Rabindranath Tagore was its student, though only for a day! It would amount to a virtual roll call of all the great men of Bengal, if one were to mention the names of all those who had something or other to do with this college. Even the first President of Bangladesh, Abu Sayeed Choudhury, was one of its illustrious pupils and its Magazine Secretary at one time.

In August 1947, I sought admission into the Presidency College, filling up the requisite forms for taking up honours in English literature with History as a subsidiary subject. Soon, however, I realised that a subject which had over the years come to acquire great importance and relevance was Economics. It had become fashionable for the comparatively better students of those days to take up Economics, which was a tough subject that posed a good deal of challenge to one's intellect.

By the latter half of the nineteen forties, the study of Economics had also acquired the potential of opening up good career prospects. The end of the Second World War had brought to the fore the question of economic reconstruction in many countries. The emergence of a number of newly independent countries in the post-war period led to an upsurge of interest in economic development with a view to bettering the lot of their poor millions. This brought in its trail an increased demand for expertise and specialisation in economic, commercial and technological subjects. Universities all over the world, therefore, started laying greater store by the study of Economics, Business Administration, Engineering etc.

Considering the pros and cons, I changed my mind about the subject of my honours course and decided to switch over to Economics. I went to the Presidency College again and submitted a fresh set of forms for admission to the honours course in Economics.

I joined the Eden Hindu Hostel, whose nearness to the college premises saved me the hassle of journeying to and from the college by bus or tram-car. I was quite impressed by this hostel that was home to a large number of brilliant students of all classes ranging from the Intermediate to the post-graduate. I was excited by the opportunity I had of rubbing shoulders with the creme de la creme of the university among the hostel's boarders. I could see how they lived, studied and played their games and how they discussed all kinds of subjects—politics, philosophy, literature, music and cultural activities. I felt proud that in some of the rooms of the Hindu Hostel, many of Bengal's and some of India's great men had lived at some time or other.

The Eden Hindu Hostel was meant for the Hindu students only. Decades later—in 1999—I read reports in the press about the bid made by a Muslim student of the Presidency College to get admission into the Eden Hindu Hostel. By then, the winds of secularism had been sweeping the academic world of West Bengal and the rest of our country. But there was some difficulty in opening the gates of the Hindu Hostel to a Muslim student. The property on which the hostel was built had been gifted by a ruler's family of Midnapore on the explicit understanding that none but Hindu students would lodge there. A prolonged agitation was launched by the secular-minded students of the college to press the demand of the Muslim student. Then the West Bengal Government's Education Department made the necessary change in the rules allowing non-Hindus to join the Hindu Hostel.

But simultaneously, another problem cropped up. There are two other hostels—the Baker Hostel for the students of the Maulana Azad College and the Carmichael Hostel for those of the Medical College—where only Muslim students could be admitted. In the face of the relaxation of rules in respect of the Hindu Hostel, the Muslim students of the Baker and Carmichael Hostels launched an agitation to ensure that no similar relaxation was made allowing non-Muslims to lodge in these hostels. The controversy in regard to the Hindu Hostel came to a formal end in December, 2001 when an undergraduate Muslim student of chemistry by name S.O. Raza was admitted as a boarder.

Many students of the Presidency College with brilliant academic records to their credit were day scholars and did not put up at the Eden Hindu Hostel. I had the opportunity of meeting them at the college. It was for the first time that I met so many brilliant students, some of whom were better than I. Like Wordsworth's 'blessed creatures', they had in their eyes 'the visionary gleam, the glory and the dream', because they had arrived at the Presidency College, 'trailing clouds of glory'.

Among the alumni of the college who had attracted notice was Amartya Sen, who became a Nobel laureate in Economics decades later. A few years junior to me, he joined the B.A. (honours) class in Economics when I was a post-graduate student at the Calcutta University. Even at that initial stage, he had hogged much limelight as a brilliant student by virtue of an article in Bengali he had written for the Presidency College magazine, which, I vaguely recall, was entitled "Vijnapaner Arthaniti" (i.e. the economics of advertisement). He had tried to show in this article that the expenses incurred on advertisement by a firm selling a commodity got added to its cost of production and were thus passed on to the consumer. (I must add here that I do not have this article before me as I write all this. Since I am drawing upon my memory for writing all this, I must request the reader to bear with me if I am found to be wrong in making these points.)

Classical economics based on the ideas of Adam Smith and Alfred Marshall that held the field for a very long time assumed that perfect competition and monopoly represented the two models of the market economy. Then came along Prof. Joan Robinson of the Cambridge University and Prof. Edward Chamberlin of Harvard, whose seminal books 'Economics of Imperfect Competition, and 'Theory of Monopolistic Competition' respectively supplemented this hitherto accepted notion and revolutionized the thinking in this regard. Marshallian economics had posited that manufacturing cost was the dominant item on the supply side that determined the cost of production. Chamberlin's theory of monopolistic competition put forward the concept of selling cost (including the cost of advertisement) as another factor that played an important role in determining the cost of production.

Amartya Sen's article showed an awareness of these new ideas, though, after the lapse of more than half a century, I do not clearly remember if he had mentioned anything about his having read these new treatises. I do, however, clearly recall that some of us post-graduate students of the Calcutta University had informally discussed this article among ourselves and come to the conclusion that Sen was indeed a brilliant student who was destined to make his mark as an original thinker in times to come.

Before joining the Presidency College, I had heard the names of many of its eminent professors — names that still stand out such as those of Dr. P.C. Ghosh (English), Sir Jehangir Coyasjee (Economics), M. Qudrat-i-Khuda, A.K. Chanda (English) and Dr. Kuruvilla Zackariah (History). They were the last words in their respective subjects in scholarship. Prof. Srikumar Banerji of the English Department, who had left the Presidency College to head the Bengali Department at the Calcutta University, was a rare academic specimen, whose scholarship in both languages was oceanic, in sweep as well as depth. I had seen him later at the Calcutta University, where, referring to his ever serious looks, some students used to jokingly say that he surely had a quinine tablet under his tongue all the time. What he was known for among the students at large was his penchant for bombastic and poly-syllabic words and long and winding sentences, which often went over the heads of those to whom he lectured.

Among the many outstanding professors of the college in 1947 was Prof. Susobhan Sarkar of the History Department, who attracted you as much by his graceful personal demeanour as by his intellectual eminence which compelled you to pay much greater attention to your study of Marxist classics than you might otherwise have done. Professor Sarkar was a committed Marxist intellectual of an extraordinarily high calibre, whose Bengali book on history written from the Marxist view-point, I read from cover to cover.

Among the professors of English literature who taught us were Tarak Nath Sen, an intellectual giant, whose lectures on Shakespeare's 'As You Like It', we made it a point never to miss and whose indifference to things mundane symbolised his spirit of academic detatchment; S.N. Maitra with his good aristocratic looks whom I specially remember for his masterly exposition of the philosophy underlying Wordsworth's 'Intimations of Immortality from Recollections of Early Childhood'; Dr. Subodh Chandra Sengupta — who dilated in his suave and soft-spoken voice in crisp

English that avoided using a word too many—on Bertrand Russel's agnostic philosophy, which was the subject matter of a prescribed piece of English prose; Tarapada Mukherjee, whose lectures on 'Macbeth' were accompanied by appropriate gestures of his hands and face as well as by the right kind of modulation in his voice; and Sadananda Chakraborti, with his young and often unshaven face whose talks on Lamb's 'The Superannuated Man' ably brought out how deep the wood had entered the soul of the frustrated English author. The last-named professor, I learnt, had a spiritual bent of mind even at that rather young age.

In the Department of Sanskrit, there was Prof. Gauri Nath Shastri, who later became the Vice-Chancellor of the Benares Sanskrit University. His brother, Dr. Ashoke Shastri was the Principal of the near-by Sanskrit College, whose annotated notes on many important Sanskrit works of poetry and drama we used to read in college. Many students of the Presidency College with a multi-disciplinary approach to studies, who took interest in a wide range of subjects, often attended Prof. Susobhan Sarkar's lectures on the French Revolution and Prof. Gauri Nath Shastri's exposition of Kalidasa's 'Abhijnan Shakuntalam', even though these themes had nothing to do with their honours subjects.

Dr. J.C. Sinha, who, as the Head of the Economics Department and the Vice-Principal of the Presidency College, taught us Indian Economics was a great authority on Bengal's economic history. One of the professors of the Economics Department was U.N.Ghoshal, who had a degree from the London School of Economics and spoke in an impressive style. Another professor was the ever cheerful R.N. Chatterjee, who, while lecturing on economic theory, not only himself burst into peals of hearty laughter, but often had the whole class as well in splits over his humorous observations.

Durgagati Chattoraj, who taught Political Science (which was then a part of the Economics syllabus), kept on looking, as he lectured, at the rafters in the ceiling through the corner of his bespectacled eyes, while we took down copious notes from his famous talks on the 'Politics of Aristotle'. A dictum of Political Science which Prof. Chattoraj often dinned into our ears was—'Back to Artistotle'—which meant that if you did not get the right answer to some question in the realm of political philosophy, you should consult the works of Aristotle, where you are most likely to get the answer you are looking for.

Behind his look of philosophical indifference lurked a fine sense of humour of which we became aware one day when, during his lecture, seeing that some students were engaged in talking to each other in muffled voices, he ticked them off by intoning, in a sing-song voice, the first line of a popular romantic song that the famous Bengalee film actress, Kanan Devi had sung—"Yadi Bhalo Na Lage To Diyo Na Mon" (if you do not like, pay no heed to me).

Most of the professors of the Presidency College were authorities on their respective subjects and many of them used to lecture at post-graduate classes of the Calcutta University. The British had created the Indian Education Service which boasted some of the greatest names of the academic world. After we gained independence on the 15th of August, 1947, almost all Englishmen, who were borne on the cadre of this service, left the country. P.C.Mahalanobis, a member of this service and the doyen of the teaching staff was the Principal of the college when I joined it. I occasionally saw him when he entered or left the college premises or walked along the corridors towards his room. He looked suave and sophisticated.

Even before I joined the Presidency College, I had heard the story of how Prof. Mahalanobis married Nirmalkumari (also known as Rani), the daughter of Prof. Heramba Maitra, an eminent educationist and Principal of Kolkata's City College. There was a touch of romance in this affair, which had aroused quite some controversy in Kolkata's Brahmo circles. I heard many of the stories about Principal Maitra from my eldest brother, who had passed his B.A. examination from the City College.

An incident for which Principal Maitra became famous had taken place on a Kolkata street, where a young man, who was passing by, asked him about the location of the Star Theatre. Principal Maitra did not like people to see professional theatrical shows and so did not want to do anything towards helping the young man in making it to the theatre. He told the latter that he did not know where the Star Theatre was located. Soon thereafter, however, he realised that he had told a lie. So he hurried up to the young man and told him that he knew the way to the Star Theatre, but would not tell him how to go there! Such was the strength of Principal Maitra's moral fibre and the courage of his conviction.

I recalled Principal Maitra's principled stand on this issue very recently when I read a piece in a newspaper[3] on the controversy kicked up in Britain over the move to ban fox-hunting. Philosopher Bertrand Russell, who was opposed to fox-hunting, had recounted an incident that took place when, during a stroll in the countryside, he came upon a fox running away from its pursuers. The hunters, who soon arrived with their baying hounds, asked Russell if he had seen the fox. Russell nodded and pointed in a direction opposite to the one the fox had gone! Unlike Principal Maitra, he did not mind that he had not spoken the truth nor did he go back to the hunters to say that he knew which way the fox had gone, but that he would not tell them.

Soon after his return from England on completion of his studies, Mahalanobis sought the hand of Nirmalkumari, but the proposal for marriage was threatened by a controversy about the rites to be followed in solemnising it. Principal Maitra insisted on the registration of his daughter's marriage in keeping with the practice followed by the Brahmo Samaj. Mahalanobis did not like the idea of registration and wanted Hindu rites to be followed. This created a difficulty which Mahalanobis got over by adopting a course of action that gradually drew him closer to the Maitra family. He started frequently visiting Principal Maitra's house and spending a lot of time with Nirmalkumari, who was then recovering from a spell of serious illness. Sitting by her bed-side, he recited Rabindranath Tagore's poems to Nirmalkumari and in due course succeeded in papering over the cracks that had appeared in the wake of the controversy over the rites of the marriage ceremony.

The marriage took place, but not according to Brahmo rites. Principal Maitra boycotted the ceremony, but Dr. Nilratan Sircar, a maternal uncle of Mahalanobis, was there to hand over the bride in marriage to Mahalanobis. The many luminaries present at the ceremony included poet Rabindranath Tagore, who arrived there quite late after attending a cultural programme organised at the University Institute Hall on the occasion of the staging of his dance drama 'Basanta'.

Mahalanobis had started his career as a student of the Presidency College and then became a Professor of Physics there. But it is as the father of Indian statistics that he later became famous.

He founded the Indian Statistical Institute, whose random crop surveys became the fore-runner of the National Sample Survey. He launched the 'Sankhya', a journal of statistics. All these activities were carried on by him from the Baker Laboratory building of the Presidency College that was the home of the Physics Department.

His surveys and calculations were later to become the basis of his growth strategy for India with its accent on the development of heavy industry—a strategy that formed the sheet anchor of the country's Second Five-Year Plan. He laid emphasis on the optimum investment of resources in the core sectors for securing the transformation of India's backward economy to which he wanted to impart a positive social direction. His concept of self-reliance favoured the development of the infrastructure of the economy and the generation of employment.

For quite some time, Prof. Mahalanobis was playing a double role as Principal of the Presidency College and as Chief Adviser to the Government of India in regard to the application of statistical methods and organisation of statistical surveys needed for chalking out the country's economic and planning strategies. He simultaneously held important positions in the statistical bodies of the United Nations Organisation.

Among the international figures in the field of statistics, who lent unstinted support and help to Prof. Mahalanobis in organising the Indian Statistical Institute and carrying forward its activities and multi-pronged field surveys and analyses was Prof. R.A. Fisher, who paid several visits to India. Later, J.B.S. Haldane, the well-known scientist came down to live in Kolkata and work in the Indian Statistical Institute. Prof. Mahalanobis had, of course, enlisted a galaxy of brilliant Indian scientists to make their contribution to the building up and development of the Institute on a sound professional basis. I had a better appreciation of his greatness as a statistician when I later took up Statistics as a special subject of study as part of my M.A. course in Economics at the Calcutta University.

Mahalanobis was a unique example of a Professor of Physics switching over to a different discipline of Statistics and achieving much greater distinction in the latter. He took a holistic view of science and believed in using statistics as a tool for furthering research work in different branches of science—a methodology, which, he believed, was useful for both Statistics and the other disciplines. His application of statistical methods in the field of anthropometry yielded useful results in sorting out what he called the "race mixture" in Bengal. He came out with some interesting findings about the background of some typical castes in northern India and Bengal. A significant conclusion he drew was that the upper castes of Bengal including the Brahmins formed a distinct racial group and had maintained their identity throughout the centuries without being much affected by their contact with the aboriginal tribes and those who came from the Indo-Gangetic plane.

He was a multi-faceted person with a wide vision, who took great interest in art, music and literature. He used statistical tools in the study of Bengali literature, an example being his publication of Tagore's 'Chayanika', which provided an index of the popularity of the poems that formed part of this compilation. Because of his closeness to Rabindranath Tagore, he was deeply involved for long years in the affairs of the Viswa-Bharati and Shantiniketan. Tagore had dedicated poems to him. It is believed that in fashioning the character of Amit Roy, the hero of his novel, 'Sheser Kavita', Tagore had blended together the qualities of Prof. Mahalanobis, Prof. Susobhan Sarkar and Prof. A.K. Chanda—all of the Presidency College. This was indeed a great tribute to this famous college!

Such was the character of P.C. Mahalanobis, a great Principal, who left his college job to join on a whole-time basis the Central Government, which he was already serving in various capacities. His residential premises at Baranagore on the Barrackpore Trunk Road, which had been named as 'Amrapali' by poet Tagore, never failed to attract my attention, whenever I passed that way, though an additional reason for me to take a good look at that whole complex was that my father and my eldest brother worked in the office of the Indian Statistical Institute that was located there.

While Mahalanobis was the Principal of the Presidency College, the students once went on a strike over an issue that pertained to the conduct of a college professor, who also worked as the Superintendent of the Eden Hindu Hostel. This was a rather unusual event in the Presidency College and created quite some commotion among the students. I still recall hat one day I had joined the other students, who had assembled near the impressive flight of stairs that led from the ground to the top floor right across the middle of the building. A student leader stood at the spacious landing at the top of the stairs and began a long harangue, expatiating on the justness of whatever the cause of the strike was. A few girls took part in the picketing in a bid to thwart some students trying to go up the stairs to attend their classes. The strike-breakers' attempt at gate-crashing was ultimately stalled by the closure of the mighty collapsible gate on the stair-way.

Principal Mahalanobis, who happened to be out of the country, came back when he heard of this development. He asked the students to start attending their classes and assured them that he would do whatever was necessary to redress their grievances. The students listened to him and called off the strike. It must be said to the credit of the Principal that he also acted promptly and changed the Superintendent of the college hostel.

In the wake of this development, we were asked one day to assemble in the big hall of the Baker Laboratory building where Principal Mahalanobis arrived to address us. We all heard him in rapt attention as he announced that that he was leaving the college. I have a vague recollection that he had left the college in an atmosphere of unpleasantness, as he was unhappy over certain matters that had something to do with the strike.

This was the only event that affected the otherwise smooth course and the even tenor of our academic life at the Presidency College. The teachers and the students alike remained generally ensconced in their ivory tower and engrossed in the problems of their academic world. The ignoble strife of the madding crowd outside this grove of academe rarely, if ever, disturbed the solitude, whose charms were alluring enough to induce in us all a serious intellectual mood. We felt fairly well insulated from the rough and tumble of the dusty highway of ordinary human existence, as long as we were on the college premises.

I vividly remember the solemn condolence meeting that was held at the Presidency College to honour the memory of Mahatma Gandhi, who had fallen to the assassin's bullet on the 30th of January, 1948. The students and members of the staff assembled on the playground of the college. A speech or two and the rendition of some devotional numbers by the students, mostly girls, figured on the programme. It was here that I saw for the first time that the serious-minded blue stockings that the girl students of the college always looked to be from a distance were capable of rising to the occasion, when the need arose for giving expression to normal human emotions. The songs were rendered quite well with the soft musical voices of the girls quivering in the depth of their innermost feelings.

Notes

1. Taken from the brochure published in 1998 by the Calcutta Presidency College Alumni Association, Delhi.
2. *Ibid.*
3. Editorial in the Hindustan Times, New Delhi, dated September 24, 2002.

14

We Become Free : Farewell to Vikrampur, My Home in East Bengal

Our freedom that came on the 15th of August, 1947 meant the partition of the country as well as of the Bengal and Punjab Provinces and the creation of two Dominions—India and Pakistan—within the British Commonwealth of Nations. I vividly recall the fervour and excitement of those days.

However, I have nightmarish memories of the serious communal trouble that often took the form of arson, loot and killings, disturbing the peace of Kolkata till as late as a few days before independence. Hindu anti-social elements burnt down many Muslims' houses in the slums of Beliaghata, a Hindu-majority locality of Kolkata. The Muslims complained that they did not feel secure, as the Muslim police officers of Kolkata had mostly opted for Pakistan and were replaced by Hindu officers.

Gandhiji was then at the Sodepur Ashram near Kolkata, where he had come in early August to spend a few days quietly away from the festivities of the Independence Day which had brought him no great joy. Hearing of the trouble in Beliaghata, he now decided to go there in a bid to restore communal peace. H.S. Suhrawardy met Gandhiji and offered his services. Gandhiji accepted the offer, but bluntly told the bon vivant Suhrawardy that they both would have to live together in the same house in the slum area of Beliaghata without any police protection.

In his memoirs,[1] H.S.Subrawardy has given an account of this mission of peace in Beliaghata in which he claims a much bigger share of the credit than the Hindus of the city had at that time apportioned to him. His version of the violent history of those times is somewhat on the following lines. He met Gandhiji at the Sodepur Ashram and requested him to put off his visit to Noakhali, then badly affected by the local Muslims' anti-Hindu violence, and instead move over to Kolkata in order to use his influence to stop the massacre of the Muslims, as otherwise there would be terrible repercussions in east Bengal where the Muslims would surely take it out on the Hindus. It was after a two-hour-long discourse with Gandhiji that Suhrawardy succeeded in persuading the former to proceed to Kolkata but on the condition already mentioned – that Suhrawardy join him in Beliaghata.

A couple of days before independence, Mahatma Gandhi and Suhrawardy reached Beliaghata and started their work from a dilapidated building located in a dirty and stinking area which was made available by its Muslim owners. The Hindus of the locality took offence at what they called Gandhiji's attempt to save the Muslims, pointing out that he had done nothing of the kind to save the Hindus during the Muslim League's Direct Action programme on August 16, 1946. They staged angry demonstrations against Gandhiji's so-called pro-Muslim bias and his association with Suhrawardy, whom they dubbed as the killer of the Hindus. Gradually, Gandhiji managed to cast his spell over the angry people of the locality. Suhrawardy appeared before an agitated Hindu mob and took all the blame upon himself, accepting responsibility for the Great Calcutta Killing of August 1946. In fact, he publicly apologised for his lapses and this humility made an instantaneous impact on the crowd. The whole atmosphere changed and bitterness and hatred gave way to friendship. Thus, on the eve of the Independence Day, Hindus and Muslims joined hands in taking out processions in different parts of Kolkata and lustily shouted slogans exhorting both the communities to forget the past and live in harmony.

Unprecedented excitement and euphoria marked the advent of freedom at midnight on August 14, 1947. In Kolkata, Hindus and Muslim forgot for the time being their animosity and embraced on another like brothers and citizens of a free country. I kept awake the whole night and. along with my friends, went from place to place to see the scenes of jubilation and the numerous joint processions of the Hindus and Muslims.

On the morning of August 15, 1947, I heard that the Government House in Kolkata i.e. the palatial residence of British Governors, was being thrown open to visitors, who would be allowed a walk-through as a gesture to show that even the ordinary man would have access to the highest places in free India. This was an opportunity I did not want to miss. I rushed to the Government House, travelling by tram-car, in which a free ride was allowed to all to mark the occasion. There were milling crowds around the Government House and it was with great difficulty that I could get inside to see the big rooms and halls with chandeliers hanging from their high ceilings, the immaculately maintained gardens, the manicured lawns, the fountains, the marble statues — things which I had never seen before.

Then I saw a small procession of dignitaries with C. Rajagopalachari, the newly appointed Governor of West Bengal, at the head, making a ceremonial entry into the Government House. I was thrilled to see from such close quarters an important statesman and the first Indian to boot to have just taken over as the Governor of West Bengal. This made me feel that we had really become free. Standing there and seeing the procession headed by the first Indian Governor of West Bengal that was wending its way through the crowds, I felt that I was very much a part of our country's history that was unfolding itself before my eyes. But what pained me on this solemn occasion was the disorderly behaviour of the crowd, which, I learnt later, had broken some precious furniture of the Government House and even indulged in acts of petty pilferage.

Close on the heels of the Independence Day, came Id on the 18th of August, 1947, which again was an occasion for joyous celebration and for public display of Hindu-Muslim fraternisation in Kolkata. Hindus and Muslims exchanged gifts and articles of food. I joined some of my friends in attending an Id function in a Muslim-majority area, where till only a few days ago, no Hindu in his senses would have ventured to go.

But the euphoria of freedom proved rather evanescent as communal riots were soon to engulf Bengal and Punjab with their inevitable repercussions in different parts of India as well as Pakistan. Muslims, on the one hand, and Hindus and Sikhs, on the other, started killing one another in Punjab forcing the latter to flee Pakistan in their thousands and seek refuge in India, particularly Delhi. The resultant communal tension led to riots and killings in Delhi. In Kolkata also, communal trouble flared up again. On August 31, 1947, some Hindus attacked the house where Gandhiji was camping with his followers and some persons, who were believed to be Muslims. A brick hurled by a Hindu youth whizzed past Gandhiji, narrowly missing him. Gandhiji commenced a fast unto death on September 1, 1947, which he called off on the 4th of September only after the riots stopped and the authorities as well as representative groups of both communities assured him in all seriousness that they would do everything possible to ensure communal peace.

Referring to this fast, Suhrawardy pays the following handsome tribute to Gandhiji in his memoirs: "Mahatma Gandhi undertook a fast unto death. He would not break it, even though perilously near breakdown, until I assured him that I was satisfied — for it was my personal satisfaction that he insisted on — that the Hindus were really penitent and that the government and the police had taken adequate steps to prevent any further recurrence. It showed the greatness of his heart and his magnanimous spirit that at every meeting, preaching the doctrine of communal harmony, he gave the credit for the new spirit of brotherhood and toleration to me and said he would not have been able to achieve anything had I not been by his side." In paying this compliment to Gandhiji, Suhrawardy has usurped a big chunk of the credit for himself !

Mahatma Gandhi's appeal to the humanistic and moral urges of the common Kolkata man had some impact no doubt, but yet this touched no more than the fringe of the problem. H.S. Suhrawardy had turned penitent and joined the Mahatma's entourage to campaign for peace. He participated in the Mahatma's prayer meetings at many places, where the latter preached his spiritual message in an attempt to bring the people back to the path of sanity. Suhrawardy's sharing of the Mahatma's platform and his participation in the singing of 'Ramdhun', the popular song in praise of Lord Rama that enjoins on all to live in communal peace and harmony, aroused derisive laughter in many quarters, as the people thought that his claim of having undergone a real change of heart was nothing but sheer hypocrisy.

However, a completely different and almost hagiolatrous assessment of Suhrawardy's role has been given by Mohammad H.R.Talukdar in the "Memoirs of Huseyn Shaheed Suhrawardy" in the following words:

"In the Gandhi peace Mission, Shaheed Suhrawardy worked and lived like a mendicant, at a great risk to his life. He turned down five tempting offers from Jinnah, in order to undertake the safety and salvation of Indian Muslims. No other Muslim League leader came forward to save the helpless Indian Muslims. Thus instead of going to Pakistan for a life of position and peace, he attended, with Gandhi, colossal peace meetings in Kolkata and in other parts of West Bengal, East Punjab, Alwar, Bharatpur, Delhi and the United Provinces. Everywhere he asked Muslims to accept partition as settled fact and live as loyal citizens of India.

Through the untiring and courageous efforts of the two of them, they were able to create a strong public opinion in India in favour of peace and communal harmony. The mission saved Pakistan from possible economic disaster by checking the potential unabated migration of Indian Muslims, sustained the integrity of East Bengal and saved the lives of millions of Indian Muslims."

Noted Bangladeshi author, A.F. Salauddin Ahmed,[2] has projected H.S. Suhrawardy as a secular and democratic leader, who started his political career as a disciple of Deshbandhu Chittaranjan Das, but later veered towards the separatist politics of the Muslim League when he realised that there was no future for the poor and educationally backward Muslim masses of Bengal unless special measures were taken for raising them to the level of the more advanced Hindu community. The communal holocaust that preceded and followed the partition of the country is said to have brought about a further change in his outlook and political thanking, bringing him in close proximity to Mahatma Gandhi and his peace mission and leading him to put forward the plan of an independent Bengal as the homeland of both Hindus and Muslims. After the creation of Pakistan on the basis of religion, he made a passionate plea for keeping religion out of politics and launched a campaign for the establishment of a democratic order in Pakistan. His disciple, Bangabandhu Sheikh Mujibur Rahman, steadfastly pursued the same ideals and brought them to fruition by realising the goal of an independent Bangladesh. There is considerable truth in this assessment.

It was when my college closed for the Puja holidays in September-October, 1947 about a month after partition that I could pay one last visit to my native village in Vikrampur that now formed part of East Pakistan. During the couple of weeks that I spent in my village, I saw the big change that had already transformed the whole atmosphere in the short span of hardly a month after partition. As I travelled from Kolkata by train, then by steamer and finally by boat to reach my village, I saw many panic-stricken Hindus, who were on their way to East Pakistan with a view to transporting their families and earthly possessions over to West Bengal. The tension was heightened as a result of the harassment caused and the searches of their luggages conducted by vigilante groups that were a law unto themselves.

In our village, just a couple of Durga Pujas were observed, but since many of the Hindus including the priests had already left for West Bengal or were in the throes of making arrangements for their departure for West Bengal for good, only the barest of religious rites were observed. There was no fervour, no festivity.

However, what pleased me was the fact that there had been no communal trouble in my village. I learnt that no incident involving communal violence had taken place there. The Muslims still behaved as courteously with us as ever before. Many of them came to see me and enquired about the welfare of the other members of our family, who had stayed behind in Kolkata. A Muslim school friend of mine, who had given up studies after reaching the tenth class, saw me as often as he could.

I paid no visit to my school since it was closed for the Puja holidays. From whatever I could ascertain from my village friend, there had as yet been no great change in the school. The Head Master and most of the Hindu teachers were still on the staff. However, it was not long before the Hindu teachers and students started leaving the school and migrating to West Bengal with their families.

When the day of my departure for Kolkata came, I felt like crying, as I knew that there was hardly any possibility of my coming back to the village in the foreseeable future. Our neighbours, most of them Hindus, belonging to the lower castes, had no intention at that time of leaving the village, as they would have had no means of livelihood, if they migrated to West Bengal. They as well as many Muslims of our village repeatedly implored us not to leave for good, but visit the village from Kolkata from time to time, whenever it suited us.

So, some time in the month of October, 1947, I, along with some of my relations, left our village for Kolkata. I could not suppress my tears as I cast my last, lingering looks at our house, the village and our neighbours before taking leave of them. It was a poignant moment of my life, because it was in this Shyamsiddhi village of mine that I had grown from a child to a college-going boy, braving many natural calamities and surviving the ravages of epidemics, one of the worst famines of recorded history and a devastating world war. And so we said good bye to our village for evermore, leaving behind all our properties, apart from all the people whom we knew so intimately.

Some members of the families of my uncles stayed behind in our village for some time, but they also migrated to West Bengal at different points of time, depending on the arrangements they could work out.

What made the impact of partition so painful for us was that we could not sell our properties and homestead for which there was no buyer, as they were located in an area that remained submerged under water for more than half the year.

We had a trusted Muslim servant, who lived in our house with his wife and performed many of our domestic chores in lieu of food and a monthly pittance of five rupees. We handed over everything to them and told them to live in our house as long as they liked. Some years ago, I learnt that this Muslim servant was no more, but that his sons were still living in our house in the Shyamsiddhi village of Vikrampur. We had also a Hindu barber whose descendants now live in another part of the house that once belonged to my uncles.

Notes

1. "Memoirs of Huseyn Shaheed Suhrawardy" edited by Mohmmaad H.R.Talukdar.
2. *Ibid.*

15

Was the Partition of Our Country Inevitable?

Since the upheaval associated with the partition of our country, more particularly that of Bengal and the attendant trauma had so vitally affected me personally, a question that has often rankled in my mind over the past six decades is whether this partition was something that was inevitable. Was it something that could have been avoided if this or that course of action was followed by the main actors who strutted on the country's political stage at that critical juncture of our history?

This raises another pertinent question about the essential character of nationalism and whether the Indian people constituted a nation on the eve of the country's division in 1947. If India was a nation—so the argument ran at that time—then it should not or rather need not have been partitioned. The argument that India should not have been partitioned because it was one nation was not at all valid, because the 'state' and the 'nation' are two different entities. A nation can be divided into two states. The German nation had once been divided into the East and West German states.

Sometimes a part of a nation can form an independent state, while the other part remains in another state. This is the case with the Irish nation. The Republic of Ireland is an independent state, while a part of the Irish nation is in the United Kingdom. The case of the Bengalees is somewhat similar because one section has formed the independent state of Bangladesh while another section lives in West Bengal, Tripura etc. in the Indian Union. In fact the latter section of the Bengalees, while sharing a common language and culture with the people Bangladesh, forms an integral part of the Indian nation and of the Indian state as well.

In pre-independence India, many used to say that India was a nation in making. There was a lot to be said for this characterisation of India, because in the state of mutual relationship between the Hindus and Muslims that prevailed at that time, it was difficult to say anything more positive than this.

Territorially, Hindu India was never completely united. Mauryan India had achieved a great deal of political unity, which was rent asunder by foreign invaders, who established their authority over large tracts of our country. The succeeding Gupta dynasty again brought the whole of north India under a united political authority, but the southern parts of the country remained beyond their control. In the seventh century A.D., India remained fragmented into three main territorial divisions, namely north India under Harshvardhana, the Deccan under the Chalukyas and the far south under the Pallava rulers, with rivalries among them forming the dominant leitmotif of India's history of that period. The cultural and political unity of India in the Gupta age, that is known as the Golden Age or alternatively the Periclean Age of Indian history, might have given rise to something like an "Aryavarta consciousness"[1], which, however, did not even remotely approximate to what could be called a feeling of Pan-Indian nationalism.

When I read Pandit Jawaharlal Nehru's Glimpses of World History as a college student, I was much impressed by his argument that the establishment by Shankaracharya of the temples at the four corners of India—at Dwarka, Puri, Srinagar and Sringeri—symbolised the spiritual unity of India. This, though true, did not mean the same thing as Indian nationalism in view of the absence of territorial integrity and the division of the country into many kingdoms, whose rulers relentlessly fought one another.

Moreover, a feeling of commonness based on religion is not always the same thing as nationalism. Both Nepal and India are predominantly Hindu and yet the bond of nationalism never united the two territories. In the Buddhist era of Indian history, many countries of Asia embraced Buddhism that spread from India; there was, however, no common nationalist consciousness among these countries.

Even after the Muslims came to India and conquered the greater part of its territory, no all-India nationalist consciousness developed among the people. As historian Sirajul Islam has observed:[2] "Evidently, we were not a nation during Nawabi period or before. Our polity and economy and social outlook were cosmopolitan in character. The king of our country assumed the unrecognised epithet of 'proconsul of the world', such as Jahangir, Shahjahan, Alamgir, Shah Alam, and so on, all meaning king of the globe". Further on, Sirajul Islam points out that after the advent of the East India Company in Bengal, the Mughals kept the door open to foreigners, allowing the Company to settle down in Kolkata and to fortify their settlement there in 1698 A.D. This, according to Sirajul Islam, established the cosmopolitan rather than the nationalist credentials of the Mughal power in India.

The sentiment of nationalism started taking shape in India during British rule. To quote historian Niharranjan Ray: "One cannot but take note of the historical fact that nationalism happens to be primarily a politico-economic concept and secondarily, a cultural one, which arose in Europe at a given time in a given politico-economic situation, and that this kind of situation was never present in India of the ancient and medieval past. That this imported concept could find a soil and strike its roots in India was due to the fact, first, that India had been drawn by the British into the colonial stream of nineteenth century British polity and economy, and secondly, because of its geographical unity which was buttressed by the British by one central political authority and one common administrative system, and thirdly, the process of its evolution was to an extent helped by the historically conditioned over-all cultural unity at its lowest common measure".[3]

But as is generally known, the development of a common nationalist outlook in pre-independence India was thwarted not only by the already existing differences between the Hindus and Muslims, but also by British machinations that aggravated these differences in diverse fields by fostering mutual suspicion and made them adopt antagonistic positions on various issues, thus furthering British colonial interests.

After Bangladesh came into being in 1971, some historians of that country have looked at the question of nationalism from the point of view of Bengalee nationalism, as distinct from Indian nationalism as well as from Pakistani nationalism represented by Pakistan. It has been suggested by them that the feeling of Bengalee nationalism that existed during the rule of the Nawabs of Bengal was stultified during British rule, but again came into its own after Pakistani rule was overthrown in 1971. It has, therefore, been observed by Mohammad Shah[4] that "the concept of Bengali as a distinct nationality or an ethnic and cultural group was rooted in the pre-colonial society of Bengal", that it "suffered a set-back in the colonial period" and that it "revived and fulfilled under the anti-Bengali Pakistani government".

As regards the phenomenon of a distinct Bengalee identity that has been alluded to by many authors of Bangladesh, it can perhaps be said that such a concept, as applied to the period of the Nawabs' rule in pre-colonial Bengal, can serve as a hypothetical proposition to start with. The Hindu-Muslim harmony that was maintained during the rule of the Nawabs in Bengal was adversely affected with the advent of British rule. The spread of English education among the Hindus, their monopolisation of government jobs by virtue of the introduction of the Permanet Settlement which catapulted many Hindus to the status of Zamindars, the oppression of the peasants, mostly Muslims, by the Zamindars, mostly Hindus, and deliberate British policy of 'divide and rule' created disharmony between the Hindus and Muslims. An inchoate common feeling of nationalism among the Hindus and Muslims thus receded into the background. All through this period, however, the Bengalee Hindus' common identity with the Hindus in the rest of India continued to remain as strong as ever.

When the Congress leaders were sent to jail in the aftermath of the Quit India movement in 1942, Jinnah and the Muslim League had the field entirely to themselves. Their support to the war effort of the British Government helped them to get recognised by the latter as the party that represented the Muslim community. This marked an important change in the political equation between the Muslim League and the Congress Party, which came to be regarded as the parties of the Muslims and Hindus respectively.

The Muslim League's growing strength in Bengal was reflected in its victory in the elections to the Bengal Legislative Assembly held in March 1946 and in the decline of A.K. Fazlul Huq's Krishak Praja Party, though he himself maintained his earlier record by getting elected from two constituencies. H.S.Suhrawardy formed the Muslim League Government in Bengal in April 1946 and gradually consolidated the party's hold over the Muslim community and leaving the Hindus in no doubt that political power in Bengal had gone beyond their reach for all times to come.

I have discussed in earlier chapters the series of developments that took place in the wake of the British Cabinet Mission's proposals made in May 1946, leading to heightened Hindu-Muslim tension all over the country.The partition of India became inevitable in 1947 as the Muslims wanted a separate state where they would be immune from competing with the more advanced members of the Hindu community and because the better educated and more prosperous Hindus refused to share a common political destiny with their less fortunate Muslim brethren.

M.A. Jinnah was suffering from tuberculosis and lung cancer to which he succumbed about thirteen months after the creation of Pakistan. However, he had managed to keep the fact of his ailment a closely guarded secret. Had this fact become generally known, many players in the partition drama might have chosen to delay matters hoping for Jinnah's disappearance from the scene. Would the other leaders of the Muslim League have been able to keep up their bargain and bring to fruition their struggle for Pakistan?

Dominique Lapierre, the well-known author, disclosed in an interview to an Indian journalist5[5] that he had seen an X-Ray of Jinnah's lungs in 1947 in the course of a research project on the basis of which the doctors had not given him more than six months to live. Lapierre claimed to have brought this fact to the notice of Lord Mountbatten, who reportedly observed that had he known this earlier, he would have delayed the withdrawal of the British from India, thus averting its partition. This also raises the basic question as to whether Lord Mountbatten was at all interested in averting India's partition.

There was no alternative to partition because the Hindus and the Muslims had drifted apart. The role that the Congress, the Muslim League and the British authorities played accelerated the process of alienation. The anarchic conditions that developed in different parts of the country in the wake of the communal holocaust led the British authorities to advance the date of their departure. They took fright from the mutiny in the Royal Indian Navy and the other wings of the armed forces. The pace of developments was greatly hastened by the replacement of Lord Wavell by Lord Mountbatten, who, always a man in a hurry, thought that he had a job of vivisection to do as fast as he could. Add to this the considerations of material gain and of sharing the loaves and fishes of office after the transfer of power that weighed with the Congress and Muslim League leaders and you would get a good idea of the reasons that made partition inevitable.

Many have criticised Mahatma Gandhi for accepting the partition of India and cited this as evidence of the failure of his life's mission. They have faulted Gandhiji for not having effectively resisted it and shrugged off the issue by merely saying that "nobody listens to me". They refuse to believe that Gandhiji was not consulted by the Congress leaders about the partition of the country before finally agreeing to accept it.

It is no use blaming Gandhiji for the fractured freedom we got in 1947.The late Prof. Hiren Mukerjee, the eminent communist ex-M.P., rightly observed in an article on the occasion of the golden jubilee of our independence: ".......... our freedom struggle had an irresolute leadership, fearful of an engineered and incendiary communal situation and it was with a tired gesture that partitioned freedom was accepted. Let not the Left which often adopts a 'holier than thou' attitude be exonerated from responsibility for the truncated and, therefore, tainted independence that came to us. In different proportions, of course, responsibility for the event has to rest on all of us". (Times of India, New Delhi, dated August 29, 1997). It was good to hear a top-ranking Indian communist leader speak in this confessional strain, though it took his other friends some more years to disabuse their minds of the view they held in our post-independence years and admit that the independence that we got in 1947 was not a 'fake', but a true one, at least politically and in terms of international law.

After partition, West Bengal, the new Province of India, became a much smaller entity than the erstwhile Province of undivided Bengal. West Bengal's economy received a great shock as a result of the influx of millions of Hindu refugees from East Pakistan that took place in spasmodic waves, depending on the occasional outbursts of communal violence there. There was a related issue of the exchange of population between India and Pakistan, which had been suggested by many people, particularly the Hindus of east Bengal, at the time of partition. In the western wing, the compulsion of circumstances forced most of the Hindus to migrate to India and most of the Muslims to Pakistan in the immediate aftermath of the partition of the country. India's political leaders, with their commitment to the ideal of a secular India being the home of both Hindus and Muslims, did not accept the suggestion for the exchange of population. We had heard at that time that M.A. Jinnah had in fact proposed such a course which indicated that he had foreseen the communal carnage that followed in the wake of partition.

When lakhs of Hindus from East Pakistan poured into India from time to time after the partition of the country, a movement had developed in West Bengal to press the demand that an equal number of Muslims be sent away from West Bengal to east Bengal to make room for the Hindu refugees from East Bengal. This demand was rejected by Delhi on the ground that it militated against India's secular credentials.

It was argued by many that M.A.Jinnah was basically a secular-minded political leader, who harboured no malice towards the Hindu community. Given to eating pork and wearing Savile Row suits, he was a typical and quintessential Englishman in his outlook and life-style in which the Qoran had hardly much place. He had started his political career in the Congress Party. When Mahatma Gandhi gave a call for the Khilafat movement in 1920 to press the demand for the restoration of the Sultan of Turkey as the Caliph of the Muslim world and thus to capitalise on the resentment of the Muslims, M.A. Jinnah had opposed Gandhiji saying that the national movement should be guided by nationalistic principles rather than by obscurantist and narrow religious considerations. Jinnah's view that religion and politics were not to be mixed was on all fours with what the protagonists of secularism preach today.

Jinnah got disillusioned when, at the 1928 session of the party held in Kolkata, all his suggestions were rejected on the plea that he was championing the sectarian cause of the Muslims. This caused him great humiliation and marked the beginning of the process of parting of ways between him and the Congress Party. Jinnah now began to put forward the demand for recognising the Muslims as a separate nation and for creating Pakistan as their homeland so that the vast numbers of the poor and backward among them could have access to education and the means for bettering their lot without being hindered by the dominant position of the Hindus in a united India.

However, once Pakistan was created, M.A. Jinnah visualised a state where the Muslims and non-Muslims would live together as equal citizens, with religion being treated as a private affair of the individual. To quote from his speech in the Constituent Assembly of Pakistan on August 11, 1947 : "You are free to go to your temples, you are free to go to your mosques or to any other place of worship in this State of Pakistan. You may belong to any religion or caste or creed that has nothing to do with the business of the State – – – – –

— —we are all citizens and equal citizens of one State— — — — — you will find that in course of time Hindus would cease to be Hindus and Muslims would cease to be Muslims, not in the religious sense, because that is the personal faith of each individual, but in the political sense as citizens of the State."

At the first conference of the Muslim League held in Karachi after partition, Jinnah had urged the Muslims of the India and the Hindus of Pakistan to be loyal to India and Pakistan respectively. He had said : "I still consider myself to be an Indian. For the moment I have accepted the Governor-Generalship of Pakistan. But I am looking forward to a time when I will return to India and take my place as a citizen of my country"

An echo of this sentiment of M.A. Jinnah reverberated throughout India in June 2005, when L.K. Advani, the BJP President, in a speech during a visit to Pakistan, quoted from the statement made by Jinnah in Pakistan's Constituent Assembly on August 11, 1947 which projected a secular image of the latter. This went counter to the generally held view in India that Jinnah had used the communal plank to carve out the sovereign State of a Muslim Pakistan out of India. Even across the BJP and the Sangh Parivar, the predominant view was that Advani had wrongly vouched for Jinnah's secular credentials. The BJP's parliamentary board agreed in a statement on June 10, 2005 that what Advani had done was to remind the people of Pakistan of its founder's commitment to ensure full freedom of faith for all citizens and avoid any discrimination between its citizens on grounds of religion. But the board's statement made it clear that the BJP had always condemned the division of the country on communal lines and continued to steadfastly reject the two-nation theory championed by Jinnah.

The left parties, by and large, did not find anything wrong in Advani's statement and took the view that he had not directly characterized Jinnah as a secularist but had merely quoted Jinnah's speech of August11, 1947 with a view to advising the Pakistani leadership to adopt the secular path as Jinnah had envisaged. Jyoti Basu, the CPM patriarch was, however, critical of Advani's praise of Jinnah whom he held responsible for the Great Calcutta Killing of August 16, 1946 and for the partition of India on the basis of his two-nation theory.

Some people have referred to the characterization of Jinnah as 'an ambassador of Hindu-Muslim unity' by Gopal Krishna Gokhale as well as by Sarojini Naidu, but this assessment had been made years before Jinnah began to show his communal fangs. Even the RSS leader, H.V. Seshadri had in his book, 'The Tragic Story of Pakistan', described Jinnah as a secular leader, who believed in the Hindu concept of 'Dashavataras' and practised Hindu social customs and laws of succession. Quoting from Seshadri's book, Atal Behari Vajpayee, the veteran BJP leader, said at a meeting in Delhi on August 21, 2005, that Jinnah, like many other nationalists, later became a communal and religious fanatic.

Mahmood Farooqui, a political analyst, expressed the view (Times of India, June 10, 2005) that Jinnah's pro-partition stance was a response to majoritarian politics. Jinnah, according to him, spent at least two decades of his political life (from 1910 to 1930) to bring about an agreement between Hindus and Muslims, before retiring in disgust from public life and settling down in England. Farooqui considers it wrong to accuse Jinnah of cant when he chose to set himself up as the sole spokesman of the Muslims in the 1940's, when he had over 99% of the eligible Muslim vote to show for that claim. Farooqui raises a very pertinent question in his write-up: "Can one espouse the cause, exclusively, of one single community and still remain secular in one's political life? If secularism implies a separation of religion from the political sphere, does it also involve repudiating any effort to seek the betterment of any one community? These are questions that independent India, almost 60 years after the death of its principal antagonist, is still struggling to answer. It would not be possible to resolve them without reappraising Jinnah and his place in our history."

Taking all these facts into account, it would be reasonable to conclude that Jinnah's political mood had alternated between two extremes one of which had the flavour of lily-white secularism in the early phase and the other of rabid communalism in the penultimate stage before he again switched over to the secular path in his capacity as the head of the new sovereign State of Pakistan.

In recent times, books by some eminent historians have gone into the various issues that figured prominently during the tumultuous days preceding the partition of our country. In his "Eminent Churchillians", Andrew Roberts has ventured the opinion that Lord Mountbatten deserved to be impeached for his failure to forestall the holocaust during the partition of our country. He attributes this failure to the advancing of the date of transfer of power by the British authorities by about 10 months from June 1948, the time originally fixed by the British Government. He also accuses Mountbatten of a clear bias in favour of the Hindus and against the Muslims, an attitude which is traced by the author to the great clout which Pandit Jawaharlal Nehru had with Edwina Mountbatten, the Vicereine.

Mountbatten's daughter, Pamela Hicks does not agree that he had worked against the interests of the Muslims. As was generally believed at that time, Mountbatten had set his heart on becoming the Governor General of both India and Pakistan after the vivisection of the country. According to Pamela Hicks, an important reason which impelled her father to put forward such a proposal was his hope that this would have enabled him to live down the general suspicion that he was partial to the Hindus and to display his impartiality as between the Hindus and the Muslims. While some important Congress leaders were believed to be willing to go along with this proposal, M.A.Jinnah put his foot down!

An important functionary of the Government of India in those days, namely Sir George Cunningham, ex-Governor of the North-West Frontier Province and Private Secretary to the Viceroy, has come out recently with the view that the large-scale disturbances in the Punjab were due to Mountbatten's decision to advance the date of partition, without making the requisite precautionary arrangements to meet the grave threat to the law and order situation.

The contrary perception has been provided by Brian Hoey in his "Mountbatten: the Private Story". His assessment is that when Mountbatten arrived in India in March 1947, the differences between the Hindu and Muslim leaders had become so irreconcilable that the longer the negotiations were delayed, the greater was the likelihood of bloodshed. Mountbatten, therefore, cut down the period of negotiations, particularly because the steel frame of the Indian Civil Service was breaking down very fast.

The politics of partition has continued to remain the subject matter of speculation and research by scholars, as is evident from several books and research papers on this subject that have been published subsequently. An important book that deserves mention is "The Sole Spokesmen: Jinnah, the Muslim League and the Demand for Pakistan" by Ayesha Jalal of the Cambridge University (1985). She has delved deep into the official records of Pakistan and Jinnah's private papers to come out with a thesis which sought to demolish the commonly held view that it was the Muslim League and M.A.Jinnah who had asked for and got away with Pakistan and, secondly, that the Congress Party and its leaders were opposed to the division of the country.

Ayesha Jalal marshals a series of facts to establish the point that the Lahore Rresolution, the basis of the demand for Pakistan, refrained from using the word and was purposely kept vague, because Jinnah did not in fact want Pakistan but merely wanted to use this demand as a 'bargaining counter' for safeguarding Muslim interests and resolving the Muslim problem within the constitutional framework of a united India.

Jalal also makes the other point that it was the Congress Party which wanted the vivisection of the country. She argues that the "Congress was not ready to offer him (i.e.Jinnah) terms which might have prevented a brutal amputation of the subcontinent". According to her, the experience of the Interim Government had shown the Congress that the presence of the Muslim League in the government would undermine its authority in an independent India. This, in her view, led the Congress to eject the Muslim League from the future constitutional dispensation that was being worked out. To quote her: "It was the Congress that insisted on partition. It was Jinnah who was against partition".

Many analysts are not prepared to go along with Ayesha Jalal's view that Jinnah was against partition though her stand gets some measure of support from Joya Chatterjee's book "Bengal Divided: Hindu Communalism and Partition", according to which, the Hindu leaders campaigned actively for the partition of Bengal, the "Bhadralok" class forming the backbone of this movement.

An article by Ashim Roy in "India's Partition Process, Strategy and Mobilization" edited by Prof. Mushirul Hassan, dwells on what he calls the "twin partition myths", namely "the League for partition" and "the Congress for unity". After acclaiming Ayesha Jalal's work as a valuable contribution to demolishing these myths, Roy concentrates particularly on demolishing the second of these myths by giving a detailed account of how the Congress Party, at various critical stages of the long and tortuous process of constitutional negotiations, took decisions that militated against the party's so-called commitment to the unity of the Indian sub-continent. The Congress Party's disillusionment with the intransigence of the Muslim League and its leaders made it adopt a stance that sought freedom for the country first, even at the expense of its unity.

The view-points of Ayesha Jalal and Asim Roy differ in some respects from Maulana Abdul Kalam Azad's thinking as reflected in his 'India Wins Freedom' (including its 30 sealed pages that were opened in 1988). In his book, Azad has put the blame for the partition of the country on Lord Mountbatten as well as on the Congress Party and some of its leaders. It was Mountbatten who started impressing upon the Congress leaders the inevitability of partition. Sardar Patel was so fed up with M.A. Jinnah's clamour for Pakistan that he was the first Congress leader to agree to the suggestion for the partition of India and was, in this sense, according to Maulana Abul Kalam Azad, 'the founder of Indian partition'.

In a seminal book "The Hindu Phenomenon"(1994), the late Girilal Jain put an interpretation on the significance of partition that reflected a typical Hindu mind. He regarded the partition of India as a "victory" for the Hindus that had put an end to the stalemate between the Hindus and Muslims in the greater part of the Indian sub-continent. The obverse side of the coin was seen by him as an indication of the tragedy of Islam in India, signifying what he called the world-wide retreat of Muslim power and civilisation. This interpretation ignored the sentiments of those who lay great store by the composite and multi-ethnic character of Indian society. Then, there are many intellectuals, mostly Muslims, who view the partition of India as a fulfilment of the aspirations of the Muslims rather than as a tragedy.

Top secret documents 6 of the British Government pertaining to pre-independence India, which have now been de-classified, have thrown fresh light on the circumstances that led to the partition of the Indian sub-continent in 1947. From these documents, it is clearly seen that as early as in 1946, the British authorities had made up their minds in favour of the partition of the sub-continent and the creation of a Muslim state of Pakistan.

In this regard, some startling revelations have been made by Narendra Singh Sarila, formerly ADC to Lord Mountbatten, 7 on the basis of his study of these documents in his book "The Untold Story of India's Partition". As he explains, the British supported Jinnah's demand for partition in order to safeguard their own strategic interests in Asia rather than the interests of the Muslims of the Indian sub-continent. In view of what was then perceived to be Soviet designs on the oil-fields in the Gulf, Great Britain did not like to lose control over the entire Indian sub-continent and sought to build a base for counter-action against possible Soviet intrusions and to safeguard the sea-lanes in the Indian Ocean.

It is now quite clear that the plan for the Balkanisation of India had been drawn up by Lord Wavell, Governor-General of India, in a telegram he sent to the British Government indicating the predominantly Muslim areas of India which were to form the future State of Pakistan. Wavell also warned the British Government that if India was not partitioned, the interests of the Muslims of India as well as in other parts of the world would be adversely affected, possibly leading to a civil war in India and enmity to the British in other Muslim countries. In response to a query on April 11, 1946, Sir Stafford Cripps, chief of the Cabinet Mission team, Clement Attlee, the British Prime Minister, clarified that the Cabinet Mission should work towards the creation of Pakistan if that was the only way to ensure an agreed settlement. The British Chiefs of Staff to whom the matter had been referred for their views also agreed that the creation of Pakistan was a better alternative than no agreement at all.

It is thus evident that the British Government had already decided in favour of the creation of Pakistan long before the Cabinet Mission Plan was made public on June 3, 1947. It was V.P. Menon, who, at the instance of Lord Mountbatten, drafted the final plan that was announced on June 3, 1947.

It has now become evident that after the Congress Party rejected the Cripps Plan (against the advice of C. Rajagopalachari), launched the 'Quit India' movement in 1942 and gave clear signals that it was against the Nazis and Fascists of Germany and Italy towards whom the British were then getting increasingly friendly, the British felt that the Congress Party would be of no help in their war effort. On the other hand, M.A.Jinnah had met Viceroy Lord Linlithgow in September 1939 and pledged to Great Britain the support and loyalty of the Indian Muslim troops during World War II. After World War II, when the western world perceived a communist threat from the Soviet bloc, it apprehended that India was likely to be pro-Soviet while Pakistan was looked upon as a better ally in this regard. In these circumstances, the British encouraged the Muslim League to seek the partition of India so that the country's north-west abutting Afghanistan and Iran could be placed in the hands of the Muslims who were willing to support the British strategy.

Many related developments can now be seen in proper perspective in the light of the disclosures made by Sarila. It is now easily understood why the Attlee Government decided to ignore the provisions of the Indian Independence Act passed by Westminister in respect of the accession of the Maharaja of Kashmir to India. It was to safeguard British strategic interests in the region. That is why the British Government bypassed the relevant statute and created the Kashmir problem. As the Times of India editorialled (March 18,2000): "The blatant bias of Britain and the US towards Pakistan on the Kashmir issue could logically be traced to Cold War objectives". It was further learnt 8 that George Marshall, the then US Secretary of State, had accepted the validity of Kashmir's accession to India but that Marshall's successors were successfully indoctrinated by the British on the basis of the Cold War logic so that Pakistan became an ally of the US, which began to favour Pakistan on the Kashmir issue.

On the basis of a top secret appreciation prepared in the Commonwealth Relations Office at that time, Sarila mentions the contemporary view in British circles8 that an independent India was unlikely to survive because it had no real background on which to build and unite a nation, there being no real affinity between its North and South, the existence of disruptive elements like the Sikhs and the likelihood of the Communists with their own agenda, growing in numbers and influence. On the other hand, the appreciation mentioned that Pakistan, weak in financial and material resources, though comfortable in food and manpower, had 'a definite background'. Islam, on which to build up a nation and to unite the people .... and has less to fear from internal disruptive forces than the government of India, and less to fear from secessionist tendencies."

However, as we all know, the situation moved in quite the opposite direction over the last several decades. India has remained intact and is a thriving democracy. Pakistan lost its eastern wing in 1971 as Bangladesh came into being. Today, strong centrifugal forces are at work in Pakistan. Sindh, Baluch and Pakhtoon leaders now resent the domination of Punjab, the factor that led to the secession of east Pakistan.

A book that throws new light on the role of M.A.Jinnah in the creation of Pakistan is Humayun Mirza's 'From Plassey to Pakistan', which is essentially the biography of his father, Iskander Mirza, who became the first President of Pakistan in 1958 after suspending its constitution. Mirza is a descendant of Mir Jafar, whose betrayal during the Battle of Plassey led to the establishment of British rule in our country. That is why Mirza invokes the memory of Plassey in assigning an appropriate name to his book. The burden of his story is that Jinnah was hell-bent on securing Pakistan.

Apparently on the basis of what his father Iskander Mirza had told him, Humayun says that Jinnah had cultivated several Muslim officals in the pre-independence era including Iskander Mirza whom Jinnah would have liked to play a crucial role in running Pakistan after it was created. In February 1947, Jinnah had told Iskander Mirza that the prospects of securing Pakistan were not particularly good, as he apprehended that the British could hand over the whole country to the Congress Party. Jinnah felt that if Pakistan could not be secured through negotiations, it would have to be won by the will of the Muslims and by demonstrating their anger. If the negotiations failed by the middle of May 1947, Jinnah wanted Iskander Mirza to resign from the Indian Political Service, return to the tribal territory of the North West Frontier Province which he knew very well and work up a Jehad (holy war) against British.

Sikander Mirza is said to have been stunned by Jinnah's suggestion, as he thought that,apart from leading to bloodshed, such a course would strain his friendship with many of his Hindu colleagues. But since he could not "refuse" Jinnah, Iskander Mirza fell in line and asked for a considerable sum of money to accomplish "this immense task". Iskander was given Rs 20,000 for immediate expenses. The rest, he was told, would be provided by the Nawab of Bhopal. As for the cover, it was said that Iskander would be told at the right time. Jinnah assured him that he would take care of the former's family. Iskander prepared a plan of action, which he was about to submit to Jinnah. At this stage, Jinnah informed him that there was no longer any need for Jehad, as Pakistan had been won.

In the words of Humayun Mirza, Jinnah was prepared to go to any length to achieve Pakistan. This shows how meticulously Jinnah had pursued his goal of Pakistan. Against this background, one cannot agree wholly with the views of Ayesha Jalal, Joya Chatterjee and Ashim Roy, according to whom, it was the Congress Party that was responsible for the creation of Pakistan. Jinnah was quite serious in chasing his dream of Pakistan.

Whatever might have been the initial postures of the main actors in this drama – the Congress, the Muslim League and the British –

by the time partition materialised in 1947, it had become inevitable because all the actors on the stage wanted the drama to end that way.

Notes

1. History And Culture of the Indian People, General Editor, R.C.Mazumdar, Vol-III, page 23
2. History of Bangladesh(1740-1971) edited by Sirajul Islam, Volume-I, page 3.
3. Nationalism In India, P.11-12.
4. "Social and Cultural Basis of Bengali Nationalism" by Mohammed Shah, Associate Professor of History, University of Chittagong, in Volume III of "The History of Bangladesh" edited by Sirajul Islam, page 761.
5. Times of India, February 25, 1999.
6. Times of India, March 17, 2000.
7. Narendra Singh Sarila, Times of India, March 17, 2000.
8. Article in the Times of India, March 17, 2000.

16

The Prince of Shovabazar

For the first 16 years of my life, I was innocent of the game of cricket. Not to speak of playing the game, I had not even seen either a bat or a ball or an actual game of cricket being played anywhere. The reason was quite simple. In Vikrampur's water-logged fields, where was the question of playing cricket?

It was after I shifted to Kolkata in 1945 that I saw for the first time how people played cricket in the Maidan. During the politically volatile period of 1945-1947, I saw the Kolkata boys play cricket not only in the lanes and by-lanes of the city, but sometimes even on the main arterial streets where all traffic stopped whenever there was a general strike.

I was greatly excited in 1948, when I had the first opportunity of seeing a first class cricket match—the one between the Indian Universities team and the West Indies team played in the famous Eden Gardens of Kolkata, the paradise of cricketers. I reached the place quite early in the morning in the company of some cricket-savvy and knowledgeable boys of our neighborhood. The Eden Gardens and its surroundings which I saw for the first time made a deep impression on my mind. According to an account[1] that I read later, the first cricket match in India was played here in 1804 A.D between the Eton Boys (that had come from Great Britain) and the Rest (i.e. the Indian side). The ground was created for this match in what was then known as the Govindapur village that was not very far from the Fort William.

The area was first named Auckland Circus Garden and renamed as Eden Gardens on April 1, 1854. The match was organised by the East India Company's civil servants in Bengal and was won by the Eton Boys. The grassy patch that had just begun to take shape at that time was located at the centre of 1178 Bighas of alluvian soil in the Gangetic delta, which was then a dense jungle infested by tigers. Pools of stagnant water dotted the whole area. Later, an area of 57 Bighas out of this land was reclaimed to develop a cricket ground along with a race course and some football grounds. Statues and monuments were put up to beautify the area.

An important reason for my eagerness to see the match between India and West Indies was the news that Pankaj Roy of the famous Bhagyakul family of east Bengal was going to play as a member of the Indian team. Bhagyakul was only a stone's throw from my village, Shyamsiddhi, which was now located in East Pakistan. In a chapter of my earlier book, 'In Sun And Shower', I have written at length about the Roy family of Bhagyakul of which our family was a sub-feudatory.

Pankaj Roy, born on July 11, 1927 in Kolkata, lived in the family's palatial premises in the Shovabazar locality of the city, but he visited Bhagyakul every year during the Pujas. The Roys of Bhagyakul were looked upon as 'Rajas' because of their fabulous wealth. In fact some members of the family had been given the title of 'Raja' by the British authorities. In my childhood, I fancied Pankaj Roy as a prince—the prince of Bhagyakul! But in Kolkata, he was the prince of Shovabazar, because it was in that part of the city that the Roy family lived. It used to be said of Col. C.K.Nayudu, the famous Indian cricketer, that he was a prince among cricketers and a cricketer among princes. I thought that the same could be said of our Pankaj Roy as well. More recently, Maharaja Saurav Ganguly, the southpaw from Kolkata, has been christened as the Prince of Kolkata by Geoffrey Boycott.

Now back to the cricket match between India and the West Indies. As the Indian players turned up on the field, I saw one of them with what looked like a cloth bandage around his head. I was told that he was none other than Pankaj Roy of Bhagyakul fame. Did he nurse an injury on his head? How would he play in that case? These and many other questions assailed our minds. Then, someone in the crowd sitting close to us, who seemed to be in the know of things, gave an explanation that, I heard later, was nearest to the truth. Roy's father, Khirode Lal Roy, had succumbed to a heart attack in Bhagyakul village, which had just a few months ago become a part of East Pakistan. Roy had rushed to Bhagyakul from Kolkata and spent some time there, strictly observing all the rites that were incumbent on a devout Hindu in the event of his father's death.

It was after observing the 'Shradh' ceremony that Pankaj Roy left Bhagyakul, when he was informed of his selection as a member of the Indian team to play against the West Indies in Kolkata. Since his head had to be shaved for the 'Shradh' ceremony, he had it properly covered when he appeared on the Eden Gardens to play the match. I felt my stock soaring when I saw him on the field, though in the batting order he figured at number 11! I proudly told everyone around that Roy was from Bhagyakul that almost adjoined my village in East Pakistan's Vikrampur Pargana!

How did the prince of Shovabazar blossom into the great cricketer that he was? His village Bhagyakul had nothing in common with cricket. Nor did the Shovabazar locality of Kolkata where he lived have anything to do with cricket. All that Shovabazar was famous for were the open grounds of Kumartuli, where the skilled potters used their deft fingers to give shape to the idols of gods and goddesses that were worshipped by the Bengalees all the year round.

But where there's a will, there's a way. In front of his Shovabazar house, there was a big park which, however, was nowhere near the size of a normal cricket field. It was in this park that he started practising and perfecting the game of cricket in his boyhood with single-minded devotion and determination. It was on the playing field of Shovabazar that the future of India's opening batsman was shaped. I had occasion to see this piece of unpretentious ground tucked away inside the busy and congested Shovobazar area and was surprised to learn that it was here that three test cricketers of West Bengal had their initiation in the game. The other two test cricketers were Pankaj Roy's son, Pranab Roy, and his nephew, Ambar Roy.

As Pankaj Roy grew up, he started playing for the team of the Vidyasagar College of which he was a student. The college went all out in supporting his bid to develop into a first-rate cricketer and provided him with facilities of various kinds including the playing gear and, most important of all, loads of encouragement. As his game started improving, he began to feel that there was no reason why he would not he able to attain the standard of the world's best cricketers. Hard work and determination lay at the root of his greatness as a cricketer.

Simultaneously, Pankaj Roy used to play foot-ball in which also he excelled. In fact, football was his first love. A premier Kolkata football club, the Sporting Union, picked him up for playing as right-in. In 1947, he had the honour of playing football as a member of the Indian team against a European side hich was called the International Team. In 1948, he represented the Indian Football Association in a match against the Burmese team—a match that I saw and greatly enjoyed. Roy was a football blue of the Calcutta University and the Captain of the University's football team, apart from being its cricket blue and also the Captain of its cricket team. In fact, Roy was an all-rounder with a natural flair for sports and games of all kinds. For some time, it was not clear which of the two games, cricket and football, he would finally take up as his prime choice.

Then something happened which tilted the scale in favour of his opting for cricket. Once while playing for the Sporting Union against the Mohammedan Sporting, the famous Calcutta football team, he suffered an injury in the left arm, though he had managed to score a goal. As his arm had to be plastered, he could play neither cricket nor football for some time. It was at this stage that his well-wishers suggested to him to give up professional football, which was a rough game, and instead concentrate whole-heartedly on cricket, a sophisticated game in which there was much less chance of getting his limbs broken.

This is how Pankaj Roy switched over finally to cricket. Because he was also a good footballer, he found it easy to develop his exquisite footwork in cricket. This was the time (1948) when he was called upon to play for the Indian Universities team against the West Indies. The latter team included two of the three famous 'W's, which are not to be confused with either wine or woman. They were Weekes and Walcott. The third 'W' represented by Frank Worrel did not take part in this match, but played later in India, when I saw him also in action.

Pankaj Roy made his debut in an official test match in 1950 against the MCC team in Delhi. He played his second official test against the same team in Bombay, when he scored 140 runs—his first test century. After that, he scored several test centuries.

For ten years, Roy was our opening batsman in matches played in India and in many other countries. He was a great stroke player famous for his square cuts and cover drives. He was said to be a "solid opener". He played in 49 test matches (44 official and 5 unofficial), scoring 5 official centuries and an unofficial one as well. A world record that has still to be broken was the 413 runs yielded by the first wicket partnership of Roy and Vinoo Mankad against New Zealand in Madras in 1955-1956. Pankaj Roy scored 21 centuries in Ranji Trophy, which, in his days, was a knock-out tournament, and, therefore, made it quite difficult for a cricketer to score many centuries. V.S.Hazare held the record of 22 centuries in Ranji Trophy.

Later in life, when I made the acquaintance of Pankaj Roy, he told me why it was difficult for players from Bengal to excel in cricket. Because of rains and the soggy ground, there was cricket for only four months in Bengal, while western India played cricket for eleven months and Delhi almost all the year round. This being the case, the Kolkata players could score fewer centuries. When trial matches were held for the selection of all-India teams, players from Bengal, with hardly much practice, found it difficult to compete with their peers from the other States, who performed better because of long and continuous practice. Against this background, it is easy to appreciate the superb performance of Pankaj Roy.

There were fewer test matches in those days with the result that the players could score fewer centuries. Vijay Merchant and Mustaq Ali had scored only two test centuries each! Lala Amarnath had scored only one test century in his life time. Hazare had seven centuries to his credit, Mankad five and Vijay Manjrekar and Chandu Borde six centuries each. Poly Umrigar had 13 test centuries to his credit—the highest in those days.

I had heard some people of Bengal complain of discrimination against Pankaj Roy on the part of cricket officials at the national level. In 1959, he was made the Vice-Captain of the Indian team that toured England. D.K.Gaekwad was made the Captain, one reason for which, it was alleged by some, was that the Maharaja of Baroda was the team's manager. But in the Second Test played at the Lord's, Gaekwad could not play as he was ill. There was no alternative but to make Pankaj Roy the captain on this occasion. Unfortunately, the

Indian team lost this test even though it had put up a good show. Roy told me that a partisan decision given by the umpire lay at the back of India's defeat.

It was felt by many that Roy should have become the team's Captain, because not only was he senior to Gaekwad, but, what was more important, he was in top form. Even as late as in 1963, Roy was chosen as the best batsman of the year by the 'Hindu', the well-known Madras daily. However, when I discussed this matter with Roy, I saw no trace of bitterness or regret in him. Like a true sportsman, he refused to criticise anybody.

Pankaj Roy was dropped from the Indian team that played against Pakistan in 1960. Thus came to an end the test career of a brilliant cricketer at the young age of just 32 years! I was very happy to have had the opportunity of listening to Pankaj Roy's own account of many interesting episodes of world cricket. For example, he told me how sad he felt when he lost the opportunity of scoring a double century in the test match against New Zealand played in Madras in 1956.Though he and Vinod Mankad set up the world record of a first wicket partnership of 413 runs in this match, he failed to score a double century on which he had set his heart. Mankad had already scored a double century. Pankaj had scored 173 runs and was looking forward to a double century. At this stage, Captain P. Umrigar sent in a slip to Pankaj, asking him to hit out without bothering about getting out. As Pankaj threw caution to the wind, he was soon out before he could score a double century. According to Pankaj Roy, Vinoo Mankad had later told him that he should not have got out by playing his reckless shots at the instance of P. Umigar.

Honours came to Roy as prolifically as runs flowed effortlessly from his bat once upon a time. In 1975, he was awarded the Padmashree. The same year, he was made the honorary life member of the M.C.C. – an honour that few Indian cricketers got. In 2000, he was made the Sheriff of Kolkata.

In course of time, Pankaj Roy and his wife had moved over to a highly spiritual plane, after having been initiated by the great saint of Bengal – Sitaramdas Onkarnath, who, alas, is no more.

Roy was an avid photographer. In his living room, one could see many specimens of his professional skill on the cricket ground. But the most eye-catching object that used to adorn a wall of the room was the life-size photograph of Sitaramdas, who stood there like a guardian angel, smiling benevolently at those who looked up to him in a spirit of reverence and surrender.

I used to hold Pankaj Roy in high esteem for his many human qualities and, above all, because he was a perfect gentleman. This was not surprising, because in those goods days, cricket used to be a game of gentlemen. "That's not cricket" is an old saying which used to bring out the cricketer's spirit of fair play, that is also the hall-mark of a gentleman. Match fixing was a much later phenomenon that had still not tarnished the image of cricket.

Some years ago, I was surprised to read an article in the Times of India (Delhi—March 30, 1995) by Gautam Adhikari in which a critical reference was unjustly made to Pankaj Roy. Adhikari praised the self-confidence and determination with which Sunil Gavaskar met the challenge of the many rival cricket teams against which he played. There is no doubt that the tribute that Adhikari paid to Gavaskar was well deserved. But what Adhikari said about Pankaj Roy and Nari Contractor in the same context was highly deplorable.

To quote Adhikari: "From the beginning of our republican life, we Indians have been a nation of whiners, displaying far too often in our international interactions a certain shortfall in self-confidence which we have betrayed by repeated wailing against foreign hands shaping innumerable conspiracies to cow us down. In cricket, we revealed it in the way we shuffled away from fast bowlers throughout the 50s and 60s. A Pankaj Roy would back off towards the square leg umpire, grinning all the way, while Roy Gilchrist and Wesley Hall pounded their ferocious bouncers in. And when a Charlie Griffith delivery nearly smashed Nari Contractor's head in a match in the West Indies—he had to have five stitches in his skull and retire from test cricket—too many of us tended to whine against the nature of fast bowling instead of asking why we could not face up to it or why we couldn't produce genuine speed bowlers of our own so that we could give it right back to our opponents around the world. Then came Sunil Gavaskar. The rest is history."

In order to make his point, Adhikari need not have gone out of the way to make these underserved and uncharitable remarks against Roy and Contractor. Those who are conversant with the history of cricket will agree that Pankaj Roy did not cower before the bowling of Roy Gilchrist as alleged by Adhikari. In a match played in February 1963 in Kolkata, Pankaj Roy had batted valiantly against the bowling of Gilchrist and scored a century in each of the two innings! It was a Ranji Trophy match between Bengal and Hyderabad played in Kolkata. The players from West Indies – Gilchrist and King- – had played in this match as members of the Hyderabad and Bengal teams respectively.

When I heard the news of Pankaj Roy's death in Kolkata on February 4, 2001, I felt a deep sense of personal loss. In his death, Indian cricket has lost one of its greatest batsmen ever and a gentleman par excellence.

Note

1. Account given by Shri Yadavendra Sahai, Director, Maharaja Sawai Mansingh Museum, Jaipur, as quoted by the Press Trust of India in a report in The Hindustan Times dated March 10, 2001.

17

Further on the Presidency College

I returned to Kolkata in the latter half of October,1947 after paying my farewell visit to Vikrampur. The Presidency College re-opened after the Puja holidays and our classes began in right earnest. As studies in the college picked up, I realized that for a proper study of Economics, the subject of my honours course, it was necessary to have a good grounding in Mathematics, as mathematical tools of analysis had come to acquire a good deal of importance in the realm of theoretical Economics. The names of Jan Tinbergen and Ragnar Frisch, pioneers of the science of econometrics, had begun to be bandied about with increasing frequency in academic circles. I, therefore, took up Mathematics in lieu of History as my subsidiary subject, not because of any great liking for the 'music of the spheres ' – the name given by Byron to Mathematics – but in genuflection to the cold logic of academic necessity.

The professors of Economics as also of Politics, which still formed an integral part of the syllabus of the Economics honours course, were an outstanding lot. The way they guided us in our studies created in us the urge to drink deep at the fountain of knowledge. Some of them helped us with books from their personal collections. What they aimed at was the full development of our intellectual potential and fostering in us the hankering for the acquisition of knowledge, but knowledge not merely of the specialized kind, but also of a generalised nature as Plato had visualised for the pupils of Greece, whom he expected to govern wisely.

I had a feeling that the atmosphere in the Presidency College was not as cosmopolitan as was generally believed. Often, the average Bengalee student made no secret of his faith in the greatness of Bengal's culture. About this greatness, there is no doubt in my mind nor perhaps in the minds of many others. But the way this feeling was expressed and flaunted led people from other Provinces to sometimes make sarcastic remarks, though sotto voce. It was perhaps natural for an average Bengalee to harbour feelings of this kind in an environment where the values of the Bengal Renaissance of the 19th century still held sway and the intellectual advances made in other parts of the country were still to be taken note of by the intelligentsia of Bengal.

The college had a well-stocked library, whose holdings of books on economic subjects were much superior to those of most other colleges. One could take some books home, apart from studying important reference books in the library's reading room during and sometimes even outside college hours. I also drew heavily upon the near-by library of the Calcutta University, courtesy the help of some senior students of M.A. classes whose acquaintance I had been able to make. For reports of Commissions set up by the Government of India or any Provincial Government, some of which we required for study, we often went to the famous book store on Hastings Road near the Government House, where we could buy them at nominal prices.

In 1947 when I joined the Presidency College, the number of girl students was far less than that of boys. There is a long history behind how girl students gained admission into the Presidency College, which initially was an exclusive male preserve. It was in June 1896 that one Miss Flora Patrick made the first move with a letter to the Principal of the Presidency College enquiring if girls could be admitted as its students. A copy of the letter is reproduced below[1]

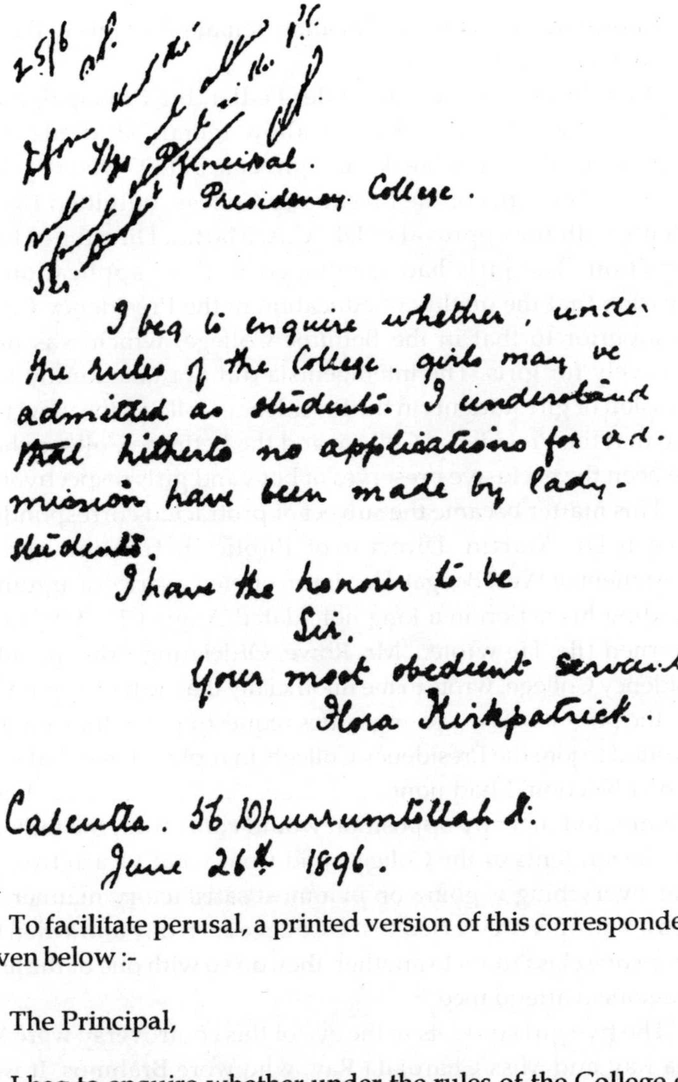

The Principal.
Presidency College.
Sir,
I beg to enquire whether, under the rules of the College, girls may be admitted as students. I understand that hitherto no applications for admission have been made by lady-students.
I have the honour to be
Sir.
Your most obedient Servant.
Flora Kirkpatrick.

Calcutta. 56 Dhurrumtollah St:
June 26th 1896.

...

To facilitate perusal, a printed version of this correspondence is given below :-

To

The Principal,

Sir,

I beg to enquire whether under the rules of the College girls may be admitted as students. I understand that hitherto no applications for admission have been made by lady-students.

I have the honour to be,

Calcutta, 56 Dhurrumtollah St. Sir,
June 26th 1896. Your most obedient Servant
Flora Kirkpatrick
26/6

Inform that the rules do not allow female students in the P.C.
AP (Alexander Pedlar)

As indicated above, Alexander Pedlar, the Principal, passed the order that the rules did not allow female students in the Presidency College. The break-through came in 1897 when F J Rowe, Officiating Principal of the Presidency College, admitted two girl students with the approval of DR. C.A. Martin, Director of Public Instruction. The girls had mentioned in their applications for admission that the quality of education in the Presidency College was superior to that in the Bethune College, which was meant exclusively for girls. The intelligentsia did not take kindly to the admission of girl students in the Presidency College, the view taken being that the Presidency College and the Bethune College should have been the exclusive preserves of boys and girls respectively.

This matter became the subject of protracted correspondence between Dr. Martin, Director of Public Instruction and the Government of West Bengal. Dr Martin offered a series of arguments defending his action in a long note dated August 17, 1897 on the concerned file. He wrote: "Mr. Rowe, Officiating Principal of the Presidency College, wrote to me unofficially that he had applications from the parents of two young ladies requesting that they might be permitted to join the Presidency College. In reply I stated that if they had no objection, I had none.. I never contemplated that any opposition would come from the fathers of the male students of the College, and from what I learn from Mr. Rowe, everything is going on in a most satisfactory manner. The ladies are properly escorted to the College each day and when they go from one class room to another, they do so with one of the junior Professors in attendance."[2]

The two girl students in the eye of this controversy were Miss Amia Ray and Miss Charulata Ray, who were Brahmos. It was a Brahmo paper, "Cosmopolitan and Liberal", which denounced this move as retrograde, commenting inter alia : "While the universities of Oxford and Cambridge have shown themselves peculiarly orthodox in matters of female education, it is to be deeply regretted that some unwilling advocates of radical reform in India have rushed in where angels dare not tread."[3]

Dr. Martin, a courageous man, presented the government with a fait accompli. The Lieutenant-Governor of Bengal wrote on the file: " Write demi-officially to Dr. Martin and say that the Lieutenant-Governor thinks that an important change of the kind should not have been made without obtaining the orders of Government. Now that it has been made, and that it is reported to be working satisfactorily, the Lieutenant-Governor will not interfere, at all events for the present." After this, sporadic but unsuccessful efforts were made towards securing the admission of girls into this college. It was in 1944 that this was permitted when Prof. A.K. Chanda was the Principal.[4]

Thus in 1944, girls started getting into this college and their number rose slowly but steadily. In most other Kolkata colleges, there was no co-education at that time. In the late nineteen forties, the view taken in academic circles was that mixed colleges provided an atmosphere for the growth of better adjusted personalities, whereas uni-sex colleges produced more aggressive boys and girls with a more prudish and demure disposition. However, in practice, most of the Kolkata colleges refused to switch over to the system of co-education, the only exceptions being the Calcutta University and a few colleges like the Presidency College and the Scottish Church College.

It was a new experience for me to get to see some girl students, who added a touch of colour to our classes. The strict discipline of the Presidency College provided hardly any occasion for boys and girls to speak to one another or exchange greetings even inside the class room. Their eyes hardly ever met. Outside the class room, there was hardly any contact or interaction between them. There was a separate common room in the college for the girls to spend their leisure time in between classes.

As the bell rang signalling the beginning of a period, the boys first entered the class room and took their seats. Soon thereafter, the teacher entered the room with the girls trooping in behind him. The girls then sat on a few benches on one side of the room, which were exclusively meant for them – an extension of the system that obtained in Kolkata's buses and tram cars, where also special seats were earmarked for girls with the words 'ladies only' emblazoned on them.

The girls never entered the class room unchaperoned by a professor. We often saw how patiently the girls waited in the corridor, outside the class room, looking away from the boys and gazing at the sky, if the professor was delayed for some reason in arriving at the appointed time for his tryst with the girls before leading them into the class room. When the bell rang at the end of a period, the boys waited for a minute or so to allow the teacher to leave the room, again with the girls in tow. After making sure that the girls had all left, the boys then came out, which left no chance for a mix-up at the door-way between boys and girls, whether intended or otherwise, at the time of departure.

Looking at those days through the rear-view mirror of life, I have often laughed at myself, wondering how we all co-operated in so scrupulously clinging to these Victorian values in a post-independence India from which the British had already departed. There was nothing extraordinary in such unabashed display of Victorianism in contemporary Kolkata society, because the process of social change took quite some time to catch up with what was happening in the rest of the post-war world. One must remember that there was still a legal ban in our country on a book like D.H. Lawrence's "Lady Chatterly's Lover", whose unexpurgated version it was difficult to get, even though by today's standards, themes of this kind would look quite unappetising.

The boys and the girls of the Presidency College invariably addressed one another as 'Aapni' (which was the most formal manner of addressing a person), hardly ever as 'Tumi' (which is less formal) and never as 'Tui' (the most informal mode of address). In those strait-laced times, there was no question by boys and girls holding hands in the college premises.

The girls being overwhelmingly outnumbered by the boys, the situation bore close resemblance to that described in Maxim Gorky's famous story "Twenty six Boys and a Girl". Like Tania, the charming girl of Gorky's story, the Presidency College girls of our days moved about among the boys with consummate skill, evading entanglement of any sort. The boys, like Gorky's 26 men, were all admiration for the girls. They were not openly ogling at the girls all the time; however, they were not above casting occasional glances at them, not furtively, but in a gawky straightforward manner, which made them look innocent.

The students of the Presidency College came from different socio-economic backgrounds. Some came from villages and district towns, some from east Bengal districts with their different local Bengali dialects and some from the English-medium schools of Kolkata and elsewhere. Many of the students hailed from Kolkata's aristocratic and wealthy families. It can be said in a general way that these differences in their backgrounds did not create any lack of harmony or friendship among the students.

Games and sports were a sphere of activity which was somewhat neglected during my days in the Presidency College. Though the college grounds were properly maintained and some facilities were provided, very few boys and practically no girl took advantage of them. Occasionally, there were friendly cricket matches between the teams of two classes of the college. We had an outstanding cricketer in Govinda Roy, a student of our class, who was the brother of Pankaj Roy, India's opening batsman of a bygone era. We had a special reason to exult over the batting prowess of Govinda, who used to play for the West Bengal cricket team in the Ranji Trophy matches. Sometimes his mighty strokes lashed the cricket ball on to the windows of the Baker Laboratory building, smashing their glass-panes.

More than half a century has elapsed since I left the Presidency College. Going by whatever I now read and hear, I think that the elitism of this college is now a thing of the past. After the communists came to power in West Bengal, they began to transfer the professors of the Presidency College to colleges in the districts and replace them with those from the latter colleges – obviously to level everything down rather than up in pursuance of the communist principle of egalitarianism! If this was my own view alone, I could have been wrong. This is a view that has been expressed by many including no less a person than Dr. Amartya Sen, a distinguished alumnus of this college and the recipient of the Nobel Prize in Economics. In August 1998, interviewed by the associate publisher of Business India, Dr. Sen mentioned many institutions of academic excellence in India such as the IIT's, the Delhi School of Economics, the Indian Statistical Institute and the Jawahar Lal Nehru University of Delhi.

But Sen excluded from this list his own under-graduate college in Kolkata – the Presidency College, about which, when questioned, he observed: "I think the issue really is why these institutions grow up and then don't seem to survive in that position. I have a very good example. My under-graduate college in Calcutta, Presidency College. What a great undergraduate college! And it is in pretty hard times now and I think that to some extent public policy has not helped really because there was inadequate recognition of the special nature of the college. It is criticised for being elitist. Now I think there is real tension in supporting elitism in a situation in which equity cries for attention. Elitism is seen as the enemy of equity. Unfortunately, great academic institutions are to some extent elitist institutions. A particular problem we are having in Britain right now is a good comparison. There, one of the problems is that the present government, the Labour Government, is more favourable to education in many ways, even to university education. But it has not been favourable to Oxbridge, it's seen as privileged".[5]

The so-called Brahmanism of the uppity colleges of Oxford and Cambridge is said to be out of sync with the changing times, which call for a change in outlook. That was the reason behind the British Labour Party's plea for certain measures of levelling down in the field of education. I have no doubt in my mind that the Calcutta Presidency College is the victim of a similar process of levelling down.

In April 1999, I was shocked to read reports in the press that some students of the Presidency College were addicted to marijuana and alcohol and that a few of them were seen smoking marijuana in the college canteen. The Principal of the college had reportedly rushed to the canteen to upbraid these students. The student fronts of rival political parties took sides on this issue and took to the streets, assaulting the members of rival students' unions. These clashes led to the 'Gherao' of the college Principal by some students which was lifted only after certain assurances were given by the former and the police also intervened.

A few months later, in August 1999, I read a report in the press that the Presidency College had been closed indefinitely as an explosive situation had developed following the alleged molestation of a girl student by one of the teachers! In the course of this agitation, the students had kept the Director of Public Instruction as well as the Principal of the college confined in a room throughout the night. I did not keep track of further developments. Taking these events into account, can anybody now talk of the Presidency College's elitism?

An important institution of our college days was (as it still is to a certain extent, I understand) the India Coffee House run by the Coffee Board on the first floor of a big building called Albert Hall at the academic nerve-centre on the College Street just opposite the Presidency College. It was the ambition of every young student to enter the Coffee House and sip a cup of coffee sitting around one of its many tables along with his friends during an interval between lectures in the college. This coffee house reminded me of what I had read in a college text book about Dr. Samuel Johnson, the nineteenth century British intellectual. It was said that Dr. Johnson and his friends used to gather at coffee houses in London to discuss not only newly published books but also political developments and social scandals. At these coffee house sessions, Dr. Johnson's celebrated biographer, James Boswell, the Scotsman, often gave him company, sitting there in a mood of constant adulation, ever anxious to take note of whatever tit-bits, he hoped, would come in handy for incorporation in his hagiography of Dr. Johnson.

I had heard that Paris was also known for its many coffee houses, one of which had become famous after having been the favourite haunt of luminaries like Guillaume Apollinaire, well-known French poet and inventor of the term 'surrealism', Ernest Hemingway, the novelist, and Zhou en-Lai, the communist revolutionary.

Many students of the Presidency College and the Calcutta University took enormous pride in cutting classes and whiling away their time in the Coffee House on the College Street. Some boys smoked cigarettes in the Coffee House, often merely to show off. There were some, who posed as proletarian intellectuals by occasionally smoking 'Bidis' in the Coffee House, though they were affluent enough to afford the best cigarettes. Not at all of them relished their 'Bidis' as often became evident from the coughing bouts that followed, making them look red in the face.

Cigarette smoke that curled up in billows clouded the big hall of the Coffee House. Mingling with the aroma of freshly percolated coffee, it created the right atmosphere for intellectual stimulation in which students – both boys and girls, but usually in gender-exclusive groups – used to discuss and debate the pros and cons of various issues, covering the whole spectrum of all conceivable subjects – economic, social, political, philosophical and scientific.

Often these discussions scaled great intellectual heights – whatever the matter under review – be it the dialectical materialism of Karl Marx, the Categorical Imperative of Kant, the thesis-antithesis-synthesis of Hegel, the Freudian interpretation of dreams, the ideas of Sartre, Kirkegaard or Bergson, the paintings of Picasso (which, alas, I had not seen at all), the works of Bernard Shaw, Maugham, Wodehouse, Dostoevsky, Maupassant, Huxley and Bertrand Russel or the poetry of Rabindranath Tagore and Jibanananda Das, or oriental and Western erotica represented by the Kamasutra, Tantras and Taoism of China on the one hand and the writings of Havelock Ellis on the other, or the multiplier of Keynesian economics, the theoretical under-pinning of the Indian communists' diatribe against the role of the I.N.A. and Netaji Subhas Chandra Bose or the latest Western film showing at Kolkata's Metro Cinema in Chowringhee. Terms such as the sub-conscious mind, sublimation and existentialism were freely bandied about across the table, as the students waxed eloquent on a theme that had cropped up. While the subjects ranged from the sublime to the ridiculous, often I was not sure how much we really understood of what we constantly chattered about.

The gossip in the Coffee House acquired a transcendental character from the very nature and level of the discussions held and differed qualitatively from what the Germans call Kaffeeklatsch – the composite noise produced by the mingling of high-decibel gossip and the clatter of coffee cups and spoons. But in the midst of this din and bustle, one could on occasion spot in a quiet corner a solitary figure, perhaps a poet, treating himself to coffee at a leisurely pace, trying to "see through all things with his half-shut eyes", as the English poet Pope had said. The Coffee House was as much for budding and established poets as for fire-brand revolutionaries including – as I heard much later – those of the Naxalite brand.

The Coffee House was a favourite haunt of Bohemians of different kinds – students, teachers, professionals and even some political figures. They were mostly unconventional people with peculiar habits and dress and a life-style that sometimes looked wayward. Many of them posed as intellectuals. Some of them were not at all well-to-do, as their unpolished worn-out shoes, unpretentious clothes and unkempt looks proclaimed. An important reason for the Bengalee intellectual's patronisation of the Coffee House was that it satisfied his innate urge for 'Adda' or gossip at the theoretical plane for which Bengalees have a natural weakness.

'Adda' was a sort of talkfest that helped the participants to unwind. There were various levels of 'Adda' in Kolkata. Whatever might have been the themes of gossip at other places, 'Adda' that thrived in the Coffee House was not, generally speaking, of the prurient kind nor was it marked by excessive pre-occupation with romantic themes about "who's whose". It was mostly innocent gossip and intellectual in character. Many years later, I read a piece [6] on 'Adda' that quoted the following saying: "A good thing about gossip is that it is within everybody's reach/And it is more interesting than any other form of speech". Ogder Nash has said: "Oh, I do like a little bit of gossip/It seems to lend savour to my tea ".[7]

I visited the Coffee House rather infrequently during my under-graduate days. I went there more frequently and almost regularly during my stint at the Calcutta University as an M.A. and Law student during 1949-52. At least one renowned professor of the Calcutta University had taken a class for a group of about a dozen of us at the Coffee House, thus putting the seal of informal recognition on our rendezvous at the Coffee House. I learnt a lot from the hours that I spent at the Coffee House. The numerous sessions there helped to build up my self-confidence and my over-all personality.

The India Coffee House had a branch in New Delhi's Connaught Place. When I came to Delhi to appear at the personality test for the Indian Administrative Service etc. examination in December 1952, I did not miss the opportunity of paying a visit to this branch along with some friends. To our utter surprise, a bearer serving coffee to us, recognised me and expressed great jubilation, saying that he had recently come to Delhi on transfer from Kolkata and that he had recognised me, because he used to see me at the Coffee House in Kolkata. I thanked him for his kind recognition and the humble tribute that he paid to my coffee-drinking habit of long standing which my Delhi friends, in whose company I had gone there, also recognised on the basis of the collateral evidence tendered by the bearer of the Coffee House.

Apart from the Coffee House on College Street, there was another on Kolkata's Chittaranjan Avenue. Both places were the favourite haunts of Bengalee intellectuals, who were regular coffee-imbibers. In the former, students and academicians predominated and in the latter, the clientele included a sizeable number of government officials as well as boxwallahs. In the early nineteen fifties, I heard a story – true or apocryphal I did not know – that some high-brow officials of the Indian Civil Service and the Indian Police used to drink infusion during lunch hours at the Chittranjan Avenue Coffee House, while they solved the difficult crossword puzzles of the 'Statesman', the famous Kolkata daily that passed for the last word in good writing in the Englishman's language after the days of the Raj came to an end.

I had heard in the late nineteen fifties that the College Street Coffee House was about to shut shop owing to a financial crisis arising from the demands put forward by the workers led by A.K. Gopalan, the communist Member of Parliament. Pandit Jawahar Lal Nehru's intervention was reported to have saved the day for the Coffee House. Again in 1996, I heard that the Coffee House was threatened with closure because of its inability to undertake essential repairs to the building and the likelihood of the Land Reforms Department of the West Bengal Government de-requisitioning the premises unless the Co-operative Department paid it a huge sum of money that had become due.

I was relieved to hear in September 1996 that the Left Front Government of West Bengal had bailed out the Coffee House by making a sum of over 26 lakh rupees available as part of a plan to convert it into an institution of cultural importance (or national importance?). It was then to be run by a workers' cooperative society on the basis of a 99-year lease.

Quite some years ago, I read a Bengali poem on the India Coffee House penned by Gauri Prasanna Majumdar, a famous lyricist, and then one day I heard its masterly rendition by Manna Dey, the popular musician, in an emotional voice that reeked of nostalgia and with a heart that sounded heavy from a sense of loss, because he himself used to hang out at the India Coffee House many decades ago. The song struck a chord deep in my heart and brought back memories of a bygone era. A few lines from Majumdar's poem that I have paraphrased with some difficulty into English would read like this:

"Gone are those days of 'Adda' (gossip) at the Coffee House. Where have those golden afternoons vanished? Nikhilesh is in Paris, Moidul inDhaka. D' Souza, the Goanese guitarist of Grand Hotel, lies in his grave. Roma Roy, who gave her heart to someone and then got the shock of her life, has lost her mind and is now in a lunatic asylum. Sujata is the happiest of all. Her millionaire husband—posh house and car, he has them all—has covered her body from top to toe with diamonds and jewels.—We used to sit for hours on end at the Coffee House table with 'Charminar' (a cheap brand of cigarette) dangling from our lips. Sometimes Bishnu Dey (the well-known Bengalee poet), sometimes Jamini Roy (the famous painter) formed the themes of our gossip. Sun or rain, we made a point of turning up at the Coffee House at the appointed hour from wherever we happened to be.—"

Some years later, I gave up my habit of regularly going to coffee house. But I used to hear that people in different parts of the globe, who continued to throng coffee houses, felt deeply moved by Bob Dylan's famous song, as he sat sipping coffee. "One more cup of coffee before I go to the valley below." Even at home, I did not remain untouched by the mordant melody of Dylan's lyric as it sometimes came over the radio. And my mind at once flew back to my glorious coffee house days of Kolkata.

Having been an ardent votary of the coffee culture early in my life, I feel sad to read in the newspapers that in recent times coffee houses in many parts of the globe are fast losing out to the lure of pizza parlours and fast food joints. The brown brew that once counted among its votaries such great names as Samuel Johnson, Voltaire and T.S. Eliot does not appear to hold the same appeal for the modern intellectual who does not have enough time to spare for long sessions at coffee houses. It is particularly disconcerting to be told that in Paris, the pioneer of the bean culture, the number of coffee houses is on the decline.

On the flip side of all this is the news that there are some coffee bars in New York which are meant for singles and which, therefore, serve as centres where one can go and scout before picking up a companion of one's choice from the opposite gender![8]

Notes

1. Taken from brochure published in 1998 by the Calcutta Presidency College Association, Delhi.
2. *Ibid.*
3. *Ibid.*
4. *Ibid.*
5. *Ibid.* A tribute paid by the Calcutta Presidency College Alumni Association, Delhi, to Nobel Laureate Dr. Amartya Sen.
6. Editorial in the Times of India, New Delhi, dated July 28, 2000.
7. *Ibid.*
8. Middle in the Times of India, New Delhi,dated June 20, 2001, written by Mohinder Singh.

18

M.N. Roy: Comintern Hero and Humanist

During my Calcutta University days, I often saw the one-time Comintern hero, M.N. Roy, and his German wife, Ellen Roy, who lived on an upper floor of the Albert Hall building on the College Street. Sometimes I saw them when they came down for coffee, generally in the afternoons, to the famous India Coffee House located on a floor of the same building. We all looked at them from a distance with a feeling of awe and reverence that their presence spontaneously aroused in us.

The India Coffee House had the honour of being visited by many other great personages such as Rabindranath Tagore and Pandit Jawahar Lal Nehru and, at a much later date, by Satyajit Ray. But unlike them, the Roys were regular visitors to the place and in fact its habitues. In this context, it is worth mentioning that I had heard of a famous coffee house in Paris, where eminent personalities like Jean-Paul Sartre, the French existentialist philosopher an left-wing intellectual, and Simone de Beauvoir, also an existentialist, author of the famous book, 'The Second Sex', and a pioneer of the femininist movement used to live in the nineteen forties.

From occasional discussions with some adherents of M.N. Roy and my study of books about him, I knew that he was not only an intellectual stalwart with an extra-ordinary analytical ability and a deep understanding of political ideology, but also a great practical revolutionary, who remained in constant touch with and gave concrete shape to the political reality on the ground. He had his initial baptism of fire in our country's nationalist movement, particularly of the insurrectionist and underground brand that was incarnated in the Yugantar and Anushilan groups of Bengal. He courted repeated incarceration for political dacoities committed in furtherance of the nationalist cause.

Clandestine peregrinations that subsequently took M.N.Roy to different parts of the globe in search of arms and funds to give teeth to the struggle for India's freedom, his role in organising and guiding the communist movement in countries as far apart as Mexico, the U.S.S.R., China and India and his pioneering effort in laying the foundation of a radical humanist movement in India had endowed him with a rich fund of revolutionary field experience. This enabled him not only to thoroughly grasp the essentials of communist and non-communist ideologies, but even to make an original contribution to them in the light of his own experience that was trans-continental and global in its sweep and spread. It may not be wide off the mark to say that in those days, he was the only Indian with an original mind, who bestrode the world of communist ideology and practice like a colossus.

Roy was a great frontiersman, whose role in the formulation and implementation of policies that guided the destinies of incipient communist movements in the under-developed countries of the world placed him in the same revolutionary pantheon as Lenin, Stalin and Mao Tse-tung. It is with such world figures as Mahatma Gandhi, Pandit Jawahar Lal Nehru, Lenin, Stalin, Trotsky, Borodin, Zinoviev, Bukharin, Mao Tse-Tung and Ho Chi Minh that he rubbed shoulders. It will not be an exaggeration to say that no contemporary political leader of India could rival the universality of his experience and exposure. Even without the benefit of formal college education, he was an original thinker par excellence, from whose pen flowed a ceaseless stream of seminal writing. Some of the numerous books that he authored are regarded as classics in the literature and philosophy of revolution.

To have the opportunity of seeing such an outstanding figure in flesh and blood so often was a unique privilege. Not that I agreed then – as I do not even now – with all that he had preached in theory or done in practice; but then, when all is said and done, he was a great man, much greater than most of the figures that strutted on our country's political stage.

Some of my communist friends used to taunt him, branding him as a "left sectarian", "right deviationist" or "counter-revolutionary" according to their own lights. Many years later, I heard that after the split in Communist Party of India, the right faction of the party had traced the Maoist deviation of the Chinese party to the seeds of left sectarianism that had once been sown by M.N. Roy. After Roy founded the Radical Humanist Party, some political workers, who were loyal to him, often distributed pamphlets, particularly the weekly organ of the new party among students and members of the public in the College Square area of Kolkata. One of the political workers, whom I came to know closely in course of time, gave me these pamphlets and some other publications, which threw light on Roy's many-splendoured revolutionary activities, particularly those during the nineteen twenties and thirties, when he was at the zenith of his career in the Comintern. As I read them in between my college books, whenever I had some time to spare, I could not but admire the depth and sweep of Roy's practical experience and theoretical knowledge.

It was but natural that the British authorities and their intelligence agencies in India and the rest of the world would keep a constant tab on M.N. Roy's movements, contacts and multifarious activities. Years later, when I was in a position to get access to all that the British did to keep track of his activities, I was not amused to see their characterisation of Roy as "the arch conspirator and Indian agent of the Comintern in Russia".[1]

Roy's original name was Narendra Nath Bhattacharya. When he went to the U.S.A. to seek arms for our freedom struggle, he changed his name to Manabendra Nath Roy in order to evade the sleuthsof British intelligence, who were ever on his trail. His underground life in the U.S.A. had a tinge of romance, as he had an affair with an American girl, Evelyn Trent, whom he later married. But they separated after about ten years.

Before this, M.N. Roy's efforts to get arms from Indonesia, Japan, China and the Philippines had ended in failure. He had also had a hand in what was called the "German plots" for importing arms into India in 1915. A report prepared on this subject by the Government of Bengal in 1933 made the following observations on these plots: " The plot was successfully frustrated—The most important Bengal names connected with these plots are those of Heramba Lal Gupta, Amarendra Chatterjea, Naren Bhattacharya (M.N. Roy), Abani Mukherjea and Rash Behari Basu".[2]

Roy's companion in the Coffee House was a German lady, Ellen Roy (nee Gottschalk), his wife by second marriage, whom he had met and courted in Europe. She had followed him to India where they married in 1937. Looking at her in the Coffee House from close quarters,I got an opportunity of seeing how a European lady spoke, ate and generally behaved. Roy and his wife had a dignified demeanour, which greatly impressed us.

It is hard to believe that Roy, who once ranked among the world's top-most communist leaders, should have in the initial years drawn inspiration from another Indian revolutionary, V.D. Savarkar, who was a great nationalist no doubt, but at the same time a firm believer in the supremacy of the Hindus in India's political destiny—a sectarian attitude which went ill with the internationalist outlook of communist revolutionaries. Roy had once even toyed with the idea of renouncing the world and had travelled to many places in different parts of India on foot, a la Swami Vivekananda. But he soon outgrew this renunciatory mood and switched over to the very different life of an underground political revolutionary branded as a terrorist in contemporary parlance. In due course, he, along with several others including Muzaffar Ahmed, prepared the ground for launching the communist movement and a peasant organisation in Bengal.

In the USA, Roy developed friendship with Lala Lajpat Rai and some other Indians who were working for Indian independence. Many of these persons were arrested and tried in what was called the Hindu Conspiracy Case. Roy and Evelyn were also questioned in this case, but they succeeded in convincing the US intelligence of their non-involvement in the conspiracy. They escaped from the USA to Mexico in 1917 and established contact with the Germans, who helped Roy with funds some of which he managed to send to Rash Behari Bose, an Indian revolutionary operating from Japan, and to some other Indian revolutionaries in the U.S.A.

It was in Mexico that Roy turned over a new leaf in his revolutionary career by embracing communism. There, he founded the Communist Party of Mexico—the first such party outside the

Soviet Union. It was there that he met the Soviet communist leader, Borodin, who was masquerading as a commercial representative from the USSR. Soon thereafter, Roy was invited by Lenin to see him in Moscow.

Travelling across several European countries, Roy reached Berlin in 1920. Following Germany's humiliation in World War I, Berlin was then seething with the fervour of an imminently anticipated red revolution that, however, ultimately failed to materialise and came to nought. Roy came in contact with many German communist leaders as well as with the luminaries of the Indian Revolutionary Committee in Berlin among whom were such well-known figures as Virendranath Chattopadhyaya, Bhupendranath Dutta and Hardyal. Virendranath was the brother of Sarojini Naidu, India's nightingale and freedom fighter. Their family originally hailed from Vikrampur in east Bengal (now in Bangladesh). Their distant Vikrampur connection was a matter of some pride for me in as much as I also belonged to the same place.

An important member of the Indian Revolutionary Committee in Berlin was Bhupendranath Dutta, brother of Swami Vivekananda and editor of 'Yugantar', the mouthpiece of India's revolutionaries. Another Indian whom Roy met in Berlin and who became his lieutenant was Abani Nath Mukherjee. Later, Roy and Mukherjee fell out. A contemporary report of the Intelligence Bureau, Government of India described Mukherjee as " a self-opinionated scoundrel, who has been completely over-shadowed by Roy in Indo-Bolshevik intrigues".[3]

From Berlin, Roy proceeded to Moscow in 1920 and met Lenin, who gave him an important position in the Comintern. From there, he helped the Indian communist movement with funds and guidance and played a key role in the formulation and implementation of the Comintern's policy, particularly in the Asian countries. The Indian Military School, which he set up at Tashkent, imparted training to some Muslim pilgrims from India, who had sneaked into Afghanistan when the Khilafat movement was at its height in India. He was instrumental in bringing into being an emigre Communist Party of India at Tashkent, though some people were of the view that Indian revolutionaries such as Acharya and Abdul Rab, who were already there, had played a big role in the formation of this party. In

1921, he set up the Communist University of the Toilers of the East, which trained many Indians in the theory and practical strategy of ushering in a communist revolution.

At the Second Congress of the Comintern held in Berlin in 1920, M. N. Roy made a great impact by virtue of a thesis he presented on the role of the communist party in the national liberation movement in the colonial countries—a thesis which was a landmark in the evolution of communist thinking over this issue. Lenin had already circulated a thesis over this issue. Since Roy had mentioned to Lenin an alternative view in this matter, he was told by the latter to put forward a separate draft, which he did. There were thus two drafts for consideration by the Second Congress—Lenin's Theses on the National and Colonial Question and Roy's Supplementary Theses on the National and Colonial Question.

Lenin's thesis suggested a strategy that enjoined on the communist party in a colonial country to actively support the bourgeois-democratic national liberation struggle. Roy did not agree with Lenin's formulation, as, in his view, the bourgeoisie in many colonial countries including India was reactionary in character and was likely to deceive the masses. His thesis was that in the colonial countries, the communist party should give a wide berth to the bourgeoisie and instead join hands with the landless peasants and industrial workers in furtherance of a revolutionary national liberation movement.

It was paragraph 11 of Lenin's draft which was the bone of contention between him and Roy. This paragraph of Lenin's draft relating to backward countries said :"11(a)–The necessity of all communist parties to render assistance to the bourgeois-democratic liberation movement in such countries: especially does this duty fall upon the workers of such countries upon which the backward nations are colonially or financially dependent."

Roy, as already stated, was of the view that the Communist International should ignore the bourgeois-democratic movement and exclusively help the communist movement in such countries. Lenin went through Roy's draft and amended it by scoring out some passages which did not fit in with his own assessment. Reproduced below are some paragraphs of Roy's original draft signed by him showing the passages which Lenin scored out :[4]

Photostat of Roy's Original Draft Supplementary Theses On The National And Colonial Question

[illegible] [illegible] NATIONAL [illegible] COLONIAL [illegible]

1. To determine the relation of the Communirt International to the revolutionary movements in the countries [illegible] by capitalistic imperialism is one of the most important questions before the Second Congress of the Third International. The history of the World revolution has come to a period when the a proper understanding of this relation is indispensable; the great European War and its results have shown clearly that the masses of the non-European subjected countries are inseparably connected with the proleterian movement in Europe, as a consequence of the centralized world Capitalism.

2. The fountain-head from which European Capitalism draws its main strength is no longer to be found in the industrial countries of Europe, but in the colonial possessions and dependencies. Without the control of the extensive markets and vast field of exploitation in the colonies, the capitalist powers [illegible] their existence even for a short time. England, the stronghold of Imperialism, has been suffering from over-production since more than a century ago. But for the extensive colonial possessions acquired for selling her surplus products and as a source of raw materials for her ever-growing industries, the capitalist structure of England would have crushed under its own weight long ago. By enslaving the hundreds of millions of inhabitants of Asia and Africa, English Imperialism succeeded so far in keeping the British proletariat under the domination of the bourgeoisie.

3. Super-profit gained in the colonies is the mainstay of modern capitalism, and so long as this is not deprived of this source of super-profit, it will not be easy for the European working class to overthrow the capitalist order. [illegible] the possibility of intensive and extensive exploitation of the human labor and natural resources in the colonies, the capitalist nations of Europe are trying, not without success, to recuperate their present bankruptcy. [illegible] exploiting the masses in the colonies, European Imperialism will be in a position to give concession after concession to the proletariat at home. It will [illegible] to go to the extent of sacrificing the entire surplus value in the home country so long as it [illegible] in the position to gain its huge super-profit in the colonies.

4. Without the breaking up of the colonial empire, the overthrow of the Capitalist system in Europe does not [illegible] possible. Consequently, the Communist International must widen the sphere of its activities. It must establish relations with those revolutionary forces that are [illegible] for the overthrow of Imperialism in the countries subjected politically and economically.

5. Such relation of the Communirt International with the revolutionary movement in the subject countries is not tantamount to the former's upholding the doctrine of Nationalism. The Communist International is the concentrated will of the world revolutionary proletariat. Its mission is to organize the working class of the whole world for the overthrow of the capitalist order and the establishment of Communism. The Third International is a fighting body which has outgrown the realm of pure doctrinairianism

[illegible] Dominated as it was by a group of politicians, permeated with bourgeois culture, the Second International failed to appreciate the importance of the colonial question. For them, the world did not exist outside of Europe. They could not see the necessity of coordinating the revolutionary movements in Europe with those in the non-European countries. Instead of giving moral and material help to the revolutionary movements in the colonies, the members of the Second International themselves became imperialists.

6. Foreign Imperialism imposed on the Eastern peoples prevented them from developing socially and economically side by side with their fellows in Europe and America. Owing to the imperialistic policy of preventing industrial development of the colonies, a proletarian class in the strict sense of term could not come into existence until recently. The indigenous craft industries were destroyed to make room for the products of the centralized industries in the imperialistic countries; consequently a big majority of the population was driven to the land to produce food grains and raw materials for export to foreign lands. On the other hand, there followed a rapid con-

[illegible]ntration of land, the proprietary right of which was vested in the state, thus creating a huge landless peasantry. The great bulk of the population was kept in a state of illiteracy. As a result of this policy, the spirit of revolt latent in every subject people found its expression only through the small, educated middle class.

The foreign domination has obstructed the free development of the social forces, therefore its overthrow is the first step towards the revolution in the colonies. So, to help overthrow the foreign rule in the colonies is not to endorse the nationalist aspirations of the native bourgeoisie but to open up the way to the smothered proletariat there.

7. The revolutionary movements in the colonies are essentially an economic struggle. The bourgeois democratic nationalist movements are limited to the small middle class which does not reflect the aspirations of the masses. Without the active support of the masses, the national freedom of the colonies will never be attained. But in many countries, especially in India, the masses are not with the bourgeois nationalist leaders, they are moving towards revolution independently of the bourgeois nationalist movement. There are to be found in the dependent countries two distinct movements which every day grow farther and farther apart from each other. One is the bourgeois democratic nationalist movement, with a program of political independence and the other is the mass action of the ignorant and poor peasants and workers. The former endeavor to control the latter and often succeed to a certain extent, but it would be a mistake to assume that the bourgeois nationalist movement expresses the sentiments and aspirations of the general population. For the overthrow of foreign imperialism, the first step towards revolution in the colonies, the cooperation of the bourgeois nationalist elements may be useful. But the Communist International must not find in them the media through which the revolutionary movement in the colonies should be helped. The mass movements in the colonies are growing independently of the nationalist movements. The masses distrust the political leaders who always lead them astray and prevent them from revolutionary action.

8. The real strength of the liberation movement in the colonies is no longer confined to the narrow circle of bourgeois democratic nationalists. In most of the colonial countries there already exist organized socialist or communist parties, in close relation to the mass movement. The relation of the Communist International with the revolutionary [illegible] in the colonies should be through the medium of these parties or groups, because they are the vanguard of the working class in their respective countries. They may not be very big today, but they reflect the desire of the masses and the masses will follow them to the revolution. The Communist Parties of the different imperialistic countries must work in conjunction with these proletarian parties of the colonies and through them, give all the moral and material support to the revolutionary movements in general.

9.

~~The supposition that, owing to the economic and industrial backwardness, the peoples in the colonies are bound to go through the stage of bourgeois democracy is wrong. The events and conditions in many of the colonies do not corroborate such a supposition. It is true that~~ The revolution in the colonies is not going to be a communist revolution in its first stages. But if from the beginning, the lead of the revolution is in the hands of a communist vanguard, the revolutionary masses would not be led astray but would go straight ahead through the successive periods of development of revolutionary experience. Indeed, it would be [illegible] in many of the Oriental countries to solve the agrarian problem along pure communist principles. In its first stages, the revolution in the colonies must be carried with a program in which will be included many petty-bourgeois reform clauses, for instance, division of land etc. But from this it does not [illegible] follow that the lead of the revolution will have to be surrendered to the bourgeois democrats.

10. The bourgeois national democrats in the colonies strive for the establishment of a free national state, whereas the masses of workers and poor peasants are revolting even though in many cases unconsciously, against the

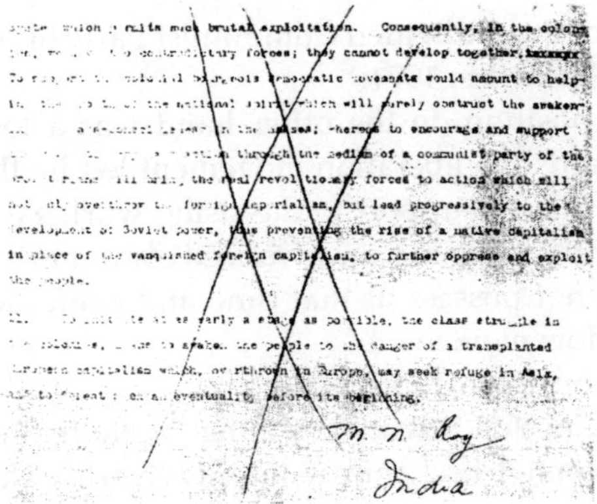
[illegible] which [illegible] such brutal exploitation. Consequently, in the colon[illegible] [illegible] contradictory forces; they cannot develop together. [illegible] To support the colonial bourgeois democratic movements would amount to help[illegible] [illegible] the national spirit which will surely obstruct the awaken[illegible] [illegible] in the masses; whereas to encourage and support [illegible] through the medium of a communist party of the [illegible] will bring the real revolutionary forces to action which will not only overthrow the foreign imperialism, but lead progressively to the development of Soviet power, thus preventing the rise of a native capitalism in place of the vanquished foreign capitalism, to further oppress and exploit the people.

11. [illegible] at as early a stage as possible, the class struggle in the colonies, [illegible] to awaken the people to the danger of a transplanted [illegible] capitalism which, overthrown in Europe, may seek refuge in Asia, and to defeat [illegible] an eventuality before its beginning.

M. N. Roy
India

Lenin's own draft was adopted by the Second Congress of the Communist International with a slight modification of its paragraph 11 mentioned above. This amended paragraph now read as below: "11. With regard to those states and nationalities where a backward, mainly feudal, patriarchal or patriarchal-agrarian regime prevails, the following must be borne in mind: (1) All Communist Parties must give active support to the revolutionary movements of liberation, the form of support to be determined by a study of existing conditions, carried on by the party wherever there is such."

It will thus be seen that Lenin's draft as amended and adopted by the Second Congress dropped the expression "bourgeois-democratic liberation movement" and instead urged all communist parties to support revolutionary movements of liberation. Though this no doubt accommodated Roy's point of view, Lenin did not think that this change of terminology meant anything great on the ground, because, as he believed, in the absence of any communist party worth the name in the backward countries, revolutionary movements in such countries were all bound to be spear-headed by bourgeois-democratic parties.

Ever since Roy fell from the Comintern's grace, it has been the unceasing endeavour of the communists in India and elsewhere to make it appear that Roy's stand was utterly sectarian and wrong and that, in the controversy over the communist party's role in colonial countries, Roy's thesis had been drastically amended by the Comintern, while the change effected in Lenin's thesis was depicted as a very minor one. For example, Dr. G. Adhikari, a top theoretician of the undivided Communist Party of India, observed in a book published in 1971:[5]

"Roy's position on the other hand was a totally negative attitude towards the liberation movement led by the bourgeoisie and of an exclusive support to the rising workers' and peasants' movement, attributing to it an advanced communist consciousness which it did not possess at that time and contraposing it to the national freedom movement."

Further on, Dr. Adhikari said:[6]

"The claim that Roy makes in his Memoirs that his original draft was accepted by Lenin with only "verbal alterations" and adopted by the congress together with Lenin's theses, because his Supplementary Theses were a corrective to those of Lenin, is totally unjustified and false. It is clear from a comparison of the original draft of Roy's theses with its amended version as finally adopted, as well as from the record of the proceedings of the plenary session and of the colonial commission of the congress, that the amendments were not verbal but fundamental and involved the elimination of all dogmatic and sectarian formulations which contradicted the general line of Lenin's theses. The only amendment introduced in Lenin's preliminary draft clarified the general line contained therein which was further concretized by the addition of the amended Supplementary Theses."

Roy's opposition to the idea of collaborating with bourgeois-democratic parties, which in India meant the Indian National Congress, might have derived from his earlier links with the underground revolutionary groups of Bengal. Another reason may have been his hostility towards Virendranath Chattopadhyaya, who was the brother of the Congress leader, Sarojini Naidu, and who, Roy, therefore thought, could have got a boost and preference over Roy if the Comintern were to decide in favour of the communists joining hands with the Indian National Congress. Chattopadhyaya's plea for Russian assistance in bringing together all nationalist groups in India on a common platform as part of India's struggle for freedom was not accepted by the Russians, who preferred to recognise and help M.N.Roy and his communist group.

This was succinctly brought out in the book "Communism In India" (1919-1924)[7] compiled by Sir Cecil Kaye, Director of the Intelligence Bureau, Government of India. Sir Kaye was the predecessor of Sir David Petrie, whose later compilation on the same subject has already been referred to. To quote from Sir Kaye: "Roy had the first word with the Soviet, and appears to have made a good impression upon Lenin, with whom he seems to have been on very friendly terms. He represented to the Soviet Government that Chattopadyaya's party was Nationalist, not Communist: and that it was contrary to Communist principles to help Nationalists. He declared his willingness to co-operate with Chattopadyaya's party if they would accept his terms; but, when the latter arrived at Moscow, they discovered that Roy had already signed a contract with the Soviet Government on behalf of the 'Indian Nationalists', under which he had agreed to accept Bolshevism as the only possible organisation that could be introduced into the 'New India' and had pledged himself to further the cause of Bolshevism, not only in India but throughout the world."

"The Conference of Indian revolutionaries proved a fiasco, Roy and Chattopadyaya disputing leadership and being unwilling to work together. – As the Conference did nothing but quarrel among themselves, the Soviet intervened. They decided in favour of Communism as against Nationalism, though agreeing to help the latter through the former: the decision being in favour of the policy of only recognising and giving help to Communist parties: who were themselves permitted, should they so desire, to aid Nationalist movements. Roy's group was unconditionally recognised as the one with which the Communist International would work in future, and it was agreed to start 'intensified propaganda in India' for which the Soviet Government undertook to provide ample funds. Chattopadyaya objected, and presented a 'thesis' in dissent – saying the first necessity was the overthrow of the British Government in India, after which Communism could be introduced, not only in India but in England, where the loss of India would produce poverty and consequent discontent. The Communist International should undertake this itself – it is incumbent on the Communist International to exploit to the utmost extent every available revolutionary tendency in and outside India. Chattopadyaya, however, in the end accepted the decision, since the Soviet Government refused to afford help under any other conditions."

At that point of time, Roy was critical of Mahatma Gandhi's role in India's freedom movement, which, according to him, smacked of obscurantism. He believed that Gandhiji often mixed religion with politics, collaborated with the capitalists and landlords and advocated policies, which were socially reactionary. Gandhiji's faith in non-violence was not to the liking of Roy, who, like all communists, plumped for a violent revolution.

The importance that Roy had by now acquired in the affairs of the Comintern became clear to the members of the Berlin-based Indian Revolutionary Committee such as Virendranath Chattopadhyaya and Bhupendranath Dutta, who were asked to see the former, when they met Lenin in Moscow on the eve of the Third Comintern Congress to seek his help in promoting the cause of the revolution in India. However, they refused to work with Roy, saying that the latter was hand in glove with Abani Mukherjee, whom they accused of being a British spy. Roy and Abani had later parted ways and the former had the upper hand.

The real reason for their hostility to Roy was traceable to the instigation of an American lady, Agnes Smedley, who nursed a grudge against him for his refusal, while in the U.S.A. in the second decade of the twentieth century, to help her and her Indian boyfriend with funds for what they claimed to be activities in furtherance of the Indian revolution. Incidentally, Agnes Smedley had later discarded her Indian paramour in the U.S.A. and started living with Virendranath Chattopadhyaya in Berlin. Most of these Indian leaders went back to Berlin a disappointed lot, as Lenin insisted that they route their plea for help through proper channel i.e. through M.N. Roy! One of them, Nalini Gupta, who stayed behind in Moscow, came in handy to Roy in maintaining contact with the leaders of the communist movement in India.

However, at the Fourth and Fifth Congresses of the Comintern (1922, 1924), Roy failed to get his strategy for communist revolution in colonial countries accepted by the majority of the delegates, who were inclined to credit the bourgeoisie with some revolutionary potential. The Fifth Congress went a step further by depriving Roy of the onus of exporting communism to India, which was now placed on the shoulders of the Communist Party of Great Britain. Roy's influence in India received a set-back. He and Evelyn Roy also separated at this time.

Before being finally cut down to size, Roy was entrusted with an important mission – that of overseeing the implementation of the

Comintern strategy in China. This looked like a deliberate ploy by the Comintern to remove Roy from having anything to do with the Indian communist movement, while the Communist Party of Great Britain was gradually taking over control the movement in India. He had by now been elevated to the Comintern Presidium and made a member of the Chinese Commission. Soon, however, differences arose between Roy and Borodin, the representative in China of the Comintern, who was providing political guidance to the Chinese communist movement. Borodin wanted to put off the agrarian revolution (which would have gone against the interests of the land-owning class represented by the Kuomintang) and to support the northern expedition that the Left Kuomintang was then seeking to launch. Roy reckoned that this expedition was fraught with grave risks and pleaded for intensification of the agrarian revolution.

Eventually, Roy's views were accepted by the Congress of the Chinese Communist Party held in 1927. But these were not implemented on the ground, as Borodin kept on promising all the while to take necessary action without doing anything of the sort. Soon, the Chinese Communist Party and the Kuomintang fell out and large-scale arrests and execution of Chinese communists followed.

In the early nineteen fifties, reading M.N. Roy's "Revolution and Counter-Revolution in China", I got some idea about his point of view in the controversy over the resultant set-back to the communist movement in China. How could he have kept up the alliance with the Kuomintang and at the same time pursued a radical agrarian programme in furtherance of the peasants' interests? Yet, this as the pretext on which Stalin blamed the failure in China squarely on Roy and even refused to see him in Moscow. That Roy had fallen from grace was also evident from the holding of the Congress of Oppressed Nationalities in Brussels in February 1927—apparently at the instance of the Comintern and despite the opposition of Roy, who had no opportunity of even attending it. Virendranath Chattopadhyaya, Roy's sworn rival, played a prominent role in this Congress to which Pandit Jawaharlal Nehru came as a delegate, representing the Indian National Congress. Pandit Nehru, who held high opinions of both Roy and Chattopadhyaya, used to affectionately call the latter 'Chatto'.

In the nineteen twenties, M.N.Roy, who was based at Moscow, made serious efforts to build up a communist movement in India with the help of his trusted followers such as Gopendra Chakrabarti, Sachindra Nath Sanyal and several others some of whom made a bid for reorganising the Anushilan Samiti, an underground revolutionary group of Bengal, on Bolshevik lines.

When I lived in Kolkata in the latter half of the nineteen forties, I had occasion to attend some public meetings addressed by Saumendra Nath Tagore, a prominent leftist leader of Bengal and a good orator, who hailed from the family of poet Rabindranath Tagore. He was at that time a leader of the Revolutionary Communist Party of India and a political opponent of M.N. Roy. In view of his past communist background with international links, his activities had been closely monitored by the intelligence agencies of the Raj, as I came to know some years later. The following excerpt from a report of the Intelligence Branch, Government of Bengal, in 1927 throws some light on Tagore's activties:

"Emissary sent abroad: In May, Saumendra Nath Tagore, a nephew of Rabindra Nath Tagore, sailed for Europe. This man is a prominent member of the Indian Communist Party and the Bengal Peasants' and Workers' Party, and, as alresy stated in the section of this note dealing with the New Violence Party, is a person of pronounced terrorist tendencies. He took with him credentials from the Indian Communist Party with which to get into touch with the Communists in London, Paris and Berlin. There he intends to study the workings of the Communist Party in order to evolve a satisfactory system, adapted to the needs of India. He also hopes to arrange for the training in Europe of young Indian Communists and the regular remittance of funds to India. He arrived in Paris on the 23rd of May, met Mahommad Ali alias Sepasis and Clemens Palme Datta, and then went to Berlin. The German Communist Party made arrangements for them to visit Moscow where he intends to establish direct relations between the Comintern and the Indian Communist Party".[8]

I went through some of the works of Saumendranath Tagore, who, in one of his books[9], had stated that Roy's prestige in the Comintern had suffered a serious set-back as a result of the complaint made by the former, during a visit to Moscow in 1927, that very little of the funds and literature given by the Comintern to Roy to help the communist movement in India had been received in India. Tagore also told the Comintern that Roy had given an exaggerated picture of the growth of the communist movement in India, because, as he said, the only communists in India at that time were those who figured on the list of the party's Central Committee, namely, Soumendranath Tagore, S.A. Dange Shaukat Osmani, Muzaffar Ahmed, Ghate and a couple of others. The main reason for the bad blood between Tagore and Roy was the former's pro-Trotsky views as against what Tagore described as the latter's pro-Stalin stance.

Contemporary reports of the Intelligence Bureau at the disposal of the Government of India (which have become accessible to members of the public) provided some confirmation that the strength of the Indian communist movement was much less than what Roy had been reporting to the Comintern and also that sizeable sums of money had been made available by the Comintern for work in India.

Several secret reports of the Intelligence Branch, Government of Bengal, compiled in the hey day of the Raj had drawn attention to the misappropriation by M.N. Roy of funds he used to receive from Russian sources for the Communist Party's work in India. Nalini Bhusan Gupta, a communist leader, who had been convicted in the Kanpur Conspiracy Case, had told the police that " Narendra Bhattacharya alias M.N.Roy was not an honest man and that he was he was misappropriating money he received from the Russian Government."[10] The Intelligence Branch of the Government of Bengal, which had been intercepting the mail of M.N. Roy, had reported that Jatindra Mitra, who had returned to India in December 1925, had sent a letter to M.N. Roy in Moscow stating that " in spite of many requests, M.N. Roy had sent no money, for the simple reason that his sole desire was to swell his own bank balance with the money received from Russia."[11]

A similar accusation made against M.N. Roy by another communist leader, Satya Bhakta, was mentioned in a report of the Intelligence Branch, Government of Bengal, which said: " In May, Satya Bhakta published a manifesto in which he exposed M.N, Roy in his true colours as an unscrupulous, hired agitator, whose sole object in joining the Communist movement was to fill his own pockets and whom a certain number of young men followed merely to extort money either from him or the Comintern.

This charge could very well be made against most of the Communist leaders. R.C.L. Sharma in Pondicherry has been exposed as a swindler, B.V. Joshi in Bombay has misappropriated money collected for the defence of the Cawnpore Bolshevik conspiracy case, and Muzaffar Ahmad has had to write to Mr. Saklatwala, M.P., for help in tracing a sum of money sent out from England for the same purpose which seems to have evaporated in India. Muzaffar Ahmad is in correspondence with Mr. Lansbury, M.P., in England."[12]

Gopen Chakrabarti, another communist leader, who was trying to put the communist movement on a firm footing in Bengal as directed by M.N. Roy from Moscow, had also made a similar complaint against the latter, as pointed out in a report of the Intelligence Branch, Government of Bengal, that was obviously based on an intercepted letter: " Gopen Chakrabartti's letter opened with the announcement of his release, for which he pitied the police, and then went on to accuse M.N. Roy of caring more for his own interests than for those of the party and to complain of his not sending either money or literature."[13]

But not all political leaders of India fell for the lure of Russian funds. The report of the Intelligence Branch, Government of Bengal (for the period from the 1st July to the 31st December 1927) drew attention to V.V. Giri and observed: " Until the end of the year, however, the influence of foreign money on communist activity in Bengal has been negligible. In December, 3000 was sent by the U.S.S.R. to V.V. Giri, President of the All-India Railwaymen's Union Federation, for the relief of strikers on the Bengal-Nagpur Railway at Kharagpur, but the money was returned by the bank as it was not claimed. In the same month, N. M. Joshi, Secretary of the All-India Trade Union Congress in Bombay, received some rs. 20,000 from Moscow, part of which was spent on the relief of Kharagpur Railway workers. The attention of Bengal communists has now been drawn to this source of funds, and there are signs that they will try to benefit thereby."[14]

The British authorities closely monitored the activities of M.N. Roy and his 'agents' in India undertaken at the instance of the Communist International based in Moscow. The Intelligence Bureau, Government of India, had at that time perceived[15] "a definite Communist plot against India" stemming from the "Thesis" of the Second Congress of the Communist International held in 1920, which stated that "the nationalist movement in the colonial and semi-colonial countries was objectively fundamentally a revolutionary struggle, and as such it formed a part of the struggle for world revolution". In a subsequent study[16] on the same subject compiled in 1927 in the Intelligence Bureau, when D. Petrie was its Director, it was observed: "The Bolsheviks are convinced that in the British Empire the most vulnerable point is India .... and they cherish it as an article of faith that till India is liberated, Russia will not be rid of the menace of England".

The British authorities wanted to put the communists out of action in India by prosecuting Roy and some of his adherents in the Kanpur Conspiracy Case of 1924. While convicting them in this case, the court came to the finding, on the basis of the evidence that was marshalled, that Roy and his "fellow-conspirators" had not succeeded to any great extent in implanting Bolshevism in India or in doing anything that was likely to endanger the public safety.[17]

Analysing the causes of the communists' failure, the Intelligence Bureau's study in 1927 observed: "The first, and possibly the chief, cause of Roy's lack of success in founding a live Communist Party in India arose out of the special circumstances of the years during which he was most active. Roy, as a John the Baptist of Communism, endeavored to introduce into India the idea and practice of mass action for the enforcement of political demands; but he could scarcely have got to work before he must have realised that 'a greater than John the Baptist' had already forestalled him. This was no other than 'Mahatma' Gandhi, whose Non-co-operation campaign produced a mass movement which, while owing nothing in spirit and conception to Communism, was far more widespread and formidable than anything that Roy could possibly have created, even if he had had a completely clear field."

Further on, the study added: 'Thus, during all the time that Roy was busiest sowing the seeds of the mass idea, there was gradually ripening in India such a harvest as even Moscow could scarcely have dreamt of. With a demi-god like Mr.Gandhi leading the non-co-operation movement, there was no one to harken to the purely secular preachings of a puny earthling like Roy. The non-co-operation movement finally collapsed, and it left an exceedingly bitter taste in the mouth of the people."

Subsequently, some communist leaders of India acknowledged the signal contribution Gandhiji had made to the country's freedom struggle by bringing about the awakening of the masses. For example, the late Prof. Hiren Mukerjee observed in article written on the occasion of the golden jubilee of India's independence in the Delhi edition of the Times of India dated August 29,1997: "............in adolescence, I had fallen prey to the Gandhi 'magic'. We had the unforgettable exhilaration of experiencing a little of the grand days of non-Cooperation (1920-22) ...." Proceeding further, Prof. Mukerjee praised Gandhiji for highlighting the British Government's exploitation of the Indian masses and voicing his concern for the condition of the people.

The report of the Intelligence Bureau further added: "Another important cause that contributed to Roy's failure was the indifferent quality of himself and his agents. Practically all of them, and Roy also is included, have proved to be greedy opportunists, lacking in scruples and principles and even in common honesty............. Mota Singh, the well-known Akali, applied purely to his private uses the money he received from Moscow. Similarly, Ghulam Hussain, Roy's Lahore 'centre', not only appropriated a great deal of what he received, but considered that he ought to have acquired merit in the eyes of Government for so preventing this money from being devoted to the purposes for which it was sent. There also clear evidence, obtained from intercepted correspondence, to show that some of the money sent to India for the defence of the Cawnpore conspirators stuck to the fingers of those who had the handling of it, with the natural result that not a little heart-burning ensued among some of the intended and legitimate beneficiaries. In the same way, Singaravelu, with his jackal Velayudham, contrived to dispose of the press provided for the work of the 'Labour and Kishan Party', and so far has never disgorged the proceeds, an act of peculation which has brought about his complete estrangement from Roy. But, in point of fact, Roy's own reputation for clear-handed dealing in money matters stands scarcely higher among his followers."

"Apart from their bankruptcy in ordinary honesty, another radical defect in Roy's team was that, while every one was prepared to lead, few or none were prepared to follow. The section headed 'New Parties in India', as well as subsequent sections in the last

Chapter, have shown how each centre produced a separate scheme, and how Singaravelu, Dange, Ghulam Hussain, etc., seemed each to consider that he himself above all others was cut out for the leadership. There were thus almost as many 'leaders' as 'parties', a state of affairs which is not entirely without a parallel in the annals of Indian revolutionary conspiracy; for it may be recalled that Obeidullah's 'Army of God', which comprised no fewer than twelve Field-marshals and forty-eight Generals of various grades, could muster no more than two Captains and one Lieutenant. Nor was any one of Roy's recruits, so far as would appear, possessed either of the necessary influence, ability or 'drive' to make himself felt, or to lay any sort of enduring foundation for a Bolshevik movement. All these agents were of ordinary calibre, and, while they were quite prepared to strut in the borrowed plumes of Bolshevism, gulping down whatever of its money came their way, and mouthing glibly its claptrap phraseology, they seemed scarcely to know which way to turn in the matter of making a beginning in anything constructive or practical."

The Intelligence Bureau's study further observed: "There was no evidence at all of the existence in India of a well-financed organisation—rather the contrary, for the Cawnpore 'Bolsheviks' never got more than small sums out of Roy and were constantly asking for more...........In regard to the supposed existence of two distinct organisations, it was possible to say definitely, almost from the outset, that Roy at least had not been able to create any agency of the dimensions suggested by the lists. His own letters, after the conclusion of the Cawnpore case, contained plenty of evidence to show that he was having the utmost trouble in maintaining touch even with his few surviving agents, and that he was feeling himself grievously hampered in the matter of achieving further progress in India. That this attitude of Roy's was not an assumed one would seem to be established by the fact that at the end of 1924 he was still unaware of the identity of one Satya Bhakta, a professed Communist of Cawnpore, who, if of no great importance, was at least tolerably well-known in India."

In regard to M.N.Roy's claim made to the Comintern about the strength of the communist movement in India, the intelligence report doubted "how far Roy was playing straight with Moscow, that is, whether he was dealing with them honestly, or whether he was making his living (and probably large expenses) out of them by representing that he had established in India a vastly larger organisation than in reality existed".

The intelligence report drew attention to M.N. Roy's undertaking given to Zinoviev that in the course of the struggle against the British Government, the Communist Party of India would subscribe one million pounds sterling and observed: "For Roy, therefore, to represent to his employers that a mere handful of rather rugged and disreputable Indian agitators were likely to be able to collect a million pounds sterling, was to reveal himself as capable of the grossest deception and falsehood."

The Intelligence Bureau referred to an observation made by Percy E. Glading, a British communist, after his visit to India in February 1925 that he had not met any communist and had finally decided that those with whom he had come in contact were useless so far as the party work was concerned. Reference was also made in the report to the view expressed by George Allison alias Donald Campbell, another British communist, who came to India in April 1926 to organise labour unions on revolutionary lines and found that there was no worthwhile communist activity in India except at Bombay, where K.N. Joglekar had been doing some work.

An atmosphere of mutual distrust pervaded India's communist circles at that time as would be evident from the following observation made in the intelligence report: "At the end of April 1926 a number of Indian Communists, then assembled at Calcutta, wrote to Roy, roundly abusing him for his failure to supply them with funds and hinting that he was putting into his own pocket money meant for "the cause". In deference to all this, Roy promised to remit a sum of £200 in July. In the course of his letter, copies of which were sent to several comrades in India, Roy betrayed an almost painful anxiety to disabuse the Indian Communists of the idea that they could look to the Indian Communist Party in Russia for financial backing. Roy said that he had received "fragmentary reports" of the Calcutta Conference, and expressed his regret that such "an atmosphere of disgust and mistrust towards us prevailed".

The Intelligence Bureau's report concluded: "It will be seen, therefore, that not only did Roy not succeed in establishing a live, working Communist Party in India, but that even those persons who grouped themselves together under that title were a poor enough semblance of any kind of a "party". Thus Satya Bhakta was distrusted and repudiated by Roy; while Roy, in his turn, was suspected by the party of Begerhotta, Muzaffar Ahmad, etc., of diverting to his own uses funds he should have remitted to India........ The whole of this evidence, in fact, almost completely negatives the possibility of the existence in India of any unknown organisation of Roy's".

In his report on communism in India, D. Petrie, Director, Intelligence Bureau, observed: "I have dwelt at this length on the result of M.N. Roy's campaign, because he seems to have been the instrument through whom the Soviet elected to put forth their main effort—-the sparking-plug by which they hoped ultimately to explode the violent-minded elements in the country. It would be quite erroneous, however, to suppose that Roy's singularly barren record can be taken to mean the Communism has obtained no footing whatever in India. For instance, many recent articles in Indian-edited papers could be cited to show that the Press is becoming increasingly alive to the immense power of mass action as a political weapon. Communism, as expounded by Mr. Saklatvala during his recent tour, earned appreciative comment in several quarters which could not all be dismissed as irresponsible........There are many clear evidences also of a growing recognition on the part of the Indian National Congress (and cognate political bodies) of the need of organising the labouring masses in order to associate them with the general movement for the country's political advancement. Then there are the organisation of Workers' and Peasants' Parties, and the growing intrusion into Labour movements of persons working for avowedly Communist purposes. The address of Bhupendra Nath Dutt to the Political Sufferers' Conference at Gauhati, no less than the association of individual revolutionaries with Communism, could be fittingly quoted to support M.N. Roy's contention that the "tendency of 'going to the masses' is gaining ground among the nationalist intellectuals of advanced views".

Even in the latter half of the nineteen twenties, the communist movement in India failed to make much impact. By early 1929, M.N.Roy was expelled from the Comintern and so when the British authorities in India arrested 31 communists in the Meerut Conspiracy Case launched that year, Roy's break with the communist movement was already complete. But in the case that was made out by the prosecution, Roy's name figured prominently as one of the main agents through whom the Comintern organised the conspiracy in India, though he was not cited as an accused.

By the time of the Meerut Conspiracy Case, Roy's effort to organise the communist movement in India had made hardly much progress. Philip Spratt, an English communist worker, who had been sent to India for the party's work and was arrested and convicted in this case, says in his book, "Blowing Up India", written after he ceased to be a communist: "In Bengal we were not very successful in bringing about or prolonging strikes, though we must have caused a good deal of loss. In Bombay, the party group, Dange, Nimbkar, Mirajkar and Bradley, were highly effective, and they had the cotton mills completely tied up for five or six months". Further on, he adds: "......... this party work seemed downright sordid. We were convinced, as we informed the Comintern (through a bulky document smuggled out of jail), that for the sake of prestige, the new party leaders were claiming bigger successes than they had actually achieved."

The judgment in the Meerut Conspiracy Case also mentioned that the communist movement in India had not attained any considerable dimension at that time.

In 1927, Leon Trotsky and Zinoviev were expelled from the Communist Party of the Soviet Union primarily for their opposition to Stalin. On one important issue – opposition to collaboration with the bourgeoisie during the phase of the communist party's struggle in the colonial and semi-colonial countries – both Trotsky and Roy used to hold an identical view. But when Trotsky was expelled from the party, Roy deserted him and put the weight of his support behind Stalin for reasons which were not very clear.

At the Sixth Congress of the Comintern (1928), a further ground for the onslaught on Roy was found in his alleged siring and espousal of the theory of 'decolonisation', even though he protested vehemently that this charge was absolutely without any basis. It was at the instance of the Comintern that Roy had taken up the task in 1927 of formulating a policy for the communist movement in India in the context of rapid industrialisation and the consequent emergence of an Indian bourgeoisie. In the report that Roy prepared, he drew attention to the plight of the Indian bourgeoisie in the face of the stiff competition that it was encountering from the manufacturers of the imperialist country, which was compelling the former to demand concessions from the authorities. The circumstances thus forced the Indian bourgeoisie to compromise with the imperialist power and at the same time to hold out the threat, if certain concessions were not provided, of joining hands with the people at large in their struggle for national liberation. The imperialist power responded by offering some concessions to the indigenous bourgeoisie. This, according to Roy, resulted in the exploitation of the Indian people by the imperialists as well as by the national bourgeoisie and was so clearly anti-people in its impact as to deserve whole-hearted condemnation by true revolutionaries.

But by 1928, Roy had become a prime target of Stalin's displeasure. The Comintern quite wrongly and unjustly accused Roy of having propounded the theory of 'decolonisation' that was said to imply a lessening of the imperialist exploitation of India— something which Roy had not done at all. By falsely ascribing the so-called concept of decolonisation to Roy, the Communist International also held him guilty of making a plea for softening the fight against the Indian bourgeoisie.

It was a travesty of truth to charge Roy with having ever visualised that the so-called 'decolonisation' policy of British imprerialism would lead to the weakening and dissolution of the British Empire. Roy was expelled from the Comintern, a tragic denouement which probably was a sequel to the internecine struggle that had broken out within the Communist Party of the Soviet Union in the wake of Lenin's death, resulting, in due course, in the assumption by Stalin of almost absolute power and the elimination of several luminaries including Trotsky, Bukharin and Zinoviev. The machinations of the Communist Party of Great Britain, which was anxious to bring the communist movement in India under its exclusive control, may also have contributed partly to hastening the process of Roy's ouster from the Comintern.

Saumendranath Tagore, Roy's arch political rival, attributed the latter's expulsion to what he termed as his violation of discipline and his role in a conspiracy to malign Abani Mukherjee rather than to any political or ideological difference with Stalin.[18] Tagore in fact dubbed Roy as a careerist and a servile agent of Stalin, though such sweeping observations do not stand close scrutiny. Roy's differences with the Comintern in regard to the attitude of the communists towards the bourgeoisie were widely known. Nor was there any justification in accusing Roy of servility, because the way he expressed his disagreement with Lenin, Stalin and the Comintern over ideological issues clearly brought out his intellectual pride and the courage of his ideological conviction. It is, however, true that Roy, despite all his differences with Stalin, was loyal to the latter and extended to him his full support on many occasions. There was a ring of sincerity in the tribute that Roy paid, when Stalin died, in his write-up in the weekly Radical Humanist, describing him as a "great man of history" and the "greatest military genius and the tallest personality of our time".

Expelled from the Comintern, Roy returned to India incognito, a disillusioned revolutionary. It took the Indian police several months to trace him and put him behind bars for all the assistance and guidance that he had rendered to the communist movement. The irony was that he had by now turned completely against the totalitarian communist regime in the U.S.S.R., which Stalin then presided over as also against the communists back home in India, who launched a vicious tirade against him and condemned his views and writings as the worst specimens of political and ideological heresy, like those of Trotsky.

The resolution adopted by the Sixth Congress (1928) of the Comintern called upon the communists to organise themselves on the basis of their own strength, build on the solid foundation of peasant-worker alliance and distance themselves from the national bourgeoisie (which in India meant the Indian National Congress) – a line that Roy had been advocating right from the beginning against the continued opposition of the Comintern. Ironically, by now Roy himself had started moving to the right in the light of his understanding of the contemporary situation on the ground and displaying a softer attitude towards the national bourgeoisie in India. It is quite possible that Roy was influenced in his thinking by the growing ascendancy of the leftists in the Indian National Congress under the leadership of Pt. Jawahar Lal Nehru for whom he had all along a soft corner.

After his return to India, Roy started pleading for collaboration with the Indian National Congress to forge an anti-imperialist front in order to usher in a democratic national revolution, a line that the Comintern did not approve of at that time, but was going to adopt a few years later. Had the Comintern given the signal to the Indian communists to take part in and identify themselves with the civil disobedience movement of the Indian National Congress during 1930-32, they would not have laid themselves open to the charge that has all along been levelled against them of their having betrayed the national liberation struggle at every critical moment of our history.

In July 1931, Roy was nabbed by the police and sent to jail. On his release in 1936, he joined the Congress and was elected a member of the All-India Congress Committee. While in this party, he adopted a stance that was anti-Gandhi in its orientation.

In 1937, many workers of the Yugantar, a revolutionary organisation of Bengal, who were released from the jails as a corollary to the Congress Party assuming power in the Provinces, decided to join the Congress, using it as an open platform, but preserving their secret organisation and strenghening their group.[19] A description of M.N. Roy given at this time by the Intelligence Branch, Government of Bengal, makes interesting reading: "Publicly, the Jugantar party announced that it had abandoned terrorism but would work in the Congress in collaboration with Mr. M.N. Roy, an old Bengal terrorist and dacoit whose real name is Naren Bhattacharji. (He was deeply implicated in the Indo-German plot in 1914-15 and absconded. He was subsequently arrested in Bombay in July 1931, convicted the same year in the Cawnpore Conspiracy case and released in November 1936. He has been in Russia, Germany, China and other countries and has betrayed most of the causes with which he has been assciated. He was disowned by the Russian communists for that reason.) M.N. Roy in a speech in Bombay on the 2nd of December 1937, said that the declaration of the intention of the old revolutionaries to join the Congress did not mean that they had ceased to be revolutionists but that as a result of their studies and experiences, they had acquired a clear conception and had become even more confirmed revolutionists."[20]

The close rapport between M.N. Roy and the Yugantar is clearly reflected in the following excerpt from the report of the Intelligence Branch, Government of Bengal: " The Jugantar State prisoners in Hijli Detention Camp sent out instructions to the members to keep the party intact and to work on socialist lines until the State prisoners were released. The State prisoners further instructed them to bring M.N. Roy, a former Jugantar leader, to work with the Jugantar and implied that they would accept Roy's programme. The leaders were attracted to Roy because of his more attractive programme of action, his hostile attitude to Mr. Gandhi, his potentialities as a leader of the middle class revolution as a preliminary to subsequent mass seizure of power and because he was backed by Dr. Jadu Gopal Mukharji, an old and greatly respected leader of the Jugantar party. The doctor was one of Roy's c'-conspirators in the Indo German plot referred to above. M.N. Roy visited Bengalin 1938 with the "blessings" of Dr. Jadu Gopal Mnkharji and announced his programme for reorganising the Primary Congrees Committees for active and practical work and for educating the masses to make their own demands."[21]

With the out-break of World War II in 1939, M.N. Roy launched a campaign against Fascism. At the Ramgarh session of the Indian National Congress held in 1940, he unsuccessfully tried to get a resolution passed, calling upon the people of India to extend whole-hearted support to the war against Fascism. This, along with his stand on some other issues which differed from that of the Congress Party, led to his expulsion from the latter. His image was somewhat tarnished following vague rumours that he was allegedly receiving assistance from the British Government in lieu of the help and cooperation he was extending to the war effort.[22]

M.N. Roy formed the Radical Democractic Party in 1940 and in 1946, he put forward his thesis called "New Orientation", which, while rejecting both bourgeois liberalism and communism, projected radicalism as an alternative ideology, its central idea being radical humanism, which visualised a country-wide network of People's Committees with the Parliament at the apex and a large number of producers' and consumers' co-operatives alongside the People's Committees. It envisaged a decentralised system of radical democracy marked by the diffusion of power rather than its centralisation. The Twenty Two Theses, which embodied his theory of "New Humanism", were explained in an abstruse philosophical language in publications, some of which a worker of his party once gave me for study. This concept of direct democracy based on decentralisation of power has a lot in common with Gandhiji's ideas and underlies the system of Panchayati Raj institutions that have come into being in our country.

At a conference of the Radical Democratic Party held in Kolkata towards the end of 1948, the party was dissolved, as the general view was that, for ushering in New Humanism, there was no need for a political party, which, according to Roy, prevent people from exercising what he called their 'sovereignty' and in reality obstructed true democratic revolution. His concept of democracy was based on party-less politics, because a political party in a parliamentary from of government which ruled by virtue of its majority in the parliament, might represent only a minority of the voters. In such a system, the individual had to submit himself to the dictates of the party machinery, thus forfeiting his freedom, which was inconsistent with the idea of true democracy. Laudable ideas indeed. But how practicable are they?

Roy's economic prescription steered clear of both the capitalist and State capitalist models. In the cooperative economy that he envisioned, it was the people rather than the capitalists or the State that would own the means of production.

I had once heard him speak at a gathering in Kolkata in 1948. It was some time in 1949 (when I had time to spare after my B.A. examination) that I read the issues of the 'Radical Humanist', the journal in which Roy publicised his illuminating views on contemporary national as well as international issues. As I understood it, New Humanism was not a philosophy of mere contemplation, but also embodied a programme of political action.

As Roy put it: "A brotherhood of men attracted by ideas, keenly conscious of the urge for freedom, fired with the vision of a free society of free men" will show the way out of the crisis of modern civilisation. Education of the citizen is the condition for such a reorganisation of society. New Humanism is cosmopolitan. A cosmopolitan commonwealth of spiritually free men will not be limited by the boundaries of national States-capitalist, Fascist, socialist, communist or of any other kind-which will gradually disappear under the impact of the twentieth century Renaissance of Man". One can discern an element of romanticism in this revolutionary philosophy of M.N.Roy, who, in the words of a British humanist leader, was propelled by some kind of "Shelleyan fire".

Roy believed in morality and ethics, but not in denominational religion. Though he was born a Brahmin, he was an atheist.

For all his disillusion with communism, Roy continued to be a Marxist in so far as his understanding of Marx's theory of evolution of the history of mankind and of the future of humanity was concerned. But he gradually deviated from Marxist ideas and developed an outlook of total opposition to the regimentation and totalitarianism of the Bolshevik regime that obtained in the U.S.S.R., particularly the Stalinist model under whose ponderous wheels the individual's freedom was mercilessly crushed.

Initially, Roy used to bitterly criticise Mahatma Gandhi, branding him as a religious revivalist and a political reactionary. When he turned over a new leaf and started preaching the message of New Humanism, he changed his attitude towards Gandhiji. He started showing considerable appreciation of Gandhiji's ideas and his stress on morality and economic and political decentralisation and praised his role in awakening the Indian masses. Like Gandhiji, now Roy also visualised the revolution in philosophical and spiritual terms; but he laid much greater emphasis than Gandhiji on the economic aspects of the Indian revolution.

What particularly hastened the process of Roy's re-assessment of Mahatma Gandhi's role in Indian politics was the way the latter threw himself heart and soul into the task of restoring communal harmony in the wake of the Great Kolkata Killing of August, 1946, his mission of peace in Noakhali, braving all physical hazards and discomfort, his fasts against communal brutality in Kolkata and Delhi and the prayer meetings he undertook in different parts of the country to restore communal amity and peace. Roy was all admiration for Gandhiji's boldness and his spiritual and moral message, which had much in common with the philosophy of New Humanism.

Gandhiji's assassination moved Roy so much that he came out with some articles in the media in praise of all that the former had done to purify politics with his gospel of truth and non-violence, urging politicians never to forget that the end did not justify the means. Though Roy still differed from Gandhi in so far as he continued to stick to his atheistic, rationalist and materialist outlook, one could see that he had moved quite close to and developed an attitude of deep regard for the Mahatma. I read some of Roy's articles on Gandhiji after the latter's assassination and realised how sharply the Comintern hero's views had changed over the decades!

What M.N.Roy advocated was a system of partyless and decentralised democracy based on people's committees, a co-operative economy and education for all as a means to character-building and making them conscious of their rights and potentialities. What he aimed at was grass-root democracy or democracy from below in which the people world exercise effective power. His ideas have often been charcterised as Utopian, but they have not lost their relevance. Jayprakash Narain had derived some of his ideas from M.N.Roy.

It was with a tinge of sadness that I learnt some time in 1954 (when I had already become a police officer) that Roy was no more. His end came after a series of physical mishaps which included a serious fall in 1952 down a precipice at Mussourie and an attack of cerebral thrombosis that partially paralysed his body. And then his wife Ellen, whose face I could still vividly recall, met with a violent death at the hands of an assassin in December 1960. What a tragic end for a brave man and his wife!

During one of my visits to Dehradun later in life, I once went to a residential area to look up a retired senior police officer whom I knew rather well. There the 'Humanist Home", as the Roys' abode in Dehradun was called, suddenly leapt into my view and revived many an old memory in my mind. From a distance, I offered a silent homage to the great revolutionary.

Notes

1. Report entitled "Terrorist Conspiracy in Bengal" (From july 1 to December 31, 1927) compiled by F.P. McKinty, Special Superintendent, Intelligence Branch, C.I.D., Bengal, vide page 591, Terrorism in Bengal, Volume I, Govt. of West Bengal (1995).
2. Terrorism in Bengal, Government of Bengal, Volume I, page 800.
3. "Communism In India" (1924-1927) compiled by Sir David Petrie, Director, Intelligence Bureau, Govt. of India. This book is now available to members of the public.
4. Documents of the History of the C.P.I., Vol. I (1917-1922), edited by Dr. G.M.Adhikari, pages 173-177.
5. *Ibid.*, page 159.

6. *Ibid.*, page 166.
7. "Communism In India" compiled by Sir Cecil Kaye, Director, Intelligence Bureau, Govt. of India. This book is now available to members of the public.
8. Terrorist Conspiracy in Bengal (From January 1 to June 30, 1927) compiled by the Intelligence Branch, Govt. of Bengal vide Terrorism in Bengal (1995), Volume I, page 569.
9. "Yatri", a Bengali book by Saumendranath Tagore, page 136.
10. Report of the Intelligence Branch, Government of Bengal (1st September 1924 to 31st March 1925) vide Terrorism in Bengal,Government of West Bengal (1995), Volume I, Appendix VIII, page 418.
11. Report of the Intelligence Branch, Government of Bengal (1st January to 30th June 1926) vide Terrorism in Bengal, Government of West Bengal (1995), Voluume I, page 493.
12. *Ibid.* Page 902.
13. Report of the Intelligence Branch, Government of Bengal (1st July to 31st December 1926), vide Terrorism in Bengal, Government of West Bengal (1995), Volume I, page 525.
14. Terrorist Conspiracy in Bengal (From 1st july to 31st December 1927) vide Terrorism in Bengal (1995),Government of West Bengal, Volume I, page 591.
15. "Communism in India" (1925) compiled by Sir Cecil Kaye, Director, Intelligence Bureau, Govt. of India.
16. "Communism In India" (1924-1927) compiled by D. Petrie, Director, Intelligence Bureau, Govt. of India.
17. *Ibid.*, pages 69-70.
18. "Yatri", P.220.
19. Note on the Policy and Activities of the Terrorist Parties in Bengal from 1937 to August 1939 compiled from records in the Intelligence Branch. C.I.D., Bengal vide Terrorism in Bengal, Government of West Bengal (1995), Volume I, page 771.
20. *Ibid.*, page 772.
21. *Ibid.*, page 772.
22. "Quit India Movement" by P.N.Chopra, P.10.

19

The Second Crucifixion

Considerable communal tension surfaced in the two Bengals on both sides of the new international border towards the end of 1947, though for some time no major incident took place. Soon streams of refugees began to leave East Pakistan and pour into West Bengal.

We did not follow the example of many other refugees, who spent much of their time in search of land for building a shelter for themselves or doles for subsistence, which were offered by the Government to bonafide refugees from East Pakistan. My father told us not to waste time in such pursuits, but to concentrate on studies so that we would be able in the foreseeable future to stand on our own legs on the strength of our merit. I realised later in life the correctness of the path my parents had chalked out for us. If they had not guided us properly at that juncture, we might have ended up with possessing a few ill-constructed huts in one of the many refugee camps in Kolkata's suburbs or in some district of West Bengal. But, I am sure, we would not have got anything more than that in life.

Towards the end of the year 1947, I saw how badly and rapidly the communal situation was deteriorating, converting the whole country, particularly Punjab and Delhi, into a virtual tinder box. While the Muslims were fleeing Delhi for Pakistan, the mass exodus of Hindus and Sikhs in the reverse direction was also taking place. We heard that a 57-mile long convoy of millions of Hindus and Sikhs had trudged all the way from West Pakistan to Delhi to escape the atrocities that were being inflicted by the Muslim hooligans.

The presence in Delhi of so many Hindu and Sikh refugees, who had been at the receiving end in Pakistan, created a tense situation. Many Muslims were attacked and killed, their belongings looted and their houses set on fire. Gandhiji visited the houses of some Muslims in Delhi to instill confidence in them. He also visited many camps of Hindu refugees, who had poured in from Pakistan, to calm their passions. From Kolkata, we closely followed the course of these events in different parts of the country, as we felt that these were bound to have a direct bearing on our lives.

It was at this stage that rumours started circulating about a cleavage between Pt. Nehru and Sardar Patel over their respective attitudes towards the Rashtriya Swayamsevak Sangh (RSS). Sardar Patel was stern and austere and meant business; it was generally believed that he regarded the R.S.S. workers not as communally motivated, but as 'misguided patriots', while Pandit Nehru held the opposite view. Gandhiji generally agreed with Panditji in such matters.

In a speech that Patel delivered at Lucknow on January 6, 1948, he openly expressed his appreciation of the role of the RSS. To quote: " In the Congress, there are some in power who feel that by virtue of authority they will be able to crush the RSS. You cannot crush an organization by the rod—After all, RSS men are not thieves and dacoits. They are patriots who love their country, only their trend of thought is mis-directed. The Congress must win them over by their love."[1]

Though this statement did not please Mahatma Gandhi, he adopted a public posture of defending Patel, which the latter did not like. On January 16, 1948, Patel declared at a public meeting in Bombay: " I am a frank man. I say bitter things to Hindus and Muslims alike. Some of them (Muslims) went and complained to Gandhiji about my Lucknow speech. Gandhiji felt impelled to defend me. That pained me, for I am not a weak person who should be defended by others."[2]

Gandhiji had been told that in Delhi the R.S.S. workers had been instigating the Hindus to take revenge against the Muslims. He met groups of R.S.S. volunteers and pleaded with them to see what he called reason. The R.S.S. workers were angry with Gandhiji, because they believed that he was trying to protect the Muslims and was in fact asking the Hindus to turn the other cheek in, when slapped on one cheek, as Jesus Christ had done.

Gandhiji undertook a fast in January 1948 to restore peace in Delhi. He put pressure on the Government of India to pay a huge sum of money to Pakistan as its share of India's pre-partition assets including a cash balance of 375 crore rupees. Many militant Hindus did not approve of what they regarded as India's softness towards Pakistan for which they held the so-called pro-Muslim and pro-Pakistan bias of Gandhiji responsible. In Kolkata, my friends and I often held animated discussions over these issues. Gandhiji ended his fast on January 18, 1948 only after he received assurances from all quarters that every effort would be made to protect the Muslims' life and property.

Among the Hindus, there was a militant fringe which remained unreconciled to Gandhiji's beliefs and ideology. This became amply clear from the conduct of one Madan Lal, a young Hindu refugee from Pakistan. Nursing a grievance that, under pressure from Gandhiji, he had been thrown out of an old mosque in Delhi where he had taken refuge on arrival from Pakistan, he joined a group of like-minded men in working out a plot to do away with the Mahatma. On January 20, 1948, he hurled a bomb at Gandhiji as the latter was addressing one of his famous prayer meetings at the Birla House in New Delhi. The bomb missed its target and Madan Lal was arrested after a chase.

On January 29, 1948, Gandhiji sent a message to Dr. S.P. Mookerjee, the Hindu Mahasabha leader and then a Central Minister in Pandit Nehru's Government, with a view to bring to his knowledge the objectionable speeches of the Hindu Mahasabha and RSS workers that amounted to open incitement to assassinate some Congress leaders.[3]

The next day—on January 30, 1948—Madan Lal's co-conspirator, Nathuram Vinayak Godse went to Birla House, where Gandhiji was about to address his prayer meeting in the evening, walked up to him with folded hands as in a pose of salutation and made no mistake when he pulled the trigger of his pistol. Gandhiji shouted 'Hey! Ram' (Oh! God), as he fell to the assassin's bullet. Many people recalled what was said in the Old Testament: "Though He slay me, yet I will trust Him".

In the trial that was later held, Nathuram was found guilty and hanged along with Apte, another conspirator. Madan Lal and four others were imprisoned for life. Another accused, V.D. Savarkar, the Hindu Mahasabha leader, was acquitted. The R.S.S was banned. There was no doubt that this assassination was a pointer to the feeling of animosity that many Hindus harboured towards Gandhiji and their opposition to the way he was seeking to restore peace and amity between the two communities.

I still remember how deeply shocked I felt when the news of Gandhiji's assassination was broadcast over the radio that night. I was busy with my studies in the evening, when suddenly I became aware of some commotion outside. I rushed out to the street and saw big crowds moving about in great excitement, discussing in an agitated mood the news that they had just heard over the radio. There were throngs of people hovering around radio sets in the shops along the roads. Since we did not have a radio, I went out from time to time to hear the radio at the street-corner shop and keep myself posted with all that was happening in Delhi and elsewhere.

Not very far from where I lived in Kolkata was the residence of Dr. Shyama Prasad Mookerjee, the Hindu Mahasabha leader. Angry crowds had surrounded his house and from a distance I could hear the anti-Hindu Mahasabha slogans that were being raised. I could clearly see an angry mob hurling some stones that flew in the direction of Dr. Mookerjee's mammoth ancestral house. Soon, the police arrived there to deal with the situation. I lost no time in leaving the place. I was told later by some political activists that the supporters of the Communist Party of India had played an important role in fomenting this trouble. However, I did not know what the truth was.

It was generally known that the communists had blamed Sardar Vallabhbhai Patel, the Home Minister, for failure to save Mahatma Gandhi's life. In fact, P. Sundarayya, a top communist leader, was reported in the press to have openly accused the R.S.S., the Hindu Mahasabha and Sardar Patel of having planned to kill Mahatma Gandhi in order to establish what he called their Fascist regime in our country.[4]

Many years later, I read about a similar allegation made in K.L. Gauba's book 'The Assassination of Mhatma Gandhi' (1969). Gauba, has said that, according to a 'well-informed source' (who desired to remain unknown), Nathuram was alleged to have said:

" I was under the orders of Savarkar. Savarkar was under the direct orders of Vallabhbhai Patel. At one meeting I also met Patel when I accompanied Savarkar who was in disguise of a Sikh.

Vallabhbhai taunted Savarkar for coming in the disguise of a Sikh as he hated the Sikhs and their beards. That meeting was in a train, sometime in December 1947."[5]

I do not know how much faith one should repose in the statement of a person who was not prepared to disclose his identity.

However, the fact remains that Madanlal had disclosed to one Dr. J.C. Jain on or about the 7th of January 1948 the details of a conspiracy to take the life of Mahatma Gandhi. Dr. Jain had brought these details to the notice of B.G. Kher, Chief Minister (then designated as Prime Minister) of Bombay and his Home Minister, Morarji Desai, on January 21, 1948 (i.e. nine days before the assassination of Gandhiji). Morarji Desai had discussed this matter with J.M. Nagarwala, chief of Bombay's Intelligence Branch, with whom Dr. Jain was then put in touch.

No wonder that Atma Ram, the Judge, who tried the Gandhi assassination case, made the following observation at the conclusion of the trial: "I may bring to the notice of the Central Government the slackness of the Police in the investigation of the case during the period between 20th January 1948 and 30th January 1948. The Delhi Police had obtained a detailed statement from Madanlal K. Pahwa soon after his arrest on 20th January 1948. The Bombay Police had also reported the statement of Dr. J.C. Jain which he had made to the Hon. Mr. Morarji Desai n 21st January 1948. The Delhi and the Bombay Police had contacted each other soon after these two statements had been made. Yet the Police miserably failed to derive any advantage from these two statements. Had the slightest keenness been shown in the investigations of the case at that stage the tragedy probably could have been averted."[6]

However, during the hearing of the convicts' appeals, Justice Bhandari of the High Court, surprisingly condoned the indifference on the part of the police by observing: "Towards the conclusion of his judgement the learned Special Judge had made certain observations which appear to indicate that if the Police had been more vigilant in the discharge of their duties the tragedy which overtook Mahatma Gandhi on the 30th January may well have been averted. Mr. Daphtary contends that these observations are not warranted by the evidence on the record."[7]

Proceeding further, Justice Bhandari observed: "The evidence on the record satisfies me (a) that no opportunity was afforded to the

Police to explain the circumstances which prevented them from apprehending Nathuram before 30th January and thereby saving the life of Mahatma Gandhi; (b) Madanlal failed to supply the names of the conspirators to the Police; (c) that even if the names were supplied it was extremely difficult, if not impossible for the Police to arrest Nathuram, who was going about from place to place under assumed names and who was determined to assassinate Mahatma Gandhi even at the risk of losing his own life."

The Gandhi assassination case again attracted national attention after many years when, in November 1964, G.V. Ketkar, a journalist of Poone, publicly declared that he had information about the plot to assassinate Gandhiji six months before the crime was committed and that he had brought it to the notice of Morarji Desai, Home Minister of Bombay, through a registered letter. A Commission of Enquiry headed by Justice G.S. Pathak went into this matter, but before he could complete his work, he had to take up some other assignments with the result that no conclusion could be arrived at.

The one-man J.L. Kapur Commission began an enquiry into this matter in 1966. An important person to depose before the Commission was N.M. Kamte, a former Inspector-General of Police, Bombay, who said that the Police would have nipped the conspiracy in the bud if he had been given the information that was at the disposal of Morarji Desai, Home Minister of Bombay, ten days before Gandhiji was done away with.

Balkrishen, a retired Deputy Superintendent of Delhi Police, who appeared before the Kapur Commission, stated that he, along with another police officer, Jaswant Singh, had gone to Bombay and, as instructed byT.I. Sanjeevi, the then Director of the Intelligence Bureau and Inspector-General of Delhi Police, met Nagarwala whom they acquainted with all the information at their disposal. When they requested Nagarwala for help in regard to some action they wanted to take, he was said to have told them that he knew everything and that they should go back to Delhi, which they did. According to Balkrishen, the Bombay Police did not co-operate with them.[8] Rikhi Kesh, Superintedent of Police, C.I.D., Delhi, who also deposed before the Kapur Commission, also stated that J.D. Nagarwala did not help the officers of Delhi Police in conducting their investigation.[9]

As a retired police officer, I feel ashamed that with all the information at the disposal of the police and the Chief Minister and

Home Minister of Bombay, Mahatma Gandhi's life could not be saved.

While some people used to allege that Sardar Patel had a soft corner for the R.S.S., the fact remains that on September 11, 1948, he had written a letter to M.S. Golwalkar, the R.S.S. chief, in which he had clearly said: "As a final result of the poison, the country had to suffer the sacrifice of the invaluable life of Gandhiji. Even an iota of the sympathy of the Government or the people no more remained for the R.S.S. In fact, opposition grew. Opposition turned more severe when R.S.S. men expressed joy and distributed sweets after Gandhiji's death".[10] The propaganda against Sardar Patel may have been a part of the calculated design of some people, who were interested in lowering his image vis-à-vis that of Pandit Jawahar Lal Nehru, who had become the country's Prime Minister.

After an enquiry had absolved the R.S.S. of the charge of having had a role in the assassination of Gandhiji, Sardar Patel was said to have suggested the withdrawal of the ban imposed on the organisation in the wake of the Mahatma's assassination. But Panditji was believed to have disagreed saying that such a step was likely to be interpreted as encouragement given by the Government to Fascist elements in India.[11] All this clearly brought out the two leaders' different perceptions on this issue.

I was deeply moved by Panditji's highly rhetorical words that came over the radio in the wake of this tragic and earth-shaking event: " Friends and comrades, the light has gone out of our lives and there is darkness everywhere". I can still hear Panditji's voice quivering with emotion, as he paid a moving tribute to Gandhiji on another occasion in the following words: "A glory has departed and the sun that warmed and brightened our lives has set and we shiver in the cold and dark". I recall another speech by Nehru likening the Mahatma to a pilgrim marching, staff in hand, in his quest for truth, determined and fearless, and regardless of consequences.

Lord Mountbatten, the then Governor General of free India described Gandhiji in a letter to a friend, as 'a remarkable old boy' whom, he thought, history would link with Buddha and Mahomet, while Indians in general compared him with Jesus Christ. Some months later I had read the tribute the New York Times had paid Gandhiji by saying that Gandhiji had 'tried in the mood of the New

Testament to love his enemies and do good to those who despitefully used him'.

I still remember that the All-India Radio had in a broadcast highlighted the tribute that Albert Einstein had paid to the Mahatma on his 75th birthday: "Generations to come, it may be, will scarce believe that such a one as this ever in flesh and blood walked upon the earth". I much appreciated the description by the Kolkata daily, Hindustan Standard, of Gandhiji's assassination by 'people for whose redemption he lived' as 'the second crucifixion in the history of the world', the similarity between the two events being heightened by the fact that Gandhiji's end came on a Friday—'the same day that Jesus was done to death, one thousand nine hundred and fifteen years ago'.

There was a view among sections of the Hindus that Gandhiji and the Congress Party were responsible for the country's partition and the creation of Pakistan. It can be said straightaway that this view was wrong and betrayed our inability to appreciate the worth of one of the all-time greats of India and the world. To comprehend Gandhiji's greatness, one has simply to turn over in the mind the many social and political concepts that he had sired or whose value he had re-emphasised—truth, love, non-violence (Ahimsa), 'Satyagraha', passive resistance, non-cooperation, civil disobedience, the economic philosophy of trusteeship, decentralised economy as against 'industrialism' etc. His struggle against casteism and untouchability, the stress that he laid on moral values and the power of soul force as distinct from brute force and the message of communal harmony between the Hindus and Muslims that he preached are still relevant.

It was Gandhiji more than any other individual, who had helped in bringing about political awakening among the Indian masses and in getting them drawn into the struggle for freedom. This was a very important factor that eventually paved the way for and led to the country's independence. It is in this sense that Gandhiji's contribution to the winning of freedom for India was of the greatest significance.

Many interesting facts about the assassination of Mahatma Gandhi have now been made public. The First Information Report recorded at the Tughlak Road Police Station in New Delhi after this heinous act was committed is now available to anyone on request. It was written in Urdu, but was later translated into English. The Police

Station was a stone's throw from the bungalow on Tughlak Road, where I lived for ten years while I served as an officer of the Intelligence Bureau, Government of India. Birla House, where Gandhiji was assassinated is just behind this bungalow. Once I visited this spot to pay my homage to Gandhiji. Often, I looked in awe and reverence at the Birla House through the rear hedge of my bungalow.

As I learnt later, Dasondha Singh, Station House Officer of Tughlak Road Police Station, had spent most of the afternoon of January 30,1948, basking in the winter sun on the lawns of the Police Station along with some other colleagues. At about 5 pm, when he was preparing to leave for his residence, a young man rushed into his room to break the news that Gandhiji had been murdered at the Birla House. Dasondha Singh rushed there to take all necessary action. The incident took place at 5.17 pm and the F.I.R. was written at 9.45 pm by Daulat Ram. Those days, there was no telephone at the Police Station and so one Nand Lal Mehta, an eye witness, who was a resident of M Block, Connaught Place, had to come all the way to the Tughlak Road Police Station to narrate the chain of events.

Sardar Gurbachan Singh, another witness, was a resident of Timarpur. It was he who told the police that the last words uttered by Gandhiji were "Hey Ram". T.G. Sanjeevi Pillai, the then Director, Intelligence Bureau, who also functioned as the Inspector General of Police, Delhi, and D.W. Mehra, Deputy Inspector General of Police, Delhi, who was down with flu, read the F.I.R. after it was written. Both these officers had thought it necessary to thoroughly interrogate witness Sardar Gurbachan Singh.[12] Sanjeevi Pillai was the head of the Intelligence Bureau of which I also became the chief many years later after working in that organisation from 1956 onward for about 31 years. D.W. Mehra was also a top-ranking officer of the Intelligence Bureau, whom I came to know quite well in due course.

Tit-bits about the Gandhi assassination case continue to surface from time to time. In September 1998, the 'BJP Today', a mouth-piece of the BJP, published an article by R. Chandrachudan, reportedly a close associate of Devadas Gandhi,[13] alleging the presence of "two mysterious photographers from the British High Commission" at the time of Gandhiji's assassination. It was further alleged that the two-some left for London the same night. The writer of the article suggested a check of the immigration records of January 30, 1948, the date of the assassination, and a scrutiny of the record of the

British High Commission's permanent, semi-permanent and casual staff of that period. There was no indication in the article as to why its writer had not brought up this matter during the five decades during the five decades that had elapsed since the assassination.

I have read a report[14] in the press about the treatment meted out to the getaway car used by N.V. Godse in the assassination of Mahatma Gandhi. The US-made Dictator Studebaker, which was nicknamed 'killer', was prevented by Congressmen from participating in the vintage car rally held at Kanpur on February 14, 1999. The owner of the car, Abdul Kamal Karim, disclosed that in 1994, the car had been stoned by Congressmen when a bid was made for its participation in the vintage car rally at Dehra Dun with the result that it was compelled to withdraw. However, it had taken part in several such rallies held at Lucknow, Delhi etc. and bagged prizes. At Abdul Kamal Karim's instance, Rajiv Gandhi, the late Prime Minister, a few days before his assassination in 1991, had assured him that the car would be given a place in the Gandhi Museum. The promise could not be fulfilled because of Rajiv Gandhi's sudden and tragic assassination.

In February 1999, several documents connected with the trial of Mahatma Gandhi's assassination case were put up for display at an exhibition entitled "Bapu, the Undying Flame" held at the National Archives, New Delhi.[15] I had a look at the First Information Report in Urdu recorded on January 30, 1948 at the Tughlak Road Police Station, the English version of which is reproduced below:

Ex. P/248

(In Urdu)

No. 68, P.S. Tughlak Road, Delhi

Date and time of report — 30-1-1948 at 5.55 P.M.

Date and time of occurrence — 30-1-1948 at 5-10 P.M.

Name and residence of Shri Nandlal Mehta

Informant and complainant son of Shri Nathalal Mehta, caste Hindustani, resident of Connaught Circus, Building Lal Sarju Prasad, M-Block, New Delhi, 302 I.P.C.

Place of occurrence, etc. Birla House at a distance of two furlongs towards north-east

Proceedings re: investigation, etc. — No delay.

Sd/-................

STATEMENT OF SHRI NANDLAL MEHTA, SON OF NATHALAL MEHTA, CASTE HINDUSTANI, RESIDENT OF CONNAUGHT CIRCUS, BUILDING LALA SARJU PRASAD, M. BLOCK,NEW DELHI.

To-day I was present at the Birla House. At about 5.10 p.m. in the evening Mahatma Gandhi stared from his room in the Biria House for the prayer-ground. Sm.Aba Ben Gandhi and Kumari Manu Ben Gandhi were with Mahatmaji, and Mahatmaji was walking resting his hands on their shoulders. With Mahatmaji in the same row there were two more girls, Lal Brij Kishan 'chandiwale', resident of No. 1 Nirendra Place, Parliament Street,Sardar Gurbachan Singh, resident of Timarpur, Delhi, and I were also going. Besides these there some females of the Birla House and two or three members of the staff. Passing through the garden (he) climbed on the steps to reach the prayer-ground. As usual the public was standing on both sides and a passage about 3 ft. was left for Mahatmaji to pass through. According to the usual custom Mahatmaji folded his hands and greeted the people. (Mahatmaji) had gone only 6-7 steps when from the crowd one person whose name was afterwards disclosed as Nathuram Vinayak Godse, resident of Pune, came forward and fired three shots at Mahatmaji from a close distance of 2-3 ft. which hit Mahatmaji at his abdomen and chest. Blood began to ooze out, Mahatmaji feil down saying 'Ram Ram'. The assailant was immediately caught on the spot together with the pistol. Mahatmaji was taken to his residential quarters in the Birla House in senseless condition and he died at that very moment. The Police had taken the accused to the Police Station.

Sd/-

30-1-1948. N.L. Mehta

Among the papers displayed at the exhibition at the National Archives was a letter from the S.P., C.I.D., sent from Simla to the Director, Intelligence Bureau, the Inspector-General of Police, Delhi, several other officials of Delhi Police and some officials of the Ministry of Home Affairs, Government of India, New Delhi. The letter indicated that Godse's final speech at the court appeared to have moved almost all those, who were present in the hall, particularly the ladies, who were noticed shedding tears or blowing their noses and wiping their eyes. It was mentioned in the letter that Nathuram's brother, who was also present in the court, received invitations to tea etc. extended by some local people. It stated that "local opinion though not against Mahatma Gandhi, appears to be definitely favourable to NVG" and that some of the people were "openly seen sympathising with him". The counsel for the accused Madan Lal and Apte requested the court to adjourn the case on sentimental grounds for 45 minutes, but the Advocate General objected and the court refused to adjourn. Nathuram Godse who argued his own case for the last seven days concluded with eulogies to the High Court Judges, pointing out that the court was the place left in India where bribery and favouritism did not exist. How true is this today, after the lapse of more than fifty years ?

According to the letter, Nathuram pointed out to the judges that he had never put any appeal for himself nor would he appeal for mercy for himself because he had shown no mercy to the Great Man of India he had killed. The only mercy he wanted was to have a stroll sometimes during the day, because he had been confined in a cell measuring 8 feet by 10 feet which meant a sort of slow death for him. He requested the court that either he should be executed immediately or permitted to leave his cell for a short time in the evening.

Another letter put up at the exhibition was from Nathuram to the Chief Commissioner of Delhi making a fervent plea for an interview with his parents in Pune. The request was turned down. Also shown at the exhibition was the noting on the file by H.V. Iyengar, the then Home Secretary, Government of India, that he had discussed the issue with the Home Minister, who had agreed that transferring Godse to Pune would be politically "unwise".

During the 1948 summer holidays, I went to English Bazar, the headquarters of Malda distrct, where my father was posted as the officer in charge of a field unit of the National Sample Survey, a project sponsored by the Kolkata-based Indian Statistical Institute. It was a very hot and humid place, a little away from the old town of Malda, but still I was happy to get out of Kolkata and spend some time in the different climate and environment of a district town. An important landmark of the place was the river Mahananda that passed by it. Ashoke Mitra of the Indian Civil Service, then District Magistrate of Malda, was the same person, who, some years ago, had been the Sub-Divisional Officer of Munshiganj, the Sub-Division of Dhaka district (now in Bangladesh) in which my village Shyamsiddhi was located.

Once, when I was crossing the Mahananda in a big ferry boat, the District Magistrate also arrived there in his jeep, which was majestically driven over an improvised wooden platform straight into the boat. He kept sitting in his jeep, while all the passengers including me remained standing on board the comodious boat that was being propelled by a couple of boatmen with their oars and long bamboo poles across the wide river. When the boat reached the other bank, the District Magistrate's jeep was driven off again over a wooden platform, that was promptly put up by some people at the instance of an obedient minion, who was accompanying him.

Thereafter, we all trooped out of the boat and proceeded to our respective destinations on foot. Needless to say, I was highly impressed by the manner in which the District Magistrate's jeep was driven into and then out of the boat, without his getting down to rub shoulders with the ordinary passengers of the ferry boat. Years later, when I entered the service of the Government, I found that this was one of the most innocent privileges, which most officers of the Government serving in semi-urban or rural areas had been enjoying all along. In any case, the District Magistrate's suave demeanour gave no offence to the sensibilities of the simple folk on board the boat.

From Malda I visited several places of historical interest—Gaud, Pandua, Adina and Ramkeli. The Jahura Kali temple of Malda, which attracted big gatherings of people on various occasions, was believed to be one of the four temples of goddess Chandi that King Vallalasena had set up. Relics like the Masjids and the Firoj Minar of Gaud still stand out in my memory. The Firoz Minar was said to have been built as a smaller replica of Delhi's Qutb Minar in 1487 A.D. by Saifuddin Firoz Shah to commemorate the conquest of Gaud. An important landmark of Gaud that I saw was the 'Lukochuri Darwaza' of the palace said to have been built in 1655 A.D. by Shuja, son of Shah Jahan, and Subedar of Bengal (1639-1659 A.D.). It is generally believed that while entering the palace through this gateway, Shuja used to play hide and seek with his Begums. Hence the name 'Lukochuri Darwaza'.

Adina was originally known as Adinath, because King Ganesh of Bengal used to worship at a temple of Lord Shiva that was located there. I heard from some local people the romantic story of how Jadunarayan, son of Ganesh, fell in love with a Muslim girl, Asman Tara (star of the sky), whom he married after embracing Islam. He was disowned by Ganesh as well as by Hindu society. He enlisted the help of Sikander Shah, the Sultan of Delhi, in conquering Adina, but, in compliance with the terms laid down by the latter, he had to build a mosque by destroying the Shiva temple of his father. This was believed to be the biggest mosque of Asia and the third biggest in the world.

Ramkeli is famous for the visit that Shri Chaitanya, the great Vaishnava saint, had paid to this place in 1506 A.D. to meet Rup and Sanatan, the two Ministers of Hussain Shah, the Sultan of Bengal, an ardent patron of Bengali literature and a votary of secular values, who used to treat the Hindus and the Muslims alike. To commemorate Shri Chaitanya's meeting with Rup and Sanatan, a festival is held at Ramkeli every year in the Bengali month of jyastha (mid-May to mid-June).

The Madanmohan temple and the Rupsagar tank of Ramkeli were tourist attractions. The Rupsagar tank was got excavated by the saint, Rup Goswami, who used to live close by. I had a view of the impressive Baraduari Masjid of Ramkeli built in 1526 A.D. by Sultan Nasiruddin Nusrat Shah, son of Sultan Hussain Shah, who, like his father, was also a great patron of Bengali literature. Though called the Baraduari Masjid (i.e. a mosque with 12 gates), it had in fact only 11 gates.

The population of Malda district included a sizeable number of Santhals and Muslims, generally known as the Shershabadias. Maithili was spoken by a large number of people. In fact, the local people had many things in common with the people of adjacent Bihar.

Malda is known for its silk industry and its delicious mangoes, particularly the 'Fazli' variety, which is very sweet, though without any special flavour. It is so big in size that a single mango often suffices for the full meal of an able-bodied person. Since I happened to be in Malda at the peak of the mango season, I had a daily feast of mangoes, which revived in my mind memories of the plentiful mangoes we used to savour in our village in Vikrampur (now in Bangladesh), though, I must confess, these were not a patch on the mangoes that I ate in Malda. I had the opportunity of attending a couple of sessions of Gambhira, the popular folk music of Malda.

After about three weeks, I came back to Kolkata, refreshed in body and mind. I now flung myself heart and soul into my studies and then in April-May, 1949, I sat for the B.A. examination of the Calcutta University.

Notes

1. Cited at page 140, 'The Assassination of Mahatma Gandhi' by K.L. Gauba.
2. *Ibid.*, page 141.
3. *Ibid.*, page 141.
4. The Statesman, February 3, 1948.
5. 'The Assassination of Mahatma Gandhi' by K.L.Gauba, page 299.
6. *Ibid.*, page 281.
7. *Ibid.*, page 282.
8. *Ibid.*, page 290.
9. *Ibid.*, page 291.
10. Letter to the editor of the Hindustan Times, New Delhi, dated March 30, 2000, from Neelima Sharma in response to a news iem in the Hindustan Times (March 20, 2000) in which the RSS leader K.S. Sudarshan was said to have indicated that his organization might decide to take legal action against those who continued to link the organization with the assassination of Mahatma Gandhi.
11. Article captioned "Beyond the devil and the deep sea" by Rakesh Sinha in the Hindustan Times, January 7, 2003.
12. Most of this account is based on Vivek Shukla's write-up in the Hindustan Times Supplement dated January 31, 2000.
13. Taken from the Hindustan Times dated September 16, 1998.
14. Hindustan Times, February 16, 1999.
15. This and the following paragraph are based on a report in the Hindustan Times, Delhi, dated February 15, 1999.

20

Time for General Studies

Moder Garab, Moder Asha
Aamori Banglabhasha

— **Atul Prasad Sen**

(A rough and ready translation would read somewhat as follows: Our pride, our hope, our beautiful Bengali language. This translation, however, fails to adequately express the sentiment evoked in all Bengalees by this immortal couplet from one of Bengal's celebrated poets of the pre-independence era.)

In my school and college, the dominant emphasis was on the study of English language and literature. During the days of the Raj, there were several considerations favoured such a dispensation, one of which was the perceived advantage that flowed from the study of English to those seeking careers in the adminstration and in the professions.

A student normally familiarized himself with the important classics of English literature and some standard works such as those of well-known authors like George Bernard Shaw, P.G. Wodehouse, Somerset Maugham, Maupassant, H.G. Wells, Bertrand Russel and Ernest Hemingway, the much-married American fiction writer, who was famous for his philanderings.

I had also developed a keen interest in Sanskrit literature, which I studied in school and for a couple of years in college. The prescribed texts included pieces of prose and some poetical works of Kalidasa as well as a few chapters of the Geeta. Even after I left college, I enjoyed reading Kalidasa's works and kept up my interest in the study of the Geeta, which proved helpful in my subsequent study of Indian philosophy and the Upanishads. Even though most students of the arts stream did not take up Sanskrit as a subject in college, still many of them ordinarily tried to acquaint themselves with important Sanskrit works in a general way, since they thought that an educated person was expected to hark back to the primary source of the country's literary, cultural and spiritual heritage.

So far as Bengali literature was concerned, there was an element of step-motherliness in the attitude that was shown to its study in schools and colleges. As a consequence, whatever one read in the realm of Bengali literature was mostly traceable to one's own individual interest and initiative. The richness and wide variety of Bengali's literary genres being on par with the best that other literatures of the world had to offer naturally appealed to the greater bulk of the student community. But the syllabi were so designed as to leave hardly much time for a serious study of Bengali literature, even if one was inclined that way.

In my village school, I had read some of Tagore's poems, short stories and novels for which I had developed the kind of admiration that was universal amongst the Bengalees. I had been reading Tagore's works all along, though not as systematically as I would have liked to, because, as I have already explained, it was not necessary to do so to fare well in the examinations whose results determined one's success or otherwise in the academic as well as in other fields.

With the B.A. examination over in April, 1949, I was rid of the over-riding pre-occupation with prescribed college studies. I had now plenty of time to go in for general studies in which I had some interest all along, but which I had to keep on the back burner all this time. In later years, I kept up this interest and read Tagore's works and books on him as well as the works of some important Bengalee writers. The observations on Bengal's literary scene that I have made in this chapter are in the nature of random reflections based on this life-long but somewhat unsystematic and unprofessional study.

Having never been a serious student of literature, I naturally felt diffident about writing on a subject like this. Though my views may have no great literary merit and may appear to be rather abecedarian, still I have made bold to express them in the hope that these may be of some help to those who have had no opportunity of getting acquainted with the writings of some of the most important figures of Bengali literature including some Muslim literary stalwarts of both West Bengal and east Bengal (now Bangladesh).

A fact of which I was aware even in my adolescent years was that Tagore belonged as much to West Bengal as to East Bengal, though he had lived mostly in Kolkata and Shantiniketan. The ten years that he had lived at Shilaidaha—near Kustia on the bank of river Padma in East Bengal—were among the most creative years of his poetic life, considering the large volume of his works that were composed here. It was here that most of the short stories of his 'Galpaguchchha' were written.

Tagore and Sir Jagadish Chandra Bose, the great scientist, were great personal friends. It is said that Bose often visited Tagore at Shilaidaha. Bose used to request Tagore to write a short story and read it out to him each time he dropped in at Shilaidaha. This is how the famous 'Galpaguchchha' took shape. Incidentally, Tagore had composed several poems eulogizing the achievements of Bose at different stages of the latter's career. Tagore had also extended financial assistance to Bose. In 1902, he accepted a donation of Rs. 15,000/-from the King of Tripura and handed it over o Bose towards meeting the expenses of Bose's foreign travel.

Tagore had spent some time at Patisar and Shahjadpur as well, besides visiting many other places of east Bengal. Living in close proximity to the Padma and the other rivers of east Bengal, he gained an exposure to the rural life of Bengal that must have contributed greatly to the shaping of his poetic genius. The fact that both India and Bangladesh chose his songs as their national anthems served to uphold their equal claims to his legacy.

During a visit I paid to 'Thakurbari' in Jorasanko in the latter part of 1945, I saw many things associated with the poet's life that gave me the feeling as if he was still alive. It was only four years ago—in July 1941—that Tagore had breathed his last. The sun had set, but its after-glow still continued to suffuse almost all branches of Bengali literature. Just as the last half of the nineteenth century was the age of Bankim Chandra Chatterjee in Bengali literature, so was the first half of the twentieth century the age of Tagore. My visit to Tagore's ancestral home whetted my appetite to read more about him.

The texts from Tagore's works that our college syllabi prescribed did not call for a very thorough study, since all that one was expected to do was to secure pass marks at the examination. However, lectures by professors at the Asutosh College and later at the Presidency College were very illuminating and served one essential purpose, namely, that of creating in the students an awareness of the immense variety and the vast range of subjects dealt with in Tagore's works and of the diverse facets of his many-splendoured genius.

Tagore was a poet, philosopher, playwright, novelist, painter, musician – all rolled into one. There is no branch of literature which has not been enriched by him. It is not my intention here to go into the infinite range of his literary creations or to undertake an in-depth analysis of his stature as a world poet. This is not the place for that nor am I competent to do so. What I intend to do is to make some observations about how in that formative stage of my life I reacted to the phenomenon that Tagore represented and how I perceived other people reacting to it.

I undertook a study of 'Gitanjali' at this time because I considered it essential reading for any educated person in view of the fact that it was this which had won the Nobel Prize for literature for Tagore – the only Indian to have had that honour for creative literature. I was quite at a loss for the simple reason that I could comprehend very little of what was meant to be said in the Gitanjali. In the initial stages, while going through Tagore's works,I grappled with certain basic concepts of Tagore such as those of 'Jibandevata', 'Manas Sundari', 'Antaryami' – transcendental forces which guide the destiny of man and nature and with which the human spirit is believed to be in constant touch.

In Tagore's poems, one usually comes across ideas that follow as logical corollaries to his perception of life and reality as the manifestation of some transcendental force or the divine mind. Still, while going through the innumerable poems of Tagore, I often encountered words and lines, whose subtle meaning and significance I did not comprehend, despite the long hours that I sometimes spent on their study. Tagore's mysticism was only a small part of his genius. He was essentially a romantic poet, but he did not fail to take note of the problems of the real world. In 'Kari O Komal', he sang : "I do not want to die in this beautiful world; I would like to live as man amidst men". This clearly brought out his humanism .

Tagore's romanticism did not remain confined to the mental plane alone. He had a fling or two in real life too. This was something that had naturally excited our curiosity in our student days. We knew that Tagore's name was romantically linked with Victoria Ocampo, an Argentinian writer, with whom he had spent some days during a visit to Argentina in 1924 and for whom he had written a few poems that figured in 'Purabi'. His intimacy with one Anna Tarkhar, a liberated Maharashtrian lady, became quite obvious from certain sentiments he expressed in 'Sandhya Sangeet'.

It was generally known that Tagore held very liberal views about sex. Even in the early decades of the twentieth century, he had come out openly in favour of conceding to women the same rights as men enjoyed. His espousal of the use of birth control devices was in sharp contrast to the stand of Mahatma Gandhi, who saw great merit in abstinence or Brahmacharya as the legitimate means of controlling birth. Tagore believed in rational thinking and had opposed the 'Charkha' (indigenous spinning wheel), the symbol of Mahatma Gandhi's economic philosophy, which he did not consider good enough for rapid economic development. One reason why Tagore's relationship with Sarat Chandra Chatterjee, the great novelist, became strained was that the latter believed in the virtues of the 'Charkha'.

In the nineteen twenties, when Bihar was devastated by a major earthquake, Mahatma Gandhi described it as God's punishment for the sin of untouchability. Tagore was quick to protest, saying that Gandhiji was thus supporting the forces of unreason. Later, in the late nineteen thirties, Tagore voiced his criticism of what he called Gandhiji's authoritarian attitude towards Subhas Chandra Bose, who had challenged the Mahatma's supremacy in the Congress Party.

So far as Tagore music is concerned, I must confess that I was completely innocent of it when I landed in Kolkata in the middle of the nineteen forties. In Vikrampur, what we had was the rough and robust Kirtan, besides,of course, Bhatiali, the lilting music of the boatman. Tagore's music had hardly any place in my village life. I had just a nodding acquaintance with some specimens of Tagorean music from the few gramophone records that were played in our village home. It is after I came over to Kolkata that I was slowly initiated into its charms. Kolkata's air resonated with Tagore music played on the gramophone and the radio. Cultural programmes held throughout the year all over Kolkata that presented Tagore's songs and dances really opened up a new vista before me. It was the wider and more intense literary and cultural life of Kolkata as distinct from my village life that wrought a slow and imperceptible change in my outlook. Questions about the interpretation of the abstruse philosophical meanings of Tagore's lyrics did not bother me much, when it came to enjoying a session of songs and dances, because the melody and the rhythm were enough to cast their spell on you.

From the exposure to Tagore music that I was now getting in Kolkata, I realised that it was here that the poet's genius revealed itself most adequately. His songs could not be categorised either as light or as classical music, but fell somewhere in between with Dhrupad forming their structural core. He had adjusted classical music to suit the requirements of his lyrics. No one was expected to take liberties with the fixed notations and the basic structure of Tagore songs. It was his songs that gave full expression to Tagore's romanticism, the depth of his spiritualism and the beauty that he perceived in the harmony of the universe. They reflected the changes in the seasons, the beauty of nature and all the moods and sentiments of the people including their patriotic fervour. Tagore songs, therefore, came in handy for people in various walks of life to express their varying moods and thus formed an inseparable bond between the poet and the people, illuminating the diverse facets of their life and culture. It is through his songs that Tagore will continue to live in the lives of the people of at least two nations—India and Bangladesh.

I started attending cultural functions that were organised in observance of Tagore's birth and death anniversaries (on the 25th Baishakh and 22nd Shravana that corresponded to dates in May and July respectively). On these and many other occasions, programmes based on Tagore's songs and dance dramas, recitations from his poems and learned discourses on the many facets of his genius were organised. It was at such functions that I saw for the first time the typical Kolkata intellectual—gentlemen dressed in

'Dhoti' and 'Punjabi' (i.e. 'Kurta') and with books loaded in sling bags that hung from their shoulders. I had never got the opportunity in my village or in my school of attending such programmes or of seeing intellectuals with such typical accoutrement and deportment.

I did not encounter any problem of appreciating the dramas of Tagore that I sometimes attended in Kolkata. His dramas are different from the general run of dramas in Bengali and other languages in the sense that they are the vehicles of lyrical ideas, while the latter are more action-oriented. Lyricism and music are the characteristic features of his dramas such as 'Valmiki Pratibha', 'Chitrangada' etc., which are more like musical ballets. I greatly liked the Chitrangada, perhaps the best of his creations of this genre. I saw some other dramas that were written in the usual mould such as 'Bisarjan', 'Raja Rani', etc., which, again, differed from the traditional drama because of their lyrical and other qualities. Some of his other dramas appealed to me because they contained a lot of humour or were farcical and, therefore, highly enjoyable. I found that Tagore's allegorical and symbolic dramas such as 'Rakta Karabi' and 'Dakghar' were quite popular, the latter being regarded as the best of his symbolic dramas.

I sometimes picked up Tagore's novels for study in leisure hours as average Bengalees used to do in our days. These novels cover a wide range of themes. I enjoyed reading 'Sesher Kavita', a good romantic novel, and thought that his 'Gora' was a literary masterpiece. When I did not have much time to spare, I had his short stories such as the 'Galpaguchchha' to fall back upon. He ranked among the world's greatest writers of this genre of fiction such as Maupassant, Tolstoy, Chekov and Gorky.

Tagore's internationalist outlook was of a piece with his concept of the universal man (Viswamanav), of "transcendental humanity". It was his vision of a world family (Vasudhaiva Kutumbakam) that underlay the 'Vishwabharati' which he founded at Shantiniketan-a place where he sought to bring about a fusion of the cultures of the East and the Westand where the whole universe was to become one home (Yatra Viswam Bhabatyekaneedam). He was against aggressive nationalism that militated against the spirit of international co-operation and cross-cultural exchanges among the nations of the world.

Some of my college friends, who had studied earlier at Vishwabharati, lamented that after the poet's demise, this institution had started slowly drifting away from his lofty ideals – a trend that got intensified after its conversion in 1951 into a Central University, making it dependent upon Government funds.

After Tagore's demise, Abanindranath Tagore, Kshitimohan Sen, Indira Devi Choudhurani, Pramatha Choudhury and many other great personalities were still available in the early nineteen forties to guide the destiny of Vishwabharati. But slowly and imperceptibly, new values started supplanting the original ideals. In the poet's days, Shantiniketan was the fountain head of music ('Ganer Jharnatala'). It was an important centre of cultural education that laid a good deal of emphasis on Tagore songs, dance and drama. It was the source of Tagore culture that influenced the life-styles of numerous people all over Bengal and elsewhere. From the late nineteen forties onward, however, things had begun to change.

Some of my Muslim friends used to say that Tagore had not paid much attention to the life and problems of the Muslims and had generally kept himself pre-occupied with the concerns of Hindu society. In their view, the Bengal Renaissance of the nineteenth century was almost wholly a Hindu phenomenon that was restricted to the upper strata of Hindu society. Since Tagore's thinking was rooted in the Bengal Renaissance, they argued, it was not surprising that he diplayed much less awareness of the problems of the Muslim community. This logic was based on a misconception, as Tagore, besides being critical of the shortcomings of Hindu society, had also striven hard to create harmonious relations between the Hindus and Muslims. He had criticised the anti-Muslim policies of Pratapaditya, one of the twelve 'Bhuinyas' of Bengal, who ruled over Jessore (now in Bangladesh) and had challenged the might of the Mughal rulers. The character of Rahamat in his story 'Kabuliwala' is an immortal literary creation. His 'Musalmaner Galpa' brings out his faith in man which transcends his commitment to any denominational religion.

Tagore had become a cult figure in Bengal and the Bengalees in general did not take kindly to any criticism directed against him or his poetry. Like all other Bengalees, I did feel proud that Tagore had got the Nobel Prize for literature. I had also read an account given by Sarojini Naidu of an interesting sight she had seen during a tour of Europe—of five old ladies sitting in a row in a bus and going through the 'Gitanjali' in speechless seriousness—a comic scene indeed, but something that typified the respect that Tagore poetry had come to command in Europe at that time. It was, however, known that some time after Tagore got the Nobel Prize in 1913, his reputation in the West had started declining. Perhaps the Western intelligentsia wanted to distance itself from Tagore's oriental mysticism. I shall touch upon the other reasons for this decline later in this chapter.

How serious the reaction in Bengal could be to any criticism of Tagore's works became evident from the furore raised over the writings of Edward J.Thompson, an English missionary and the teacher of a school in the Bankura district of Bengal. A contemporary and a close acquaintance of Tagore's, he knew Bengali and did more than any other Englishman to enlighten the Western world about Tagore and his works through his books and translations. However, he had to incur the displeasure of Tagore as well as a section of Bengal's literary world for some of his candid observations on Tagore, though there was no doubt at all that he was as genuine a friend of Tagore and India as any foreign literatteur in his position and in those days could be expected to be.

It was when I was an undergraduate student in Kolkata that I learnt about Edward J. Thompson's book "Rabindranath Tagore: Poet and Dramatist". In the early nineteen fifties, I came by a copy of this book and, after reading it, got a general idea about how a non-Bengalee or non-Indian hailing from the Western world looked at Tagore. I found that though Thompson had made a critical assessment of Tagore's literary position, he had, on the whole, acknowledged the latter's outstanding merit.

According to Edward J.Thompson, Tagore "wrote with a skill and virtuosity hardly ever equalled, in a tongue which is among the half-dozen most expressive and beautiful languages in the world". However, Thompson criticised what he called the "monotony" of Tagore's work, arising partly from the abundance of his writing and partly from the fact that "he explores and exploits one emotion far too much, that of mother and son for each other". While labouring this point, Thompson came out with observations which were none too flattering for the Bengalee or Indian psyche. At one place, he said: " Bengali poetry reminds one too much of those streams which are choked with water-hyacinth – a sheer mass of violet bloom – so common a sight in Bengal today". Or take, for example, his observation: "Indian poetry has a monotony of tradition".

Adverting to the abundance of Tagore's writing, Thompson drew the conclusion that "he is a very unequal poet – His inequality is in his thought and matter". Thompson made no secret of his exasperation with "endless references to the first night of nuptials" and "the prevalence of all this marriage-chamber obsession " in Tagore's work, "The Golden Boat" (Sonar Tari), which, he conceded, "is crammed with beautiful and accomplished poetry". Edward J. Thompson has made many other critical references to Tagore's writings, as, for example, when he says: "We often feel there is a slackness somewhere, probably at the very springs of thought and conception. His poems rarely fail in beauty of style, but they often fail in grip. This is the special failure of Chitra, so fine lyrically .... The worst flaw of his later work is this lack of serious intellectual effort."

Thompson was also critical of Tagore's concept of 'Jibandebata' – " the presiding deity of the poet's life – not quite that even – it is the poet himself – the inner self of the poet, who is more than his earthly incarnation", though Tagore's followers "made much of it, causing widespread irritation in his own country". Thompson is all praise for Tagore's songs. "It is by his songs that he is best known", said Thompson. But about Tagore's dramas, he said that the former's countrymen" do not rank Rabindranath's dramas high". According to Thompson, the earlier dramas seem "curiously obsolete", though he praised the later dramas as they "lay bare a lofty attitude towards life, and reveal a mind moving only on the highest planes of thought and feeling".

Comparing Tagore with the best poets of the Western world, Thompson said that Tagore was not a Shakespeare or a Sophocles or a Dante, though he might be a Hugo or a Wordsworth or greater than either. Thompson was of the view that not only were life and thought circumscribed for Tagore in his land, but his genius was left without guidance. He thought that there was no literary criticism in Bengal, where "politics overshadowed all thought" and "the national sensitiveness was so quick that a book was judged, not by its honesty or ability, not by the insight it showed or the help it brought, but solely according as it flattered patriotic vanity".

Referring to Tagore's attempt to seek some guidance from English literature, Thompson said: "But it also served him badly", because "Rabindranath took over from English poetry surface qualities, metrical nuances, and a closer way of natural description". Thompson also thought that unfortunately for Tagore, English, the European language that he knew best, was not the richest in criticism. Switching over to the positive side of the balance sheet, Thompson conceded that Tagore was "the most open-air of poets". He said: "Just as life in India is more open-air than in England, so poetry also, when not a mere literary exercise, is more open-air". He characterised Tagore as a supreme landscape poet, because Bengal's villages, streams, bazaars and melas, its moon and sky found perfect expression in verse. In atmosphere and general effects, Tagore was scarcely rivalled, according to Thompson.

Thompson thought that an important reason for the failure of a non-Bengalee to fully appreciate Tagore's greatness was that translation could rarely convey the depth and colour of his verse and "its glow of imaginative interpretation of the natural world". Thompson agreed by and large with the claim of Buddhadeb Bose that Tagore was the world's greatest lyric poet. He accepted the claim often made in India that Tagore's forte lay in his interpretation of nature. Thompson was, however, less convinced of the validity of another claim made by Tagore's votaries about his gift for the interpretation of sorrow.

Making an over-all assessment of Tagore's genius, Thompson said that his place would be not simply among India's poets, but among those of the world.

Thompson's book greatly annoyed Tagore and provoked a hostile reaction. Even before this book was published in 1926, a shorter study on Tagore by the same author entitled "Rabindranath Tagore", which came out in 1921, had raised the poet's hackles because of several blunders that it contained.

Tagore and some of his admirers launched a campaign against the writings of Edward J.Thompson. Tagore did so pseudonymously and his admirers openly, though it became clear that they were doing so at the instance of Tagore, sometimes using for this purpose material provided by him. Dr. Brajendranath Seal, the eminent philosopher and intellectual, who had become a great friend of Thompson's, felt offended by the latter's first book. Rabindranath's pseudonymous article in the "Prabasi" and the attacks launched by Ramananda Chatterjee, editor of the Modern Review, his daughter Shanta Debi and Nihar-ranjan Ray showed the vehemence and intensity of the feeling in the Tagore circle.

While I was broadly aware of the trends of criticism of Tagore's work by Edward J.Thompson and of the fact that Tagore's reputation in the West had come down considerably from the level when he was awarded the Nobel Prize, I did not have the opportunity of keeping up my studies on this issue for quite some years because of pre-occupation with the exigencies of a demanding official career. My study of Bengali literature became rather casual and haphazard. Years later, I tried to pick up the thread from where I had left off. I find that latterly there has been a noticeable upsurge of interest among scholars, both Indian and foreign, in this subject with the result that there is now quite a volume of literature on it, which is quite interesting and illuminating. Among the books that one can now study are the "Selected Poems of Tagore" by William Radice, "Alien Homage: Edward Thompson and Rabindranath Tagore" by E.P.Thompson (son of Edward J.Thompson), "Imperfect Encounter" by Mary Lago, "Tagore-Thompson Correspondence" by Uma Dasgupta and Harish Trivedi's "Introduction" to the 1989 edition of Edward J.Thompson's "Rabindranath Tagore: Poet and Dramatist". There are several other books which are also relevant and some more were believed to be in the pipe-line a few years ago.

On going through some of these books, I feel happy that more than six decades after the poet's demise, there are scholars who can now make bold to come out with their true views on the literary stature of Tagore, though I do not mean that all the criticism that has been directed against him is valid.

As for the waning of Tagore's literary reputation in the West soon after he received the Nobel Prize in 1913, an important contributory factor was his nationalist outlook, which reflected itself in his lectures on nationalism and his renunciation of knighthood in the wake of the barbaric repression let loose by the British authorities on the Indians at Jalianwalabagh in 1919. Tagore was on the watch list of the police and was mentioned as "class B No.12" in the records of the Special Branch of the Bengal Police. The Intelligence Branch of the Bengal Government had drawn attention in a report to what it perceived as attempts made by the Anushilan

Samiti, a revolutionary organisation of pre-independence Bengal, to infiltrate the Vishwabharati . To quote:[1]

" Bolepur.-An institution which the Anushilon Samiti is using for the purpose of terrorist organization is Dr. Rabindra Nath Tagore's well-known educational institution at Bolepur, in the district of Birbhum. Two active members of the party are known to be there, one of whom, Mon Mohan Ghosh, has been selected as one of the two delegates of the party to be sent to Bandar Abbas to get into touch with the Bolshevik. This man was sent in May to Lucknow with Rash Behari Bose's Japanese address for Jiten Sanyal, brother of Sachin Sanyal. During his Japanese tour in 1924, Dr. Rabindra Nath Tagore met Rash Behari Bose and it is significant that in 1924, after Government had refused a passport to India to KeshhRam Sabarwal, a revolutionary of Peshawar, who was at one tme rash Behari Bose's private secretary and was cognizant of the German plots in the Far East. Dr. Rabindra Nath Tagore interceded, although unsuccessfully, on his behalf before the Governor of Bengal, suggesting that Sabarwal would be provided with a post in Bolepur. In June 1925, Narendra Sen wrote that Mr. Bose of Japan had been trying to introduce an agent into the Bishwa Bharati (Dr. Tagore's University at Bolepur), but had not been successful. In that letter he also wrote that it was necessary to place three more members of the party in Bolepur. I. B. Sen, who is known to be connected with M.N. Roy, tried in May to secure an appointment in the Bishws Bharati for an ex-detenu named Lal Mohan De, who is still an active member of the Anushilan Samiti. A reliable agent states that Mr. Lim Ngo Cheang, Professor of Chinese at the Bishwa Bharati, is the link between the revolutionaries of India and China, and it is reported that Mon Mohan Ghosh is a constant associate of his at Bolepur. As far as it is known, Dr. Tagore himself is not cognizant of the use the party is making of his institution."

Some songs of Tagore were considered to be seditious by the British authorities and figured on the " List of common Bengali Songs on Record in the Political Branch, Criminal Investigation Department (1912), Government of Bengal.[2] Among them were such popular numbers as 'Aamar Sonar Bangla, Aami Tomai Bhalabasi' (Oh my golden Bengal, I love you), 'Aamader Yatra Holo Suru Ekhan' (Our voyage has started now), 'Ekbar Tora Ma Bolia Dak' (Once you call me mother), 'Oder Bandhan Yatoi Shakta Habey'

(The more they bind the fetters fast), 'Tobu Parine Sampite Pran' (Yet we could not dedicate our lives), 'Tomari Tore Sampinu E Deho' (For your sake I have dedicated my body), 'Yadi Tor Dak Shuney Keu Na Aase Tobe Ekla Chalo Re' (If no one responds to your call, then walk alone). One of these songs—Oder Bandha Yatai Shakta Habey—was considered fit for proscription under a provision of law, but no such action was taken. Decades later, the song—Aamar Sonar Bangla—was chosen as the national anthem of Bangladesh.

Poor English translations of Tagore's poems also contributed in some measure to the decline in his reputation in the West. For one thing, it is not possible to translate a poem into a different language without allowing its quality to suffer; for another, the translations were not done well. Even Tagore's own English translations of his poems did not fully bring out the greatness of his creations. It is said that under the influence of C.F.Andrews, many of the translations were done in such a manner as to appeal to the Western mind. As for Yeats' introduction to the Gitanjali, Tagore himself thought that it was misleading, a view which Edward J.Thompson fully shared.

Vanity was also believed by some to have contributed to the cooling off in Tagore's relationship with Edward J.Thompson. This may have been the reason why Tagore said that the latter, being nothing more than a school master, should have been conscious of his limitations before venturing to criticise him.

In seeking to present a true picture of Tagore's literary status in Bengal, Thompson had highlighted the fact that the Pandits of Bengal did not like his use of colloquial Bengali as the vehicle of his expression. The Calcutta University was initially unappreciative of Tagore's colloquialism and even used to set passages from his works, asking examinees to rewrite them in chaste Bengali. Tagore felt offended by the manner in which Thompson drew attention to these facts.

William Radice in his "Rabindranath Tagore: Selected Poems" made some observations, disagreeing with Edward J. Thompson's critical stance towards Tagore. While praising Tagore's literary genius, he also drew attention to what he regarded as some of the poet's shortcomings. According to him, the main reason for the failure of the Western world to fully appreciate Tagore's works was that the lyrics translated into English were mostly songs, which were "intimate combinations of word and melody". Radice thought that it was impossible to translate songs because "the mood, the feeling, the truth of the song are all in the melody."

An important addition to the growing volume of literature on Tagore is a book by Edward J.Thompson's son, E.P.Thompson, entitled "Alien Homage: Edward Thompson and Rabindranath Tagore", which is based on unpublished papers that he inherited from his father. He has tried to present a balanced view of Tagore's genius, mentioning both his greatness and his shortcomings. However, by and large, he seeks to defend his father's attitude towards Tagore and refute the view held by many that it was his father's writings that were responsible for bringing down Tagore's image in the Western world. According to him, Tagore's reputation in the West had slumped before Thompson wrote the two books on the poet. Moreover, Edward J.Thompson is said to have always upheld Tagore's reputation in public, writing about him with generosity and reserving his 'doubts and sharp asides 'for his private correspondence. The elder Thompson, according to his son, was an admirer of Tagore, but a "critical interpreter", hoping to "give the West a pukka view of Rabi at last" i.e. "give Bengali a critism of its stuff by universal standards".

In fairness to the junior Thompson, it must be said that he does not fully approve of his father's attempt to judge Tagore's works with reference to what are called "universal standards", because, as he says, "Thompson was over-confident as to his own command of universal standards". He describes as "unforgivably brash" a letter his father wrote Tagore in December 1920, proclaiming his self-appointed mission to "revolutionze the Western notion of you as a poet". As regards his father's knowledge of the Bengali language, which Tagore had found not adequate for the tasks he had taken upon himself, he admits that though the elder Thompson had a good knowledge of spoken Bengali, "his command of classic Bengali was uncertain and his knowledge (at that time) of Sanskrit was slight".

All these concessions notwithstanding, E.P.Thompson seeks in his book to generally vindicate the stand of his father against what he regards as the unjust criticism by the poet and his disciples.The reasons to which E.P.Thompson attributes the criticism directed in Bengal against his father's attitude towards Tagore are the role of politics, the Bengalee's feeling of local pride and the poet's own sense of vanity. In this context, E.P.Thompson quotes the following observation from Partha Chatterjee's "Nationalist Thought and the Colonial World-A Derivative Discourse" : "There was no way Bengalis were going to allow Thompson to become a critic of Bengali literature : it was ruled out precisely by the colonial relation".

Edward J.Thompson's book was republished in 1991 with an erudite introduction by Prof.Harish Trivediof the Delhi University. Trivedi's observations on the Tagore-Thompson interface cover the whole ground admirably, dealing exhaustively with all the facts that are by now known to all students of comparative literature. His comments reveal his sympathy for Edward J.Thompson, who, in his view, "deals fairly evenly in both blame and praise". While conceding that Tagore was the greatest writer of modern India, he finds the vast claims made for him by Bengali-knowing scholars in English "quite insupportable by any evidence or argument they are able to offer". As an example of such exaggerated panegyric, he cites the view of Buddhadeb Bose that "Rabindranath is the world's most complete writer".

Trivedi thinks that the significance of Thompson's book lies in it its attempt to present a picture of Tagore to those who knew English, but not Bengali. To quote: "With all its defects and shortcomings, real and imputed, as well as such merits as it possesses, Thompson's book remains virtually the only one of its kind : the one book in English to discuss Tagore's poetic work extensively on the basis of a reading of the Bengali originals, from a point of view which is at once sympathetic and an outsider's". Thompson wanted to "deconstruct" the "orientalist", "mystical-lyrical Tagore" and replace him with a more fully rounded, robust and incomparably greater and more enduring Tagore".

Trivedi lambasts the campaign launched against Thompson by Tagore and his disciples in some journals of Bengal. "He was not only most indignant, he became undignified", says Trivedi. With this view, William Radice agrees when he says that Tagore's publication of a pseudonymous critical review of Thompson's book "was unworthy of the greatness that Thompson never failed to see in him".

Trivedi feels that what annoyed Tagore most was what he regarded as Thompson's lack of reverence for him, an attitude that arose, according to Trivedi, from their different cultural backgrounds.

Trivedi also traces Tagore's annoyance to his feeling that Thompson's criticism and deconstruction of his work had damaged his reputation in the West—a feeling for which Trivedi sees no justification, when one remembers that "over the following years, Thompson took every opportunity to write favourably about Tagore and Bengali literature in the English papers".

In 1994, William Radice's book on Rabindranath Tagore was reprinted along with a preface and a copy of an article by him that had earlier been published in the literary supplement to the Kolkata issue of the Statesman dated May 8, 1993, in which the author made same observations that are relevant to the Tagore-Thompson controversy and are, therefore, worth mentioning. He characterises Edward J. Thompson's book on Tagore as "the biggest and bravest attempt by a Westerner to understand and communicate Tagore's works". Adverting to E.P.Thompson's remark that Radice had distanced himself from Edward J Thompson by making some critical references to the book, Radice now admitted his mistake for which he profoundly apologised. However, Radice stuck to the main point that he had made earlier, namely that "Thompson's book misses its target and that the legacy of his work is problematic." He stood by his opinion that Thompson's study of Tagore was "by and large distressingly unsuccessful", a view with which even E.P.Thompson agrees. He also defended himself against the junior Thompson's suggestion that he had blamed the senior Thompson for the decline in Tagore's reputation in the Western world.

Radice is of the view that Tagore's sharp reaction to Edward J.Thompson's book was traceable to his feeling that Thompson had misunderstood him and to a fear that Thompson's undoubted credentials as a Bengalee scholar together with the status of the OUP (Oxford University Press) imprint "would give the book an 'authority' that could do lasting damage". Radice asserts that, considering all the circumstances, "Tagore was right to be fearful." I think that Radice is right.

Referring to Harish Trivedi's observation that "judgement criticism of the kind that Thompson attempted is essential", Radice wonders if a "critical evaluation" of Tagore will ever be successfully achieved, because "some great artists, by their copiousness and genius, elude evaluative critism." To this must be added another factor, namely the lack of adequate knowledge of Bengali on the part of a non-Bengalee or a non-Indian, without which an unbiased assessment of Tagore's works is next to impossible.

Radice quotes a comment by Sisir Kumar Ghose—"Criticise we must, but on bended knees"—and observes that just as this is done to Shakespeare, Rembrandt and Bach, we must also genuflect to Tagore. I agree with Radice that "the challenge of communicating to non-Bengalees the scale and 'strangeness' of Tagore's achievement remains enormous and perhaps insuperable". Radice concludes by saying that "Thompson's work, for all its courage and energy, its important informal content and its true sense of Tagore's greatness as a man, will remain of litle help and possibly even a hindrance to those attempting that daunting task".

I think that it is not possible for a foreigner and even for a non-Bengalee without a very sound knowledge of Bengali to fully appreciate the greatness of Tagore's genius. It is not proper to borrow the standards of literary criticism from English literature and apply them to Bengali literature because such standards are apt to overlook the divergence in the typical manner of the historical evolution of the two literatures, apart from the differences in the socio-cultural outlook of the people reflected in their different customs, traditions, living conditions and life-styles. I also feel that Tagore was right in reacting in the manner that he did to Edward J.Thompson's assessment of his works, because his knowledge of Bengali was not adequate and his attitude betrayed a lack of reverence for a world poet of Tagore's stature, apart from the fact that his writings did cause harm to Tagore's image in the Western world.

Even in Bengal, criticism of Tagore's writings was being voiced by those aligned with publications like Kallol, Shanibarer Chithi, Kalikalam etc., who were making a pitch for a new literary movement based on their own perception of realism. Incidentally, in the opinion of Nirad Chandra Choudhuri, this hostility to Tagore sprang from sheer jealousy. Critical observations about Tagore's poetry were made by the famous poet, Dwijendra Lal Roy (author of 'Dhana Dhayey Puspey Bhara'), whose patriotic songs and historical dramas had served as a source of inspiration for the freedom movement of our country. He and Tagore were contemporaries, though he was younger than the latter by two years. They were great personal friends to start with, but later they fell out and did not hesitate to give public expression to their mutual recriminations, some of which pertained to matters of poetry and some others to differing personal attitudes towards life in general. It was an unforṭunate chapter of Bengal's literary history.

Roy died young in 1913, then just 53 years of age, some time before Tagore got the Nobel Prize. Tagore continued to trail a blaze of glory, but poor Dwijedra Lal Roy's legacy did not receive the measure of recognition from posterity that his poetic and musical genius deserved. Practically nothing has been done to preserve his numerous writings and songs. Just two years after the spectacular celebration of Tagore's birth centenary in 1961, D.L.Roy's birth centenary in passed by largely unnoticed and uncelebrated.

Some other literary figures such as Buddhadev Bose, Shakti Chattopadhyaya and Sunil Gangopadhyaya have been critical of Tagore and found fault with him for some reason or other. Some have said that Tagore's poems centring around nature no longer appeal to the people in the context of the modern world's complexities. Some have found Tagore songs too slow and rigid and have urged that they should be freed from the shackles of orthodoxy and authorised notations to enhance their appeal.

Such critical views notwithstanding, Tagore bids fair to occupy his Olympian heights for a variety of reasons such as his universally acknowledged and unrivalled contribution to all branches of Bengali literature and to the evolution of the modern Bengali language that is the language of Bengali books. Above all, his music that provides the Bengalee with a song appropriate for all occasions, all the seasons of the year and all the moods of man bid fair to outlast all serious as well as flippant attempts to bring him down from the high pedestal where he has been resting securely right from the beginning of the last century.

Well-known Bengalee writers such as Pramatha Nath Bishi and Dr. Niharranjan Ray contributed considerably through their writings on Tagore's works to the correct and masterly interpretation of the poet's literary output. Had their writings been available in the English language, the Western world would have been in a much better position to appreciate the greatness of Tagore's over-all contribution.

A recent book of translations of Tagore's poems by Ketaki Kushari Dyson has greatly facilitated a proper comprehension of the poet's works by non-Bengalees, non-Indians and those from the

Western world. However, her role in the controversy over the translation of a poem Tagore had composed as a tribute to the memory of William Shakespeare evoked criticism in literary circles. The poem in question figures in Tagore's " Balaka " and was translated by Tagore himself. A few years ago, a bust of Tagore was installed at Stratford-on-Avon, Shakespeare's birthplace—a great honour for an Indian poet. When Ketaki learnt that Tagore's English translation of his poem in memory of Shakespeare was to be engraved on the stone at Stratford-on-Avon alongside his poem in Bengali, she was believed to have denounced Tagore's English rendering of the poem as below standard and pressed for the acceptance instead of her own English translation of the poem on the ground that it was superior to Tagore's translation.

I do not know whether it is correct to say, as some have done, that Ketaki went about seeking the view of English literary figures as to the excellence of her own translation vis-a-vis Tagore's. But what was evident was that the controversy gave some English scholars an opportunity to poke fun at what they called the poor quality of Tagore's English translation of his own poems. William Radice has also translated the particular poem, but when he heard that the poet's own translation was to be inscribed on the bust, he refrained from throwing his hat into the ring and chose not to press the claim in favour of his own translation in a show of deference to Tagore. I understand that the authorities concerned eventually decided—and, I think, rightly—to inscribe Tagore's own translation on the plinth.

A recent study or rather a biography of Tagore by Krishna Dutt and Andrew Rabinson that concentrates mainly on the poet's personality rather than his work and its ouvre has its quota of critical observations, which, together with some of the ill-informed reviews of the book in the British press, reflect the tendency to judge a great poet rather superficially and flippantly without a through understanding of the subject matter. All this is a pointer to a resurgence of interest in Tagore in the Western World, which, with all its shortcomings, is still welcome in view of the opportunity that it may provide in the long run for a proper assessment and appreciation of Tagore's true literary contribution.

Kazi Nazrul Islam was another popular and highly regarded poet of Bengal, whose songs and recitation from whose poems, like those of Tagore, invariably figured in all cultural programmes that I used to attend in my student days in Kolkata. I had read many of his poems besides those which figured in our school and college text books. A Havildar of the Army during the First World War (hence the epithet soldier-poet applied to him), Nazrul, the rebel poet of Bengal, gave expression through his poetry and songs to the ordinary Bengalee's emotion of passionate protest against the prevailing socio-political order. Secular and radical in his views, he also dilated at length on the theme of women's liberation. He had spent two spells in jail in the nineteen twenties and thirties for exhorting his countrymen through his writings in the 'Langal', 'Ganabani', 'Navayug' etc. to rise in revolt against imperialist rule and throw off the shackles of slavery.

In the mid-nineteen twenties, Nazrul was a member of the Labour and Peasants' Party, which wa just another name for the communist party. The British authorities had kept track of his radical political activities as is evident from the following extract from a report[3] of the Intelligence Branch, Government of Bengal: " Kutubuddin Ahmad, Hemanta Sarkar, Shamsuddin Ahmad and Kazi Nazrul Islam are the principal members of this party, which is to all intents and purposes the Bengal branch of the Indian Communist Party.. a considerable amount of Communist literature from Russia addressed to it has been intercepted in the post." Referring to the strikes by the jute mill workers of Bhatpara near Kolkata, the report observed: "There are no signs that the efforts made by the Labour and Peasats' Party to spread communism among the people have met with any success. Muzaffar Ahmad, Shamsuddin Ahmad, Kutubuddin Ahmad and Qazi Nazrul Islam paid several visits to the jute mill area during the strikes and, with Shib Nath Banarji of the Jute Workers' Association, spoke to the strikers on their grievances and urged them to join the Labour and Peasants' Party."

While Nazrul's compositions such as 'Bidrohi' and 'Agnibeena' no doubt took the people of Bengal by storm, some critics felt at a later date that they were gradually losing their appeal since they lacked in depth, without which no poetry can survive for long. His relevance today lies in his secular stance that runs counter to the appeal of fanaticism of various kinds. His songs in praise of the Hindu goddess Kali are an instance in point. His claim to lasting fame is securely based on his devotional songs as well as on his lyrics of love or 'Ghazals', which he was the first to introduce in Bengali music and which are bound to survive much longer because they have a place of their own in Bengali literature.

Nazrul's songs reflect the influence of classical and folk music as well as Carnatic music. He amalgamated indigenous and foreign tunes, as Tagore had also done. For his foreign tunes, Tagore chose particulaly those of English and American music. Nazrul's foreign tunes drew upon the music of the middle east—countries such as Arabia, Turkey and Egypt. That is why the frequent reference in his poetry and songs to wine and Saqi, date trees which thrive in the desert, the burning sun and the allure of the oasis. Thus Nazrul gave a new ambience to Bengali music and poetry. He wrote devotional songs in the form of 'Padavali' (based on Vaishnav themes) or in praise of goddess Kali as well as songs expressing the joy of a Mohammedan at the sight of the crescent moon on the occasion of Id. His famous song "Aami Jadi Arab Hotem" sung in an Arab tune evokes an atmosphere much different from what is conjured up by a Tagore song like, say, "Purono Sei Diner Katha', whose tune is the same as that of 'Auld Syne Lang".

Though Nazrul shifted to East Pakistan after the partition of the country and his body lies buried under the soil of Bangladesh whose national poet he became, he was the poet of Bengal as a whole. He stood for unalloyed secularism and is held in high esteem by Hindus as well as Muslims, who continue to express equal appreciation of his devotional themes drawn as much from the religion of the Hindus as from that of the Muslims. He is primarily regarded as a poet of rebellion, but his poems and songs cover a wide range of themes such as love, secularism and devotion to God, making sure to steer clear of the Hindu-Muslim cleavage. He drew equally on the Vedas, Upanishads and Puranas of the Hindus and on the teachings of the Qoran—a combination that is unique. It was a pity that he could not keep up his writings in the latter part of his life, as he fell prey to a paralytic stroke in July 1942 that deprived him of his creative ability.

A firm believer in Hindu-Muslim unity, Nazrul used to say that one who had faith in one's own religion could never hate the religion of another. He married in a conservative Hindu family and his wife, Pramila as well as her widowed mother regularly worshipped Hindu gods and goddesses. His children were given Hindu names.

In July 1999, a three-day literary conference was held in Kolkata by the Bangla Academy and the Sahitya Academy of West Bengal in celebration of the birth centenary of poet Nazrul. It was attended by poets and literary figures from both India and Bangladesh, who threw light on the diverse facets of the poet's genius. But the next year (i.e. 2000), which was the silver jubilee year of his death, the occasion was not observed in West Bengal with as much enthusiasm as one expected. I do not know how to explain this indifference of West Bengal's literary circles.

The name of Mohitlal Mazumdar often figured as a topic of discussion among many of my student friends during sessions of 'Adda' in college mainly because an important theme of his poetry was love, mostly in its physical connotation, which brought out the depth of emotion and the white heat of bodily desire and passion, but in a subtle way. Mohitlal was a poet as well as a literary critic known for his fearless and outspoken views.

Modernism was increasingly making its presence felt in Bengali literature even in Tagore's life-time. In fact, Tagore was the bridge between tradition and modernism, between the old and the new. In our days, students of literature used to set great store by the poetry of Jibanananda Das, who had already made his mark as one of the greatest of modern Bengalee poets. His poems bear considerable similarity with those of the English poet Gerard Manley Hopkins and the American poet T.S. Eliot in so far as they reflect their social awareness. The English poet, Y.B. Yeats had influenced him a great deal.

In Jibanananda's poetry, there is a sense of sadness and desolation and a melancholic obsession with death, which is reflected in the frequent reference to 'Hemanta' (late autumn) when the land lies bare after the harvest. A single poem from his pen—Banalata Sen—would have been enough to make him immortal in the realm of Bengali poetry, even if he had composed no other poem. Like Eliot, Jibanananda was known for his imagist poetry as also for poems that projected a symbolic picture of nature. Just as Y.B. Yeats had brought the genius of poet Tagore to the notice of the Western world, so had poet Buddhadev Bose played an important part in getting the attention of the lovers of Bengali literature focussed on the poetry of Jibanananda Das through the columns of his literary journal, Kavita.

What appealed most to me about Jibanananda Das was the typical milieu and beauty of rural Bengal that he projected. This may have had something to do with my own rural background. I read and re-read his 'Rupasi Bangla' and 'Banalata Sen' that abound with images drawn from history and myth. He was also influenced by W.B. Yeats, whose lyrical poetry drew heavily on the mythology and legends of Ireland.

Jibanananda's own life was a tragedy, as, besides facing the onslaught from the famous Bengali literary journal 'Shanibarer Chithi', he had to suffer the ignominy of being sacked by the authorities of Kolkata's City College, where he taught, for his poetry was adjudged as immoral. Then came the partition of Bengal in 1947, which resulted in privation and ruined him economically, as he hailed from the Barisal district of east Bengal. And finally on a fateful night in October 1954, he was run over by a moving tram-car in Kolkata, which led to his death a few days later.

Jibanananda's greatness as a Bengalee poet has been the subject matter of learned discourses and research papers in subsequent years. An American scholar Clinton B. Seeley, who, as a Peace Corps Volunteer, worked in East Pakistan and acquired thorough mastery over Bengali language and literature, produced a scholarly research paper on Jibanananda's poetry, which earned him some coveted literary awards. As someone has pointed out in a light vein,a significant fact that this American discovered during his research was that there is a banana ensconced into the poet's name !

A large volume of Jibanananda's unpublished writings has been discovered after his death. It will take a long time for all this to come out and become available to the people at large. This is expected to provide a fertile ground for further research by the scholars of India and Bangladesh. Some of his works have been translated into English and French, apart from several Indian languages.

The famous opening lines of Jibanananda's "Rupasi Bangla" – "I have seen the face of Bangla; now I need to see no more" – clearly bring out his quintessentially Bengalee outlook and spirit. It is these lines that inspired and sustained the people of Bangladesh in their fight against the imposition of Urdu on them by the erstwhile Government of Pakistan and during their struggle for liberation from Pakistan. In 1998, the centenary of his birth, the Government of Bangladesh brought out a special postage stamp in recognition of his strong assertion of the Bengalee as distinct from the Muslim identity of the people of Bangladesh—an assertion that is in sync with the secular credentials of the people of Bangladesh.

Another Bengalee poet who formed the subject matter of lively literary discussions among my college friends was Sudhindranath Dutta, a modern Bengalee poet, who had come under the influence of French symbolist poets, Mallarme and Valery. His poems were sometimes unintelligible because of the language that he used in keeping with Mallarme's style that depended on the choice and use of words to produce the effect. He was a romantic poet whose style revealed a regard for classicism in the use of words, which was unique, being much different from the classicism of, say, Rabindranath Tagore. His poems and essays reflected a deep concern with the problems of contemporary life. He had founded the Bengali magazine 'Parichay', which published writings with a Marxist slant. On Fridays, he took part in sessions of "Adda" (gossip) with his friends that included some of Bengal's leading intellectuals.

If the hallmark of the'Kallol' literary group of Buddhadev Bose and others was its camaraderie, that of the 'Parichay' group of Sudhindranath Dutta was its intellectual calibre-a difference that led many to regard the two groups as literary antipodes. The 'Parichay' was initially devoted to making critical reviews of literature-not only Bengali but even European-much like the 'Criterion' of T.S. Eliot. Sudhindranath Dutta's 'Kshanika' (My Passing Love) is a good example of his love poetry, which is generally characterised by intense passion and candour. He was very close to Rabindranath Tagore in whose company he had travelled widely abroad. His wife, Rajeshwari Dutta, a Punjabi lady, was highly regarded for her rendition of Tagore songs some of which I had savoured as they came over the radio many years ago.

Sudhindranath was not a committed Marxist as some people believed. Writings in the 'Parichay' reflected a Marxist bias largely because of the general outlook of his friends. In course of time, the

'Parichay' became a Marxist journal. Sudhindranath's disenchantment with Stalin's policies led him to gradually distance himself from communism and come close to M.N. Roy, then the Radical Humanist leader, though he did not get converted to the latter's anti-communist view-point.

In 1945, when I was a student of the Asutosh College, I saw a drama 'Punarujjiban' in the college hall that was based on Sudhindranath Dutta's Bengali translation of 'The Resurrection' by Yeats. Eminent personalities like Bishnu De and Jamini Roy had collaborated with the organisers to make the show a great success. I liked the drama and developed an interest in Sudhindranath Dutta that led me to read some of his works in due course.

Poet Bishnu De, who taught in the Central Calcutta College, was my colleague for some time, as I also taught there in 1952—though a different subject, Economics. I am mentioning this fact without pretending to indulge in name-dropping. He was an established poet by the late nineteen forties. I sometimes listened to his informal discussions with other senior colleagues, which gave me an insight into the changes that had come upon Bengal's contemporary literary scene. He appeared to have come under the influence of Lorca, the Spanish poet, known for his unforgettable lament over the brutal killing of a bull-fighter by Franco's sympathisers during the civil war. Love and romance often figured in his poems, though his style differed from that of the traditional romantic poets.

Samar Sen, another modern and Marxist poet, who many years later became the editor of the "Frontier", dwelt on the trials and tribulations of the poor and middle classes. His images of smoke-filled Kolkata evenings and of social degeneration echoed the frustration of the wasted youth of his generation. Buddhadev Bose, who drew inspiration from D.H. Lawrence, had proudly declared that the age of Rabindranath Tagore in Bengali literature was over! His claim to be one of the modern poets, who had freed themselves from Tagore's influence, did not rest on solid ground, as romance constituted the most important ingredient of his poems. I had followed his poetical works with special interest because he was from the Malkhannagar village of Vikrampur, which was not very far from my own village.

The writings of the leaders of the 'Kallol' group such as Premendra Mitra and Achintya Sengupta had become quite popular by the nineteen forties. The literary scene in Bengal of those days reflected the trends that prevailed in the literature of the Western countries. Premendra Mitra's poetry showed a good deal of interest in city-life and Kolkata and his 'Pramatha' can be cited in this context. A poet, who was quite close to Tagore and deserves mention was Amiya Kumar Chakraborti, whose style looked modern, but did not essentially depart from old traditions.

Subhas Mukhopadhyay, a Marxist poet, had made a great impact, particularly on Bengal's youthful intellengentsia. His poetry of protest was symbolised by his favourite image of a clenched fist. His 'Padatik' (Foot Soldiers) published in the early nineteen forties had taken Bengal's literary circles by storm, as it professed the cause of the communist party to which he belonged and avoided any reference to the theme of love and romance. He gave up 'dalliance with flowers' and sought instead to liberate mankind through a communist revolution. Years later, Mukhopadhyay's genius was nationally recognised when he received the Jnanpeeth Award, but by then he had already recanted and publicly made known his realisation of the shortcomings of the Marxist philosophy.

The young Sukanta Bhattacharya, even while in his teens, had already become a legend in Bengal. I remember having personally felt the impact made on our generation by his poem 'Runner' and by his famous line : "The full moon looks like burnt bread" ('Purnimar Chand Jena Jhalsano Ruti'). Poetry of this genre greatly helped Marxist ideology in gripping the mind of the Bengali youth in our days.

Birendra Chattopadhyay, was another eminent poet, whom I knew personally—because, as I have mentioned in an earlier chapter, he was a close relation of mine. Besides, he hailed from Vikrampur (now in Bangladesh), which is also my native place. He not only exposed the corruption in the government and the administration and the hypocrisy of the political leaders, journalists and literary figures through the biting sarcasm and satire of his poems, but also displayed his basic humanism by voicing his concern for the sorrows and sufferings of the toiling millions. He is usually type-cast as a poet of protest, but the theme of romantic love dominated many of his poems. Birendra Chattopahyay was a poet of the masses. He was a Marxist and also an anti-imperialist in the tradition of Jibanananda Das and Bishnu De, as Mrs.Sumita Chakraborty has observed in her book on Birendra Chattapadhyay's poetry.

Sometimes, it is not easy to comprehend his poetry because of the complexity and the obscurity of his style.Smt. Sumita Chakraborty has said that Birendra Chattopadhyay had imitated Jibanananda's language—a statement that is not accepted by all. Birendra Chattopadhyay had drawn upon Bengal's old folk lores and traditions in many of his poems. He did not believe in God, but brought in the idea of God, when he needed it, as the symbol of humanity. He had once told me that though there was no such thing as God, yet it was sometimes necessary to project the idea of God.

His Vikrampur connection comes out clearly in his poem "The History of Vikrampur: A Dream", which, as translated into English by his brother, Rathindranath Chattopadhyay, reads as below:

'You: Atish Dipankar ?
You're here after so many days?'
'Who ? Why cannot I come ?"
"You've seen so many homes in this world
Yet, have you failed to feel the fondness for your home?"
"I've not come to stay. Yet
This land, this is my birth place.
That's why I come back again and again"...
"Then please stay".
"I am a sage. Moreover,
I do not have a passport,
A visa".
"But you're Dipankar Srignan
You know
The history of Vikrampur.
This land is unique, this land knows no passport-visa,
This land knows only men, sons of mead
All over the World".
Moreover, we shall keep ourselves awake whole night
And listen to such stories and poems
which do not have passports
And visas". "All right. Let that be so. I know

You all are dreams, I myself am a dream; yet
Seeing the faces of human beings
And keeping awake all night—all these are
not dreams."
"Tomorrow at dawn I shall leave you all
Yet your faces
Your eyes
This sitting with you, encircled,
All night
I shall remember, so long as men have longevities."

The humour of Parasuram, the wit of Mujtaba Ali, Jajabar's satirisation of Bengal's social life through some of his dramas, which often reminded one of George Bernard Shaw's works, and the writings of 'Banaphul' (pen name of Balai Chand Mukhopadhyay), particularly his depiction of the characters of Iswar Chandra Vidyasagar and Michael Madhusudan Dutta were among the many works to which I, like the average Bengalee of our days, often turned when in the right literary mood. Syed Mujtaba Ali's book, 'Deshe Videshe', was a fascinating account of his years in Afghanistan, where he went in the nineteen twenties after completing his studies in Shantiniketan and became a teacher at a time when Amanullah, the progressive king, was trying his best to modernise that country. But Amanullah was overthrown by Bacha Sakao, whose rule was marked by the ascendancy of the Islamic fundamentalists and animosity towards the Soviet Union. I am making a special reference to 'Deshe Videshe' because of the close similarity between what happened in Afghanistan during Bacha Sakao's regime and the situation that developed in that country some years ago during Taliban rule.

In the realm of the Bengali novel, Sarat Chandra Chattopadhyay's works reigned supreme. While I had read many of Bankim Chandra's novels in school, it was after I entered college that I started reading Sarat Chandra's novels a little seriously. He dealt with the day-to-day problems of the ordinary man, avoiding by and large the theme of romantic love, which dominated the writings of Bankim Chandra Chatterjee and Rabindranath Tagore. His sympathy was reserved not merely for the common man, the weak and the oppressed, but also for those helpless women whose circumstances forced them into prostitution. I do not know if any Bengalee writer before Sarat Chandra had pleaded so strongly for the right of these women, whose immoral life had cast them beyond the pale of civilised society, to not only survive but also be treated as human beings.

When I was in college, the three Bandopadhyay novelists, namely, Bibhutibhusan, Tarashankar and Manik, had already appeared on Bengal's literary scene with a new genre of writing. Tarashankar ranks among the greatest of Bengal's novelists and was definitely the greatest Bengalee novelist in the post-Sarat Chandra era. His work reflected the ambience of mass movements and sometimes displayed a softness towards communism and the theme of class conflict. Some of his works, like those of Rabindranath, often reached the level of epic writing, considering their depth and the range of subjects dealt with in them.

Manik Bandopadhyay (whose real name was Prabodh Kumar Bandopadhyay) looked for ideological inspiration to both Marx and Freud. While Tarashankar used the landscape of West Bengal as the background of his literary creations, Manik Bandopadhyay, who hailed from east Bengal, depicted in his writings the character and motivations of the ordinary people of east Bengal, bringing into bold relief the primordial and beastly passions of both man and woman. I took a special interest in his novels because his family hailed from Malavdiya village of Vikrampur (also my native place, now in Bangladesh), though he was not born there. This is the reason why his novels depicted the social picture on the eastern side of the river Padma.

His novels often painted the primitive man in a good light and bitterly criticised the attitudes and outlook of the middle class-a line which was in conformity with his Marxist belief. He was no mere theoretical and arm-chair Marxist. He had joined the Communist Party of India and its front organisations – the Progressive Writers' Association and the Indian People's Theatre Association – and taken part in protest actions against what he regarded as the Government's undue interference with the lives of ordinary men. I still remember that in 1947, before the Pujas, he joined had many prominent writers and artistes of Kolkata, such as Tarashankar Bandopadhyay, Gopal Haldar, Suchitra Mitra and Debabrata Biswas, in taking out processions in many riot-affected areas of Kolkata and appealing to the people to restore communal peace and live in harmony. He was basically a rebel poet or a poet of protest, somewhat like Michael Madhusudan Dutta and Nazrul Islam, though they expressed themselves in their own different ways.

In his writings, Manik Bandopadhyay attached greater importance to the economic factor in keeping with his Marxist commitment than to the sex impulse that Freud had held up as the main-spring of human motivation and action. It was his realism—the realistic pictures that he drew of the trials and tribulations of Bengal's ordinary man—that accounted for the great liking displayed for his novels by people at large.

Among the women literary figures of Bengal, who had achieved fame as novelists and storywriters and with whose writings I was acquainted were Ashapurna Devi and Pratibha Bose. When Ashapurna Devi received the Jnanpith Award many years later, the news came as no surprise to me.

In the nineteen forties, Bijon Kumar Bhattacharya's drama, 'Nabanna', devoted to the theme of the Bengal Famine of 1943, used to draw large crowds in Kolkata. As a professor of Bengali literature in Asutosh College, he taught me for two years during which he had generated in us a deep interest in the study of Bengali literature.

The fact that most of the important poets and writers of Bengal I have mentioned above happen to be Hindus does not imply that I was oblivious of the signal contributions made to the development of Bengali language and literature by the Muslims in different phases of Bengal's history. Though Bengali language had its origin in the Sanskrit, Pali and Prakrit languages, yet, after the advent of the Muslim conquerors in Bengal, their languages—Persian and Arabic—began to influence the evolution of the Bengali language and eventually left a lasting impact on its character. Bengali language had its greatest patron in Alauddin Hussain Shah, the 15th century secular ruler of Bengal, who, according to some, was a Bengalee and during whose rule the concept of what is known as Bengal supplanted the earlier nomenclatures of Gaud and Vanga. Bengali language continued to receive official patronage when his son, Nusrat Shah, became the ruler of Bengal in the 16th century A.D. In the next century, two outstanding poets of Arakan—Daulat

Kazi and Alaol—who were patronised by the kings and ministers of that country composed some famous poetical works that are regarded as important landmarks in the process of the development of Bengali literature.

Mir Mosharaf Hossain, the well-known writer from east Bengal, whose long literary career spanned the latter half of the 19th century and the early years of the 20th, displayed a style which placed him in close proximity to Michael Madhusudan Dutt and Bankim Chandra, the literary giants of that period. His masterpiece 'Bishad-Sindhu' is a historical novel and the most highly rated among his many literary creations of varied forms, which focuses on a theme that draws upon the tragic events of Karbala in such a manner as to pull at the heart-strings of the secular-minded reader. Its style bears close resemblance to that of Madhusudan Dutt's 'Meghnadbadh'. He was truly a bridge between the literary worlds of the Hindus and the Muslims of Bengal.

In Bengali poetry, Kaikobad's "Mahashmnashane", an epic in the poetical form based on the Third Battle of Panipat, was marked by a non-communal attitude, which earned him the appreciation of Hindus and Muslims alike. Though a contemporary of Rabindranath Tagore, he was not much influenced by the latter's style. Sheikh Fazlul Kasim and Hamid Ali wrote verses which easily reminded one of Michael Madhusudan's style.

In pre-independence Bengal, Muslim poets like Jasimuddin and Bande Ali Mian projected themes drawn from the serene rural life of Bengal. Jasimuddin and another poet, Abdul Kadir, espoused secular ideals. Abdul Kadir found the source of his inspiration in Mohitlal Mazumdar's writings. Farrukh Ahmed's ideas based on the religious and cultural tradition of Islam represented another kind of poetry. There were other Muslim poets, who distanced themselves from the Tagorean tradition by highlighting ideas that reflected their social awareness, their commitment to the freedom of the individual and concern for the struggles of the ordinary man. In this group were poets like Ahsan Habib, Abul Hossain and Shamsur Rahman, who had begun to make their presence felt on the eve of the partition of our country in 1947.

In the first half of the twentieth century, Muslim poets and writers in Bengali had demarcated themselves into different groups which reflected their respective viewpoints from the communal, secular or progressive angles. For example, Muzaffar Ahmed, the communist leader, poet Nazrul Islam and some secular-minded and progressive thinkers had set up the Bangiya Muslim Sahitya Samiti in Kolkata, whose journals carried the writings of both Hindus and Muslims

The Muslim Sahitya Samaj, which had been set up in Dhaka in 1926, represented another secular group committed to the ideal of 'Buddhir Mukti' or the emancipation of intellect and the liberation of the mind from all prejudices and called upon the Muslims to liberalise their intellectual and social outlook. Writers like Kazi Abdul Wadud, Abul Hussein, Abdul Qadir and Motahar Hossain propagated their ideas in a journal called 'Shikha'—ideas which they had imbibed from Raja Rammohan Roy, Rabindranath Tagore, Romain Rolland, Kamal Ataturk and Derozio, the founder of the 'Young Bengal' group. Among others who joined hands with this group were Prof Humayun Kabir, Kazi Nazrul Islam and Sheikh Wajed Ali. All these intellectuals were in favour of fostering a new socio-political environment in Bengal through a fusion of Hindu and Muslim cultures. They were rationalists and accepted as their guide the rational exposition of Islam by some thinkers. Abul Hussein advocated inter-marriage between Hindus and Muslims as a mean of fostering communal harmony.

Kazi Abdul Wadud, who hailed from the Faridpur district of east Bengal, wanted the Muslims to develop a taste for classical literature, arts and music. Sanskrit was one of the subjects he had studied at the Presidency College, Kolkata, where his fellow students included such luminaries as Subhas Chandra Bose, Rama Prasad Mukherjee and Dilip Kumar Roy. For many years, he was a professor of Bengali at the Jagannath Intermediate College, Dhaka, but later he shifted to Kolkata where he spent the rest of his life till his death in 1970. He refused to move over to East Pakistan after partition since he was opposed to the creation of Pakistan and also because he thought that he would have a much better opportunity of holding on to his independence of thought and action in a secular India.

Kazi Abdul Wadud's writings reflected the deep impress of the influence of the tradition of the Renaissance. He was said to a believer in the philosophy of three R's—Raja Rammohun Roy,

Rabindranath Tagore and Romain Rolland. He also lay great store by the views of such great men as Prophet Mohammed, Kamal Ataturk, Tolstoy, Goethe and Mahatma Gandhi. The earlier writers whom he held in high esteem were Imdadul Haq, Lutfar Rahaman, Mir Mosharaf Hossain and Begum Rokeya. Though he was in close touch with Muzaffar Ahmed and Kazi Nazrul Islam, he remained impervious to communist ideas. His progressive thinking had evoked the praise of Rabindranath Tagore.

The Pakistan Renaissance Society set up in Kolkata in 1942 by Akram Khan, Abul Mansur Ahmed and some others was ideologically aligned with the Muslim League and committed to the two-nation theory. A branch of this organisation also functioned in Dhaka on the eve of partition. Another body that functioned in Dhaka at that time was the Pragati Lekhak Sangh (Progressive Writers' Association), which served as a platform for secular and progressive writers, both Hindu and Muslim.

After partition, some Muslim poets including Abdul Qadir, Ahsan Habib and Abul Hussein and a Muslim author, Sankat Osman, went away to East Pakistan. Some others like poet Ghulam Quddus and writers of prose such as Kazi Abdul Wadud, Syed Majtuba Ali and Abu Syed Ayub stayed on in West Bengal. Syed Majtuba Ali left for Bangladesh after 1971.

After the Second World War, some of the Muslim poets of Bengal such as Ghulam Mostafa, Sufia Kamal and Shahdat Hussain reflected in their poems the distinct impress of Tagore's influence. Begum Sufia Kamal, the outstanding poetess of Bangaladesh, had been influenced by Tagore and Nazrul and continued be in the creative mode for long years before she passed away in November 1999 at the ripe old age of 88 years. I still recall what a significant role she had played in the movement for women's rights and in the 1971 liberation struggle of Bangladesh. She had praised the literary effort of Taslima Nasreen, the controversial Bangladeshi writer, but she had not hesitated to criticise the latter or raking up religious controversies and cold-shouldering a plea to work with women's rights groups.

Shamsur Rahman, a popular poet of Bangladesh, has now emerged as a symbol of the ordinary people's hopes and aspirations and often comes out with ideas about the cultural unity of the two

Bengals that reflect his secular outlook. Taslima Nasreen, the stormy petrel of the Bangladeshi literary world, is all praise for Shamsur Rahman's poetry. I was happy to learn that in March 2001, Shamsur Rahman was honoured with the SAARC Literary Award for Life-Time Achievement, though some young poets of Bangladesh took exception to this saying that while he was the "right poet" for the Award, he was not the best in their opinion!

Before partition, many Muslims had a feeling that the Muslims had very little to do with the literature and culture of the Bengalees since these were said to mirror the outlook of the Zamindars and the upper classes, most of whom were Hindus.But so far as the Bengali language was concerned, they did not succeed in assigning a class or communal character to it for the simple reason that language does not have such a character; language is above both class and community. People of different classes and communities speak the same language to exchange their ideas. In August 1947, Bengal was partitioned, but not the Bengali language. The Muslims, Hindus and all sections of East Pakistan's people fought unitedly for defending Bengali language against Pakistan's bid to force Urdu down their throats.

Soon after the birth of Pakistan, some Muslim authors of East Pakistan had sought to banish Vidyasagar, Bankim Chandra, Rabindranath and Sarat Chandra and even the Bengali script from Bengali language and literature. But the people of East Pakistan did not take long to realise what they were in for, as the Pakistan authorities started oppressing them and tried not only to impose Urdu on them, but also to distort the Bengali language by weeding out from it words that had their origin in Sanskrit and increasingly incorporating into it Arabic and Persian words.

The Muslim intellectuals of East Pakistan carried on a fierce struggle for the preservation of their language with which Bengali culture was inextricably linked. While even a well-known poet like Ghulam Mostafa plumped for Urdu, many prominent men of letters like Dr. Enamul Huq took up the cause of Bengali language. The sacrifice that the students of East Pakistan made on February 21,1952 in the cause of their language eventually led to their victory and the creation of Bangladesh in 1971. The people of Bangladesh and West Bengal have a common language of which they are fiercely proud.

The study of Bengali literature cannot be split up, because it is an integral whole that is being continuously re-invigorated by the advances made on both sides of river Padma.

But language and literature alone do not create harmony among the people. There has to be a community of ideals. If people belonging to different religious backgrounds have faith in some common socio-economic and cultural ideals, they can live as good neighbours in peace and amity. Linguistic and cultural identity alone is not sufficient for this purpose. The socio-cultural symbiosis in Indonesia is a good example. There, the Hindus and the Muslims live together in harmony, because the Muslims claim the Ramayana as a part of their cultural heritage, while the Hindus unreservedly accept as their own many social practices derived from the Muslims' heritage.

Notes

1. Terrorist Conspiracy in Bengal (From 1st April to 31st December, 1925) vide Terrorism in Bengal (1995), Government of West Bengal, Volume I, page 456.
2. Terrorism in Bengal (1995), Government of West Bengal, Volume IV, page 121.
3. Report entitled "Terrorist Conspiracy in Bengal (From 1st January to 30th June, 1926) by R. E. A. Ray, Special Superintendent, Intelligence Branch, C.I.D., Bengal, vide Terrorism in Bengal (1995), Government of West Bengal, Volume I, pages 503-504.

21

Kolkata's Cultural Ambience

" A great city is that which has the greatest men and women"

—**Walt Whitman**

When I lived in Kolkata (1945-1953), it was a cosmopolitan city which was home to not only the Bengalees but also to people from all continents and many other countries of the world, besides, of course, those from the other Provinces of India. Many families in different parts of our country whose bread-winners lived and worked in Kolkata were thankful to this city for keeping their home fires burning. Naturally, this cosmopolitan composition of its population invested Kolkata with a varied cultural outlook that tolerated, rather fostered, all shades of opinion and reflected all the colours of the cultural rainbow.

For all his cosmopolitanism, the Bengalee of Kolkata was a staunch Bengalee at heart, who set great store by culture in its varied forms—dance, drama, music, poetry and literature. By and large, he set his face against excessive materialism and took a lively interest in intellective pursuits as well as in political developments, local and global. He was passionate and emotional and his effusiveness found expression in 'Adda' or idle, harmless and sometimes highly intellectual gossip. His relationship with fellow citizens and people from other places who came to live in Kolkata was marked by warmth, sincerity and readiness to be helpful provided, of course, the other person reciprocated his sentiments. That is why people from elsewhere who lived in Kolkata for some time developed a liking for the local people, despite whatever reservations they might have had initially about going to live in a city bedevilled by a host of problems—congestion, traffic jams, pollution and what have you. However, over time, Kolkata grew on them and entered their very being with the result that when it was time for them to leave Kolkata to live elsewhere, they felt rather unhappy and thereafter missed Kolkata, which primarily meant the people of Kolkata.

Politically speaking, what Kolkata, or rather Bengal, thought at that time still showed the way to the rest of the country. People all over the country still gratefully acknowledged that Kolkata had held the first meeting in 1833 of the Indian National Conference which in due course paved the way for the birth of the Indian National Congress to which again Kolkata gave its first President in the person of the venerable W. C. Bonnerjee; that Kolkata gave the country not one but two national songs namely 'Vande Mataram' and 'Jana Gana Mana'.

Sir Asutosh Mookerjee, the Vice-Chancellor of the Calcutta University had assembled a number of eminent academicians in different faculties of the University. C. V. Raman, the world-renowned scientist, who had joined the Calcutta University as the Palit Professor of Physics in 1917, got the Nobel Prize in 1931 for the research work he did in Kolkata. He had rightly said (in 1930) that Kolkata was still playing a leading role in scientific research that extended far beyond Bengal.[1]

Acharya Jagadish Chandra Bose had established the Bose Research Institute in Kolkata in 1917. His discovery of life in plants and the inanimate world and the demonstrations given by him in 1895 in Kolkata and London for the first time in the world of the transmission of radio waves established his credentials as a pioneer of science, though despite all this, he was unjustly deprived of the Nobel Prize which was given to Marconi for no earthly reason. Meghnad Saha's Spectral Analysis earned him international acclaim. Shyamadas Chatterjee conducted successful experiments on nuclear fission at the Bose Research Institute in 1940 after World War II started. S. Radhakrisnan, the great philosopher-statesman, who at one time, adorned the Calcutta University as King George V Professor of Philosophy, provided the ferment for philosophical research aimed at plumbing the depths of ancient Indian philosophy and culture.

What struck a country bumpkin like me transported overnight from an out-and-out rural outback in east Bengal to the great metropolis of Kolkata was the completely urban character of the city's culture which was fast losing its touch with rural life that that had so far been standing for the culture of Bengal as a whole. Gradually, Kolkata's urban culture came to represent the neo-Bengali culture that set the pattern for the rest of Bengal to imbibe.

The contemporary view of Kolkata's culture that was widely accepted among the youth and the intelligentsia was the Marxist one according to which Kolkata's culture was that of the comprador bourgeoisie. It was the culture of the 'Bhadralok' class that consisted of the land-owners, the absentee landlords who had migrated to Kolkata from the villages and the English-educated gentry drawn from the salariat i.e. officials in the administration and the boxwallas as well as the professionals.

The English rulers blocked the opportunities for local industrial capital to participate in the industrial development of the country, unlike in the western countries where the native bourgeoisie had acted as the revolutionary catalyst for the industrial revolution that destroyed the old feudal economic, social, political and cultural order. The Permanent Settlement of Lord Cornwallis had opened for India's zamindars opportunities to channelise their energies into land-owning, turning their face away from industrial enterprise, and thus emerge as a comprador bourgeoisie class, whose culture became the dominant leitmotif of the culture of Kolkata and Bengal in general.

Whatever commercial opportunities arose for the indigenous bourgeoisie in due course were mostly monopolized by non-Bengalees and Marwaris while mills and factories owned by British capital dominated the industrial scene.

It has been said that with avenues of commercial and industrial development practically closed before him, the Bengalee looked inward and sought solace in religious and spiritual pursuits, which basically reflected the failure of the bourgeoisie to evolve naturally.[2] The communist intellec tual, Gopal Haldar put it across nicely:

"A dynamic personality like Vivekananda was driven to religion and the Daridra-Narayana cult. The clue is furnished by his own words:'religion begins with a tremendous dissatisfaction with the present state of things, with our lives ...." Naturally, religion commanded the allegiance of the revolutionary spirits of the time, whom the objective socio-economic backwardness could not satisfy. In Keshub Chunder Sen too, we find the same spirit and conflict of the times, earlier and still better mirrored. Gone to the religious fold which offered the refuge for his energy, he was impatient for social reforms that bourgeois civilization required."[3]

But is that the only reason why man turns to religion? Even in the western world where the bourgeoisie had ample scope for participating in industrial enterprises, many among them sought solace in religion.

Gopal Haldar also describes how the comfortable landed bourgeoisie and the idle rich, who had been "weaned away from work", wasted themselves in drink and debauchery.[4] The salaried and professional classes diverted their energy in a different direction by deeply immersing themselves "in the learning and literature of the bourgeois civilization of the west." [5]

The Calcutta University nurtured this educated middle class of Bengal. Raja Ram Mohun Roy, a staunch advocate of English education and the Brahmo Samaj movement spearheaded this new culture and, as Gopal Haldar has said, successfully inaugurated a bourgeois revolution. The Renaissance which had made Bengal a role model for the rest of the country to emulate had still not spent itself out when I moved over to Kolkata in the mid-forties of the last century. By then, Kolkata's cultural ambience had also acquired a thin Marxist veneer.

Some of my contemporaries in college were Marxist intellectuals, who took part in inter-college debates and also acted in dramas with a pro-left tilt. The cock of the walk was Utpal Dutt, a student of St. Xavier's College in the latter half of the nineteen forties. Endowed with a multi-faceted intellect, he had distinguished himself in debate. He used to act in Bengali as well as English plays and in due course he became one of the top stars of the Bengali screen. Later, his roles in several Hindi films attracted country-wide notice and acclaim.

I had once gone to the St. Xavier's College to see 'Othello' that was staged there by a visiting British troupe. Utpal Dutt, then a student of that college, was co-opted as a member of the troupe to act in this drama—a great honour for a Bengalee student of those days. I distinctly remember his superb performance, though I fail to recall the particular role he had played. Some time after this, I saw a Bengali film on Michael Madhusudan Datta in which he played the eponymous role, depicting the tragic life of the literary giant. It was a run-away success that earned him instant fame throughout Bengal.

In course of time, Utpal Dutt blossomed into one of the country's famous actors, directors and playwrights. He became a legendary figure in the world of Bengali theatre by virtue of his creativity and his unique contribution in taking Shakespeare, Ibsen, Maxim Gorky and George Bernard Shaw to the masses through the Bengali medium. His political beliefs and commitment to Marxism-Leninism and Mao Tse-tung Thought which found expression in his anti-establishment plays and films made him a controversial figure in later years, but about his class and appeal there was never any doubt.

I recall Utpal Dutt's brilliant performance in a debate that was organised in the Kolkata University's once famous but now demolished Senate Hall with its impressive columns that faced the College Square. A team of English student debaters had come to Kolkata from the United Kingdom to take part in debates. To measure swords with them, a debating team of the Calcutta University was fielded that included (if memory serves me right) Utpal Dutt and two other brilliant students, namely, Mohit Sen and Sibendu Ghosh of the History Department of the Kolkata University.

Mohit Sen, who hailed from an upper class enlightened family, had a brilliant academic career in the Presidency College and the Kolkata University. He went for higher studies to the United Kingdom, where he came under the influence of R. Palme Dutt and joined the Communist Party there. On return to India, he became an important leader of the Communist Party of India. Later on, he left this party and joined the less orthodox communist party that was formed by S.A.Dange.

Sibendu Ghosh, also known for his leftist proclivity, later outgrew his political convictions (at least outwardly) and joined the Indian Administrative Service. He served in Bombay and Gujarat as well as at the Centre in various capacities. I last met him in Delhi in the early nineteen eighties, when he was the Secretary to the Ministry of Defence, Government of India, and I was the Additional Director of the Intelligence Bureau, Government of India. We both took part in a meeting in the room of the Union Home Minister to discuss a case of espionage in which a Western country's intelligence agency was involved.. Not long after this meeting, I received the shocking news that Ghosh had breathed his last. He had just a couple of years to go to reach the retirement age of fifty eight years. What an abrupt and tragic end to a brilliant career! Some time ago, Mohit Sen also breathed his last in Hyderabad.

There were some others among my college friends who had made a name in the debating world. One of them was Sudhangsu Kumar Dasgupta, a brilliant scholar, who qualified for one of the

Central Services of the Government of India after passing the combined competitive examination held by the Union Public Service Commission, but was disqualified on physical grounds. He later became the Secretary to the Kolkata Improvement Trust, but died prematurely before retiring from service.

I attended many inter-college debates that were an important feature of Kolkata's academic life in our days. Some students and professors had become famous for their debating skill. The names that readily come to my mind in this context are those of Sadhan Gupta, a blind advocate, Prof. Amlan Datta, Prof. Nirmal Kumar Bhattacharya and Viswanathan, a student of the ST. Xavier's College, apart from Utpal Dutt, Mohit Sen, Sibendu Ghosh and Sudhangsu Kumar Dasgupta, whom I have already mentioned.

Kolkata in the late nineteen forties was still the country's leading centre of music, dance and drama. Uday Shanker, the renowned dancer was at the peak of his form and used to hold big audiences in thrall with his innovative ballets. His dance in the company of Pavlova, one of the greatest ballerinas of those days, thrilled people everywhere. His later dance programmes with Simkie as his partner carried his fame to still greater heights, belying the apprehension of art critics that, without Pavlova by his side, he might lose his appeal. But his charm never flagged and his art gave true form and life to the ideals enshrined in the ancient Natya Shastra. His brother, the celebrated Sitar maestro, Ravi Shanker, was already making waves in the world of music.

An outstanding stage artiste of Bengal of those days was Sadhana Bose, whose dance dramas enthralled packed houses for many years. They were three highly talented sisters—Bentia, the eldest, who was a playwright; the next, Sadhana, who was an accomplised danseuse; and Nilima, the youngest, who later came to be known as Naina Devi, the name she assumed after she married into the Patiala ruling family and shot into fame as the queen of 'Ghazal' and 'Thumri'.

When I used to listen to Naina Devi's music as part of Delhi audiences many years later, sometimes sitting very close to her, I failed to take the opportunity of telling her that my wife and I were from Kolkata to which she also once belonged and how much, once upon a time, we once used to admire her sister Sadhana's dances in Kolkata. Very few in Delhi knew of Naina Devi's Bengalee identity and of her links with Kolkata.

The three sisters were the grand-daughters of Keshab Chandra Sen, one of the founders of the Brahmo Samaj, and grew up in the artistic atmosphere at the latter's sumptuous Kolkata residence that was the favourite haunt of the renowned artistes of those days such as Hafiz Ali Khan, the classical musician, K.L.Saigal, Rai Chand Boral, Ahindra Choudhary, the actor, and Manmatha Ray, the author. It was there that Sadhana Bose met Madhu Bose, the famous director. The two fell in love and married against the wishes of Sadhana's family. This is how Sadhana Sen acquired the surname of Bose.

Sadhana Bose's "Alibaba" and "Raj Nati", both musical comedies, were great hits. "Raj Nati" was dubbed in Hindi with a slightly different name "Raj Nartaki" and also in English under the name "The Court Dancer". The famous Timir Baran provided the music for many of her dance dramas. Later, she earned high praise for her role in "Bhookh" that highlighted the grim tragedy of the Bengal Famine of 1943. I remember having seen and highly appreciated her roles in the ballets, "Birth of Freedom" and "Freedom Festival", towards the end of the nineteen forties. Despite all this success and glory, she turned into a tragic figure of Bengal's stage and screen as she became so deeply addicted to alcohol that, as the rumour went, she was sometimes found lying drunk on Kolkata's streets unable to take care of herself. Divorce from Madhu Bose followed and eventually excessive alcohol led to her death in circumstances that were truly pathetic.

Kolkata was an important center of Indian classical music where top-notch 'Ustads' of different schools lived and gave live performances on various occasions. On occasions, there used to be night-long music conferences in Kolkata where the country's top musicians considered it a privilege to perform. Those, who had money, could afford the pleasure of attending these soirees by buying tickets that were expensive. But the poor middle-class music lover of Kolkata did not miss much; he would sit somewhere on the near-by footpaths and pavements, defying the cold which could be quite freezing outside the hall even in the mild Kolkata winter – the season when those conferences were generally held.

Over the microphone, the music of the maestros came floating through the air to reach the much bigger and perhaps a more appreciative audience outside the hall that burst into loud and spontaneous applause, whenever the subtle twists and turns of the musician's voice called for such open approbation. Where else in the world could an artiste hope to get such an exultant and supportive audience? It was as a member of such al fresco audiences that I had learnt to appreciate good classical music.

Kolkata's stage, screen and studios made it a premier center of art and culture.The people of Kolkata were great theatre fans. The National Theatre established in Kolkata in the 19th century was the first public theatre which was open to members of the public who could buy tickets for admission and relish theatrical performances marked by excellence of a high order. Some young men of Baghbazar (north Kolkata) including the great Girish Chandra Ghosh had taken the lead in setting up this theatre. Later, Sisir Kumar Bhaduri ushered in a new era in Bengali stage. When I was in Kolkata, it had several theatres, such as the Star and the Minerva, where, every evening, Bengali plays were staged by highly professional groups of well-known actors and actresses. One could go to any of these theatres, buy a ticket, which was rather expensive by contemporary standards, to gain entry and enjoy an evening packed with the thrill and suspense of a gripping Bengali drama. I had the opportunity of savouring some of these performances, whose excellence I have ever cherished. The leading actors and actresses of Kolkata's stage of those days are names to conjure with and rank among Bengal's all-time greats.

Artistes of the calibre of Hemanta Mukherjee and Sachin Deb Burman had still not migrated to Bombay and were available to perform at music programmes (called 'Jalshas') that were a regular feature of Kolkata's cultural scene. The "Jalsha" was a unique 'Para' programme (neighbourhood programme) of Kolkata in which all the people of a locality formed the audience and were treated to superb music that came for free. This is how I had heard the best musicians sing on such occasions, sitting quite close to them, without paying a penny. And yet, the whole atmosphere was peaceful enough for the artistes to perform properly and the audience to listen in rapt attention. In the nineteen forties, Salil Chowdhury's radical music had started casting its spell on the young generation of Bengal.

In the world of cinema, Satyajit Ray was still to appear on the scene in a big way. He had started the Kolkata Film Society in 1947 to promote good cinema. I saw Vittorio de Sica's "Bicycle Thief", a good film which, I learnt later, had made a deep impact on Ray and brought home to him the point that it would be possible for him to make his epoch-making film "Pather Panchali" with a cast of amateur artistes. In the nineteen forties and fifties, Kolkata prided herself on the New Theatres, a host of able film directors like Bimal Roy and a galaxy of actors and actresses, whose class was typified by the likes of K.L.Saigal, Ashoke Kumar, Chhabi Biswas, Ahindra Chowdhury, Jahar Ganguly, Pahari Sanyal, Kanan Devi, Chhaya Devi, Chandravati and Molina Devi. Saigal's famous song 'Babul Mera' in the Bengali film entitled 'Street Singer' had enchanted the music lovers of Kolkata, as in the rest of the country.

I had the good fortune of seeing both the Bengali and Hindi versions of the epoch-making tragic film Devdas based on a Sarat Chatterjee novel. The roles of Pramathesh Barua and K.L. Saigal had left a deep impression on my mind. I have seen the latest Hindi version of Devdas starring Shah Rukh Khan, Aishwarya Rai and Madhuri Nene. I reserve my comments because it would be wrong to compare this new version with the old ones, keeping in view the fact that people's ideas have changed radically during more than half a century that has elapsed.

Bengali films fell on evil days with the partition of Bengal, which led to the shrinking of the market for them. Soon Bengal's film stars started drifting to Bombay.

The people of Kolkata were no less zealous in their commitment to Hindi films, some of which, including the famous 'Barsat' ran for weeks and months on end in full houses. I remember seeing this film along with my college friends in the packed Paradise cinema hall of central Kolkata. Hindi film stars had as much fan following in Kolkata as anywhere else in the country. Raj Kapoor, Dilip Kumar, Ashok Kumar, Nargis, Madhubala, Suraya, Kamini Kaushal and many others were household names in Kolkata as in the rest of the country. Dilip Kumar, the tragic hero of Indian cinema, and Raj Kapur, the romantic icon, were the idols of the ordinary Indian. I still recall what a spell had been cast on me by the film Kismet featuring Ashok Kumar.

Aother film with Ashok Kumar as hero that had made waves was Mahal, which had as its heroine Madhubala of distractingly bewitching beauty, who was often called the Venus of the Indian screen. In this film, Madhubala acted as an elusive ghost whom Ashok Kumar chased till the end when it was found that she was not a ghost at all, but a woman with all the frailties of the human flesh. The mystique of her immortal song "Aayega Aanewala" in this film must be still haunting the cinema-goers of that by-gone era.

The story of Madhubala's life—her unsatiated romance with handsome Premchand and thespian Dilip Kumar, eventual marriage with fun-loving Kishore Kumar and premature death in painful circumstances that had left her shattered and heart-broken—was a real-life tragedy whose pathos had moved the people of Kolkata as much as those in other parts of the country. Using some oft-quoted words, it can be said that time has not been able to wither nor custom stale her beautiful face caressed by a strand or two of stray wind-blown hair, which still stares at you from the past.

The music of Bengali and Hindi films of that era has bequeathed to the subsequent generations some of the hummable tunes marked by superb melody, many of which are now being served afresh in the modern garb of remix music.

With the Englishmen still around in Kolkata in the nineteen forties, life in the city reflected the Western ethos in various fields. It had plenty to offer to those with a taste for Western classical music. Kolkata's middle class intelligentsia was known for its addiction to English films. We never missed a good English film that was shown in Kolkata. Films like 'Gone With The Wind', 'Hamlet', 'The Lost Horizon', 'How Green Was My Valley', 'Marie Antionette', 'Samson and Delilah' and outstanding fim stars like Humphrey Bogart, Cary Grant, Sir Lawrence Olivier, Douglas Fairbanks, Clark Gable, Gregory Peck, Olivia De Haviland, Ava Gardener, Vivien Leigh and Norma Shearer remain clearly etched in my memory and still ring a bell in my mind.

The golf course In Kolkata's Tollygunge opened in 1829 was the second oldest in the world. British company executives played golf there as well as on the courses which, I learnt, were maintained by some jute firms in Kolkata's suburbs. It was not open to Indians to play in some of these courses until the restrictions were withdrawn just on the eve of our independence or soon thereafter.

The Englishmen, ever fond of club life, found Kolkata to be an immensely clubbable city—to use an epithet applied by Dr. Samuel Johnson to London, the first city of the British empire. Among their favorite haunts were the Calcutta Club, Bengal Club, Saturday Club and a couple of clubs in Tollygunge. The Bengal Club had been founded as early as on February I, 1827. One Boris Lissanevitch, a Russian, who used to be a pilot and a dancer, was the person who set up the 300 Club with the help of some native rulers on the lines of the prestigious 400 Club of London. During World War II, it was frequented by servicemen from the Allied countries, whose conduct dealt a severe blow to the club's exclusivist image. The lush green tennis courts of the South Club were immaculately maintained, as I saw during a visit to the area in the course of an expedition to see the houses of Subhas Chandra Bose and his elder brother Sarat Chandra Bose, who lived in the vicinity of the club.

In the mid-nineteen forties, some of the indigenous Maharajas of eastern India still added a touch of glamour to Kolkata's social life, as I gathered from newspapers, which reported on important social and cultural events. One often read of the activities of the Cooch Behar family as also of Uday Chand Mahatab, the doyen of the Burdwan family, who patronised polo and equestrian sport. The Maharajas of Darbhanga and Cossimbazar were known for their patronage of learning and higher education. I benefited personally from a Calcutta University scholarship which the Maharaja of Cossimbazar had instituted.

In the latter half of the nineteen forties and the early nineteen fifties when I lived in Kolkata, the world of art had changed radically. In the realm of painting, the Bengal School represented by Abanindranath Tagore, Gaganendranath Tagore, Nandalal Bose, Asit Halder and Mukul Dey had come to a dead end and Rabindranath Tagore, whose modern paintings had made quite some impact in the nineteen twenties and thirties, was no more. But Jamini Roy attracted a good deal of attention. He hailed from Bankura, whose famous folk art he drew upon as the source of his inspiration. Debi Prasad Chowdhury, the renowned sculptor was a name to reckon with. The Academy of Fine Arts under the stewardship of Lady Ranu Mukherjee patronised the exhibition of paintings at its famous gallery in Kolkata.

In literature, Kolkata was legitimately proud not only of Tagore, Bankim Chandra and Sarat Chandra, but also of a number of other literary stalwarts whom I have already mentioned in an earlier chapter.

Kolkata's young 'Bhadralok' (gentlemen) hopefuls belonging to the middle and upper middle classes were known for their antipathy to taking the risk of going in for industrial and commercial ventures. They either turned to the colonial rulers for providing them with secure jobs in the bureaucratic, police or judicial hierarchies or chose the career of the boxwallah in the then British-dominated private sector. Some went for the legal, medical or journalistic professions. Their life-style left some space for a wide range of intellectual and cultural pursuits such as spending a part of their earnings on the purchase of books, Indian and foreign, talking interest in exhibitions of paintings, Bengali as well as English film shows, professional Bengali theatrical performances, dance recitals and music programmes that encompassed Tagore and Nazrul songs, modern Bengali songs, Indian classical music and also a bit of Western music.

Occasional trips to one or the other of the restaurants and hotels in Chowringhee typified by the Firpo's, the Grand Hotel and the Great Eastern Hotel, which were known for their continental cuisine, added flavour to the middle class Bengalee's life-style, which on the whole was not so humdrum.

Notes

1. Calcutta Municipal Gazette, Anthology Number (1924–1947), page 37.
2. *Ibid.*, Article captioned "The Nature of Bengali Culture and Calcutta" by Dhurjati Mukerji, page 69.
3. *Ibid.*, Article captioned 'This Calcutta Culture" by Gopal Haldar, page 88.
4. *Ibid.*, page 86.
5. *Ibid.*, page 89.

22

Calcutta University : My Alma Mater

I was having a great time, thoroughly enjoying my literary pursuits, which were occasionally laced with films, theatre shows and music programmes. And then one fine morning, the B.A. results were out. I was thrilled to find that I had not only got a first class in Economics honours, but had also stood first. I felt somewhat like Byron, because I woke up one morning and found myself at the top.

The second position in the first class went to my friend, Alak Ghosh, also of the Presidency College, who, decades later, became the Head of the Economics Department of the Calcutta University. We were the only two to get first class in Economics honours. I felt extremely sorry for another class-mate, Amaresh Bagchi, a brilliant student, who narrowly missed first class. However, in due course, he distinguished himself as an eminent economist of our country becoming successively the Director of the Indian Institute of Public Finance and Taxation in Delhi, a member of the Finance Commission and also a member of the Prime Minister's Economic Advisory Council.

When I joined the M.A. course in Economics at the Calcutta University in 1949, the Economics Department of the Calcutta University underwent a split and yielded place to two Departments-Economics and Political Science – subjects which had all these years been studied together in the Econonmics Department. Now, a student could go in for either Economics or Political Science at the post-graduate level. I chose the former while some of my friends went in for Political Science. This change facilitated a proper study of both Economics and Political Science, as rapid advances in these subjects, particularly in the field of Economics, called for greater specialisation.

The M.A. course in Economics had eight papers of which six were compulsory and common for all the students. The other two optional papers were on what was called a special subject, which had to be chosen out of a list of such subjects. I took up Statistics as my special subject. I started applying myself to my studies very seriously right from the beginning.

An important academic project of the Calcutta University's Economics Department that was launched in our days was the'Economics Seminar'. The main idea behind this project was to organize periodical seminars and to bring out a weekly wall paper that was displayed on the wall outside our class room. Articles on various economic subjects written by the students figured on this wall paper. The seminars organised occasionally on economic and political subjects aroused a good deal of interest among the students. I was elected as the Secretary of the Economics Seminar to look after its activities.

The professors, who taught us in the M.A. class, were well-known authorities in their respective fields of specialisation. Apart from the whole-time teachers on the staff of the University's Economics Department, there were several part-time Lecturers chosen from among those who taught in under-graduate classes in in one or the other of the many Kolkata colleges. They were devoted academicians, who had not left the University even when they got offers of better jobs elsewhere. Some of them had earned great fame by virtue of their scholarly books. Some became Vice-Chancellors of Universities in due course Among our teachers were D.N. Ghosh, J.P. Niyogi, Panchanan Chakraborti, Bhabatosh Dutta, Saroj Kumar Basu, P.C. Ghosh, Amlan Datta, Panchanan Sinha, H.G. Gupta and H.C. Sinha.

There were some girl students in the Economics Department of the Calcutta University, but they were numerically much stronger in some other disciplines such as Bengali, Philosophy, History etc. Their number was the highest in the Bengali Department. At cultural functions that were held occasionally in the University, the girls took a leading role, particularly when it came to the singing of songs at the beginning or at the close. Many among the girls were good at Tagore songs, which it was customary to sing at such functions. In the Calcutta University, there was much greater mixing of boys and girls than in the Presidency College, because they became more mature by the time they reached the post-graduate level.

Dramas were sometimes staged by the students of the Calcutta University, but these were generally uni-gender enterprises of the boys. The girls were left out of the cast, though many of them used to be present in the audience. It was during our term at the Calcutta University that (if I remember aright) this age-old male chauvinism gave way to what we regarded as a revolutionary change with the boys and girls sharing the stage for the first time in a drama whose name I fail to recall. This heralded an era of comparatively free and frequent social intercourse between boys and girls, sweeping away the cob-webs of many past prejudices and meaningless inhibitions. This may not look so very revolutionary now, but it was really so at that time when our society was quite conservative.

By this time, like most other post-graduate students, I had become a more regular visitor to the near-by India Coffee House on College Street. In between classes, I went there, usually once, sometimes even twice a day, to gossip with fellow coffee-drinkers. There were some who spent more time in the Coffee House than in the class. Like T. S. Eliot, they perhaps measured their life in the University in coffee spoons. A few years later, when we all had passed out of the University, I met one or two of these old friends at the Chittaranjan Avenue Branch of the Coffee House in central Kolkata, which was known in intellectual circles as the House of Lords as against the appellation of House of Commons given to the College Street branch.

In the realm of agitational politics, the boys and girls of the Calcutta University of our days took the lead over those of many other universities in the rest of the country. Most of the political parties had their student fronts in the Calcutta University and their competitive wooing had politicised the students. Prominent leaders of these student organisations, who included both boys and girls, attached much greater importance to their political activities than to studies. In time, some of these student leaders evolved into key political figures of West Bengal. Considerable tension and excitement used to be generated when meetings, rallies, processions and demonstrations were organised in the congested University campus to protest against or endorse the policies and actions of the Government, which at that time was in the hands of the Congress Party, both at the Centre and in West Bengal.

In the University campus, one often bumped into many eminent figures of the academic world. One could see, for example, Dr. Kalidas Nag, Professor of History and Culture, who, ever since he had done his doctoral thesis in French on Kautilya's 'Artha-Shastra' at the University of Sorbonne in France, was in close touch with such great minds of the world as Romain Rolland, Professor of Music at Sorbonne and Herman Hesse, the German author, whose novel, 'Siddhartha' became the cult book of the hippies or the flower children at a much later date. You often ran into the bespactacled Dr. Suniti Kumar Chatterjee, the great authority on linguistics, walking ponderingly with his dignified gait towards the Asutosh Building and then patiently waiting for the giant lift till it touched the ground floor and then went up again with a gasp, creaking noisily before delivering its load of distinguished passengers at their respctive destinations on the upper floors.

A student could literally rub shoulders in this lift with a figure like Dr. Srikumar Bannerjee, who, once a professor of English literature at the Presidency College, was now adorning the chair of the Department of Bengali Literature in the Calcutta University. Of the same ilk were Prof. Niharranjan Ray and Prof. Hiren Mukherjee. Shortly before I joined the University, Prof Benoy Sarkar, who had popularised the teaching of political economy and political science in Bengali language, had left for some academic assignment in the U.S.A. Among the outstanding professors from the affiliated colleges, who came to deliver lectures at the University were Prof. Susobhan Sarkar of the Presidency College, Prof. Nirmal Bhattacharya of the Scottish Church College and Prof. Panchanan Sinha, Principal of the Asutosh College, whose long hair and flowing beard gave him the look of an Indian savant of ancient times.

Alongside the two-year M.A. course in Economics, I had also joined the three-year Ll.B. course at the Calcutta University Law College. The law course was to extend a year beyond my M.A. course that was to finish in 1951. One had the option of joining the law class either in the morning or in the evening; I chose the latter. The M.A. classes in Economics were from 11 a.m. to 4 p.m. and the evening law classes from 6 p.m. to 8 p.m. This schedule left just enough time for office-goers also to join the law course, as they could rush to the University to attend their law classes after office hours.

Leaving home at 10 a.m., I attended my M.A. classes and then spent the two hours from 4 p.m. to 6 p.m. either in the library or in the Coffee House, where I refreshed myself with a cup of coffee and snacks, before walking over to the law class. Occasionally, I took a stroll around the tank in the College Square, while eating a couple of delicious bananas or some peanuts, which were cheap but substantial. There I often watched the swimming and diving exploits of young boys, who were sometimes joined by a few girls.

On occasions, I savoured tea and snacks at some restaurant in the neighbourhood. There were several restaurants, whose names should even today ring a bell in the minds of the former students of the Calcutta University and the Presidency College. These were the tea shop of Jnan Babu, the restaurant on the ground floor of the Y.M.C.A. building near the crossing of College Street and Harrison Road (whose names alas! have now changed), the famous sweet house of Punti Ram at the inter-section of College Street and Mirzapur Street and the 'Paragon' and the 'Paramount' known for their cool, refreshing drinks of diverse flavours and of as many hues as there are in the rainbow. One could get a wide variety of snacks at these places at prices kept low enough to suit the purses of college students. When I wanted to eat something more substantial, and if my purse permitted, I walked across the Harrison Road to the famous sweet house of Dwariknath Ghosh.

Well-known barristers-at-law and advocates used to deliver lectures at our law classes where the atmosphere was quite different from that in the M.A. classes. Over half the students of the law class were elderly and practical men of the world, who had families to support and were mostly office employees. They had none of the academic and intellectual pretensions, which one came across in the high-brow students of the M.A. class. One could not miss the intellectual flavour of the lectures and discussions in the M.A. class and the idealism as well as the cheerful disposition of the young lotus-eaters inclined to look at life through tinted glasses.

An important feature of the law college syllabus was the holding of 'moot courts' in the class, which were designed to impart practical orientation to the lessons. It was in eighteenth-century Kent in England that the institution of moot court had its root. People used to assemble there under the open sky to hold "moots" with a view to discussing local issues and sorting out mutual problems. This system subsequently became the model for practical training in law in different parts of the globe. For moot courts held in our class room, some important cases already decided by the High Courts or other judicial bodies were usually picked up. Plenty of material that had been relied upon by the contending parties before the court in such a case used to be available in old law journals. We had to study all this material and, on a day fixed by the Lecturer, he held court in the class room, and acted as the judge while some students chosen by him appeared as advocates for the rival parties. Some of the students acted as witnesses, who were subjected to cross examination.

The Lecturer, deputising as the judge of the moot court, conducted the proceedings as in a real court. The students chosen as advocates locked horns and matched their skill, as they argued the case on behalf of their respective parties. This often gave rise to a serious atmosphere, as if a real case was being tried in a court. There was great fun in the class room on such occasions, which gave us an opportunity of learning the art of advocacy as well as the procedure of conducting a case in a court in real life.

In the Presidency College, I had become quite intimate with two other class-mates at the Presidency College, namely, Sripati Goswami and Dilip Kumar Mukherjee, both of whom also hailed from Vikrampur near Dhaka, which is now the capital of Bangladesh. All three of us had taken up honours in Economics and later took up the same subject for the M.A. course at the Calcutta University. We used to help one another a great deal by exchanging books and notes, which made our friendship academically quite fruitful.

Sripati and I chalked out plans of visiting some places of historical and cultural interest in northern India during the Puja holidays in September-October 1949, since neither of us had ever ventured beyond the confines of Bengal. Each of us arranged a princely sum of about a hundred rupees. For this, I drew upon the scholarship money which I was getting regularly every month. Out of the sum of rupees one hundred, I spent about fifty rupees on buying third class return tickets for travel by train. The rest of the money—about fifty rupees—I spent mostly on food during the twenty days that I was away from Kolkata. Wherever we had relations, we stayed and ate with them, which helped to reduce the strain on our meagre resources. Where we had no relations or even acquaintances, we spent most of the nights at railway stations, moving about during the day, seeing places and eating whatever food was available at wayside eateries.

It was on a shoe-string budget that we visited a number of places such as Jamalpur, Monghyr, Patna, Danapur, Gaya, Allahabad, Kanpur, Lucknow, Benares, Agra, Fatehpur Sikri, Mathura, Vrindaban, Panipat and Delhi. Some of the places figured on the itinerary for the simple reason that either I or Sripati had a relation or an acquaintance there or because it did not involve too much of a detour from the straight line from Kolkata to Delhi, which would have inflated the expenditure on the railway fare.

It was our first long distance travel by train through the heartland of north India and was a great education for both of us. I still cherish the old memory of how the trains we travelled by roared along through the country-side by day as well as by night, hooting from time to time and then suddenly screeching to a noisy halt at railway stations.

At Gaya, we put up at the Dharamshala of the Bharat Sevashram Sangha, where board and lodging were free. One could, however, donate to the funds of the Sangha according to one's capacity. The Sadhus of this Ashram, founded by Swami Pranabananda, rendered great social service by helping out numerous Hindu pilgrims, who went to Gaya to offer 'Pinda' to their ancestors. It was a great institution, which sought to spread Swami Pranabananda's message of 'Mahasamanvaya' or universal integration, awakening, synthesis and emancipation of the humankind through self-discipline, self-sacrifice, devotion to truth and continence. The Sangha had provided training and guidance to many priests known as 'Pandas' so that they could render assistance to the Hindu pilgrims, who came to Gaya from all over the country for ancestor worship.

As is generally known, Gaya is one of the most important Hindu pilgrimages of India. The place is said to have derived its name from Gaya, a king, who had performed a big 'Yagna' (sacrifice), which had so greatly pleased the gods that they ordained the naming of the place after him. The other and more widely accepted view is that the place was named after a demon Gayasur, who had done long penance to get a boon from the gods that whoever saw or touched him would be assured of a place in heaven. This resulted in an unprecedented increase in the population of heaven. Alarmed at this, Brahma asked Gayasur to lie down so that he could sit on him and perform a 'Yagna'. Gayasur obliged by lying down and Brahma commenced his "Yagna'. But Gayasur's body moved from time to time, making it difficult for Brahma to concentrate on the 'Yagna'. At this stage, Vishnu hit Gayasur on the head with his club and placed a big slab of stone on his chest so that he could not move. Vishnu also ordained that 'Pinda' offered by anybody at this place would result in the emancipation of his ancestors.

The foot-print of Vishnu is still to be seen inside the Vishnu temple built at this spot and it is here that that 'Pinda' is offered by devout Hindus. This temple is located on the bank of the Falgu river that is supposed to be flowing underground. We paid a visit to this temple, which, we were told, had been renovated in 1787 A.D. by queen Ahalyabai of Indore. We walked around the place to see if there was any trace of a river, but could see none! We saw several other temples in and around Gaya.

We paid a visit to the famous Buddhist pilgrimage, Bodh Gaya, about six miles from Gaya. The ancient name of this place was Uruvilva. It is located on the bank of river Nairanjana. It was after taking a dip in its waters that prince Siddharth had partaken of a sweet dish called 'Payesh' offered by a girl, Sujata, and then proceeded to sit for meditation that led to his enlightenment. This place is known as Bodh Gaya, where now stands the Mahabodhi temple. The Pipal tree under which he had sat for meditation is known as the 'Mahabodhi' tree. Was this the original tree? Some say that it is the offshoot of the original tree brought from Ceylon, where Ashoka had sent a cutting of the original tree. A big slab of stone on which he sat for meditation is known 'Bodhi Pallanka'. We felt very happy to see all these sacred spots which figured so prominently in history and literature.

About twelve miles from Gaya are the famous Barabar caves in the hills over which stands the Siddhwaratha Shiva temple. The Pandavas are said to have come to these hills in course of their travel undertaken during their exile from Hastinapur. We could not make it to these hills on account of certain logistical problems.

In Delhi and some other towns, we saw many settlements that had been hastily built to accommodate the refugees who come from West Pakistan. During train journeys, we often struck up conversation with the passengers in our broken Hindi. Many of the passengers were refugees who openly spouted venom against the Muslims and Pakistan and were critical of what they called the weak-kneed policy of the Government of India over various issues. Some of them were full of appreciation for Dr.Shyama Prasad Mookerjee's views.

It was a rewarding experience to see the temples and 'Ghats' of Benares and the labyrinthine reticulam of its lanes and by-lanes. It was, I was told, the city of Lord Shiva where the Hindus from across the country came and settled down in old age, secure in their belief that death here meant exemption from re-birth and liberation from the cycle of life and death. We visited the near-by Buddhist pilgrimage of Sarnath and spent quite some time there. We felt supremely happy to visit Mathura and Vrindaban in the heartland of Brajbhumi, about whose folk lore and legends we had read so much in literature. There we saw some foreign tourists who were being regaled by the guides with many anecdotes about Krishna's dalliance with Radha.

At Agra, we visited the Taj Mahal, heart-broken emperor Shahjehan's eternal love-memorial to his departed queen that was famously compared by poet Rabindranath Tagore to a white, glittering drop of tear on the cheek of Time. I recalled the description of the Taj by another poet, Sir Edwin Arnold, to whom it was "not a piece of architecture, as other buildings are, but the proud passions of an emperor's love wrought in living stones".

Some of the other landmarks that still linger in my memory are the fort that Akbar had built at Fatehpur Sikri, the Governor-General's residence along with the North and South Blocks, the Red Fort and the Qutb Minar of Delhi and the open spaces near Panipat that were shown to to us as the battle ground, where India's destiny had been decided at se several critical junctures of our country's history.

Near Allahabad, we visited Prayag, also called 'Tirtharaj' (the holiest of all pilgrimages), where Brahma, the Master Creator, had performed the 'Yajna' of creation. This was the place that was sanctified by the drops of holy nectar that fell from the 'Kumbh' (pot), which was retrieved by the gods, in the course of their fight with the demons, from the ocean after its churrning by Lord Shiva. It is here that Brahma, Vishnu and Shiva, the holy trinity of the Hindu pantheon, are believed to come down from their celestial heights to bless the millions of pilgrims from far and near, who congregate on the occasion of the 'Kumbh Mela' that comes off once in twelve years.

At Prayag, we took a small boat to reach the spot where the streams of the Ganges, Yamuna and the mythical and sub-terrestrial (hence invisible) Saraswati mingle and flow in a united stream. I was reminded of poet Kalidasa description of this confluence in his Raghuvamsham, which was prescribed for our study in college: "Like the white ash-besmeared countenance of the great Shiva sporting the black coils of His serpent ornaments, so shines Ganga's snow-white stream, mingling with Yamuna's deep blue billows ..... You look like a flight of white swans from lake Manasa, intermingling with a flock of dusky geese".

I had also a read a mythological story about how Ganga (i.e. the Ganges) happened to mingle with the Yamuna at Prayag. It is said that initially the Yamuna flowed alone by this place and Ganga came there only after she was brought down to the earth through the prayers and penance of Bhagirath. When Ganga arrived there, Yamuna came to welcome her with an appropriate religious offering, which Ganga refused to accept, saying that if she did so, her flow would get lost into that of Yamuna because Yamuna was elder than Ganga. This, Ganga said, would result in her losing her separate name and identity. Upon this, Yamuna urged Ganga to accept her offering because she was the former's guest. She assured Ganga that it was she who would get merged into the flow of Ganga. She further said that for the first 400 'Kroshas' (i.e. over 800 miles), the river consisting of their combined streams would be known as Ganga after which Yamuna would flow as a separate stream. Ganga accepted these terms as a result of which the two rivers mingled at Prayag. Beyond this point, the name of the river is Ganga, but its colour is that of Yamuna. Because Ganga is the daughter of the Himalayas, her water is cool; and because Yamuna is the daughter of the Sun, her water is warm.

Our travels helped to fill our minds with down-to-earth pictures of a miniature India and brought home to us the cultural unity of our country that runs like a thread through the diversity of many languages, religions, climates and customs.

In the Preliminary Law Examination of the Calcutta University held at the end of a year, I secured a first class as a result of which my academic stock went up a notch higher. I got a scholarship from the Calcutta University, which, however, was not paid in cash, but had to be used for buying books on any subject that I chose to study. This was a good opportunity for me to go in for some books on history, philosophy, economics and English literature. From the famous Kolkata book-store, Dasgupta & Company, I thus acquired some books by authors like Bertrand Russel, Arnold Toynbee, Joan Robinson and Dr. S. Radhakrishnan. These books even today form part of my personal collection.

The book houses on College Street were very well stocked. One could walk over to any of them and buy any book published anywhere in the world at reasonable prices. Besides, one could fall back upon the numerous shops that sold second-hand books where one could get most of the important books published in India and abroad at much lower prices. I often browsed through the old books that were spread out on the pavements on both sides of the College Street. There, if you were lucky, you could get a really valuable book that you were looking for at an unbelievably low price.

I also attended the next two years' lectures at the law college, but could not appear at the Intermediate and Final Law examinations, as my whole-hearted attention was claimed by the M.A. examination held towards the end of 1951 and the Indian Administrative Services etc. examination that was to be held in the latter part of 1952.The result was that, though I completed the Ll.B. course, I passed only one of the three prescribed examinations, thus getting no degree and forfeiting for ever the opportunity of trying my luck at the bar, if not at the beginning of my career, at least after my retirement from Government service, as some of my friends with a law degree have done.

23

Prof. Maurice Dobb of Cambridge

A memorable event of the Calcutta University's Economics Department in our days was the visit of Prof. Maurice Dobb of the Cambridge University, a leading economist of the world and an authority on Soviet economic development, whose writings on the subject including his book "Studies in the Development of Capitalism" formed part of our prescribed study. I had read the works of many renowned British, European and American economists, but had had no occasion to see any of them in person or attend their lectures. It was a great experience for us, therefore, to not only see Prof. Dobb but also to hear him speak, though, I must confess, I could not properly follow the English that he spoke.

Prof. Dobb was an Englishman, but his saintly visage, simplicity and lack of superciliousness impressed me a great deal and disabused my mind of many wrong notions, which I had harboured till then, about the so-called superiority complex of all white men. He had put up in a well-known hotel in Chowringhee, which by our standards was one of Kolkata's best; but I learnt that he was not very comfortable there. This brought home to me the fact that often our best was not good enough for others.

As I listened to the series of erudite lectures on the Soviet economy delivered by Prof. Dobb in our class room, I understood where students like us actually stood in relation to him and how insignificant our own academic attainments were. As he spoke, we took down copious notes, which proved really useful for our subsequent study of the subject.

Later in life, I came to know of another facet of Prof. Dobb's activities at the Cambridge University.[1] It has been said that after a visit to Moscow in 1925, Prof. Dobb made no bones about his communist sympathies.[2] In the twenties and thirties of the twentieth century, he had become a leading light of the university's pro-communist group from which the Soviet KGB recruited some of its 'moles', whose names earned great notoriety all over the world. I must, however, add that I do not know for certain whether he had a direct hand in such activities. It was a revelation for me to know that Prof. Maurice Dobb of Pembroke College, Cambridge, was a member of the Communist Party of Great Britain as well as of the pro-communist Union of Scientific Workers at the Cambridge University—an organisation whose professed aim was to prevent science from serving the interests of capitalism and make it a tool for strengthening the hands of the Soviet Union and its people.

Another doyen of the scientific community at the Cambridge University, who shared these views, was Prof. J.B.S. Haldane. Dobb played an important role in proselytising the students of Cambridge's Economics Faculty. His lectures on Soviet economic development openly and ably preached the superiority of the communist economic model, but did so in a manner that did not make him appear partisan. This had reportedly alerted the British Security Service to what it was said to have regarded as his subversive role.

Reports of the British Special Branch and the MI5 that are believed to have come to light are said to bring out the elaborate measures that were taken to monitor the activities of Maurice Dobb, who was looked upon as Moscow's "leading spokesman for the new version of the classless, scientifically run society. [3] His lectures at Cambridge Economics classes and his interpretation of Soviet economic policy were "models of clarity and memorability" and "earned this former student's gratitude because attendance at his biweekly Soviet Economic History class enabled me to confound my college tutor's predictions of a "third" because I had skipped most of the other economics lectures!" [4]

British counter-intelligence officers monitoring the activities of Dobb and his Cambridge associates were said to have revealed a 'sinister' plan of cultural rapprochement through Soviet film propaganda. [5] Intercepted correspondence reportedly revealed that Dobb, who had met one Pudovken in London, was making arrangements with a local supporter named Poynter to hire a projector to show a film "The Mother". Enquiries had shown that a left-wing socialist and a final-year undergraduate student by name

P.A. Sloan had been helping Dobb in making arrangements for showing "The Mother".[6]

A copy of the intercepted correspondence is reproduced on the following page from John Costello's book "Mask of Treachery".[7]

All this was believed to have even invited a query [8] from King George V of Great Britain as to why Maurice Dobb with his known Marxist proclivity was allowed to brainwash Cambridge's undergraduates. It has been said that from his position as a leader of the British Society for Cultural Relations with the Soviet Union, Dobb served as an important figure in the Soviet propaganda machinery in the United Kingdom.

I have devoted a separate chapter of this book to Prof. Maurice Dobb because very recently I got a confirmation of the important role that he played in imparting ideological guidance to and eventually getting recruited to the

Communist Party many foreign students including Indians, who used to go to Cambridge for higher education. This confirmation has come from a book "A Traveller And The Road" (Rupa & Co., New Delhi, 2003) written by the late Mohit Sen, a well-known communist leader of India.

Sen clearly says that among those who had greatly influenced his thinking and led to his becoming a votary of communism were two celebrated professors—Susobhan Sarkar of the Presidency College, Kolkata and Maurice Dobb of Cambridge. From what Sen has revealed, it is evident that a well-organised world-wide system of recruiting the bright students of different countries to Communist Party had been evolved. Sen has said that he was already a candidate member of the C.P.I. when he went to the United Kingdom in September 1948 for higher studies at Cambridge. Before he left Kolkata, Prof. Susobhan Sarkar got him the clearance from the C.P.I. and gave him a letter of recommendation to the authorities of the King's College, Cambridge.

Sen was entrusted by the C.P.I. with the task of carrying the party's documents along with a 'coded' letter (obviously a secret message) addressed to R. Palme Dutt, the British eminence grise on Indian affairs. When Sen met Dutt in London, the latter asked him not to be a communist too openly for some time, not to join the Party and wait to see if the intelligence agencies had any inkling of his acted as a courier of the C.P.I. In the mean time, Sen was told to be in touch with Prof. Maurice Dobb for whom Dutt gave a letter of introduction.

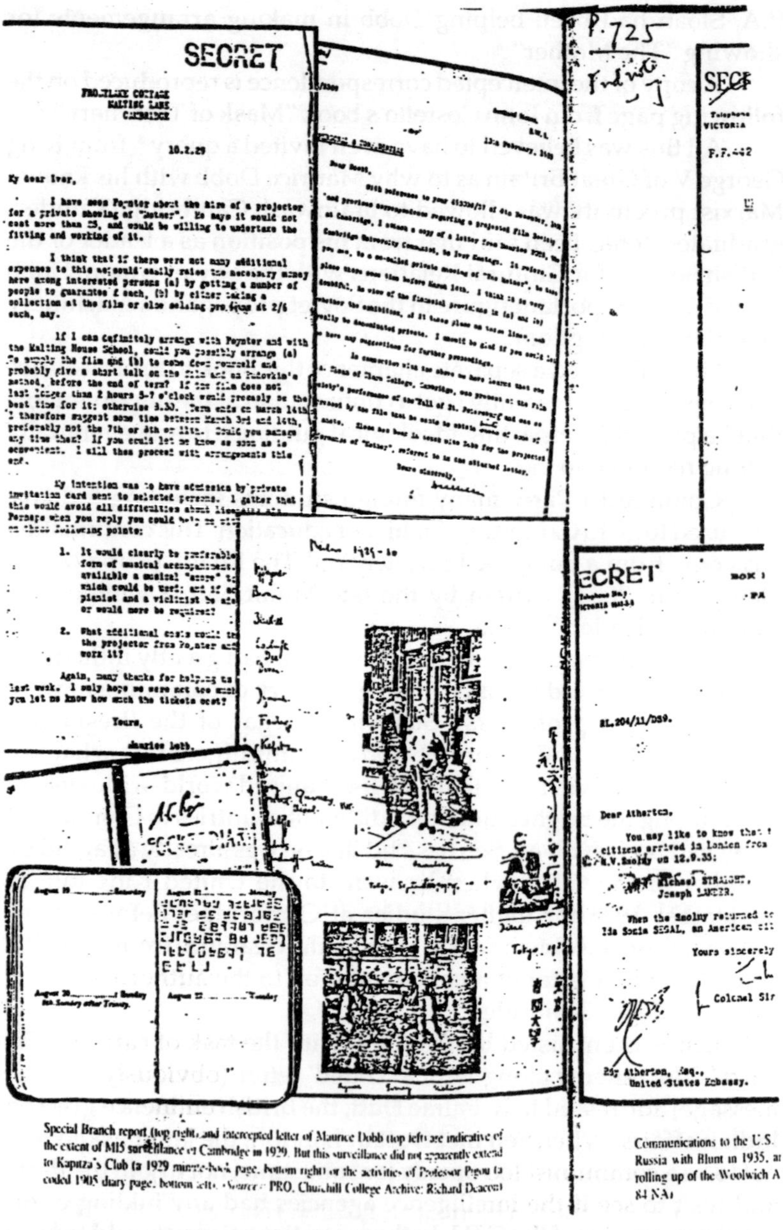
SECRET

FROGNALE COTTAGE
MALTING LANE
CAMBRIDGE

10.2.29

My dear Ivor,

I have seen Poynter about the hire of a projector for a private showing of "Mother". He says it would not cost more than 25, and would be willing to undertake the fitting and working of it.

I think that if there were not many additional expenses to this we could easily raise the necessary money here among interested persons (a) by getting a number of people to guarantee £ each, (b) by either taking a collection at the film or else selling programmes at 2/6 each, say.

If I can definitely arrange with Poynter and with the Malting House School, could you possibly arrange (a) to supply the film and (b) to come down yourself and probably give a short talk on the film and on Pudovkin's method, before the end of term? If the film does not last longer than 2 hours 5-7 o'clock would probably be the best time for it; otherwise 8.30. Term ends on March 14th. I therefore suggest some time between March 3rd and 14th, preferably not the 7th or 8th or 11th. Could you manage any time then? If you could let me know as soon as is convenient, I will then proceed with arrangements this end.

My intention was to have admission by private invitation card sent to selected persons. I gather that this would avoid all difficulties about licensing etc. Perhaps when you reply you could help me on these following points:

1. It would clearly be preferable ... form of musical accompaniment ... available a musical "score" ... which could be used; and if ... pianist and a violinist be ... or would more be required?

2. What additional costs would ... the projector from Poynter and ... work it?

Again, many thanks for helping ... last week. I only hope we were not too much ... you let me know how much the tickets cost?

Yours,

Maurice Dobb.

Dear Atherton,

You may like to know that ... citizens arrived in London from ... S.V. Smolny on 12.9.35:

Michael STRAIGHT,
Joseph LUTER.

When the Smolny returned to ... Ida Sonia SEGAL, an American cit...

Yours sincerely

Colonel Sir ...

Ray Atherton, Esq.,
United States Embassy.

Special Branch report (top right) and intercepted letter of Maurice Dobb (top left) are indicative of the extent of MI5 surveillance of Cambridge in 1929. But this surveillance did not apparently extend to Kapitza's Club (a 1929 minute-book page, bottom right) or the activities of Professor Pigou (a coded 1905 diary page, bottom left). *Source:* PRO, Churchill College Archive; Richard Deacon)

Communications to the U.S. ... Russia with Blunt in 1935, ar... rolling up of the Woolwich A... 84 NA)

When Sen met Dobb in Cambridge, he realized that the latter took R.Palme Dutt's instructions very seriously. For example, Dobb told Sen not to join the Cambridge branch of the Communist Party of Great Britain at least for two terms, though he was allowed the option of joining the Cambridge University Socialist Club. Sen was told by Dobb to attend the fortnightly after-dinner meetings in his rooms at the Trinity College, Cambridge, where discussions were held on various topics. Dobb used to take a class on imperialism at the Cambridge Party School. He prevailed upon Sen to take this class to which Dobb continued to come, staying there throughout. What Sen has said shows that his continuance and steady advance in the communist circuit were being closely monitored by Prof. Susobhan Sarkar in Kolkata, R. Palme Dutt in London and Prof. Maurice Dobb in Cambridge.

One of the greatest Soviet spies of the last century, Kim Philby, was reported to have accused Dobb of having been the principal Soviet talent-spotter at Cambridge. Yet, I must confess that I do not know the basis on which he had made such an allegation. It is generally believed that there was no valid ground for Philby's characterization of Prof. Dobb as the principal Soviet talent spotter at Cambridge. [9] Mohit Sen also said in his recent book that Dobb was unlikely to have been a recruiter for the KGB because he was far too well-known as a member of the Communist Party of Great Britain to engage in such clandestine activity.

Cambridge in the nineteen thirties and forties was known as the hot-bed of communists and homo-sexuals, though its reputation as a centre of academic excellence continued to remain unsullied. A.C. Pigou and Dennis Robertson of the Cambridge Faculty whose works on Economics I used to study seriously were both communist sympathizers and homosexuals to boot. [10] Mohit Sen also referred to this theme in his book and admitted the possibility of E.M. Forster having been a homosexuality. Sen thought that it was perhaps part of the influence of Grecian aesthetics and defiance of Victorian hypocrisy. Sen agreed that the King's College, Cambridge, "almost made a cult of homosexuality—Keynes, J.T. Sheppard (Provost of College in my time) and G.H. Rylands were known homosexuals."

It was from among Cambridge students with impeccable public school backgrounds and with high academic distinction to their credit, who hailed from Britain's privileged aristocratic class that Moscow recruited its most infamous spies, who betrayed their own country. Among them were Anthony Frederick Blunt, Guy Burgess,

David McClean and Kim Philby (who incidentally was born in India, where his father was employed in the service of the British Government).

There was a secret society of the Apostles of Cambridge, which Anthony Blunt had joined. Prominent among the Apostles were John Maynard Keynes, E.M. Forster, Rupert Brooke and Dennis Robertson, who was later knighted for his contribution as an economist. Many members of this society were Marxists. As regards Keynes, however, it was known that he had tried to reform capitalism in a bid to stem the tide of communism that was advancing in some countries.

Some scientists of the Cambridge network were believed to have helped in making the secrets of the atom bomb available to the Soviet Union. One Philip Spratt, who was charged in the Meerut Conspiracy case against the Indian communists in 1929, was a graduate of the Cambridge University.

The Oxford University did not lag very much behind Cambridge in fostering communism, though there is hardly any evidence of its having thrown up any well-known Soviet spy. Many of Oxford's dons and students did profess their faith in communism and had even been friendly to and intimate with some Cambridge-educated Soviet spies. There was a member of the Indian Civil Service—Michael Carritt of the Bengal cadre—who was from the Oxford University and had served in Bengal in the nineteen thirties till he voluntarily resigned in 1938 after having done his bit in the cause of communism. He had established clandestine links with the communist underground in India.

This gentleman, despite his veneer of 'Oxbridge sophistication and classical scholarship'—qualities which he claims for himself in his autobiographical book 'A Mole in the Crown'—developed into what he calls 'a starry-eyed activist in the Indian Independence Movement and, in particular, its communist-led trade union and peasant committees'. Even while he was holding the key position of Special Officer in the Political Department of the Government of Bengal, he was conducting secret parleys with top-ranking leaders of the Communist Party of India such as P.C. Joshi, its General Secretary, Ajoy Kumar Ghosh, who also at a later date became the party's General Secretary, and Michael Scott, who was Chaplain to the Bishop of Bombay and an underground communist activist.

Carritt has given an account of the secret briefing that he had received, while he was holding this post under the Bengal Government, about Dimitrov's exposition of the United Front tactics at the VII World Congress of the Communist International. He pokes fun at having all the while fooled the Intelligence Branch of Bengal Police for its failure to uncover his secret links with the proscribed Communist Party of India. He kept in touch with communist leaders both in India and the United Kingdom through secret channels of communication. Under the assumed name of Daniel Thackeray, he sent messages to communist leaders in India.

After his voluntary retirement from the Indian Civil Service in 1938, he went back to London and joined hands with some communist leaders there, playing an important role along with R. Palme Dutt in providing guidance to the Indian communist movement. He assisted B.F. Bradley, the British communist leader, in organising the Indian Communist Students' Secret Group in the U.K., which helped in initiating many Indian students in that country in the theory and practice of communism. He regularly contributed articles to the organs of the Communist Party of India and the international communist movement. As he himself says of his conversion to the communist ideology, he had suffered no sudden flash of Pauline conversion; it was the effect of a series of shocks to his liberal conscience that produced a change in his attitude to the British Raj in India and his outlook on life generally. Mohit Sen said in his recent book that his first meeting in London with R. Palme Dutt was arranged by Carrit, who was then Dutt's Secretary.

It was in this atmosphere of Oxford and Cambridge Universities that many of our country's top communist leaders had their initiation in the communist ideology along with whatever studies they had gone there for as bright young hopefuls hailing from well-to-do bourgeois families. However, I do not wish to say anything uncharitable about them. Most of these communist celebrities came from the upper strata of Indian society. That despite their aristocratic upbringing and Oxbridge background, they devoted themselves on their return home to the rough and tumble of agitational politics was a measure of the depth of their ideological commitment.

Notes

1. For much of the information in this and the next few paragraphs, I have drawn profusely on "Mask of Treachery" by John Costello, published by William Morrow & Co. Inc., New york.
2. *Ibid.*, page 117.
3. *Ibid.*, page 164.
4. *Ibid.*, page 165.
5. *Ibid.*, page 167.
6. *Ibid.*, page 169.
7. *Ibid.*, page 726.
8. *Ibid.*, page 165.
9. *Ibid.*, page 615.
10. *Ibid.*, page 149.

24

Indian Communists : Quo Vadis

When I was a college student in Kolkata, I got to know some student and youth workers of various political parties including those of the Communist Party of India, some of whom lived in my neighbourhood in Bhowanipur while some others were my class-mates in college. I realized that the pro-communist students were somewhat demoralized as a result of the widespread public antipathy towards the communists arising from their earlier opposition to the Quit India movement which pitted them against the dominant national sentiment. The communists' denunciation of Netaji Subhas Chandra Bose's role had exposed them to the wrath of the people.

The communists were unceremoniously expelled from the Congress Party in December, 1945. There were public demonstrations against the Communist Party of India, sometimes accompanied by attacks on their supporters and offices in different parts of India in early 1946.

The people's disenchantment with the communists was clearly reflected in the poor showing of the latter in the Central Assembly and Provincial Assembly elections held respectively in December, 1945 and March, 1946. When the personnel of the Royal Indian Navy rose in mutiny at Bombay in February, 1946, the people in general believed that the Communist Party of India had triggered the incident as a step towards its switching over to a militant line. There was no doubt that several communists among the naval personnel had a hand in this incident, but the Communist Party of India later denied that it had anything to do with the mutiny and that whatever the communists did was in their individual capacities. The participation of the workers of the Communist Party of India in the 'Direct Action' programme of the Muslim League on August 16, 1946 badly tarnished their image.

While the tension between the Congress and the Communist Party of India was thus continuing, voices emanating from the Soviet and British experts were in the mean time suggesting a different policy for the C.P.I. A. Dyakov, a Soviet expert, clearly indicated in a couple of articles (January, March, 1946) in the New Times published from Moscow the need for the C.P.I. to cultivate friendly relations with the Congress. Similarly, R. Palme Dutt conveyed in an article in the Labour Monthly (March, 1946) the view of the Communist Party of Great Britain that the C.P.I. should establish rapport with the Congress. Dutt also came to India in March,1946 as a representative of the Daily Worker along with the Cabinet Mission and met the leaders of the Congress with a view to lending a hand in improving Congress-C.P.I. relationship. There was thus a dichotomy between the C.P.I.'s practical political line and the ideological stance of the international communist movement—something which took me some time to grasp fully despite the great effort that some of my well-informed communist friends made to explain the whole matter to me as lucidly as they could.

The Cabinet Mission's Plan announced on May, 16, 1946 was criticized by both the C.P.I. and Moscow on the ground that the Plan did not offer immediate independence to India but was designed to strengthen the British imperialist grip over India. By August,1946, R. Palme Dutt changed his stance vis-à-vis Congress-C.P.I. relationship as he realized that his interaction with the leaders of the Congress had failed to disabuse the latter of their reservations about the C.P.I. He had paid a visit to Kashmir in June, 1946, and met Sheikh Abdullah, which had convinced him of the correctness of the path being followed by Sheikh Abdullah namely a militant struggle for independence and democracy that was directed against the ruler of Kashmir. Dutt's meeting with the leaders of the C.P.I.'s Central Committee in Bombay helped in persuading the latter to switch over to a more militant line in August, 1946, that marked a departure from the softer policy of P.C. Joshi, the party's moderate General Secretary.

Thus in 1946, the Communist Party of India began to follow a militant line that took the form of strikes by the working class and peasants' struggles in the rural areas as part of a broad-based struggle for the revolutionary seizure of power. The party adopted a policy of inciting the workers and peasants to resort to large-scale violence.

By the end of 1946, the communists had succeeded in raising the tempo of their agrarian struggle in Telengana, Malabar and several areas of Travancore-Cochin State, where they seized crops and lands by indulging in lawless activities. In Bengal, the 'Tebhaga' movement gathered momentum in the rural areas where the share-croppers demanded two-thirds of the grain they produced. 'Tebhaga Committees' set up in the rural areas of some districts of Bengal guided the movement and in some areas parallel courts also functioned. But eventually, the movement failed largely because even the rural people got affected by the canker of communalism that had vitiated the relationship between the Hindus and Muslims.

In February, 1947, the British Government announced its decision to transfer power to India not later than June, 1948. Though initially the C.P.I. reacted adversely to this announcement, its final stance in this regard was shaped by a resolution that was adopted by what was called the first Empire Conference of Communist Parties held in London towards the end of February, 1947, and attended by some representatives of the C.P.I. as well. The declaration of this conference that became public in March-April, 1947 suggested to the C.P.I. to extend its support to the Congress in fighting for true independence rather than a sham independence. The establishment of diplomatic relations between India and the Soviet Union in April, 1947, signalled the beginning of closer relations between the two countries.

Soon, however, indications of a reversal of the Soviet line vis-à-vis India began to be available. One such hint was the view expressed by the Soviet expert, A, Dyakov, in the New Times (June 13, 1947) that the Mountbatten plan for the transfer of power was designed to strengthen imperialist domination in India and that the Congress was a reactionary party that had accepted a plan for partial independence in view of the compulsion of circumstances. Some other Soviet experts on India such as E.Zhukov,and Balabushevich as well as the Yugoslav expert, Edvard Kardelji pleaded for a more radical line for the C.P.I.

However, the C.P.I. appeared to be blissfully unaware of what line was being prescribed for it by Moscow. This became evident from the resolution of the party's Central Committee adopted at Bombay in June, 1947 that declared the Mountbatten Plan as a step in the right direction and said that this had been extracted as a result of the Congress Party's continuous struggle as well as the pressure of the masses. This was in direct contrast to the Soviet line on this issue. Even R. Palme Dutt, the great British authority on India, seemed to be in the dark about the Soviet line as was clear from his write-up in the Labour Monthly of July, 1947, in which he called the transfer of power to India as an 'enforced retreat of imperialism' and pleaded for Congress-C.P.I. understanding. The C.P.I. directed its workers to participate whole-heartedly in the celebration of the Independence Day on August 15, 1947.

Even though the C.P.I.'s official line did not smack of radicalism, on the ground the situation was different in the sense that the party's workers had launched militant struggles right from pre-independence days. The communists' activities in different parts of the country–the Tebhaga movement in Bengal, the Punnapra-Vayalar uprisings in Kerala and the armed struggle in Telengana – had been anxiety to the authorities. From reports[1] that came to light many years later, I learnt that on January 30, 1947, E.M.Porter, Home Secretary, Government of India, had sent a communication to the Governments of Bengal and some other Provinces, holding the Communist Party of India responsible for serious acts of violence and suggesting strong measures to prevent the situation from going out of control. On February 11, 1947, the Inspector-General of Police, Government of Bengal, sent a secret note to P.D. Martin, Additional Secretary, Government of Bengal, suggesting a ban on the Communist Party of India. Martin sent a proposal to the Government of India for banning the Communist Party of India, using for this purpose the provisions of the Indian Criminal Law Amendment Act (1908).

However, a letter dated May 21, 1947, from John D.Tyson, Secretary to the Governor of Bengal addressed to P.D.Martin conveyed the rejection of this proposal on the ground that the Viceroy feared international repercussions and that, moreover, the war-time powers of the government were no longer available. What must have really weighed with the British authorities in desisting from such a course was the fact that since they were quitting India in the very near future, it had become irrelevant for them to go in for any drastic measures on the law and order front which would have amounted to fighting the future Indian Government's battle against communism.

In the mean time, B.T. Ranadive, the leader of the radical faction of the C.P.I. had begun to voice his disagreement with P.C. Joshi's policy of collaboration with the Congress and to advocate a more militant line for the party. In August, 1947, articles by some leaders of the Yugoslav Communist Party, notably Kardelji, suggested that since the bourgeoisie had turned reactionary, there was no alternative to a line involving a violent revolution.

Soon thereafter, the formation of the Communist Information Bureau (Cominform) in 1947 in the wake of the dissolution of the Communist International (Comintern) had an ominous significance for our country, as it signaled the beginning of a militant offensive on the part of the Communist Party of India against the Congress Governments at the Centre and in the Provinces. At the foundation conference of the Cominform held in Poland in September 1947 in the presence of the leaders of many communist countries, A. Zhdanov, the Soviet communist leader, gave a clarion call for the adoption of a new policy, which, shorn of all verbiage, meant a resort to armed struggle by the communists in various countries for the seizure of power. Kardelji, the Yugoslav expert, who also addressed the conference, made a powerful plea for a policy of launching attacks on the bourgeoisie, as was evident from reports published in the Communist (January, 1948), the organ of the C.P.I.

Tit-bits about these developments in the international communist movement leaked out to the press from time to time. For India, the policy meant that the country's newly-won independence was a sham because the freedom struggle that had led to it did not have the working class and the Communist Party of India at its vanguard. It further implied that the C.P.I was to over-throw the Congress Governments at the Centre and in the Provinces by forging the unity of the peasants and workers and adopting a strategy that was to rely primarily on violence. The Central Committee of the C.P.I. which met from December 7 to 16, 1947, replaced P.C. Joshi by B.T. Ranadive as the party's General Secretary, who took up the task of implementing the new policy in right earnest.

I had seen reports in the press about the holding in Kolkata in February 1948 of the South East Asia Youth Conference under the auspices of the communist international front organizations for students and youth. It was attended by many leaders of these organizations from the Soviet Union and East Europe as well as from South East Asian countries including China and, of course, India. Smt. Geeta Mukherjee, whose name was quite well-known to Kolkata's student community, was colosely associated with the organization of this conference.

From discussions among students that used to take place in Kolkata at that time, I could see that they generally looked upon this conference as a move to draw the students and the youth of these countries into the stepped-up struggle for the seizure of political power in conformity with the Zhdanov line that had been adopted a few months ago by the leaders of the international communist movement. It was also widely believed that the presence of important representatives not only from the Soviet Union and Yugoslavia but also from many countries of South East Asia provided an opportunity for transmitting the new Zhdanov line to India and the South East Asian region and in due course resulted in the outbreak of communist-inspired violence.

I recall having seen reports in the press about how the members of the Indian delegation to this conference fought among themselves over various issues that came to the fore. The pro-communist delegates from India had the upper hand, which led the pro-Congress and some other elements to dissociate themselves from the conference.

Aurobindo Bose, a nephew of Netaji Subhas Chandra Bose, who was then a member of the Forwad Bloc, and was chosen to be the leader of the Indian delegation, felt unhappy when a resolution moved by some students praising the role of Netaji Bose and the I.N.A. in Asia during the Second World War was opposed by representatives from some countries such as China, Malayasia, Burma etc., who not only refused to recongnise Netaji Bose's role in the struggle for Asia's liberation, but, on the contrary, sought to condemn him as a collaborator of the Fascist forces.

Aurobindo Bose and some other members withdrew from the Indian delegation, criticising the representatives of the C.P.I and international communist front organizations for seeking to cast aspersions on Netaji Bose's role. This was followed by disturbances and the hurling of crackers and bombs and the firing of pistols and sten guns at the delegates attending the conference. Aurobindo Bose, his brother and some others were rounded up by the police in the wake of these incidents, though many students said that the police had no evidence of their complicity in these acts of violence.

Some of the communist students, who had lent a hand in making arrangements for this conference, told us how annoyed they felt with the behaviour of many of the Indian delegates. Some student friends of mine, whom I did not see for several days, told me later that they had been enlisted for making arrangements for another very important conference held in Kolkata immediately after the South East Asia Youth Conference. This was the Second Party Congress of the C.P.I. that was held from February 28 to March 6, 1948.

Though this Party Congress was held in camera, a good deal of information about the various issues that figured during the deliberations became available from the party's published literature such as the People's Age in the course of a couple of weeks. Among the important leaders of the party who addressed the Party Congress were B.T.Ranadive and Bhowani Sen, both of whom, besides stressing the need for the adoption of violent tactics by the party, highlighted the relevance of the party's struggle in Telengana, which in their view showed the way the party should follow in the rest of the country.

The formulations of the C.P.I.'s Second Congress, as I understood from discussions with my communist friends as well as from a study of the party's published literature were that the party would try to seize power by over-throwing the bourgeois Congress Government through a 'democratic revolution' – which was the first stage of the revolution – to be accompanied almost simultaneously by a second revolution, which was characterized as the 'socialist revolution' – very much on the lines of what had happened in the Soviet Union. In pursuance of the directive of the Party Congress, the moderate phase of the C.P.I's struggle yielded place to a new adventurist line that was marked by an armed offensive against the government. On Ranadive's shoulders fell the responsibility of pushing through what came to be known as the party's 'acid bulb' line.

On March 25, 1948, Kiron Shankar Roy, the Home Minister of West Bengal, declared the CPI as an illegal party in order to put a stop to its violent activities. It was some years later that I learnt about the objection that had been raised by Prime Minister Pandit Jawahar Lal Nehru to this action of the West Bengal Government taken without informing the Central Government. Activists of the C.P.I. indulged in attacks on policemen, workers of rival political parties and of mills and factories and on landlords in rural areas. As these disturbances spread to several Provinces, the local Governments reacted by banning the C.P.I. and ordering the arrest of its workers and leaders.

I read an account of the C.P.I.'s violent activities during this period in a booklet entitled "Communist Violence in India" published in 1949 by the Ministry of Home Affairs, Government of India, New Delhi. It had listed the murders, arson, loot and acts of sabotage committed by the C.P.I. workers as part of their strategy of creating chaos all over the country. It quoted excerpts from the party's documents that revealed the detailed instructions issued by the party to its cadres on the use of fire arms and on the organization of guerrilla squads for raiding police stations, sabotaging telephone and telegraph lines and attacking the landlords. Many of these documents, which had been issued by the C.P.I. or its units in West Bengal, exhorted Indian Army personnel to turn their guns against the Congress workers and called upon the labourers to attack the houses of Congress workers.

In his recently published autobiography titled 'A Traveller And The Road" (Rupa & Co., New Delhi, 2003), the late Mohit Sen gave an account of how several C.P.I. leaders of Kolkata were able to escape arrest when the Government of West Bengal decided to ban the party in view of its planning to overthrow the government by resorting to armed insurrection. What Sen disclosed was somewhat like this. Ranjit Gupta, a senior officer of the Indian Police, connected with the Intelligence Branch, was a close friend of Sen's elder brother as well as a former student of Prof. Susobhan Sarkar, who was in touch with top C.P.I. leaders. Gupta was a strong sympathizer of the C.P.I. and wanted to warn the C.P.I. leaders of their imminent arrest. He was aware that Sen was a candidate member of the C.P.I. and was also close to Prof. Sarkar. He informed Sen about the likely crackdown on the party and told him to pass on the tip to Prof Sarkar with a view to its being communicated to the C.P.I. leaders. Sen acted accordingly and Prof. Sarkar also did what was contemplated with the result that the top C.P.I. leaders escaped arrest by going underground.

Thereafter Prof. Sarkar asked Sen to lessen his visits to the former's apartment on Kolkata's Elgin Road and never to come there to pass on any information that Gupta might provide. For that purpose, Sen was told by Prof. Sarkar to ring him up from a public call office using the name Abbas Baig and asking for an appointment. The appointment would be refused, but it meant that Sen and Prof. Sarkar were to meet at eleven next morning at the Oxford Bookshop on Park Street. Sen was to type out the information using the Comintern code. On seeing that Prof. Sarkar had seen Sen, the latter was to leave the paper containing the coded message in a book chosen at random from where Prof Sarkar would pick it up. Sen was to use the same method if any message was to be passed on to Gupta. According to Sen, this arrangement worked for nine months till he left for England for higher studies in September, 1948. As a former intelligence officer of long standing, I discovered in this plot a close similarity with the sophisticated techniques of spy cases in different parts of the world.

Sen said that he did this because he was convinced that the C.P.I. needed this service from him. He felt confident that he ran little risk as he was the son of a High Court Judge and was not working in public for the party. He, however, realized that Ranjit Gupta and Prof. Sarkar had much to lose if they were caught. But they were never caught even after Sen left for England when this work continued through some other intermediary. Bhowani Sen, a top C.P.I. leader, who used to receive the messages, did not disclose the source of his information when pressed to do so later by his opponents in the party.

Coming after a lapse of five and a half decades, this revelation by Mohit Sen proved somewhat bizarre to me because I had varying degrees of acquaintance with Sen, who was senior to me by two years in college and Prof. Sarkar, for whom I had profound regard because he was an outstanding Professor of the Presidency College, Kolkata, where I studied. Ranjit Gupta's younger brother, Dilip, was my class-mate at the Presidency College at the time when all this drama was being enacted in Kolkata. Unfortunately, Dilip died prematurely quite some years ago. I also came to know Ranjit Gupta after I joined the Indian Police Service, though I never worked with him

I often saw the scenes of violence that were enacted on Kolkata's streets in those days. I still recall the typical scenario on a Kolkata street of that era – processions winding along the streets, boys and girls marching forward, holding placards in their hands and lustily shouting slogans, the sudden crack of gun-fire, the sound of bombs exploding, police jeeps rushing through the streets, people running helter skelter at the sight of the police, the imposition of curfew that gave the streets an eerie and deserted look and the silence broken by the stuttering staccato of rifle fire or the report of explosion.

It used to be said that a Kolkata boy of those days, who had passed through the college, also learnt, in addition to what he was taught in the class room, a lot more in the school of life on the streets about what was happening in the world outside and even about how to throw a bomb at the police. It was a revolutionary era in which the students took up and fought for many causes. The smell of gun powder was in the air, which was rent by slogans that were aptly coined and chanted with a rhythm and style that were not to be seen anywhere else in the country.

Often, the college and University examinations were put off by a month or two and sometimes for much longer. This is how our M.A. examination scheduled for March-April 1951 was eventually held in November-December of that year, the results coming out after a good few months in 1952. We thus lost a whole year, which also delayed by a year our entry into the job market.

Reports in the newspapers at that time left us in no doubt that B.T. Ranadive's adventurist policy had led to widespread lawlessness at many places in the country. The Government's counter-measures were reportedly proving quite effective in meeting the challenge and turning the tide against the communists.

The communists gave a call for a Railway strike all over the country in March 1949, which was billed to be the harbinger of an all-India insurrection against the government, but it proved a dismal failure, one reason for which was the withdrawal from the strike of the All-India Railwaymen's Federation led by Jai Prakash Narain.

Undaunted by the failure of the Railway strike, the Communist Party of India kept up and even tried to step up, wherever it could, its violent offensive against the authorities and incited its workers to launch attacks on the police, the landlords and the vested interests. At this stage, Prime Minister Nehru paid a visit to Kolkata in July 1949 to offer his support and help to the local Government's efforts to put down the communists' insurrectionary activities. The communists created lawlessness at the venue of the meeting on the Kolkata Maidan and hurled bombs towards the Prime Minister, killing a policeman and injuring many others.

While passing by the Maidan on this occasion, I had a view of the unprecedentedly large crowd that had assembled to greet the Prime Minister. The rousing reception that the Prime Minister got from surging crowds put paid to the communists' bid to foil the visit, which, judging from what I saw, was a great success. These developments figured prominently in the Kolkata press and naturally formed the subject matter of lively discussions among the student community.

After the abortive Railway strike, Ranadive, in a fit of anger, launched a process of purging the party of what he called bourgeois elements as a step towards proletarianising it. Many important leaders in different parts of the country were suspended from the party and the Provincial Committee of West Bengal was dissolved.

Some communist students of the Calcutta University, whom I knew, expressed their indignation at the suspension of Jyoti Basu. In fact, the party's West Bengal unit had even earlier expressed disagreement with Ranadive's adventurist line.

Some West Bengal party leaders were blamed for leaking out party secrets and some were dubbed as petty bourgeois intellectuals with no genuine commitment to the proletarian cause. S.K. Acharya and Bhupesh Gupta were accused of maintaining links with outsiders. Dr. Ranen Sen and Bishwanath Mukherjee, members of the party's Central Committee, were expelled at a later stage. One of the charges against Bishwanath Mukherjee was that he had sought temporary release from jail and performed the 'Shradh' ceremony of his father, which was described as a 'revolting' religious rite that betrayed lack of a revolutionary and materialist outlook. What, one may ask, about the participation of Bengal's communist leaders and workers in the Durga and Kali Puja festivals during all these past years?

I learnt that as early as in 1948, some communist leaders of Andhra had formulated a thesis recommending the Chinese model of 'new democracy' for India in preference to the Soviet strategy. The main plank of this thesis was the launching of guerilla warfare in the rural areas on the Chinese pattern as part of the liberation struggle for the seizure of power. At that time, I saw many of my student friends take a lively interest in the developments taking place in China, particularly after the Chinese Communist Party seized power on October 1, 1949. Like many other students of that era, I read with avid interest Edgar Snow's 'Red Star Over China' and Pearl S. Buck's 'Good Earth' in order to gain some background knowledge about China and its people.

In the meantime, the Soviet party had started sending out signals of new thinking and conveying its perception that the communist parties of colonial and semi-colonial countries should adopt the Chinese path of revolutionary struggle. Indications of the change in the policy of the communists were available in Kolkata in bits and pieces in the communist press and published literature which my communist friends showed to one another and discussed among themselves.

Ranadive took hardly any notice of the change of strategy that was being recommended for the Indian communists. He not only condemned the thesis of the Andhra communists, but also made critical remarks against Mao Tse-tung. His criticism of Mao, published in party literature barely a few weeks before the epoch-making success of the Chinese revolution, caused considerable embarrassment to the Indian communists. My communist friends told me that the West Bengal party leaders were furious, but could do nothing to bring Ranadive to his senses.

It was in January, 1950 that the Cominform formally recommended the Chinese path to India and other colonial and semi-colonial countries. This prescription came in the form of an editorial in the January 27, 1950 issue of the Cominform journal "For a Lasting Peace, For a Peoplee's Democracy". Some time in the middle of 1950, Ranadive was removed from the post of General Secretary and Chandra Rajeswara Rao, the veteran Andhra leader, appointed in his place to implement the new policy, which regarded India as still a colonial country—this characterisation of India coming a good three years after the country's independence. The new policy placed almost the whole accent on armed guerilla struggle in the countryside to be conducted from rural bases. The armed fight against the Congress Governments was to be kept up with the emphasis shifted from cities to the countryside. Telengana's armed struggle was the model to be replicated all over the country.

However, though the party had theoretically armed itself with a new strategy, practical difficulties on the ground stared it in the face. The entry of Indian troops and police forces into Telengana forced the communist guerillas to retreat. In West Bengal, the party leaders did not agree with the new line and demanded the convening of a new Party Congress to remove the ideological confusion in the party's ranks. In Bombay, S.A. Dange, the veteran party leader, issued a statement to the press (which my friends had shown me at a later date), denying that the C.P.I. believed in a policy of armed struggle—a statement from which the C.P.I.'s central leadership dissociated itself.

Signals from overseas started coming to the C.P.I., suggesting a careful re-assessment of the line it was following. R. Palme Dutt, the leader of the Communist Party of Great Britain (CPGB), was reported to have conveyed to the C.P.I. that while it could rely on armed struggle as a means of seizing power, as was the case in China, the reality on the ground was that the party in India was not yet in a position to build up and sustain any armed struggle worth the name and that the objective conditions were not yet conducive to the launching of such a struggle. He, therefore, thought that it was necessary for the C.P.I. to organise a series of struggles in various forms, which could, over a period of time, culminate in a bigger armed struggle over a wider area. He also saw some progressive features in Pt. Nehru's foreign policy, which went against the interests of the imperialist powers and, therefore, deserved the support of the C.P.I.

Maurice Dobb, the British expert on Soviet economic development, was in India at about this time as a visiting professor of the Delhi University and had come to the Calcutta University to deliver lectures to us in the Economics Department, as I have mentioned in the previous chapter. He had, I learnt much later, taken this opportunity to advise the Indian communist leaders in January 1951 against clinging to the line of armed struggle for the seizure of power. He had reportedly suggested to the party to switch over to a policy of developing mass struggles as a step towards building its base among the people at large, before it could think of resorting to more revolutionary tactics. Incidentally, Prof. Dobb had again come to India in 1975 and met some C.P.I. leaders in Delhi. The same year, he fell unconscious near a bookshop in Cambridge and passed away.

Some of my communist friends told me that they were vaguely aware of a visit to London that a few important C.P.I. leaders had paid in the first half of 1951 for holding discussions with R. Palme Dutt in order to thrash out a new strategy for the Indian communists. Some others told me that it was to Moscow that these leaders had gone in secret for consultation. I did not know what the truth was. Be that as it may, in the light of the fresh international guidance it was said to have received, the C.P.I. chalked out in 1951 a new tactical line which some people called a Swadeshi communist line designed to suit the Indian situation, though, to my mind, the foreign inspiration behind this was all too clear.

In later years, when I undertook a study of the C.P.I.'s policies and programmes, I came across several party documents not all of which were immediately available at that time. For example, a document to which the title 'tactical line' was assigned by Dr. G.M.

Adhikari, a top party idealogue, had been drafted by the C.P.I. in consultation with the leaders of the Communist Party of the Soviet Union and adopted by the Central Committee of the C.P.I. in April 1951. This was circulated 'illegally' 2 and a 'legal' version was released in May 1951 before being formally adopted later by the party's Kolkata conference in November 1951.

The document captioned 'tactical line' that was adopted in April 1951 clearly stated that the party's objectives "cannot be realized in peaceful, parliamentary way. These objectives can be realized only through a revolution, through the overthrow of the present Indian state and its replacement by a people's democratic state"............. "therefore, the replacement of the present state upholding the imperialist feudal order by a people's democratic state is possible only through an armed revolution of the people".3

This tactical line steered clear of the controversy about the suitability of the Russian or the Chinese path and focussed on the development of sectoral struggles in the towns and villages of India by the industrial workers and peasants respectively with a view to building up the party's mass base. It envisaged the setting up of underground units in the rural areas and the raising of volunteer groups consisting of militant cadres. The party was told to shun the idea of going in for premature uprisings, but where the conditions were considered suitable, it was expected to launch partisan warfare. This document was not made public as the party perhaps thought that its open plea for armed revolution might provide the government with justification for taking action against it.

In May 1951, the C.P.I. released a document entitled "Statement of Policy of the Communist Party of India", which was published in the journal of the Cominform in June 1951, which meant that it had the stamp of Soviet approval. This document which was later adopted by the party's Kolkata conference in November 1951 omitted all references to armed revolution and instead observed: "But it would be a gross exaggeration to say that the country is already on the eve of armed insurrection or revolution, or that civil war is already raging in the country. If we were to read the situation so wrongly, it would lead us into adventurism and giving slogans to the masses out of keeping with the degree of their understanding and consciousness and their preparedness, and the government's isolation. Such slogans would isolate us from the people and hand over the masses to reformist disruptors."

This softening of the party's policy was in sync with the line that the leaders of the Communist Party of Great Britain had earlier suggested for it. Moreover, with the first general election under the new Constitution of India looming on the horizon, the party considered it necessary to adopt a line that would bring it closer to the masses whose support it needed for a good showing in the election. That is why the Statement of Policy made it clear: "We must fight the parliamentary elections and elections in every sphere where the broad strata of the people can be mobilized and their interests defended. We must be wherever the masses are and would like us to be."

The C.P.I. also released in April 1951 its Draft Programme, whose publication in the journal of the Cominform in May 1951 signalled its approval by the Soviet authorities. This programme, which was adopted with some changes by the party conference held in Kolkata in October 1951, lambasted the Nehru Government for having belied the hopes of the people. Like the Statement of Policy, this programme also came to the conclusion that it would not be prudent for the party to go in for a socialist revolution in India immediately in view of the weakness of the mass organizations of the peasants, workers and the toiling sections of the intelligentsia. It, however, considered it feasible to replace the anti-democratic and anti-popular government by a government of people's democracy formed on the basis of a coalition of all democratic anti-feudal and anti-imperialist forces in the country.

To give effect to the change in the party's policy, Rajeswara Rao was replaced by Ajoy Kumar Ghosh, a veteran leader from Kanpur, as the party's General Secretary towards the end of 1951.

Soon the C.P.I. plunged into the first general election held in January 1952. The party's new line adopted in1951, which had shifted the emphasis on mass work, was designed to equip it ideologically to face the election. It joined hands with some other leftist parties, but kept away from the Socialist Party of Ram Manohar Lohia and Jai Prakash Narain. As I had just completed my M.A. examination, I had ample time to follow the course of the election campaign of the various political parties, to study their election manifestoes and even to attend some election meetings . I did this in order to make up my mind about which candidate it would be appropriate for me to vote for. In fact, I was quite excited over this matter, because it was the first time I was going to cast my vote in the first election held under the new Constitution of free India!

Some of my communist friends got extremely busy with election work and were rarely to be seen. The election results were welcomed by the C.P.I., which emerged as the second largest party in the Lok Sabha as well as in many State Assemblies. It was second only to the Congress Party, which, of course, left it far behind. The post-election period was one of euphoria for the communists, who rejoiced over their so-called success, though I thought that their over-all performance was nothing much to gloat over.

Notes

1. Report in the Pioneer dated August 24, 1997
2. Documents of the History of the Communist Party of India, Vol. 8 (1951-56), edited by Dr. G.M. Adhikari, page 19.
3. *Ibid.*, pages 19-20.

25

I Become A College Lecturer : My Tryst with the Imperial Bank of India

The results of the M.A.examination in Economics came out in early 1952. Tragedy struck, as I narrowly missed the first class, obtaining 59.5% of the marks as against the requisite 60%. Two boys got first class, which meant that I had stood third in order of merit. This rather unspectacular showing surprised me as much as my friends and relations. I, therefore, made up my mind to take up a teaching job as a stop-gap arrangement and then to try my luck at the Indian Administrative Service examination held by the Union Public Service Commission.

I joined the Central Calcutta College as a Lecturer in Economics in August, 1952. This was a respectable job in a government college, which had been set up by the British authorities under the name of the Islamia College to cater specially to the needs of Muslim students. It was renamed as the Central Calcutta College after independence and thrown open to all communities. The college building's Sarasenic architecture gave it a distinctive look. The Baker Hostel accommodated the Muslim students of both the Islamia College and the Presidency College.

It was the second government college in Kolkata, the other being the prestigious Presidency College. The staff of these colleges was inter-changeable and there were some among the Lecturers of the Central Calcutta College, who had earlier served at the Presidency College.The Principal was F.F.Pereira, a strict disciplinarian, who managed the affairs of the college rather well. He became the Principal of the Presidency College after some years. The pay that I drew was higher than that of the Lecturers of many private but better-known Kolkata colleges.

To teach under-graduate, specially honours classes in Economics, I had to keep abreast of the latest advances in this subject. Preparing for the I.A.S. etc. examination and delivering lectures at the Central Calcutta College, for which also I had to do some spade work, besides journeying by bus to the Calcutta University to attend law classes, I found myself completely pre-occupied from early morning till almost mid-night. Working under great strain, I completed the law course and also managed to appear at the written test of the I.A.S. etc. examination. As I had done fairly well in the written test, I was called for interview for the I.A.S./I.F.S. at the Dholpur House in New Delhi, the headquarters of the Union Public Service Commission, on a date towards the end of December 1952.

In the mean time, I had also appeared at a competitive examination held in Kolkata for the post of a Probationary Assistant in the Imperial Bank of India. On passing the written test, I was interviewed by two successive boards and selected along with eleven others. I was asked to join the branch of the bank at Kanpur in the first week of January, 1953. It was a good job with attractive emoluments, besides being considered quite prestigious, as the Imperial Bank, the predecessor of the present-day State Bank of India, was a British bank with some Englishmen still on its staff.

I decided to proceed to Delhi to appear at the interview for the I.A.S./I.F.S. towards the end of December, 1952 and then travel to Kanpur to take up my job at the Imperial Bank. The very thought of saying good-bye to Kolkata pained me, because I had lived in this city for over seven years that spanned my entire college life. It was here that I had nurtured my intimate friendships and forged close links in social, political and academic circles. There was another reason for my feeling so bad: for the first time, I would have to live on my own not only in a different city, but also away from my parents, brothers and sisters, whom I was going to miss very much.

When I resigned my Lecturer's job at the Central Calcutta College, many students and professors urged me to desist from such a course, as they saw a bright future for me in an academic career, considering my aptitude and mental make-up. However, in the specific circumstances in which our family was placed and in view of the limited prospects of an academic career, I reasoned in my mind that I should go in for the bank job.

It was with a heavy heart that I left Kolkata for Delhi in the last week of December 1952, though I felt somewhat recompensed by the call I had received from the Union Public Service Commission to appear for an interview for the I.A.S./I.F.S. In Delhi, I put up with Nirmalendu Nath, a close relation of our landlord, Nandalal Roy, who lived at Anand Parbat. Two years my senior in college, he treated me like his younger brother. All the members of our family had become quite close to Nirmalendu Nath, his brothers and parents, who were very good people and ever helpful to us.

On the afternoon of the appointed day, Satu Da (that is how I addressed Nirmalendu Nath) took me to the Union Public Service Commission's headquarters on New Delhi's Shahjehan Road in a three-wheeler (a ride in which was a new experience for me). The board was presided over by the veteran civilian, R.N. Bannerjee, the then Chairman of the Union Public Service Commission, and consisted of about ten members – all eminent men – who grilled me for over half an hour.

I answered most of the questions which the board members asked, though, from the way some members of the board reacted to the answers, I thought that my pronunciation of English with a typical east Bengal intonation and accent perhaps had appeared rather queer to them. I had a feeling of extreme unease with the neck-tie, which, if I correctly recall, I had worn for the third time till then, the two earlier occasions being my interviews for the job of the Imperial Bank of India. I kept on tightening the noose around my neck in a desperate bid to put the knot in its place, but the noose kept on slackening for no rhyme or reason with the result that the knot constantly slid down a notch or two.

This might have given the members of the board an impression of unsmart bearing and sartorial sloppiness on my part. These were shortcomings in my personality, which I had not yet been able to outgrow in the typical circumstances and environment of my life – shortcomings which I took a long time to shed. Those who had the advantage of studying in public schools or urban schools, or living in a more sophisticated environment, were not handicapped by such drawbacks, which were peculiar to the upbringing of many a youth like me.

I was one among six candidates interviewed that afternoon. After each of us was interviewed separately, all of us were asked to take part in a 'group discussion' on the pros and cons of cow slaughter—a subject that was given to us by the board on the spot. We were asked to articulate our views in a free and frank manner, chipping in with whatever observations we wanted to make as the discussion progressed. The members of the board sat in a corner of the room as silent observers, leaving the field free for us. Their idea seemed to be to see how each candidate fared in relation to the other members of the group during mutual discussions and whether a candidate could establish the validity of his stand-point by clearly, coherently and concisely putting forward what he had to say.

With the 'group discussion' over, we were allowed to go. And so I came out of Dholpur House into the cold air of that December evening, not sure of what was in store for me. I could see the redoubtable members of the board soon troop out of the building one after another and getting into their respective cars, which whizzed past me, raising a haze of the red brick dust that lay thick over the pathway leading out of the gate. Outside, on the Shahjehan Road, streams of vehicles, bi-cycles and office employees trudging back home on foot, presented a picture of New Delhi's bureaucratic life-style, which, within less than four years, I was going to embrace as my own, though at that point of time, there was no way I could have foreseen such a possibility.

I left Delhi for Kanpur by train on the forenoon of December 31, 1952 to take up my job at the Imperial Bank of India there. It was a dismal and squally weather marked by a continuous drizzle when I left Delhi. By evening when I reached the Kanpur Railway Station, it was already dark and the drizzle had intensified into a steady downpour, causing a big drop in the temperature. I shivered in the bone-chilling cold as I came out of the Station and engaged a cycle-rickshaw that brought me to a residential-cum-commercial area of Kanpur city.

After making enquiries from some passers-by, I arrived at what was known as the 'Calcutta Hotel' located on Birhana Road, which was a wide arterial road of the city. It was a typical Bengali hotel meant for middle class people. There were about half a dozen rooms, each shared by several boarders. I insisted on a single room for myself and the manager obliged by converting a tiny store room with a small window into a bed room, charging me a little extra on that score. The bath room and the toilet were, however, to be shared with the others. Charges for food and accommodation amounted to a hefty four rupees a day.

After I reported for duty at the Imperial Bank of India, I was sent for by J.C. Thukral, the Agent, as the Branch Manager of the Imperial Bank was called those days. Thukral was a soft-spoken, good-mannered gentleman, who, after asking me a few general questions about my academic and family background, told me in plain terms that capacity for hard work, a spirit of obedience and a sense of discipline were the sine qua non for a successful career in the bank. I think that what he had told me on that day holds good even today and epitomises the cardinal principles that a person must follow to do well in life and in any sphere of work.

The Agent put a veteran officer of the bank in charge of my training for which an elaborate syllabus and a time-bound schedule had already been chalked out by the bank's headquarters. Each day, like the other officers of the bank, I had to reach office half an hour before time. This was the time when the officers had a tete-a-tete with the Agent about various matters connected with the day's work and even about non-official matters in an atmosphere of friendly gossip. This informal chit-chat gave me a useful insight into the bank's working and contributed greatly to the building up of my outlook and background as a budding bank officer.

At the stroke of ten, the officers and all other employees of the bank used to be on their seats. The customers were treated very politely. The officers kept an eye on what was happening at each counter so that, if there was any problem or clogging of the wheels that was causing delay, the concerned supervisory officer reached the relevant counter and saw for himself what could be done to smooth away the difficulty and ensure easy transaction of business.

I had to sit at each counter of the bank for some days to learn the work that was done there and then moved over to another counter. At the end of each day, the bank's account books had to be balanced. If an employee in any of the bank's various sections committed even a minor error, the over-all receipts and disbursements would not balance, a sure pointer to the fact that something was wrong in the state of Denmark and that someone was at fault. The whole staff would then set about the task of tracing the mistake or mistakes. A practice that was strictly observed was that no employee left the bank before the books were balanced, howsoever, late it might be in the evening or at night. On odd occasions, the staff had even to sit till midnight to balance the bank's books.

Working in the bank with the officers and other employees, who represented a cross section of people from different parts of the country, I gradually developed a wider mental outlook and outgrew many prejudices of a typical Bengalee. I had to dress like an officer, flaunting a suit and a tie, and communicate with the others in English, occasionally trying to speak in colloquial Hindi, which I started picking up quite fast.

I discovered that seeing Hindi films was a good way of learning the language. However, I was still unable to follow complicated dialogues. In the matter of food, while I largely subsisted on Bengali dishes at the Calcutta Hotel, I also learnt at the same time to relish the north Indian cuisine that I occasionally savoured in some restaurant or at some of my colleagues' places.

There was another Probationary Assistant, who had joined the bank six months before me. He was V. Atal, a Kashmiri young man, who was a good sportsman with a smart bearing. He maintained a good standard of living and was elegantly dressed. He had many of the qualities that an officer and a gentleman was expected to possess. He lived in a good hotel, which served as a respectable address and was far superior to and more expensive than my Calcutta Hotel. Naturally, we became good friends. After more than three decades, I was happy to learn that Atal had become the Managing Director and eventually the Chairman of the State Bank of India.

My work in the bank kept me pre-occupied throughout the day. I could leave office late in the evening long after normal office hours. Since this work involved calculations and figure work, I had to remain very alert all the time, because the slightest carelessness could lead to some error that was bound to be detected at the end of the day when the bank's books were balanced. By and large, the bank's work appeared to me to be rather drab. Frankly speaking, I did not like the work, though I grew fond of the company that I kept there. I had made friends with some of my colleagues, who had good personal qualities.

Then one fine morning, when I saw on the front page of a newspaper a list of the names of those, who had been selected for the I.A.S./I.F.S. My name was missing from the list. Nor did I see in it the name of any of my friends from Kolkata whom I knew. It was obvious that the candidates from Kolkata had not fared well. It was a rude shock to me.

It was not a working day. All that I remember is that it was either a Sunday or perhaps a holiday on account of some Hindu festival. Not having to go to office, I was in no hurry that morning. I took my own time to get ready, trying all the while to figure out in my mind the reasons for my failure to make the grade.

Many of the Bengalee boarders of Calcutta Hotel, who knew that I had appeared at the I.A.S. etc. examination, had already scanned the newspaper and on seeing me conveyed their sympathies – each in his own characteristic way. I thanked them all politely and after some time went out of the hotel.

I walked down the wide Birhana Road without giving any thought to where I was going. Soon I noticed that throngs of people were moving in a particular direction. Following in their trail, I found that they were all making a bee-line towards the Ganges, which was not very far from the city. I gathered that they were all going for a dip in its holy waters, the occasion being some Hindu religious festival. Soon, the Ganges with its swirling waters loomed into view, giving me a sense of deja vu, because it was the same river that flowed past the city of Kolkata and also through east Bengal, by which time it assumed the name of Padma which I used to see in my childhood surge along in all its fury, inundating vast tracts of land that included my own village and sometimes my house as well.

Men and women of all age groups were taking their dips in their thousands in the Ganges, braving the cold weather. I saw many of them going back in droves, shivering in their wet clothes, but still supremely happy as I could see from the radiant glow on their faces that reflected the sense of spiritual bliss deep in their hearts. As I stood there for a while, listening to the melody of the Ganges that was rushing down its course, I tried to make up my mind as to what I should do in the wake of my missing the I.A.S./I.F.S. bus. I had no doubt that I would not relish working in the bank for the rest of my life for the simple reason that I found the job rather mechanical and uninteresting.

Over the next few days, I thought over the various options that were open to me.

Finally, I made up my mind and decided to give up my career in the bank, go back to Kolkata and make one more bid for the I.A.S./ I.F.S. for which there was still some time.

I did not eat my heart out nor disclose to anyone either in Kanpur or in Kolkata that I had decided to quit Kanpur and my job in the bank. I waited for the month of March to be over and then one day in the first week of April, 1953, after I received my pay for the month of March, I wrote out my letter of resignation from the bank's service and sent it straight to the Agent.

This virtually stunned the Agent, who sent for me after a while and tried to draw me out on the circumstances that had impelled me to take such a drastic decision. He spoke to me very kindly and tried his best to talk me out of giving up a career, which, according to him, had very good prospects. I explained my position to him, arguing that I had not acted on impulse. I could clearly see that he was not convinced by my logic. He said that he would forward my letter of resignation to the bank's regional headquarters in Kolkata for necessary action. I told him that I was not going to wait for the bank authorities' acceptance of my resignation, but would be leaving Kanpur immediately for Kolkata. Having said this, I took leave of him, thanking him for the kindness that he had shown me and for all that I had learnt from him and in the course of my work in the bank.

By this time, the other officers and employees of the bank had come to know what I had done and, as I came out of the Agent's room, many of them tried to dissuade me from taking what they called a rash and disastrous course of action. I thanked them all for their kind advice, but told them that I was not going to change my mind.

Leaving the bank's premises, I walked to Calcutta Hotel, paid off my bills and after collecting my bags and belongings, proceeded to the Kanpur Railway Station at about mid-day. I felt greatly relieved that I was again a free human being. I caught a train in the evening and next morning I was in Kolkata.

Kolkata looked vastly different after the interval of over three long months that I had spent in Kanpur—which incidentally was my longest ever absence from the city that had become my home. Breathing the air of Kolkata again, I felt supremely happy, though I knew that I was now one among the vast multitude of the jobless youth, whose ranks—I consoled myself—I had joined of my own volition. It was the biggest gamble of my career. I had let the bird in my hand fly, with no likelihood of any in the bush being in sight in the very near future!

26

June 1953 : An Eventful Month

All the members of my family were taken by utter surprise to see me back home from Kanpur one fine morning, as I had not informed anyone of what I was up to or of what my plans were. Their surprise was all the greater when I told them of my resignation. Most of them did not approve of what I had done. My father was positively unhappy.

I lost no time in commencing preparations for the next I.A.S. examination. I again got an offer of a Lecturer's job in a government college, not in Kolkata this time, where there was no vacancy, but at Krishnagar. Acceptance of this offer would have necessitated my leaving Kolkata which would have made it difficult for me to prepare for the I.A.S. examination. And so I turned down this offer most reluctantly and preferred to remain unemployed for the time being, hoping to make it big in the not too distant future.

Even before I left Kanpur for Kolkata in April 1953, I had heard the news of the death of J.B. Stalin, the Soviet leader. In Kolkata, when I met my communist friends, they expressed their concern about the impact of this event on the future of the communist world. This was interpreted by some as marking the beginning of a process that was going to result in a definite decline in Moscow's authority over the international communist movement—a process that was accelerated by the growing importance of Mao Tse-tung and Peking, particularly in the countries of South East Asia.

June 1953 was an eventful month that yielded quite a lot of excitement. First came the news of the conquest of the world's highest peak—Everest—by a British team. Tenzing Norgay from Darjeeling and Edmund Hillary from New Zealand were at the summit on May 29, 1953. It was an unprecedented achievement that was hailed all over the world, but particularly in India and West Bengal, because Tenzing was from Darjeeling. This spectacular success came after 32 years of unsuccessful human endeavour to reach the top of the world, the first bid having been made in 1921. I used to lap up every bit of news that reached us through the press and the radio about this feat that symbolised the triumph of human spirit and endeavour.

The news that the peak which had remained virgin since time immemorial had now yielded to man's indomitable spirit, perseverence and endurance thrilled us all. It was broken to the world at large by the team leader Col. John Hunt on June 2, 1953, the day of the coronation of Her Majesty Queen Elizabeth II of Great Britain. It was said to have been deliberately delayed and timed to coincide with the Queen's coronation in a manner that made it look like the gift of the British team to the nation and the new Queen. For us in India, both Norgay and Hillary became instant heroes, adulation for whose pioneering feat remains as great even today as ever before.

The coronation of Queen Elizabeth on June 2, 1953 was another event that generated considerable public interest in India. Only a little over five years had passed since we had gained independence. We had declared ourselves a Republic only two and a half years ago, freeing ourselves from allegiance to the British monarch. Even the minutest tid-bits about the British Queen, therefore, still aroused no end of interest amongst India's intelligentsia. Apart from the daily dosage of news dished out by Kolkata newspapers, there was the reportage in the foreign press to which I had now secured regular access by visiting the British Council Library on Theatre Road and the United States Information Service Library in Chowringhee. In fact, the latter place had become a favourite haunt and rendezvous of Kolkata's student community by virtue of its central location and the free availability there of refrigerated water, which, in summer months, became a highl, rized attraction for us.

In these libraries, I had the opportunity of browsing through the many glowing accounts of the preparations for the Queen's coronation and of the ceremony when it eventually took place in the Abbey Church of St. Peter Westminster on June 2, 1953. The elaborate drill that was followed during the ceremony began with the royal procession of the queen and her family members and the royal and other representatives of foreign countries. The Queen, with her slim and graceful figure, sported a 'diadem of precious stones' on her head and looked resplendent in her royal habiliments of "crimson velvet, trimmed with ermine and bordered with gold lace". She took the coronation oath, kneeling by the side of the altar and "laying her right hand on the Holy Gospel in the great Bible, tendered to Her Majesty by the Archbishop of Canterbury". She was then anointed with "holy oil" by the Archbishop.

Then followed her investiture with "the Colobium Sindonis the Supertunica and the Girdle" and presentation of the 'Spurs' and the 'Sword', the putting on of the 'Armills', the investiture with the 'Stole Royal' and the 'Robe Royal', the delivery of the "Orb", the putting on of the'Ring' and the 'Glove' and the delivery of the 'Royal Sceptre' The next steps in the ceremony were the placing of King Edward's Crown on the head of the Queen and the pronouncing of "Benediction" by the Archbishop. Then the Queen ascended the throne. After a few more ceremonies that culminated in the singing of the national anthem – "God save our gracious Queen, Long live Queen Elizabeth............" – she left the church and returned to the Buckingham Palace.

The coronation of Queen Elizabeth II was an occasion for great jubilation among the English people that showed itself in the large crowds which gathered in different parts of London and its suburbs on the routes of four post-coronation State drives by the Queen and the Duke of Edenburgh on different days during the first half of June 1953. The whole of London became "en fete" with many houses, buildings, statues and gardens either illuminated or flood-lit. Programmes were conducted by the BBC and on television (which had still to make its appearance in India). There were dances in clubs and hotels and on the streets. A great marquee was erected for a public ball in Hyde Park. Bands played in hotels and on the streets. There were fireworks as part of night-long rejoicing.

Strict dress orders were issued for guests attending the coronation ceremony. Ladies had to wear a head covering, which was not to cover the face but was more like a veil. It could be of any colour except black. If tiaras were worn with evening dress, the veil could be dispensed with. The dress code for gentleman prescribed full evening dress or dress of any of several other permissible kinds and clearly laid down: "No mourning will be worn".

As the London Times put it, the British people took "a holiday from reality" for a few weeks on the occasion of the coronation. But even at that time, despite all the euphoria over royalty, the volume of Republican rhetoric was considerable, though it was nothing compared to the royalty bashing of today by the tabloids that indulge in scurrilous attacks on royal peccadilloes and see nothing wrong in encroaching on the privacy of the members of the royal family.

The Prime Ministers of the Commonwealth countries including Pandit Jawaharlal Nehru, who were in London for the Commonwealth Prime Ministers' Conference, also attended the coronation ceremony. Pandit Jawaharlal Nehru, India's Prime Minister, also attended it. In the invitation card for the coronation ceremony, only Pt. Nehru was mentioned as "Mr." to signify that India had become a Republic, though continuing as a member of the Commonwealth. All the other countries of the Commonwealth, whose Prime Ministers attended the coronation ceremony, still owed allegiance to the British sovereign. It was to get over the problem created by India's adoption of a Republican constitution that the "British Commonwealth of Nations" was converted into the "Commonwealth of of Nations" by dropping the prefix "British".

A couple of years later, I married Anita, the foster daughter of Shri B.N. Mullik, the then Director of India's Intelligence Bureau, and his wife Smt. Pratima Mullik. From the Mulliks, I heard a first-hand account of this event. Since Shri Mullik had gone to London in connection with the Commonwealth Prime Ministers' Conference, he and Smt. Mullik had received an invitation to attend the coronation ceremony in London. They had also been invited to an 'Afternoon Party' in the garden of the Buckingham Palace on the 28th May, 1953 hosted by the Queen. I saw the invitation cards that they had received for these functions. I reproduce below the invitation card for the garden party on May 28, 1953:

EIIR

The Lord Chamberlain is commanded by Her Majesty to invite

Mr and Mrs B N Mullick

to an Afternoon Party in the Garden of Buckingham Palace on Thursday 28th May, 1953 from 4 to 6 o'clock.

(Weather Permitting)

Morning Dress or Uniform or Lounge Suit.

The coronation ceremony was solemnized on June 2, 1953 at the Abbey Church of Westminster. The invitation to the Mulliks for the coronation ceremony came along with a communication from the Earl Marshal's Office, which is reproduced below:

EARL MARSHAL'S OFFICE
14 BELGRAVE SQUARE, LONDON, S.W.1
Sloane 0877 *Telegrams: Cepro London*

By the Queen's Command

The Earl Marshal has the honour to enclose an Invitation to be present in Westminster Abbey at the Coronation of Her Majesty upon the 2nd June next.

A reply should be forwarded as soon as possible on the enclosed card or cards, so that, if necessary, the Cards of Admission and Instruction may be sent to you in due course.

Shri & Shrimati B. N. Mullick

The invitation for the coronation ceremony, which was quite ornamentally designed, is shown below:

These communications show how formal and convoluted the language of invitation can be in Great Britain. Those not well versed in the niceties of the language of royalty may mistake such an invitation for a "command" or a "direction", which, however, is not the true spirit of the communication.

I learnt from Shri Mullik that the then Director of Pakistan's Intelligence Bureau had also been invited to the coronation ceremony and that the language of the invitation card that the latter received was slightly different from that used in the invitation that Shri Mullik had received. The difference in the language arose from the fact while the Director of Pakistan's Intelligence Bureau was an official of a country that still owed allegiance to the British sovereign, Shri Mullik was from a country that owed no such allegiance.

Very recently, when Prince Charles of Great Britain married Camila Parker Bowles in April 2005, I read in the newspapers that the invitations were sent by the Lord Chamberlain saying: "The Queen commands the Lord Chamberlain to invite ...." The language was identical with that for the Queen's coronation in June 1953. When I read this news, my mind went back to the events of June 1953

In June 2002, when I saw television pictures of the enthusiastic celebrations in the United Kingdom marking the golden jubilee of the reign of Queen Elizabeth II, I recalled the excitement all over the Commonwealth countries that was reflected in the coverage by the press in most countries of the world. This time around, there was much less euphoria and very little hype and hoopla in the countries of the Commonwealth. In London, however, the golden jubilee celebrations evoked a very good response among the people, as became evident when the Queen's appearance on the balcony of the Buckingham Palace was lustily greeted by a million-strong cheering crowd that milled around the area in a spirit of great jubilation.

In this matter, the personal factor plays an important role, as the Queen is generally looked upon as a benign presence, while the foibles and peccadilloes of some of the other members of the royal family have struck a sad blow to the image and prestige of the royalty. Queen Elizabeth II, who enjoys good health, is in good company, as by virtue of having completed fifty years on the throne, she has joined the ranks of some earlier British monarchs such as King George III (from 1760 A.D. to 1820 A.D.) and Queen Victoria (from 1837 A.D. to 1901 A.D.).

Towards the end of June 1953, an event that sent shock waves throughout our country and specially in West Bengal was the tragic death of Dr. Shyama Prasad Mookerjee in prison in Srinagar, where he had been detained after being arrested on the ground that he had entered the territory of Jammu and Kashmir without the requisite permit. The news of Shyama Prasad's death came like a bolt from the blue and aroused deep anger not only against Sheikh Abdullah, Chief Minister of Jammu and Kashmir, but also against the Central Government.

I remember how eagerly the crowds that had formed along the long route from the Dum Dum airport to the Bhowanipur residence in south Kolkata of Dr. Mookerjee waited throughout the hot and humid afternoon of June 23, 1953 to have a glimpse of the cortege of their beloved leader. Nobody knew when exactly the body of the leader would reach Kolkata. Continuous jostling and shouting of fiery slogans by the people to give expression to their pent up feelings added to the all-pervasive heat. It was at night that the body finally arrived and was brought to Dr.Mukerjee's residence in Bhowanipur. Thousands of people joined the funeral procesion to the Keoratala burning Ghat where the body was consigned to the flames on June 24, 1953.

I lived very close to Dr. Mookerjee's residence and turned up there on the afternoon of June 23,1953 as soon as I heard the tragic news. I returned home quite late that night after seeing the cortege enter Shyama Prasad's house. The next morning, I was there again to see the long slow-moving funeral procession. I recalled that it was from him that just three years ago, I had received the certificate of my B.A. degree at the convocation of the Calcutta University held in the Senate Hall. I had not forgotten what a bright and dynamic person he was and what an inspiring address he had delivered on that occasion to show us the way to the future. His voice was now stilled for ever.

It was natural for all Bengalees to feel deeply sad. They had not forgotten the contribution and the pioneering role of Dr. Mookerjee's father, Sir Asutosh Mookerjee, the Royal Bengal Tiger as he was called, in the field of education and culture. Two great stalwarts whom Sir Asutosh had nurtured early in their careers in the Calcutta University where Sarvapalli Radhakrishnan and C.V. Raman.That was the measure of the supreme contribution that Sir Asutosh Mookerjee had made to the building up of the country's intellectual and scientific edifice.

Dr. Shyama Prasad Mookerjee was an outstanding academic figure, who, at the age of 33, was the youngest Vice-Chancellor of the Calcutta University, the biggest university of the country. In the political field, he had never failed to take up the cause of the Hindus, which, in his view, was often neglected by the Congress Party in its eagerness to woo the Muslims.

In 1939, when I was a young school boy, the Muslim League had engineered communal riots in some areas of east Bengal including several places in my home district of Dhaka – Keraniganj, Munshiganj and Dhaka town. These developments struck a blow for the Hindus in his mind. He gradually veered towards the Hindu Mahasabha, which he then joined, but this did not detract in the least from his secular and nationalist credentials as was evident from the good personal equations he continued to maintain with Subhas Chandra Bose and several important Congress leaders of Bengal, poet Kazi Nazrul Islam and A.K. Fazlul Huq of the Krishak

Praja Party. In December,1941, Dr. S.P. Mookerjee joined the Bengal Ministry led by A.K. Fazlul Huq as Finance Minister in order to prevent the Muslim League from gaining the upper hand in Bengal politics.

Soon thereafter in August, 1942, the Congress Party gave the call for 'Quit India' which was instantaneously followed by the arrest of almost all its leaders and unprecedented repression let loose by the British authorities to put down the movement. Dr.S.P. Mookerjee, though a Minister of the Bengal Government and a leader of the Hindu Mahasabha, which was not a party to the 'Quit India' call, took up and espoused the cause of the freedom struggle on behalf of the Congress Party, whenever the occasion demanded.

Dr. Mookerjee raised his voice against the repressive action of the administration and particularly against the conduct of the officials. In 1942, when an unprecedented cyclone caused havoc in Midnapore district, specially Contai, Shyama Prasad lambasted the British authorities and the district administration for deliberately refusing to take relief measures as a punishment for the role the people had played in imparting a militant thrust to the 'Quit India 'movement. Shyama Prasad and Fazlul Huq cocked a snook at the British authorities and launched special relief measures which were highly appreciated by the people.

Shyama Prasad submitted his resignation from the Bengal Ministry in November, 1942 in protest against the repressive measures taken by the British authorities to crush the 'Quit India' movement and against the conduct of the British Governor of Bengal in allowing the advice of the officials to override that of the Ministers. Simultaneously, he also pressed his demand for the grant of independence to our country. He charged that Provincial autonomy had been reduced to a farce as a consequence of the interference of the Governor and the officials with the police and the general administration. His statement in the Bengal Legislative Assembly on February, 12, 1943 to explain the circumstances that had led him to resign created a deep impact on the public mind all over India, particularly in Bengal.

When the Bengal Famine was at its worst in 1943, the British administration tried to prevent the press from bringing the facts to the notice of the world at large. Dr. Mookerjee issued a statement about the grim situation in Bengal, which received wide publicity in the newspapers and aroused nation-wide indignation against the ineptness and the failure of the administration. The British authorities threatened Dr. Mookerjee with legal action, but he challenged them to do whatever they could.

After his release from jail in 1944, Mahatma Gandhi expressed deep appreciation for all that Shyama Prasad had done to provide relief to the people affected by the Bengal Famine. It was largely at Gandhiji's instance that Shyama Prasad was inducted into Pt. Nehru's Cabinet in August, 1947, when the country became free. But Shyama Prasad had to continuously fight from within the Government over its policies on various issues such as those pertaining to Kashmir, Hyderabad and the fate of the Hindus and Buddhists of East Pakistan. Shyama Prasad's espousal of the cause of the Hindu and Buddhist minorities of east Bengal had greatly endeared him to the latter.

Shyama Prasad vehemently protested against the oppression of the Hindus of east Bengal by the Pakistan authorities and repeatedly drove home the point that Indo-Pak agreements including the Nehru-Liaqat Pact of April 1950 had not been seriously implemented by Pakistan with the result that these had failed to put a stop to successive waves of exodus by lakhs and lakhs of Hindus from east Bengal to India. I had read with avid interest newspaper reports on the statement he made in the Parliament on his resignation on April 8, 1950 from Pt. Nehru's Ministry, in which he gave a succinct analysis of the state of Indo-Pak relations at that time. This was an issue that vitally affected me personally because we had migrated to India from East Pakistan.

This was Dr. Mookerjee's second resignation from a Ministerial position, which immensely raised his stature in the estimation of the people, particularly those of Bengal. What particularly struck us was his emphatic re-iteration that the Hindus of east Bengal were entitled to India's protection, not on humanitarian considerations alone, but by virtue of the sacrifices they had made in the cause of India's freedom. Speaking in the Parliament, Dr. Mookerjee had drawn attention to Panditji's assurance given to the Hindus of east Bengal in a speech delivered on the 15th of August, 1947, an extract from which is reproduced below:

"We think also of our brothers and sisters who have been cut off from us by the political boundaries and who, unhappily, cannot share at present in the freedom that has come. They are of us and will remain of us, whatever may happen in future, and we shall be sharers in good and ill fortune alike".

After the assassination of Mahatma Gandhi on January 30, 1948, Dr. Mookerjee had dissociated himself from the Hindu Mahasabha. He was instrumental in the formation of the Bharatiya Jan Sangh, which, he thought, would be open to non-Hindus as well. After the 1952 general election, he was returned to the Parliament on the ticket of this party, which, however, got only a few seats. In view of his stature and ability, he became the de facto leader of the opposition, though he lacked the numerical strength to be given such a position de jure. His oratory and fearless espousal of various national causes earned him applause all over the country as an able parliamentarian. It was only he who could tell Panditji on his face in the Parliament that the latter was wrong on a particular issue. I always read newspaper reports of Dr. Mookerjee's speeches in the Parliament with great interest and delight.

From 1952 onward, Dr. Mookerjee remained almost completely pre-occupied with the situation in Jammu and Kashmir. He lambasted Sheikh Abdullah's vision of an independent Kashmir. In the course of a hard-hitting speech he made in the Parliament on June 26, 1952, he asked: "Who made Sheikh Abdullah the King of Kings in Kashmir? It is because Indian troops went there. Did we do it for creating a sovereign republic within a sovereign republic?"

Dr.Mookerjee wholly supported the popular agitation launched by the Praja Parishad in Jammu to secure the fullest integration of Jammu and Kashmir with the Indian Union-an agitation which invited brutal repression from Sheikh Abdullah's Government. He expressed admiration for the spirit with which the people of Jammu were making sacrifices and suffering untold misery to realise their dream of 'Ek Nishan, Ek Vidhan, Ek Pradhan' – one flag, one constitution, one President. I read with great interest a newspaper report of a speech Dr. S.P. Mookerjee had made in the Parliament, an extract from which is reproduced below:

"Are Kashmiris Indians first and Kashmiris next, or are they Kashmiris first and Indians next or are they Kashmiris first, second and third and not Indians at all?"

Some years later, I read what Dr. Mookerjee had written in a letter to Sheikh Abdullah. After mentioning the tragic division of the country as a corollary to the two-nation theory, he had written:

"You are now developing a three-nation theory, the third being the Kashmir nation. These are dangerous symptoms ....". I was later surprised to learn that the supporters of Sheikh Abdullah's line had contradicted the report about this by saying that no such letter existed among the papers of the Kashmiri leader

As the protest movement launched in Delhi against the repression let loose on the Praja Parishad agitation in Jammu gathered momentum, Dr. Mookerjee and some other leaders of the Bharatiya Jan Sangh were arrested and detained in Delhi in March 1953. There were lathi-charges on the workers and supporters of the party in Delhi. On release from detention after some time, Dr. Mookerjee decided to proceed to Jammu to protest against the introduction by the Sheikh Abdullah Government of a system that enjoined on anyone from India desiring to enter Jammu and Kashmir to obtain a permit from the prescribed authority. The devoted son that he was, he first went to Kolkata to seek the blessings of his old mother and then returned to Delhi before proceeding to Jammu. Little did he know that this was going to be his last visit to Kolkata and his last meeting with his mother.

And so Dr. Mookerjee left for Jammu on the 8th of May 1953 along with some others including Atal Behari Vajpayee. On the 11th May, 1953, Dr. Mookerjee reached Pathankot, where he was assured by the Deputy Commissioner of Punjab's Gurdaspur district that, though he did not have a permit for entry into Jammu, the Government of India had sent word to him (the Deputy Commissioner) to allow Dr. Mookerjee to proceed to Jammu.[1] But as soon as Dr. Mookerjee reached the Madhopur Check Post, the Jammu and Kashmir police arrested him for having no permit. From there, he was driven to Srinagar, where he was kept detained in a small cubicle.

A few days later, I read in the press that Shri N.C. Chatterjee, M.P. (father of Somnath Chatterjee, a leader of the CPM and now the Speaker of the Lok Sabha) had raised this matter in the Parliament and asked why Dr. Mookerjee was arrested in view of the fact that the Deputy Commissioner of Gurdaspur had communicated to him the decision to allow him to proceed to Jammu. The press report said that the Central Government had contradicted the news of any meeting between the Deputy Commissioner and Dr. Mookerjee.

Dr. Mookerjee's closest relations were denied permission to meet him in Srinagar. His health started deteriorating, but proper medical facilities were denied to him. He died of a heart attack at 3.40 am on June 23, 1953. A demand for an enquiry into the circumstances leading to his death was made by several political leaders cutting across party lines as well as by many eminent persons and, of course, by his mother, Jogmaya Debi, but to no avail.

After Dr. Mookerjee's death, when his personal papers were made available to his family members, they were surprised to see that these included a note[2] in his own hand-writing, which showed that he had detected a suggestion of malafide. His hand-written note made the following points:

"Court can certainly intervene. Malafide is suggested by the following

(1) My telegram to Abdullah and his reply-he did not then consider my visit to be so dangerous (it was inopportune) as to bring it within the scope of the P.S. Act.

(2) Conspiracy between Govt. of India and J & K Govt – the circumstances under which my entry was facilitated by Indian officials.

(3) Keeping both orders ready beforehand – specially the 2nd order – which when signed, mentioned certain alleged facts which could not possibly then be in existence."

Dr. Mookerjee was kept confined in a special jail where no facility was provided even for taking a short walk to which he was accustomed. Lack of exercise led to loss of appetite. No arrangement was made for proper medical treatment for the first several days after he fell ill nor was there any nurse to look after him. Medical facility should have been rushed to him there or he could have been sent out of Jammu and Kashmir, as was pointed out by Dr. Naliniranjan Sen, an eminent Kolkata physician, who also observed: "To keep a man so obviously ill with such a fatal illness in charge of people who cannot even diagnose such severe attacks and, if diagnosed, handle him so roughly like a quack is a blunder which definitely cost the patient's life and cannot be condoned or pardoned".

Another well-known physician of Kolkata, Dr. Amal Kumar Roy Chowdhury was of the view that "there must have been bungling somewhere and that proper attention had not been paid to the case". Injections that were administered to Dr. Shymaprasad Mookerjee were contra-indicated in the opinion of some medical experts. The fact that a patient suffering from coronary attack was removed to a hospital at a distance of ten miles showed an attitude of callous neglect on the part of the doctors treating him.

Dr. B.C. Roy, Chief Minister of West Bengal, reportedly requested Pt. Jawaharlal Nehru to concede the public demand for an impartial enquiry into the circumstances of Dr. Mookerjee's death, taking into account the public feeling in West Bengal over this issue. Atulya Ghose, the Congress leader, in a communication to Panditji, brought to his notice the feelings of the Congress leaders of West Bengal over this issue and took exception to the blunt manner in which the news of Dr. Mookerjee's death was communicated to the members of his family without any consideration for the feelings of the aged mother, Jogmaya Debi. Contemporary newspapers provided a lot of detailed information which I religiously went through every morning with great interest.

I had heard that the news of Dr. Mookerjee's death was communicated to his family members in a rather queer manner. Very early in the morning on June 23, 1953, the telephone at his south Kolkata residence started ringing abruptly. Justice Ramaprasad Mookerjee, the eldest brother of Shyama Prasad, who picked up the receiver was informed by the telephone operator that a call was coming from Srinagar. All the family members got up from their beds and assembled near the telephone hoping to get the latest news about Dr. Mookerjee. Jogmaya Debi, his old mother, sat there hoping to talk to her son, who was in jail in far-away Srinagar. Then the bomb-shell was dropped. The operator said that since the person at the other end in Srinagar was unable to speak directly to Justice Mookerjee, he was passing on the message from Sheikh Abdullah, which was that Dr. Shyama Prasad Mookerjee was dead and further that Sheikh Abdullah wanted to know what arrangements were to be made about the disposal of the body!

In the absence of any earlier information about Dr. Mookerjee's illness, the news of his death came like a bolt from the blue. On a query from Justice Mookerjee, the operator said that according to what Srinagar had told him, Dr. Mookerjee had an attack of pleurisy a few days ago and that the previous day, he had been removed to hospital, where he had a heart attack and had expired at 3.40 am i.e. a couple of hours before the telephone message came. Justice Mookerjee was also informed by the operator that the person at the other of the line in Srinagar was no less than Durga Prasad Dhar, the Deputy Home Minister of Jammu and Kashmir. Justice Mookerjee told the operator to inform Srinagar that his brother's dead body should be sent to Kolkata immediately.

It took an inordinately long time for the body to reach Kolkata, because it was taken to Adampur and then to Kanpur on short flights and finally flown to Kolkata in another plane.

The news of Dr. Mookerjee's death was received with shock and surprise all over the country. People from all walks of life and belonging to almost all political parties including the Congress Party expressed profound grief over this tragic event. The resentment in Bengal, which cut across party lines, was reflected in the letter that the veteran Congress leader, Atulya Ghosh, addressed to Pt. Jawaharlal Nehru. Dr. B.C. Roy, Chief Minister of West Bengal, who was also the family physician of Dr. Mookerjee, sent an indignant telegram to Sheikh Abdullah, asking the latter why he had not been informed of Dr. Mookerjee's illness in time.

Of the many tributes paid to Dr. Mookerjee, I specially remember the one by poet Harindranath Chattopadhyaya, who, though on the other side of the political fence, in an obituary number, aptly described him as a 'giant' and 'colossal intellect' and lamented that the nation would miss his "speech which thundered every time he rose to speak" and his "high oratory, packed with lightning flashes". Many years later, I read another write-up on Dr. Mookerjee by the late Prof. Hiren Mukherjee, a communist Member of Parliament, who, despite his ideological differences with the former, had no hesitation in saying that "he could not, however, be glibly branded as a mere communalist" in view of his 'catholicity and also, within limitations, the rationality of his outlook". Prof.Mukherjee admitted that for all his reservations against socialism, there was in Dr. Mookerjee an innate liberalism. Citing one of the many instances of Dr.Mokherjee's capacity for giving rapier-sharp retorts, Prof. Mukherjee mentioned that once when the former was criticising the Congress Government in the Parliament for detaining political opponents without trial, he heard someone from the government side say: "Face the Truth". Dr.Mookerjee instantly roared: " How can I, for I face the Treasury benches!"

In Dhaka, A.K.Fazlul Huq, a pre-independence Chief Minister of Bengal in whose cabinet Dr. Mookerjee was once a Minister, exclaimed in utter grief: " The loss of the only brother I had in this world has driven me mad with sorrow".

Jogmaya Debi, the broken-hearted mother of Dr.Mookerjee, remained unreconciled to the plea that her son, a Member of Parliament and de facto leader of the country's Opposition, had no right to enter Jammu, a part of Indian territory, without a permit, which, she learnt, had been verbally given, but not officially acknowledged. She considered it to be nothing but deception which left her unconsoled till the end. When I thought of her agony, I was reminded of the poem "Home They Brought her Warrior Dead," in which poet Alfred Tennyson described how the shell-shocked mother reacted on seeing the dead body of her warrior son that had been brought home from battle front.

Jogmaya Debi wrote in a foreword to a book[3] published at that time: "Death is inevitable. But death in detention – and a detention without trial – is neither normal nor inevitable. Yet, such was the death of my son. Imprisoned by persons whose political activities he had the courage to oppose, surrounded by armed guards till his last moments in the hospital, for away from his near and dear ones, without even one familiar face within his last sight, my gallant son – for whose life many would have offered their own lives – met his tragic end .... I demanded justice from Shri Jawaharlal Nehru. I asked for an immediate, impartial, open enquiry into this whole tragic episode. But he has failed and failed miserably".

In a letter to Panditji, Jogmaya Debi wrote: "In your letter you have tried to impress that Kashmir Government had done all that should have been done. You base your impression on the assurances and information you have received.

What is the value, I ask, of such information when it comes from persons who themselves should stand a trial?"

In another letter to Panditji, Jogmaya Debi wrote: "Your experience in jails in known to all. It was at one time a matter of great national pride with us. But, you had suffered imprisonment under an alien rule and my son had met his death in detention without trial under a national Government. What would have happened if such a tragic and mysterious end had come behind the prison bar during the British rule?

It is futile to address you further. You are afraid to face facts. I hold the Kashmir Government responsible for the death of my son. I accuse your Government of complicity in the matter".

Some years later, I read an account in a book[4] by Dr. Mookerjee's younger brother, Umaprasad Mookerjee, of his journey to the Himalayan shrines of Badrinath and Kedarnath, during which he happened to meet the former Queen of Kashmir, that is, King Hari Singh's wife and mother of Dr. Karan Singh, who became the Sadr-i-Riyasat after his father. The venerable lady, while returning from Badrinath with her entourage, came across Umaprasad Mookerjee and party, who were also coming down from the same pilgrimage.She stopped in her track and sent a person to Umaprasad Mookerjee, communicating her desire to speak to him.

When Umaprasad Mookerjee walked up to her, she said that she was so anxious to meet him because, as she said, she had heard that he was the brother of the late Shyama Prasad Mookerjee. She enquired about his mother and was told that the latter was at Puri. Then she said that Dr. Shyama Prasad Mookerjee was known to her family while he was alive, but when he fell ill in the Srinagar prison, she did not know of it nor did she come to know of his death in tragic circumstances till after his dead body had been flown away from Srinagar. She checked her emotion with great difficulty and then said that Shyama Prasad was a great well-wisher of Jammu and Kashmir, which owed him a debt of gratitude for all that he had done.

The former Queen of Kashmir said that she had told her son—Dr. Karan Singh—that much of the glory of the position that he was enjoying as the head of the State of Jammu and Kashmir was attributable to Dr. Mookerjee's efforts and sacrifices. She had, therefore, asked her son, she continued, to go to Kolkata to meet Dr. Mookerjee's mother, give her his regards and personally bring it to her notice that even while being in Srinagar, they all were as unaware of the happenings during the last days of Dr. Mookerjee's life, as she was. This tragic feeling, she said, was something which she would never be able to get over.

As she spoke these words, her voice became choked with emotion and tears welled up in in her eyes. After a silence of a few minutes, she said that she had asked her son whether, during a visit to Kolkata that he had paid, he had met Dr. Mookerjee's mother. And her son told her that he could not summon enough moral courage to go and meet Dr. Mookerjee's mother. Then she said that she realised her son's moral plight. She concluded with a request to Umaprasad Mookerjee to communicate her feelings to his mother and with a salutation to the bereaved mother in token of which she joined the palms of her upraised hands. I was deeply moved when I read this account in Umaprasad Mookerjee's travelogue.

Later that very year (1953), after Shyama Prasad's death, Sheikh Abdullah was arrested for hatching a conspiracy with the agents of Pakistan to establish an independent Kashmir. The case against Sheikh Abdullah was based on very strong evidence, but was later withdrawn on political grounds, though against the advice of many important persons. Ashoke Sen, the then Union Law Minister, was believed to have tendered his resignation in protest against this decision and withdrawn it on the persuasion of some political heavy weights of those days.

In July 2000, several political parties including the BJP and the Trinamool Congress celebrated Dr. S.P. Mookerjee's birth centenary in Kolkata. Addressing a meeting in Kolkata on July 6, 2000, on this occasion, Prime Minister Atal Behari Vajpayee paid glowing tributes to the departed leader and recalled his services to the nation. The leaders of the CPM boycotted the function on the ground of what they called the communal outlook of Dr. Mookerjee.

This view of the CPM leaders smacked of political bias. Dr. Mookerjee had functioned as a Minister in the government led by A.K. Fazlul Haque, fought against the communalism of the Muslim League and provided full support to the Quit India movement launched by the Congress Party in 1942, when the leaders of that party were mostly in jail. It was he who had, in his capacity as the Vice-Chancellor of the Calcutta University, helped in including Islamic Culture and History as a subject of post-graduate studies. As pointed out by some political leaders, had Dr. Mookerjee been communal, Kazi Nazrul Islam, the secular poet would not have expressed his appreciation of the contribution made by him. Prof. Hiren Mukherjee's tribute to Dr. Shyama Prasad that I have already referred to should have sufficed to nail the CPM leaders' lie about the so-called communalism of the departed leader.

Notes

1. Shyamaprasader Diary O Mrityuprasanga (Bengali) by Uma Prasad Mukherjee, page 121.
2. "Shyama Prasad Mookerjee, His Death In Detention–A Case For Enquiry", edited by Uma Prasad Mukherjee, page 70.
3. *Ibid.*
4. Himalayer Pathe Pathe (Bengal) by Umaprasad Mukherjee, pages 29-32.

27

Proud to be A Policeman

"The policeman must be the eternal sentinel standing at the crossroads of right and wrong, pointing the path to right and obstructing the path to wrong. He must show his fellow brethren the path in darkness. He should be the guide who should lead people by the hand over difficult and dangerous paths. If sometimes he is left alone, he should not be dismayed; he should go forward."

—B.N. Mullik in his "A Philosophy For The Police", page 162

A couple of days before I received the shocking news of Dr. Shyama Prasad Mookerjee's tragic death, another piece of news reached me—on June 21, 1953, if I remember aright—through the columns of newspapers that had published a list of candidates, who had been selected for the Indian Police Service and several Central Services on the basis of the combined competitive examination held the previous year by the Union Public Service Commission. I was happy to see my name in the list, though there was no indication of the particular service for which I was selected. It meant that I could be offered any of these services.

Soon a communication reached me from the Government of India, offering me the Indian Police Service. Neither I nor the members of my family felt particularly happy about my joining the police, since in the then prevailing atmosphere in West Bengal, it was not a service that was held in very high esteem by the ordinary people.

A mighty popular agitation against an increase of a pice in the fares of Kolkata's tram cars was then sweeping the city like a storm. This one-pice war, as it came to be called, was marked by considerable violence necessitating a firm response from the police in the form of frequent tear-gassing, lathi charges and firing that had resulted in many casualties. There was strong public resentment against the tough handling of the situation by the police, which had led the government to order a high-level enquiry. In the surcharged atmosphere of those days, the image of the police did not look too bright to the man in the street, though, I am sure, there must have been enough justification for the police to have acted in the manner it did.

Initially, I was cool about joining the police service, because I was aware of the unsavoury reputation the police had acquired primarily as a sequel to its oppressive role in the pre-independence era in seeking to smother the freedom struggle. My reservation also stemmed from the fact that I did not know much about the police, its hierarchy, its role and functions and its relative position vis-a vis the other services in the administrative set-up. However, considering the pros and cons, I finally decided to join the police in the belief that the outlook of the police must have changed a great deal in an independent India.

I was one of the five candidates selected for the West Bengal cadre of the Indian Police Service. Among them, apart from me, were Nirupom Som, who was my class-mate at the Calcutta University and Parthasarathi Basu Roy Chowdhury, who was in the same class with me at the Presidency College. I did not know the other two namely R.N. Bhattacharaya and S.K. Datta. None from West Bengal had made it to the I.A.S., but some of us had fairly high positions in the list of candidates declared successful for the other services.

There were several Central Services like the Indian Audit and Accounts Service, Indian Income Tax Service, Indian Customs Service, Indian Railway Accounts Service, etc. whose pay and prospects were the same as those of the Indian Police Service. Some of them had even better prospects of promotion than the Indian Police Service. Moreover, the conditions of work in none of these Central Services were as rigorous as in the Indian Police Service. It is for this reason that most of those, who failed to get into the I.A.S. or the Indian Foreign Service (whose pay and prospects were definitely better than those of all other services), were generally anxious to join any of the Central Services rather than the Indian Police Service.

The result was that only those, whose positions were not high enough in the Central Services list, joined the Indian Police Service, while in fact the challenges that the police had to face made it necessary to enlist into it candidates with sufficiently high positions in the list. It was in recognition of this necessity that the Government changed the rules of selection from 1952 onward. It was now stipulated that in case a candidate failed to qualify for the Indian Administrative Service or the Indian Foreign Service, but had qualified for the other services, the government could compel him to join the Indian Police Service rather than any other Central Service, even in disregard of the order of his preferences that he had indicated before sitting for the competitive examination. If he refused to join the I.P.S. in such circumstances, he could be deprived of the opportunity of joining any other service, even though he had qualified for it.

Some years later, I heard that there was one more reason why some of us were made to join the Indian Police Service. Dr. B.C. Roy, Chief Minister of West Bengal, was reported to have insisted that he would prefer Bengalee I.P.S. officers in his State, as, in his view non-Bengalee police officers would not be able to properly understand the sensitivities of the Bengalee people – an understanding, which he regarded as an essential pre-requisite in a police officer, if he was to successfully handle complex law and order situations arising from diverse political agitations and protest movements into which West Bengal's youth and student community was being increasingly drawn, having come under the influence of several brands of leftist political ideology. I do not know if what I had heard about Dr. B.C. Roy's stand in this regard was true or not.

Despite initial reservations, I made up my mind to join the Indian Police Service. Parthasarathi, my old class-mate, was the son of a police officer, who had started his career as a Sub-Inspector of Police in pre-independence Bengal and had gradually risen to the rank of Superintendent of Police, before retiring from service a few years after independence. Through Parthasarathi's good offices, I met his father, a veteran of many battles, and had my first battle inoculation. This is the first time in my life that I sat face to face with someone who had held responsible and important positions in the course of a long career in the police and was in a position to give me a good low-down on the police service, mentioning its good as well its bad points. He foresaw a great future for those who would work with zeal and dedication in the police service of independent India. His persuasive talk that eventually helped me make up my mind in favour of joining the police service.

In the meantime, I got a communication from the Central Police Training College at Mt. Abu (then in Bombay State, now in Rajasthan), asking me to report there for training by the fifth of October, 1953 and carry with me the items of uniform which were specified in the letter. I got these items stitched by the famous Kolkata tailors, F.C. Lewis and Co., as recommended by my friend Parthasarathi. When I got these clothes, I put on some of them and looked at myself in the mirror. I felt that I looked somewhat strange in them; my brothers and sisters were in splits to see me in my new image.

But before joining the police, I completed the written test for the next I.A.S. etc. examination held in September-October, 1953. There was nothing in the rules to prevent me from switching over from the I.P.S. to the I.A.S., if I qualified for the latter service. My last paper, as far as I remember, was on the third of October, 1953. The same evening I left Kolkata by train reaching the Delhi Railway Station the next night; then I took a metre gauge train that chugged along till it reached Abu Road Railway Station the next day. About 20 miles from there was Mt. Abu on top of a hill. I availed myself of a bus to go up the winding hill road and reach Mt. Abu on the evening of October 5, 1953. I felt a chill in the air which was refreshing.

The next morning i.e. on the forenoon of October 6, 1953, I joined my duties as Probationary Assistant Superintendent of Police in the junior scale of the Indian Police Service at a salary of Rs.350 to which was added a sum of Rs.40 per month by way of dearness allowance to neutralise the impact of high prices. It was my third job and a second switch in my career.

This was the beginning of a career which drew to a close on March 31, 1987, when I retired as Director, Intelligence Bureau or D.I.B., as I was generally known in Delhi's bureaucratic and Ministerial circles. Little had I dreamt, when I hesitantly joined the Indian Police Service with a certain measure of trepidation, that one day I would become the top police officer of the country and simultaneously the head of its internal security and intelligence organisation, which, evolving through the various stages of its transformation in the course of almost a century of its existence, had acquired a great prestige readily conceded not only in our own country but also by similar organisations in other countries of the globe.

And then I reached the climactic point of my career. In February 1988, I was appointed the Governor of Haryana, whose Chief

Minister was the veteran freedom fighter and elderly statesman, Chaudhury Devi Lal, who voluntarily gave up the post of the country's Prime Minister and chose instead to become Deputy Prime Minister in December, 1989 in the wake of a general election that saw the ouster of Rajiv Gandhi as Prime Minister, his replacement by Vishwanath Pratap Singh of the Janata Dal and the removal of the Congress Party from power at the Centre for the second time in the post-independence era. In between, I was also sworn in as the Governor of Himachal Pradesh for a very short period, thus holding a double gubernatorial charge. But of these developments, more anon. Looking back, all that I would like to say is that I was proud to be a policeman and that if I were to begin my career again, I would choose to be a policeman once more!

Index

B

D

N

O

S